Globalization: Theory and Practice

2

9

99

Globalization: Theory and Practice

Edited by

Eleonore Kofman and Gillian Youngs

PINTER

Pinter

A *Cassell imprint*
Wellington House, 125 Strand, London WC2R 0BB
127 West 24th Street, New York, NY 10011

First published 1996

British Library Cataloguing-in-Publication Data
A CIP catalogue record for this book is available from the British Library.

ISBN 1-85567-346-0 (hardback)
1-85567-347-9 (paperback)

Library of Congress Cataloging-in-Publication Data

Globalization: theory and practice / edited by Eleonore Kofman and
Gillian Youngs.
p. cm.
Includes bibliographical references and index.
ISBN 1-85567-346-0. — ISBN 1-85567-347-9 (pbk.)
1. International relations. I. Kofman, Eleonore. II. Youngs,
Gillian, 1956– .
JX1391.G528 1996
320.1'2—dc20   95–49671
                                                      CIP

Typeset by York House Typographic Ltd, London
Printed in Great Britain by Biddles Limited, Guildford and King's Lynn

Contents

Part 3   Trading Places or Gendering the Global

Part 4   Other Domains of the Global: Issues of Inequality

Acknowledgements

———

The idea for this volume developed from a conference entitled 'Global Politics: Agendas for the Year 2000', organized by the editors at the Nottingham Trent University in the UK in July 1994. Seventy delegates, including postgraduates, from universities in Europe, the USA, Canada and Australia took part in what proved to be a productive and stimulating event. The editors would like to thank all those involved including Mandy Morris, Richard Davies, Margaret Law and Audrey Brougham, whose efforts were vital to the planning and smooth running of the proceedings, and the Department of International Studies of the Nottingham Trent University and colleagues for their support. Eleonore Kofman also thanks the IBG Political Geography Study Group, which provided funding for postgraduate attendance, and Gillian Youngs thanks Roger Tooze for his support of the conference and her academic work in general, Pauline Tomblin and Keith Baldock for varied and valued assistance, and the many friends and colleagues in the International Studies Association and British International Studies Association who keep the spirit of academic community alive.

About the Contributors

Philip G. Cerny is Professor of International Political Economy at the University of Leeds. His published works include *The Changing Architecture of Politics: Structure, Agency, and the Future of the State* (London, Sage, 1990) and 'Globalization and the changing logic of collective action' (*International Organization*, Autumn 1995).

Simon Dalby is an Associate Professor at Carleton University in Ottawa, where he teaches political geography and international affairs. Author of *Creating the Second Cold War* (London, Pinter, 1990), his current research interests are in critical geopolitics and environmental security.

Chris Farrands is Principal Lecturer in International Relations at Nottingham Trent University, where he specializes in foreign policy, foreign economic policy and international political economy. His publications include articles on technology and change, *Regional Blocs in Global Politics* (1997) and a co-edited book on *Technology, Culture and Competition* (1996).

Gerhard Fuchs is Research Fellow at the Center of Technology Assessment, Stuttgart. His research interests cover communication and information technologies, and international political economy. His recent publications include 'Policy-making in a system of multi-level governance – the Commission of the European Community and the restructuring of the telecommunications sector' (*Journal of European Public Policy*, Autumn 1994).

Richard J. Harknett is Assistant Professor of International Relations in the Department of Political Science at the University of Cincinnati. He has written on conventional and nuclear deterrence theory and is currently completing a book on the impact of types of deterrent threats on security decision-making environments.

Ahmet Icduygu is an Assistant Professor in the Department of Political Science, Bilkent University, Turkey. His recent research interests include the root causes of international migration and the social and demographic status of ethnic and racial minorities.

Andrew Koch teaches in the Department of Political Science and Criminal Justice, Appalachian State University, Boone, North Carolina. His research interests are Max Weber, postmodernism and comparative politics. His recent publications include 'The ontological assumption of Max Weber's methodology' (*Texas Journal of Political Studies*, Winter 1994–5).

Eleonore Kofman is Professor of Human Geography at Nottingham Trent University. She is review editor of *Political Geography* and co-edited a special issue on gender and political geography in 1990. Her current research interests are gender and the politics of immigration and integration in Europe, and new directions in political geography, particularly feminism and political theory and spatiality. She is writing a book on political geography for Routledge.

Jill Krause is Lecturer in International Relations at the University of Keele. Her current research interests are gender and international theory in the post-positivist debate. She is writing a book entitled *Perspectives on International Relations*, to be published by Polity Press, in late 1996.

Marianne Marchand is Lecturer in International Relations at the University of Amsterdam. She has written on gender and NAFTA and is co-editor of *Feminism/Postmodernism/Development* (Routledge, 1995).

Giles Mohan is a Research Fellow in the New Economic Geography Unit at Portsmouth University. He has recently published articles in *Political Geography* and *Review of African Political Economy* and is co-authoring a book on the varied impacts of adjustment programmes in sub-Saharan Africa, to be published by Routledge in mid-1996. He is also an editor for a series of readers on African development published by Pluto Press.

Geoffrey Parker is Senior Lecturer in Political Geography and Geopolitics at the University of Birmingham. He has a particular interest in European political geography and Western and Asiatic geopolitical thought. He has written a number of books on these subjects and has contributed to journals, books and reference works, including the *Dictionary of Geopolitics* (J. O'Loughlin, ed., Westport, CT, Greenwood Press, 1994).

Hélène Pellerin is Assistant Professor of Political Science at Glendon College, York University, Toronto. Her research focuses on international migration, transformation of the production process, and the theorization and practice of organizing resistance and responses to global capitalist restructuring.

V. Spike Peterson is an Associate Professor in the Department of Political Science at the University of Arizona. Her published works include the edited volume *Gendered States: Feminist (Re)Visions of International Relations* (Boulder, CO, Lynne Rienner, 1992). She is co-author, with Anne Sisson Runyan, of *Global Gender Issues* (Boulder, CO, Westview, 1993) and is currently working on a manuscript provisionally entitled *Globalization and Gender: Beyond Sovereign States/Men.*

Jan Jindy Pettman is Senior Lecturer in Feminist and International Politics at the Australian National University. She is the author of *Living in the Margins: Racism, Sexism and Feminism in Australia* and *Worlding Women: A Feminist International Politics.* She is currently working on women's roles in nationalist and identity politics, and on the international traffic in women of South-East Asian states.

Anne Sisson Runyan is Associate Professor of Politics and Director of the Women's Studies Program at the State University of New York at Potsdam (and will be Director of Women's Studies and Associate Professor of Political Science at Wright State University, Dayton, Ohio, from Fall 1996). She has written extensively on gender and international relations, is the co-author of *Global Gender Issues*, and has served as the Chair of the Feminist Theory and Gender Studies Section of the International Studies Association.

Jan Aart Scholte is Lecturer in International Relations at the University of Sussex. He is the author of *International Relations of Social Change* (Buckingham, Open University Press, 1993) and *Globalization: A Critical Introduction* (Basingstoke, Macmillan, forthcoming).

Tracey Skelton is a Lecturer in the Department of International Studies at Nottingham Trent University, where she teaches Geography and Cultural Studies. She is currently editing two texts on *Culture and Global Change* (with Tim Allen, of South Bank University) and *Geographies of Youth Cultures* (with Gill Valentine, of Sheffield University). Her individual research focuses on Jamaican Reggae music and its interrelationship with gender identities for the people of the Caribbean diaspora.

David Slater is Professor of Social and Political Geography at Loughborough University. He is author of *Territory and State Power in Latin America: The Peruvian Case* (Macmillan/St Martin's Press, 1989) and editor of two special issues on Social Movements and Political Change in Latin America, published in *Latin American Perspectives* (Sage, 1994). At the present time, he is working on geopolitics and North-South relations, and questions of decentralization and democracy in Latin America.

Roy Smith is Course Leader and Lecturer in International Relations in the Department of International Studies at Nottingham Trent University. He is co-director of the NTU Centre for Asia Pacific Studies, and has published work related to various aspects of critical security studies. In particular his research has focused on the interests of small island states. He is a contributor to *Global Agendas: Towards the Year 2000* and *Size and Survival: The Politics of Security in the Caribbean and the Pacific* (P. Sutton and A. Payne eds, Frank Cass, 1994).

Peter J. Taylor is Professor of Geography at Loughborough University. He is author and editor of several books on political geography and world-systems analysis including *Political Geography: World-Economy, Nation-State and Locality*, 3rd ed. (London, Longman, 1993) and *The Way the Modern World Works: World Hegemony to World Impasse* (London, Wiley, 1996). He is editor of the journals *Political Geography* and *Review of International Political Economy*.

Marc Williams teaches International Relations at the University of Sussex. His current research focuses on contemporary international theory, and the political economy of global environmental degradation. His most recent book is *International Economic Organisations and the Third World* (London, Harvester Wheatsheaf, 1994).

Gillian Youngs has recently been lecturing and researching in the field of International Relations and has a background in journalism and communications consultancy. Her interests include the relationship between political, economic and cultural dimensions of globalization and the role of theoretical discourses in this context. She is author of *From International Relations to Global Relations. A Conceptual Challenge* (Cambridge, Polity Press, forthcoming).

Introduction: Globalization – the Second Wave

ELEONORE KOFMAN AND GILLIAN YOUNGS

Globalization is no longer a new phenomenon in the academic world. It has become part of the established conceptual vocabulary for addressing social relations on a global scale. The hype has been put on one side and it has been recognized that it is time to start moving away from its generalizing tendencies to the specificities of what globalization actually means when used in particular contexts for declared and undeclared purposes.

This volume represents the second wave, as it were, of globalization studies. These are characterized by a dissatisfaction with the current state of global play, both theoretical and practical. They reject the universalizing characteristics of much of the discussion about globalization. They are circumspect about its euphoric nature and question the problematics of its roots in particular traditions of thought and structures of power. Contributions to this volume signal the range of critical issues which need to be addressed in relation to the theory and practice of globalization. In varied ways they demonstrate that interconnections between theory and practice have distinctive importance when thinking about globalization and its differential impacts upon those involved in its processes.

Globalization relates as much to a way of thinking about the world as it does to a description of the dynamics of political and economic relations within it. Globalization has opened up new imperatives for investigating power linkages between thought and action, knowledge and being, structure and process.

Intrinsically this volume seeks, from a range of perspectives, to politicize and historicize present considerations of globalization. Just as theories of globalization cannot be considered in a vacuum – as if they were isolated from traditions of thought on which they have drawn, directly and indirectly – the phenomena they address have their roots in long-term developments in international capitalism and the inter-state system. In many ways, arguments put forward in this volume emphasize globalization's theoretical and practical associations with the past as vital dimensions of understanding its implications for the future.

The human dimensions of globalization remain to the fore throughout this volume. The authors do not present globalization as some kind of anonymous force. They investigate its discourses and processes, including their effect on individuals in differentiated positions of power. The opening chapter by Spike Peterson affirms globalization's links with the 'politics of identification' and argues: 'When we neglect identities, and cultural dynamics more generally, we cannot account for significant social practices.'

The theory/practice imperative of globalization as a field of study

The imperatives which globalization, as a field of study, presents for a much more detailed analysis of theory/practice relationships is a recurrent theme of this volume. The interdisciplinary and multidisciplinary characteristics of the field emphasize the complexities of addressing such issues. They make clear that the exchange of intellectual resources between disciplines is fraught with risks. The conceptualizations and theorizations developed by different academic disciplines cannot be regarded as abstract tools to be utilized without close regard to the discursive histories characterizing their formulation and hierarchization. Theoretical traditions as well as structures of debate need to be addressed in examinations of what it means to adopt particular concepts and theories in particular ways.

This volume features analysis from two disciplines, international relations and political geography, whose political, economic and spatial preoccupations draw them into the heart of globalization's concerns and problematics. It may be, however, a recent orientation as in political geography's return to global preoccupations in this new *fin de siècle* (Taylor, 1993). A number of the chapters demonstrate that political geography and international relations have generated a vast amount of *knowledge* about world politics and economics, and they communicate fascinating parallels and differences between preoccupations and patterns of theorizing across the two disciplines.

States, order and system are common focuses, and although thinking about them in political geography and international relations has distinctive trajectories, Simon Dalby asks us to consider the degree to which these disciplines can be regarded as having been 'complicit in the power relations of empire, and more recently of American hegemony'. His chapter prompts us to think about a direct historical relationship between geography and international relations in this context. It demands that we think about the politics of academic practice and ask questions about the implications of the relationship between academic fields and domains of practice. It is commonplace to understand the role of geography in mapping the world, but to think how and why this may be politically and economically important at any time is to take the matter further. Dalby's discussion encourages us to think more deeply about the politics of mapping as well as the mapping of politics. The former might be said to be characteristic of the vital importance of geographic practices to the identification, articulation and control of empire. After all, geopolitics, as a strategy that sought to master space 'through geographical processes of disciplining, subjugating, exploiting and developing places' (Agnew and Corbridge, 1995), emerged with the 'closure' of the world by colonial powers at the end of the last century. On the other hand, the state-centric and foreign policy orientation of international relations might be understood as crucial to more recent hegemonic practices in world politics.

Gillian Youngs' discussion of the 'dangers of discourse' highlights the importance of recognizing that theoretical discourse is a form of practice. She presents a picture in which the theorist is deprived of the luxury, if it may be so regarded, of thinking of her or his activity as in any way abstract, but argues instead that theorizing is very much part of the *real* world, with all the responsibilities that implies. Jan Aart Scholte's chapter takes the debate further, exploring the different characteristics of 'liberal' and 'conservative' discourses of globalization. His analysis deepens our understanding of globalization, and concludes with the optimistic assessment that, in some respects at least, 'globalization has opened space for critical theory and a fundamental rethink of production, governance, ecology and community, as well as the nature and purpose of knowledge itself '. Jill Krause's chapter charts the achievements of feminist politics and describes how globalization has changed the terms of those politics. The emergence of new themes, such as gender and sexuality, make us also reflect on how they are to be incorporated into discussions of globalization processes and implications for disciplinary concerns. The inclusion of women's experiences and gender relations may lead us to re-examine the conceptualization of a discipline or sub-discipline, as Eleonore Kofman suggests in her discussion of the problematic closures practised by geopolitics. Furthermore, the political economy of sex questions what constitutes global political economy, that which is transacted and traded, and the relationship between public and private domains, as the chapters by Eleonore Kofman, Jan Jindy Pettman and Anne Sisson Runyan indicate. *Personal services* of all kinds in private and public spheres are as integral a part of the economy as are the manufacturing industries and financial services commonly studied in global political economy.

Towards a political economy of spatiality

The contributions to this volume suggest that globalization requires us to think in terms of a political economy of spatiality (Youngs, forthcoming). We need to link our consideration of the nature of political and economic relations more strongly to our interpretation of spatiality, and current conceptualizations of spatiality in the international have well-established and highly particularistic traditions. While world systems conceptualized the global in centre–periphery terms (Taylor, 1993), political space has been conceived predominantly in terms of states, and economic space has been too much an opposition – something out there, the *market*.

The following chapters fundamentally disrupt this spatial opposition of politics and economics. They examine the theory and practice of politics and economics in a global context and recognize historic as well as transformative influences. They locate political and economic relations and institutional influences and assess their various effects and meanings, taking into account specific definitions and articulations of space.

Their conclusions enable us to understand that, if globalization can be considered *new*, then in many ways it is a reformulation of the *old*. We are confronting old relations in new forms, some of which may be transitional while others may represent entrenchment. Furthermore, the issue of inequality remains central to any consideration of globalization. Far from offering positive possibilities to all, globalization signals new forms of oppression for many. A number of chapters in this volume assert that globalization represents changes in the operation of global capitalism which, if anything, has expanded its potential for producing inequalities. Anne Sisson Runyan dramatically demonstrates that those with the least power, whether defined in state, class, 'race' or gender terms, are being forced to compete on an increasingly intense basis with one another. When it comes to attracting the benefits of transnational capital, seduction is the name of the game, and the pickings for many continue to diminish.

Vital to considerations of political economy of spatiality is the kind of assessment of North–South relations undertaken by David Slater, who expresses concern about the 'absence of any critical acknowledgement of the continuing power of neoliberal ideas' in discussion of globalization. Giles Mohan too asks what dialogue there can be between the West and sub-Saharan Africa's multiple crises and marginalization, but finds that the flow of ideas from the West is very much one way. Power has been displaced, markets have been deregulated and political space re-regulated in the application of international institutions' development strategies. Small states have, nevertheless, attempted to participate and shape the debate about global environmental issues and sustainable development through their own regional grouping, as Roy Smith outlines.

The strongest focus of this volume is the state and predispositions of political geography and international relations towards it, especially as a primary focus for interpreting world politics. Theoretical and practical issues surrounding the state are identified as probably the key issue to be addressed in understanding not only processes of globalization, but also the limitations which exist to current conceptual tools for investigating them. Marc Williams and a number of chapters remind us of the enduring symbolic, and in some respects, reasserted, role of the state as a source of belonging and identity in an era of globalization. Spike Peterson notes that the realist tradition in international relations has had the 'paradoxical effect of neglecting theories of the state', while Eleonore Kofman suggests that it is more than ever necessary to engage with the full panoply of social and cultural interventions by the state that mediate and structure class, gender and ethnic relations nationally, regionally and globally.

Change and the state, which this volume stresses has been identified (through theory as much as practice) as the dominant ordering category of world politics, is therefore at the top of the agenda. Philip Cerny's answers to his question 'What next for the state?' indicate that the state cannot be regarded as a casualty of globalization, but rather as an active participant in the transformations which globalization is facilitating. He argues that the state ' ... is developing more and more into an enterprise association with key, civic, public and constitutional functions becoming increasingly subordinate to imperatives of the global marketplace – or even vestigial'. His conclusions, however, emphasize the fluidity of the contemporary situation and he demonstrates caution in predicting the future of the state. Peter Taylor's exploration of the 'exhaustive multiplicity' of the 'modern inter-state system' deepens our appreciation of its major characteristics so that we may better analyse the difference between 'ordinary' and 'extraordinary' change. According to Taylor the former can be understood as 'adaptive change' of that system and the latter, characterized by 'trans-stateness', as 'demising change'.

Were we to look at the movement of labour in contrast to that of capital, there might be slightly different conclusions about the status of the state. Here the state, or the regional institution to which it has delegated its authority, has reasserted its closure of borders, partly in response to dislocation caused by the movement of capital. Whilst capital increasingly disregards traditional borders, the state has generally reinforced the operation of borders and demonstrates its presence as one of the principal agents determining the membership of the nation. Richmond (1994) speaks of global apartheid whereby the white and wealthy countries have imposed repressive and restrictive policies to restrain the number of migrant workers and refugees in the post-Fordist era of less regulated migration flows, resulting in a form of territoriality which is neither 'state-centric nor homogeneously unfolding and structured', as Hélène Pellerin also highlights.

Migration is of course central to the study of globalization, as a number of chapters in this volume assert, but once again the risks of ahistorical approaches are identified. It is not a new phenomenon, nor a typical feature of the global era of social relations. Too often, migration is studied in a positivist form which identifies those involved as passive victims of global pressures. Distinctive to the subtleties of Pellerin's analysis is the recognition of their role as 'agents of change' and participants in global restructuring. Ahmet Icduygu's assessment of citizenship also reflects a complex approach to migration as a process which involves the migrants themselves, the countries they leave and those they enter. These kinds of investigations of migration contribute to our understanding of the changing nature of state dynamics, political and economic.

It is clear that the spatiality of globalization and maps of inequality cannot be understood simply along state lines. Powerful regional institutions, such as the European Union (EU) and the North American Free Trade Association (NAFTA), play crucial roles in facilitating the changing terms of competition. Control over movements of people and new working practices in the service of capital are key features. Yet political intervention in such processes is problematized by the 'terms of debate'. This is demonstrated in Marianne Marchand's discussion of the 'silenced gender implications' of the dominance of neo-classical economics in relation to NAFTA. The new gender regimes that are beginning to emerge (see Kofman, Marchand, Sisson Runyan) pose a 'challenge to feminist activism', although new forms of cross-border feminist resistance have been organized within NAFTA. As Anne Sisson Runyan outlines, globalization has changed the terms of these politics.

Several contributions raise the 'new world order' debate, signalling the degree to which discussions of globalization have tended to fill the 'void' left by the collapse of Cold War frameworks for understanding the world. Geoffrey Parker's comprehensive reminder that there is nothing new in the 'idea of a new world order as the structure for the implementation of a particular "vision" of a more satisfactory world' provides a vital historically sensitive perspective on the combined geographical and philosophical bases on which such 'visions' are built. Richard Harknett's assessment of the nuclear issue emphasizes crucial continuities between the Cold War and post-Cold War periods in relation to issues of security and territoriality. Underlying his whole approach is the central role of the state as the legitimate user of force in world politics, the relevance of the global reach and destructive potential of nuclear weaponry to understandings of security and territoriality, and proliferation as one of the key insecurities of post-war times. Harknett's contribution draws our attention to the darker side of globalization and indicates that any political economy of spatiality must take account of the continuing importance of the link between territorially defined states and security concerns in a nuclear age.

The multiplication of the sites of authority and the exercise of power does not render sovereignty obsolete. The diversity of actors is not necessarily replacing established structures, as Chris Farrands shows in relation to power, governance and the regulation of technology. Marc Williams' re-thinking of sovereignty concludes that 'the impact of globalization on perceptions of time and space provide a strong challenge to conventional notions of sovereignty'. Regional institutions, such as the European Union, might be seen as reshaping political identities and shifting state sovereignty boundaries in space and time (Walker, 1993) at the same time as the state is being reshaped (Müller and Wright, 1994).

Globalization is frequently analysed in terms of flows and networks, whether of media, communications, technology or finance. These flows are assumed to be placeless and disembedded, such that transmission takes place instantaneously and real time obliterates space. The result is an indeterminate juxtaposition of heterogeneous and disparate elements. Places supposedly no longer matter in the operation of global economy and culture. Thus one of the spatial discourses emanating from the West, with universal pretensions akin to the 'end of history' thesis (see Gillian Youngs' chapter), is the 'end of geography'.

> This refers primarily to the operation of financial markets for which geographical locations no longer matter ... or matter much less than hitherto ... rules no longer apply solely to specific geographical frameworks such as the nation-state or other typical regulatory jurisdictional territories. (O'Brien, 1992: 1)

Yet place still matters, as many geographers have emphasized. Global processes are articulated and concretized in particular places. For example, Sassen (1991, 1994) has forcefully argued that global cities act as the sites of control and management for the increasing dispersal of economic activities and as poles of international migration. In this way globalization has generated a new geography of centrality and power, on the one hand, and marginality and decline, on the other. It would, however, be rash to disconnect these global cities from their national contexts. We need to articulate the different scales – local, regional, national, and global – which operate simultaneously. One of the means by which the dislocation of spaces has been confronted is through the retreat to the local or the places of affective relationships. Tracey Skelton indicates how land may still hold for many people in the Caribbean an affective bond in the face of the economic and political impact of globalization. Whilst the local may be a site where it is possible to escape the relentless logic of the capitalist system, it may also encourage the idea that nothing can be done about the operation of global processes (Cox, 1992).

Indeed, many chapters demonstrate the local experiences of global restructuring of the operation of global capital, disruptions and ecological threats, and the possibility of sustainable development, in particular for small states, upon which Roy Smith focuses. Global processes, too, pose challenges to individual and collective subjectivities. A new political economy of spatiality which addresses globalization must recognize the degree to which the world is not just 'out there' but is 'here' and 'now'. If this volume contributes in some substantial way to this recognition then it has achieved something worthwhile.

References

Agnew, J. and Corbridge, S. (1995) *Mastering Space*, London, Routledge.

Cox, K. (1992) Comment: the politics of globalization, *Political Geography*, **11**(5), 427–9.

Müller, M. and Wright, V. (1994) Reshaping the state in Western Europe, *West European Politics*, **17**(4), 1–11.

O'Brien, R. (1992) *Global Financial Integration: The End of Geography*, London, Pinter.

Richmond, A. (1994) *Global Apartheid: Refugees, Racism, and the New World Order*, Toronto, Oxford University Press.

Sassen, S. (1991) *The Global City: New York, London, Tokyo*, Princeton, NJ, Princeton University Press.

Sassen, S. (1994) *Cities in a World Economy*, Thousand Oaks, CA, Pine Forge Press.

Taylor, P. (1993) *Political Geography*, Harlow, Longman.

Taylor, P. (ed.) (1993) *Global Political Geography at the End of the Twentieth Century*, London, Pinter Belhaven.

Walker, R. B. J. (1993) *Inside/Outside: International Relations as Political Theory*, Cambridge, Cambridge University Press.

Youngs, G. (forthcoming) *From International Relations to Global Relations. A Conceptual Challenge*, Cambridge, Polity Press.

Part 1

Rethinking Globalization in Theory and Practice

1

Shifting Ground(s): Epistemological and Territorial Remapping in the Context of Globalization(s)[1]

V. SPIKE PETERSON

Categorical separations between subject and object, public and private, political and economic, domestic and international are breaking down in the face of postmodern challenges, subnational and transnational political identifications, and local–national–global linkages. In this context of conceptual and empirical transformations, boundaries – and the ground(s) they mark – are shifting, forcing us to remap what recently was (or seemed to be) familiar terrain. This chapter reviews briefly what conventional maps tell us about identity, epistemology, states and markets; it considers how these are problematized by contemporary boundary changes; and it identifies critical, postmodern and, especially, feminist scholarship as resources for remapping now unfamiliar territory.

The politics of identification

Until recently, the politics of identity and identification have not been a central focus of enquiry in political science or geography. In general, accounts of individual agency take for granted a Eurocentric model of the modern subject – as unitary, autonomous, interest-maximizing and rational. And in political science, international relations and geography, accounts of collective identity generally take for granted a (Eurocentric) spatial model of public sphere agency and territorial states. In these accounts, the dichotomy of public–private locates political action in one but not the other sphere; the dichotomy of internal–external distinguishes citizens and order within from 'others' and anarchy without; and the dichotomy of culture–nature (civilized–primitive, advanced–backward, developed–undeveloped) 'naturalizes' global hierarchies of power.

These conventional accounts, however, are increasingly challenged by empirical and epistemological transformations. In terms of the former, state-centric political identity no longer monopolizes but shares the stage with a growing number of non-territorial claimants. Subnational and transnational social movements transgress territorial boundaries in favour of identities 'grounded' on ecological, anti-nuclear, ethnic, feminist, religious and other non-state-based commitments (Walker, 1988; Amin *et al.*, 1990). The globalization of production and finance undercuts national economic planning, eroding state sovereignty and the political identities it presupposes. Even as supranational forces alter state power, subnational conflicts expose the illusion of homogeneity promoted in nationalist narratives (Corrigan and Sayer, 1985; Anderson, 1991). In short, identities conventionally 'grounded' in state territoriality are losing ground to a politics of new, or even non space(s).

Zdravko Mlinar (1992: 2) refers to the transformation from territorial units as a 'transition from *identity as an island* to *identity as a cross-road*'. He also argues that, while it

> is increasingly unlikely that a territorial unit can continue to *preserve* its distinctiveness on the basis of ... 'de-linking', ... there is an increasing probability that distinctive identity may be *formed* as a unique crossroad in the flow of people, goods and ideas. (p. 2, emphasis in original).

From this vantage point, Mlinar believes that contemporary socio-spatial developments are best understood as a 'unity of opposites' – of individuation (diversification) and globalization (homogenization).

In terms of epistemological transformations, critiques of positivism have altered our understanding of agents and subjectivity. In contrast to the modernist conception of a unitary rational actor, contemporary social theory illuminates the multiplicity of subject locations (implying multiple identifications) and their dynamic interaction within the self *and* in relation to the self's environment. In short, identities are socially constructed as processes: they are embedded in and interact with historically specific social contexts composed of inter-subjective meaning systems, practices, institutional structures and material conditions (Brown, R. H., 1987; Knights and Willmott, 1985). On this view, the study of identities must be historical, contextual and dynamic, asking not only how identities are located in time and space but also how they are (re)produced, resisted and reconfigured.

Identities are politically important because they inform self–other representations, embed subjects in meaning systems and collective agency (Bloom, 1990), and mobilize purposive, politically significant actions. They are important windows on 'reality' because 'internal subjective selfchange and external objective social change' are inextricable (Bologh, 1987: 147). In this sense, identifications bridge agency and structure, are multiple and sometimes contradictory, and can be understood as strategies.[2] When we neglect identities, and cultural dynamics more generally, we cannot account for significant social practices. For instance, we lack adequate understanding of how people are willing to kill and be killed so that a particular group can thrive.

Feminists have a number of reasons for attending to political identity and the politics of identification. First, constructions of femininity and masculinity that inform our identification as women and men have unbounded implications for the lives we lead and the world(s) we live in. Bound up with constructions of sexuality and desire, these implications extend to the most intimate activities as well as the most global social dynamics. The study of gender is crucial once we recognize that 'there has been no ungendered *human* experience' (Brown, W., 1988: 190).

Second, to the extent that personal gender identities constitute a core sense of self, they fundamentally condition our self-esteem and psycho-sociological security. This means that challenges to gender ordering may appear to threaten a personal identity in which we are deeply invested (Lorraine, 1990). A fear of loss or destabilization may then fuel resistance to deconstruction of gender ideologies, with many – and mostly negative – implications for feminist movement.

Third, given the significance of gender identities in every domain of human endeavour, feminists have criticized biological explanations that essentialize maleness and femaleness and have developed alternative explanations of gender identity formation and its effects (Fausto-Sterling, 1992; Keller, 1985). Exposing the social construction of binary male and female identities involves a parallel deconstruction of Western dichotomies as gendered, culminating in feminist critiques of science and the development of alternative epistemologies.

Fourth, feminist studies have established that the identity of the modern subject – in models of human nature, citizenship, the rational actor, the knowing subject, economic man and political agency – is not gender-neutral but masculine (and typically European and heterosexual) (Harding and Hintikka, 1983). The unacknowledged privileging of élite male experience and perspective – androcentrism – has profoundly structured our conceptual categories and concrete activities. There is now a vast literature exploring the ways that androcentrism marginalizes women and all feminized 'others'.

Fifth, feminist identity itself is a problem for feminism. If a universal category of 'woman' is a necessary condition of feminist movement, then the actual diversity among women contravenes that condition (Mohanty, Russo and Torres, 1991). Essentialist characterizations of 'woman' and homogenizing effects within feminist movements have been irrevocably disrupted by the realities of 'difference'. Contemporary feminisms are both challenged and enriched by struggles to address diversity without abandoning solidarities enabled by shared experience – and necessary for emancipatory politics (Gunew and Yeatman, 1993; Grewal and Kaplan, 1994).

Finally, identity groups (whether based on ethnicity, race, religion or nationality) that have been most closely associated with political power have also been historically based on gender inequality (Molyneux, 1985; Yuval-Davis and Anthias, 1989). As members of these groups, women have interests in their 'success', including the group's acquisition of political power *vis-à-vis* competitors. But in so far as these groups reproduce masculine dominance, identification with and support for them is problematic for feminists.

For all of these reasons, and more, feminists have taken the lead in multidisciplinary and wide-ranging studies of identity, identification processes, and their relationships to power at local, national and global 'levels'. The literature critical of gender identities is extensive; most significant for the intersection of international relations and geography are studies that problematize political identities understood as exclusively public-sphere and state-centric (e.g., Pateman, 1988, 1989; Kofman and Peake, 1990; Pignone, 1992; Orloff, 1993). These issues merge with feminist and other critical analyses of citizenship (e.g., Yeatman, 1988; Heater, 1990; Meehan, 1993; Lister, 1993; Yuval-Davis, 1991; Smith, 1989; Marston, 1990) and, more broadly, the gendered politics of democracy (e.g., Rose, 1990; Phillips, 1991; Travers, 1992; Waylen, 1994). Nationalism, of course, is a particular focus of identity studies and has been well mapped by feminists (Yuval-Davis and Anthias, 1989; Parker *et al.*, 1991; *Gender and History*, 1993; Pettman, 1992; *Feminist Review*, 1993, numbers 44 and 45; Peterson, 1995a).

Given the significance of identity politics, feminists have focused considerable attention on the interaction of oppressions – racism, ablism, (hetero)sexism, ageism, classism and so on – and possibilities for solidarity in the face of diversity (Phelan, 1989; Anzaldua, 1990; Mohanty, Russo and Torres, 1991). Similarly, differences among women have compelled feminists to take a politics of difference seriously, including a politics of accountability even in the context of postmodernist theorizing. I have argued elsewhere that postmodernism permits *but does not entail* apolitical relativism (Peterson, 1992b, 1992c). Yet at present, feminists (including men who identify as feminists and take gender seriously in their work) are largely the only postmodernists undertaking the difficult but indispensable task of engaging a *politics* of difference (Young, 1990; Yeatman, 1994; Grewal and Kaplan, 1994; Gunew and Yeatman, 1993; Sylvester, 1994). Hence, in the context of shifting ground(s) – and especially for those committed to pursuing 'progressive' politics – the contributions of postmodern feminists are particularly significant.[3]

The politics of epistemology

Although it has been challenged from numerous vantage points throughout this century, positivist science, or Enlightenment epistemology, continues to dominate the study of social relations, especially in the discipline of international relations. In brief, positivist knowledge claims presuppose a correspondence theory of truth, and categorical separations of subject–object, fact–value and theory–practice. Consistent with Western philosophy's objectivist metaphysics, the binary logic of these foundational dichotomies infuses not only our scientific knowledge claims but our mental maps – our ways of thinking, imagining and expressing – more generally. Of particular significance is how dichotomies differentiate concepts both oppositionally (as mutually exclusive poles of meaning) and hierarchically (as asymmetrically privileged categories). As a consequence, positivist dichotomies frame and effectively (re)produce 'ways of knowing' that are reductionist, ahistorical and static. They are also masculinist because the privileged terms in foundational dichotomies – reason, culture, public – are associated with masculinity and the denigrated (second) terms – affect, nature, private – are associated with femininity (Peterson and Runyan, 1993).

Contemporary empirical and epistemological developments reveal significant problems with such ways of knowing. Empirically, the 'new times' we live in are marked by dynamics of fragmentation, pluralism, decentralization, flexibilization and globalization(s) (Hall, 1991). In this context, conventional reliance on monocausal, reductionist and/or teleological explanations is exposed as radically inadequate. In particular, monodisciplinary perspectives, which emerge from and reproduce positivist dichotomies, frame social inquiry too narrowly and leave too much of significance out of the picture.

For example, realist preoccupation with Cold War power politics obscured the importance of economic, socio-cultural and psychological factors that 'brought down communism'. Similarly, inattention to inter-subjective meaning systems and the politics of identification continues to impair our ability to understand the force of nationalist and fundamentalist movements. These examples illustrate how the dichotomy of politics–economics prevents an integrated and more adequate explanatory map, the dichotomy of production–reproduction leaves us ignorant of how the world is (re)made in everyday practices, and the dichotomy of reason–affect dangerously obscures the political significance of emotional attachments.

Epistemologically, the 'third debate' in international relations (*International Studies Quarterly*, 1989, 1990) acknowledges metatheoretical challenges to the discipline's foundational assumptions, including its defining dichotomies of domestic–international, order–anarchy, war–peace and realism–idealism. Critics argue that the ahistorical and oversimplifying map cultivated by dualist thought must give way to understanding concepts as interactive and *in relation* (Peterson, 1992c). On this view, order is not fixed within a spatial container called the state, to be contrasted with an outside (of international relations) where anarchy prevails. Rather, disorder also exists within states and various forms of order infuse inter-state relations. In the global context of structural violence, war is not the opposite of peace but on a continuum with it: war constitutes only the most direct, not necessarily the most systemic, devastation. Finally, realist claims to describe the world 'as it is' – a 'spectator' theory of knowledge – effectively deny theory *as* practice (George, 1994: 12, 21 and ch. 8), refusing to acknowledge the interaction of speaker (subject), representation (object, theory) and context (practice). But in fact, realist discourse at once describes *and makes* the world; in the process, it (re)produces a historically specific (and particularly narrow) 'map' of 'what's out there' that becomes a self-fulfilling prophecy (e.g., Vasquez, 1983).

Simon Dalby's (1991) 'Critical geopolitics' and Jim George's (1994) *Discourses of Global Politics* offer excellent, accessible reviews of the theoretical debates in international relations and recent critical and postmodern responses. They are persuasive in arguing that the politics of discourse is key to (re)producing – and reconfiguring – power relations (see also Der Derian and Shapiro, 1989; Klein, 1990; Campbell, 1992; O'Tuathail and Agnew, 1992; Weber, 1994).

Dalby and George acknowledge the increasing importance of feminist contributions but do not elaborate on the epistemological implications of 'taking gender seriously'. Feminists go beyond other critics of positivism to argue that the foundational dualisms of Western philosophy – including constitutive dichotomies of international relations and political geography – are conceptually and empirically gendered. Hence, feminist critiques of positivist ways of knowing are central, not peripheral, to the remapping we must do as global dynamics reconfigure territorial and other boundaries.

Because gender hierarchy pervades social relations, feminist scholarship is inherently inter- (I prefer meta-) disciplinary. It typically utilizes multilevel, multidimensional analytic frameworks that are less likely to generate reductionist and/or static accounts. Because of their critical commitments, feminists take the interaction of knowledge and power – theory *as* practice – seriously. In this sense, their theorizing is relatively more 'grounded' and relevant to daily practice, even when it emerges from postmodernist orientations. Feminists add to and go beyond non-feminist perspectives by including women's lives, experiences and ways of knowing in the construction of knowledge claims. They demonstrate how masculinist constructions of subjects and subjectivity are disembodied (abstract, void of desire and corporeality) and disembedded (ahistorical, without contextualization and relatedness) (e.g., Benhabib and Cornell, 1987; Butler, 1989; Brown, W., 1988). And they transform non-feminist critiques of positivism by exposing the masculinism of reason, science and dichotomized mapping more generally (e.g., Harding, 1986, 1991). In Susan Hekman's (1990: 8) words, 'The postmoderns see the error of Enlightenment dualisms but the feminists complete this critique by defining those dualisms as gendered' (see also Peterson, 1992c).

What I want to emphasize is that, in contrast to most non-feminist analyses, *feminist critiques of dichotomies are inseparable from their critiques of oppression.* As part of this, feminists take seriously the relational implications of rejecting dichotomies. I identify two complementary dimensions of this relational orientation: the contextual and conceptual. The former emphasizes bringing the abstract critique of dualist thought into relation with its concrete (historical, empirical) effects. Historical–empirical contextualization illuminates the contingent linkages among concepts, practices, agents and institutional arrangements, for example Merchant's (1980) study of the scientific revolution. In this sense, feminists not only theorize the masculinity of positivist concepts (rationality, objectivity) but also embed these concepts in male-dominated historical conditions (e.g. 'conquering of nature', European state formation and colonialism, industrial capitalism).

By embedding positivist science in historical context, feminists also expose how science is embedded in power relations (Harding, 1986). For example, feminists put flesh on the observation that the model of the rational individual presupposed in scientific ways of knowing is the same (masculine) individual presupposed in economic contracts and political agency (Pateman and Gross, 1986). One consequence, which feminist studies repeatedly confirm, is that females cannot be added to categories that are defined by maleness and therefore imply the absence of femaleness. To do so exposes the masculine gender of the category, demonstrated, for example, by the assumption of male experience in constructions of the public, political identity and politics *per se* (Peterson, 1992b: 17). Either females cannot be added (they are marginalized), or they must become 'like men' (they are masculinized) or *they are included, and the meaning of the category is transformed to include femaleness.* This brings us to the second, conceptual, dimension of a relational orientation.

If the contextual dimension highlights the political implications of bringing categories into relation, the conceptual dimension highlights the theoretical implications. The binary logic of dichotomies frames our thinking in mutually exclusive categories so that masculinity, reason and objectivity are defined by the absence of femininity, affect and subjectivity. Once we reject the categorical separations presupposed in dichotomies, not only does the boundary between them change but so does the meaning of the polar terms: they are not mutually exclusive but in relation, which permits more than the two possibilities posited in either–or constructions (Peterson, 1992c). Moreover, changing the meaning of the terms and bringing them into relation (exposing their interdependence) changes the theoretical frameworks within which they are embedded.

Hence, a critique of masculinity, reason or objectivity does not entail the elevation of femininity, affect or subjectivity (at the expense of former) but a recognition of their *relationship* in historically specific contexts. Rather than assuming an unproblematic categorical separation of terms, which promotes static explanations, our pursuit of knowledge requires that we specify how terms are related, which requires situating terms and events in historical context and promotes dynamic understanding. This is a complex task, but the more appropriate one for understanding – not acritically reproducing – social life. This task also suggests how a relational orientation is simultaneously contextual and conceptual: by bringing terms into relation, feminists not only contextualize the categories – politically, economically, socioculturally – but also reconceptualize the categories and theoretical frameworks, with implications for political identifications and strategies.

In sum, modernist ways of knowing are masculinist and political – embedded in and reproducing particular relations of power – because they naturalize the marginalization, objectification and corollary exploitation of that which is associated with the feminine: women, nature and colonized 'others' (Mies, 1986; Trinh, 1989). The ostensible 'naturalness' of sex difference is generalized to other forms of domination. In this sense, feminist critiques are not simply about male–female relations but about all social hierarchies that are naturalized (depoliticized, legitimated) by reference to ostensibly 'natural' sex differences.

What these points demonstrate is that masculinist ways of knowing marginalize women as agents and gender as an analytic category. A litany of dichotomies privilege (élite) male experience and androcentric accounts at the expense of female experience (in all its diversity) and the experience of all who are 'othered' by association with femininity. One consequence is distorted knowledge claims and inadequate theories, leaving us – sometimes intentionally but always dangerously – ignorant of important social dynamics. The gender-differentiated effects of these distortions are not only conceptual but concrete, reproducing identities and conditions that favour diverse but always gendered social hierarchies.

The politics of states and markets

Replicating disciplinary divisions and consistent with positivist dichotomies, conventional accounts in international relations separate political activities associated with states from economic activities associated with markets. In international relations, politics is spatially located within the territorial boundaries of the state, to be distinguished from anarchy (the absence of 'authentic politics') outside the state and/or from market activities (myriad individual decisions) that are not territorially 'grounded'. More frequently, reference to public and private spheres invokes mutually exclusive spaces for political and economic behaviour respectively. In this framework, the private sector of business operates to maximize profit while the public sector of government operates to maintain order and infrastructure.

As the dominant paradigm in international relations, realist preoccupation with power politics has had the predictable effect of marginalizing economics and the paradoxical effect of neglecting theories of the state (Halliday, 1987; Peterson, 1992a). As focuses of enquiry, the history and reproduction of states are largely set aside in favour of a discipline-defining focus on the meaning of sovereignty and security in an inter-state system already in place and assumed to be structurally unchanging. Sovereignty – the distinctive feature of the modern system – is the right of states to exercise complete jurisdiction within mutually exclusive territorial domains. In these accounts the dichotomy of public–private locates legitimate use of force in the public realm of the state and the dichotomy of internal–external projects this legitimacy outward, expressed as the state's right to make war (Ruggie, 1993: 151).

The neglect of history and presumption of territoriality have impoverished international relations theory, rendering it particularly inadequate in the context of globalization. Ignoring history has exacerbated the tendency towards static and reductionist understanding: as many critics have observed, prevailing theories deal poorly with change and simply deny fundamental transformations. On the other hand, elevation of politics (understood territorially) over economics has precluded sophisticated and critical analyses of market dynamics. In the absence of such analyses, the globalization of capital evades our understanding: we rely too much on liberal–capitalist orthodoxies, we know too little about unregulated financial markets and non-territorial power, and we lack any credible alternatives to a model of unbridled accumulation that is ultimately (ecologically, if not morally) self-destructive.

Important literatures counter these weaknesses, though only a sample can be identified here. Accessible and sophisticated treatments of political economy in the context of globalization(s) include Cox's *Production, Power, and World Order* (1987), Strange's *States and Markets* (1994) and recent edited volumes by Drache and Gertler (1991), Murphy and Tooze (1991), Gill (1993), Epstein, Graham and Nembhard (1993), Bakker (1994), and Stubbs and Underhill (1994). More broadly focused and including international politics, political theory and socio-cultural developments in the context of globalization(s) are Berry (1989), Czempiel and Rosenau (1989), Hall and Jacques (1989), Cerny (1990) Wallerstein (1991), King (1991), Robertson (1992), Walker (1993) and *International Sociology* (1994). Sassen (1991) is crucial on global cities, Dunn (1990) considers the 'economic limits to modern politics', Scholte (1993) addresses social change, Mlinar (1992) considers territorial identities, Driver (1991), Baldwin (1992) and Ruggie (1993) rethink state territoriality, and sovereignty is reconsidered in Barkin and Cronin (1994) and numerous works by Richard Ashley, David Campbell, R. B. J. Walker, and Cynthia Weber (see also chapter by Marc Williams in this volume). In the midst of celebrating the 'third wave of democratization' (Huntington, 1993), it is especially important to consider how global dynamics problematize territorial democratic theory and practice (Held, 1993; Connolly, 1991; Resnick, 1992; Peterson, 1995b).

A considerable feminist literature exists on the gendered state. This includes the gender politics of welfare states (e.g., Sassoon, 1987; Gordon, 1990), Third World states (e.g., Afshar, 1987; Agarwal, 1988; Parpart and Staudt, 1990), and states in an international context (e.g., Peterson, 1992a and forthcoming). Feminists have critically analysed state-centric security (e.g., Cohn, 1987; Tickner, 1992; Enloe, 1993) and have been at the forefront of ecological movements (e.g., *Hypatia*, 1991; Mies and Shiva, 1993). In the context of European integration, feminists have examined gendered power as it shapes diverse issues (e.g., *Feminist Review*, 1991; *Women's Studies International Forum*, 1992; Meehan, 1993). Feminist scholars are challenging conventional accounts and their foundational assumptions in both geography (e.g., Bowlby *et al.*, 1989; Kofman and Peake, 1990; Bondi, 1990, 1992; Hanson, 1992; Bondi and Domosh, 1992; Dalby, 1994; Rose, 1994) and international relations (e.g., Beckman and D'Amico, 1994; Grant and Newland, 1991; Tickner, 1992; Peterson, 1992a; *Alternatives*, 1993; Pettman, 1993; Peterson and Runyan, 1993; *Fletcher Forum*, 1993; Sylvester, 1994; Whitworth, 1994; Zalewski and Parpart, forthcoming).

Finally, and particularly telling, are feminist analyses of gendered power as manifested in global divisions of labour. A voluminous 'women and development' literature has for decades chronicled the costs of gendered economic policies (e.g., Nash and Fernandez-Kelly, 1983; Sen and Grown, 1987; Mies *et al.*, 1988; Elson, 1991). Contemporary studies examine global restructuring, its gendered assumptions and its gendered consequences (e.g., Kamel, 1990; Ward, 1990; Vickers, 1991; Smith and Wallerstein, 1992;

Review of Radical Political Economy, 1991; Beneria and Feldman, 1992; Peterson and Runyan, 1993; Bakker, 1994; Peterson, 1996). Because gendered divisions of identity are inseparable from gendered divisions of labour, and because the latter shape and are shaped by global dynamics and divisions, this literature is crucial for our (re)construction of social theory in the context of globalization.

Conclusion

This chapter has argued that we need new mapping strategies to situate our selves and effectively negotiate the unfamiliar terrain of globalized 'new times'. Empirical and epistemological challenges interact to problematize conventional accounts of identity, epistemology, states and markets. In these accounts, foundational dichotomies set the boundaries of epistemological orientations (subject–object, fact–value, theory–practice), disciplinary fields (politics–economics, political science–international relations, cultural–physical geography), politically salient identifications (citizen–alien, scholar–activist, men–women), and the meaning of politics and power (agent–structure, public–private, domestic–international). Yet precisely these dichotomies and the 'grounds' they establish are brought into question by today's empirical and epistemological turbulence.

In spite of the complexity and instability associated with new times and postmodern perspectives, they are not without pattern and meaning. Rather than paralysis in the face of postmodern challenges, we must develop strategies/theories/identifications that acknowledge complexity without abandoning commitments to human understanding and progressive politics. I find a *'three Cs'* framing device – contextualization, comparison, critical reflection – useful in this regard. From a postmodern vantage point, *contextualization* both historically (exposing how reality is made, not discovered) and multidimensionally (exposing the interaction of agents, concepts, practices and institutions) is paramount. Bringing 'objects' of study into relation (contextualization) enables us to render non-essentialist critiques by making *comparisons*, not absolute claims. Asking the question 'Compared with what?' reminds us that our actions/strategies/theories/identifications are 'choices' always shaped (but not fixed) by contingent factors, by context. Moreover, they are never 'neutral' but involve complex trade-offs with intended *and* unintended effects. Specifying comparisons then enables us to engage in *critical reflection*, to evaluate 'choices' by reference to anticipated trade-offs, not decontextualized preferences. In short, the 'three Cs' frame a provisional and pragmatic orientation born of postmodern understanding.

I have suggested that the work of postmodern feminists is particularly valuable. Briefly, a postmodern orientation is required by well-established critiques of modernist (positivist) science: ahistorical grounds – and the binary boundaries that they naturalize – are not to be found and we do well to abandon that search and its dichotomized mapping practices. A feminist orientation is required by recognizing gender as a pervasive feature of social life: ungendered identities, epistemologies, states and markets are not to be found and we do well to take seriously how feminists integrate conceptual and contextual critiques of naturalized dichotomies.

In sum, postmodern feminism offers not a definitive map (a contradiction in terms) but valuable mapping strategies – born of researching the terrain (both empirically and critically) and addressing the complexity (both conceptually and politically) of postmodernity's shifting ground(s). Consistent with a relational orientation, they have contextualized their concepts – a sound, if not grounded, strategy.

Notes

1. I pluralize globalization in order to 'mark' the complexity of today's global dynamics, specifically that their effects are both homogenizing *and* fragmenting. See the chapter by Youngs in this volume, Mlinar (1992) and the essays in *International Sociology* (1994).
2. If social theories bring agency, order and change into intelligible relation, then identifications offer *one* way of bridging agency (subjectivity, identities, micro-level), order (structure, institutions, macro-level) and change (transformations – of agency and order – as effects of action, mobilized by variants in identity salience and shifting identifications). The diverse literature underpinning this orientation is not addressed here; see the excellent account in Pignone (1992).
3. The relationship between feminism and postmodernism is extremely controversial and currently the focus of extensive debates, especially among feminists. These debates are additionally, and frustratingly, complicated because the meaning of postpositivism, poststructuralism and postmodernism varies among disciplines and authors. For example, Bondi (1990, 1992) and Bondi and Domosh (1992) argue persuasively that (what they refer to as) postmodernism in geography more often appropriates than addresses feminist issues and is therefore incompatible with a feminist agenda; they prefer a strategy of feminist poststructuralism that avoids postmodernism's 'radical relativism'. My use of postmodern in this chapter most closely resembles my use of postpositivist in Peterson (1992c).

References

Afshar, H. (ed.) (1987) *Women, State, and Ideology: Studies from Africa and Asia,* Albany, State University of New York Press.

Agarwal, B. (ed.) (1988) *Structures of Patriarchy: State, Community and Household in Modernizing Asia,* London, Zed.

Alternatives (1993) (special issue), Feminists Write International Relations, **18**(1).

Amin, S., Arrighi, G., Gunder Frank, A. and Wallerstein, I. (1990) *Transforming the*

Revolution: Social Movements and the World-System, New York, Academic Press.

Anderson, B. (1991) *Imagined Communities*, 2nd edn, London, Verso.

Anzaldua, G. (ed.) (1990) *Making Face, Making Soul/Hacienda Caras: Creative and Critical Perspectives by Women of Color*, San Francisco, Aunt Lute.

Bakker, I. (ed.) (1994) *The Strategic Silence: Gender and Economic Policy*, London, Zed.

Baldwin, T. (1992) The territorial state, in H. Gross and R. Harrison (eds), *Jurisprudence: Cambridge Essays*, Oxford, Clarendon.

Barkin, J. S. and Cronin, B. (1994) The state and the nation, *International Organization*, **48**(1), 107–30.

Beckman, P. and D'Amico, F. (eds) (1994) *Women, Gender, and World Politics*, Westport, CT, Bergin and Garvey.

Beneria, L. and Feldman, S. (eds) (1992) *Unequal Burden: Economic Crises, Persistent Poverty and Women's Work*, Boulder, CO, Westview.

Benhabib, S. and Cornell, D. (eds) (1987) *Feminism as Critique*, Minneapolis, University of Minnesota Press.

Berry, B. J. L. (1989) Comparative geography of the global economy, *Economic Geography*, **65**(1), 1–18.

Bloom, W. (1990) *Personal Identity, National Identity and International Relations*, Cambridge, Cambridge University Press.

Bologh, R. W. (1987) Marx, Weber, and masculine theorizing, in Norbert Wiley (ed.), *The Marx-Weber Debate*, Beverly Hills, Sage.

Bondi, L. (1990) Feminism, postmodernism, and geography: space for women? *Antipode*, **22**(2), 156–67.

Bondi, L. (1992) Gender and dichotomy, *Progress in Human Geography*, **16**(1), 98–104.

Bondi, L. and Domosh, M. (1992) Other figures in other places: on feminism, postmodernism and geography, *Environment and Planning D: Society and Space*, **10**, 199–213.

Bowlby, S., Lewis, J., McDowell, L. and Foord, J. (1989) The geography of gender, in R. Peet and N. Thrift (eds), *New Models of Geography*, London, Unwin Hyman.

Brown, R. H. (1987) Personal identity and political economy: western grammars of the self in historical perspective, *Current Perspectives in Social Theory*, **8**, 123–59.

Brown, W. (1988) *Manhood and Politics*, Totowa, NJ, Rowman and Littlefield.

Butler, J. (1989) *Gender Trouble: Feminism and the Subversion of Identity*, New York, Routledge.

Campbell, D. (1992) *Writing Security: United States Foreign Policy and the Politics of Identity*, Manchester, Manchester University Press.

Cerny, P. G. (1990) *The Changing Architecture of Politics: Structure, Agency, and the Future of the State*, London, Sage.

Cohn, C. (1987) Sex and death in the rational world of defense intellectuals, *Signs*, **12**, 687–718.

Connolly, W. E. (1991) *Identity/Difference: Democratic Negotiations of Political Paradox*, Ithaca and London, Cornell University.

Corrigan, P. and Sayer, D. (1985) *The Great Arch: English State Formation as Cultural Revolution*, Oxford and New York, Basil Blackwell.

Cox, R. W. (1987) *Production, Power, and World Order: Social Forces in the Making of History*, New York, Columbia University Press.

Czempiel, E.-O. and Rosenau, J. N. (eds) (1989) *Global Changes and Theoretical Challenges: Approaches to World Politics for the 1990s*, Lexington, MA, Lexington Books.

Dalby, S. (1991) Critical geopolitics: discourse, difference, and dissent, *Environment and Planning D: Society and Space*, **9**, 261–83.

Dalby, S. (1994) Gender and critical geopolitics: reading security discourse in the new world order, *Environment and Planning D: Society and Space*, **12**, 595–612.

Der Derian, J. and Shapiro, M. J. (eds) (1989) *International/Intertextual Relations: The Boundaries of Knowledge and Practice in World Politics*, Lexington, MA, Lexington Books.

Drache, D. and Gertler, M. S. (eds) (1991) *The New Era of Global Competition*, Montreal, McGill–Queen's University Press.

Driver, F. (1991) Political geography and state formation: disputed territory, *Progress in Human Geography*, **15**(2), 268–80.

Dunn, J. (ed.) (1990) *The Economic Limits to Modern Politics*, Cambridge, Cambridge University Press.

Elson, D. (ed.) (1991) *Male Bias in the Development Process*, Manchester, Manchester University Press.

Enloe, C. (1993) *The Morning After: Sexual Politics at the End of the Cold War*, Berkeley, University of California Press.

Epstein, G., Graham, J. and Nembhard, J. (eds) (1993) *Creating a New World Economy: Forces of Change and Plans for Action*, Philadelphia, Temple University Press.

Fausto-Sterling, A. (1992) *Myths of Gender: Biological Theories About Women and Men*, New York, Basic Books.

Feminist Review (1991) special issue, Feminisms and Europe, no. 39.

Feminist Review (1993) special issue, Nationalisms and National Identities, no. 44.

Feminist Review (1993) special issue, Ethnicities, no. 45.

Fletcher Forum of World Affairs (1993) special issue, Gender in International Relations, **17**(2).

Gender and History (1993) special issue, Gender, nationalisms and National Identities, **5**(2).

George, J. (1994) *Discourses of Global Politics: A Critical (Re)Introduction to International Relations*, Boulder, CO, Lynne Rienner.

Gill, S. (ed.) (1993) *Gramsci, Historical Materialism and International Relations*, Cambridge, Cambridge University Press.

Gordon, L. (1990) *Women, the State, and Welfare*, Madison, University of Wisconsin.

Grant, R. and Newland, K. (eds) (1991) *Gender and International Relations*, Bloomington and Indianapolis, Indiana University Press.

Grewal, I. and Kaplan, C. (eds) (1994) *Scattered Hegemonies: Postmodernity and Transnational Feminist Practices*, Minneapolis, University of Minnesota Press.

Gunew, S. and Yeatman, A. (eds) (1993) *Feminism and the Politics of Difference*, Boulder, CO, Westview.

Hall, S. (1991) Brave new world, *Socialist Review*, **21**(1), 57–64.

Hall, S. and Jacques, M. (eds) (1989) *New Times: The Changing Face of Politics in the*

1990s, London, Lawrence and Wishart.

Halliday, F. (1987) State and society in international relations: a second agency, *Millennium*, **16**, 215–30.

Hanson, S. (1992) Geography and feminism: worlds in collision? *Annals of the Association of American Geographers*, **82**(4), 569–86.

Harding, S. (1986) *The Science Question in Feminism*, Ithaca, NY, Cornell University Press.

Harding, S. (1991) *Whose Science? Whose Knowledge?* Ithaca, NY, Cornell University Press.

Harding, S. and Hintikka, M. (eds) (1983) *Discovering Reality*, Dordrecht, Netherlands, D. Reidel.

Heater, D. (1990) *Citizenship: The Civic Ideal in World History, Politics and Education*, London, Longman.

Hekman, S. J. (1990) *Gender and Knowledge: Elements of a Postmodern Feminism*, Cambridge, Polity.

Held, D. (ed.) (1993) *Prospects for Democracy: North, South, East, West*, Cambridge, Polity.

Huntington, S. P. (1993) *The Third Wave: Democratization in the Late Twentieth Century*, Norman, OK, University of Oklahoma Press.

Hypatia (1991) special issue, Ecological feminism, **6**(1).

International Sociology (1994) special issue, Globalization, **9**(2).

International Studies Quarterly (1989) special issue, Exchange on the third debate, **33**(3).

International Studies Quarterly (1990) special issue, Speaking the language of exile, **34**(3).

Kamel, R. (1990) *The Global Factory: Analysis and Action for a New Economic Era*, Philadelphia, American Friends Service Committee.

Keller, E. F. (1985) *Reflections on Gender and Science*, New Haven, CT, Yale University Press.

King, A. D. (ed.) (1991) *Culture, Globalization and the World System: Contemporary Conditions for the Representation of Identity*, London, Macmillan.

Klein, B. S. (1990) How the West was one: representational politics of NATO, *International Studies Quarterly*, **34**(3), 311–26.

Knights, D. and Willmott, H. (1985) Power and identity in theory and practice, *Sociological Review*, **33**(1), 22–46.

Kofman, E. and Peake, L. (1990) Into the 1990s: a gendered agenda for political geography, *Political Geography Quarterly*, **9**(4), 313–36.

Lister, R. (1993) Tracing the contours of women's citizenship, *Policy and Politics*, **21**(1), 3–16.

Lorraine, T. E. (1990) *Gender, Identity and the Production of Meaning*, Boulder, CO, Westview.

Marston, S. A. (1990) Who are 'the People'? Gender, citizenship, and the making of the American nation, *Environment and Planning D: Society and Space*, **8**, 449–58.

Meehan, E. (1993) Women's studies and political studies, in J. Evans, J. Hills, K. Hunt, E. Meehan, T. ten Tusscher, V. Vogel and G. Waylen (eds), *Feminism and Political Theory*, London, Sage.

Merchant, C. (1980) *The Death of Nature: Women, Ecology and the Scientific Revolution*, New York, Harper and Row.

Mies, M. (1986) *Patriarchy and Accumulation on a World Scale: Women and the International Division of Labour*, London, Zed.

Mies, M., Bennholdt-Thomsen, V. and Von Werlhof, C. (1988) *Women: The Last Colony*, London and New Jersey, Zed.

Mies, M. and Shiva, V. (1993) *Ecofeminism*, London, Zed.

Mlinar, Z. (ed.) (1992) *Globalization and Territorial Identities*, Aldershot, Avebury.

Mohanty, C. T., Russo, A. and Torres, L. (eds) (1991) *Third World Women and the Politics of Feminism*, Bloomington, Indiana University Press.

Molyneux, M. (1985) Mobilization without emancipation? Women's interests, the state, and revolution in Nicaragua, *Feminist Studies*, **11**, 227–54.

Murphy, C. and Tooze, R. (eds) (1991) *The New International Political Economy*, Boulder, CO, Lynne Rienner.

Nash, J. and Fernandez-Kelly, M. (eds) (1983) *Women, Men, and the International Division of Labor*, Albany, State University of New York Press.

Orloff, A. S. (1993) Gender and the social rights of citizenship: the comparative analysis of gender relations and welfare states, *American Sociological Review*, **58**, 303–28.

O'Tuathail, G. and Agnew, J. (1992) Geopolitics and discourse: practical geopolitical reasoning in American foreign policy, *Political Geography*, **11**(2), 190–204.

Parker, A., Russo, M., Sommer, D. and Yaeger, P. (eds) (1991) *Nationalisms and Sexualities*, New York, Routledge.

Parpart, J. L. and Staudt, K. A. (eds) (1990) *Women and the State in Africa*, Boulder, CO, Lynne Rienner.

Pateman, C. (1988) *The Sexual Contract*, Stanford, CA, Stanford University Press.

Pateman, C. (1989) *The Disorder of Women*, Stanford, CA, Stanford University Press.

Pateman, C. and Gross, E. (eds) (1986) *Feminist Challenges: Social and Political Theory*, Boston, Northeastern University Press.

Peterson, V. S. (ed.) (1992a) *Gendered States: Feminist (Re)Visions of International Relations Theory*, Boulder, CO, Lynne Rienner.

Peterson, V. S. (1992b) Introduction in Peterson (ed.) (1992a).

Peterson, V. S. (1992c) Transgressing boundaries: theories of knowledge, gender, and international relations, *Millennium*, **21**(2), 183–206.

Peterson, V. S. (1995a) The politics of identity and gendered nationalism, in L. Neack, P. J. Haney and J. A. K. Hey (eds), *Foreign Policy*, Englewood Cliffs, NJ, Prentice Hall.

Peterson, V. S. (1995b) Reframing the politics of identity: democracy, globalization and gender, *Political Expressions*, **1**(1).

Peterson, V. S. (1996) The politics of identification in the context of globalization, *Women's Studies International Forum*, **19**(1–2), 5–15.

Peterson, V. S. (forthcoming) Seeking world order beyond the gender order of global hierarchies, in R. Cox (ed.), *Multilateralism and World Order*, New York, Macmillan, on behalf of United Nations University Press.

Peterson, V. S. and Runyan, A. (1993) *Global Gender Issues*, Boulder, CO, Westview.

Pettman, J. J. (1992) Women, nationalism and the state: towards an international feminist perspective. Occasional Paper 4 in Gender and Development Studies, Asian Institute of Technology, Bangkok.

Pettman, J. J. (1993) Gendering international relations, *Australian Journal of International Affairs*, **47**(1), 47–62.

Phelan, S. (1989) *Identity Politics*, Philadelphia, Temple University Press.

Phillips, A. (1991) *Engendering Democracy*, Cambridge, Polity.

Pignone, M. M. (1992) On becoming a global citizen – praxis in identity politics: a participatory development education project, Ph.D. thesis, American University, Washington, DC.

Resnick, P. (1992) *Isonomia, Isegoria, Isomoira* and democracy at the global level, *Praxis International*, **12**(1), 35–49.

Review of Radical Political Economics (1991) special issue on women, **23**(3–4).

Robertson, R. (1992) *Globalization: Social Theory and Global Culture*, London, Sage.

Rose, G. (1990) The struggle for political democracy: emancipation, gender and geography, *Environment and Planning D: Society and Space*, **8**, 395–408.

Rose, G. (1994) Engendering and degendering, *Progress in Human Geography*, **18**(4), 507–15.

Ruggie, J. G. (1993) Territoriality and beyond: problematizing modernity in international relations, *International Organization*, **47**(1), 139–74.

Sassen, S. (1991) *The Global City: New York, London, Tokyo*, Princeton, Princeton University Press.

Sassoon, A. S. (ed.) (1987) *Women and the State*, London, Hutchinson.

Scholte, J. A. (1993) *International Relations of Social Change*, Buckingham, Open University Press.

Sen, G. and Grown, C. (eds) (1987) *Development, Crises, and Alternative Visions: Third World Women's Perspectives*, New York, Monthly Review Press.

Smith, J. and Wallerstein, I. (eds) (1992) *In Creating and Transforming Households: The Constraints of the World Economy*, Cambridge, Cambridge University Press.

Smith, S. J. (1989) Society, space and citizenship: a human geography for the 'New Times'? *Trans. Inst. Br. Geogr.*, **14**, 144–56.

Strange, S. (1994) *States and Markets*, 2nd edn, London, Pinter.

Stubbs, R. and Underhill, G. R. D. (eds) (1994) *Political Economy and the Changing Global Order*, New York, St Martin's Press.

Sylvester, C. (1994) *Feminist Theory and International Relations in a Postmodern Era*, Cambridge, Cambridge University Press.

Tickner, J. A. (1992) *Gender in International Relations: Feminist Perspectives on Achieving Global Security*, New York, Columbia University Press.

Travers, A. (1992) Radical democracy's feminist potential, *Praxis International*, **12**(3), 269–83.

Trinh, M. (1989) *Woman, Native, Other: Writing Postcoloniality and Feminism*, Garden City, NY, Anchor.

Vasquez, J. A. (1983) *The Power of Power Politics: A Critique*, London, Pinter.

Vickers, J. (1991) *Women and the World Economic Crisis*, London and New Jersey, Zed.

Walker, R. B. J. (1988) *One World, Many Worlds: Struggles for a Just World Peace*, Boulder, CO, Lynne Rienner.

Walker, R. B. J. (1993) *Inside/Outside: International Relations as Political Theory*, Cambridge, Cambridge University Press.

Wallerstein, I. (1991) *Geopolitics and Geoculture*, Cambridge, Cambridge University Press.

Ward, K. B. (ed.) (1990) *Women Workers and Global Restructuring*, Ithaca, ILR Press of Cornell University.

Waylen, G. (1994) Women and democratization: conceptualizing gender relations in transition politics, *World Politics*, **46**, 327–54.

Weber, C. (1994) *Simulating Sovereignty: Intervention, the State, and Symbolic Exchange*, Cambridge, Cambridge University Press.

Whitworth, S. (1994) *Feminism and International Relations: Towards a Political Economy of Gender in Interstate and Non-Governmental Institutions*, London, Macmillan.

Women's Studies International Forum (1992) special issue, Women in Europe, **15**(1).

Yeatman, A. (1988) Beyond natural right: the conditions for universal citizenship, *Social Concept*, **4**(2), 3–33.

Yeatman, A. (1994) *Postmodern Revisionings of the Political*, New York, Routledge.

Young, I. M. (1990) *Justice and the Politics of Difference*, Princeton, Princeton University Press.

Yuval-Davis, N. (1991) The citizenship debate: women, ethnic processes and the state, *Feminist Review*, **39**, 58–68.

Yuval-Davis, N. and Anthias, F. (eds) (1989) *Woman-Nation-State*, London, Macmillan.

Zalewski, M. and Parpart, J. (eds) (forthcoming) *Feminism, Masculinity and Power in International Relations*, Boulder, CO, Westview.

2

Crossing Disciplinary Boundaries: Political Geography and International Relations after the Cold War

SIMON DALBY

Global politics after the Cold War

In Hugh Gusterson's (1993: 279) choice phrase, 'the end of the cold war has destroyed our maps'. Although this may be a particularly perilous fate for geographers, Gusterson obviously had the cartographic aids used by practitioners of the discourses of international relations more clearly in focus in his critique of the conventional scholarly apparatuses of cold war. But the collapse of the Cold War is not solely responsible for the representational crisis in the cartography of contemporary global politics. The phenomena usually grouped under the convenient label 'globalization' have also further eroded some of the clean lines of national boundaries and the claims to effective sovereignty (Camilleri and Falk, 1992; O'Tuathail and Luke, 1994).

Global financial markets and the proliferation of financial instruments that can be transferred through cyberspace by a few keystrokes have increasingly made global politics about daily responses to market perturbations. Central banks now seem much less central. Traders in obscure foreign branches of venerable financial institutions can quickly cause dramatic upsets. Chiapas rebels spread the news from the south of Mexico across the world instantly on the Internet. Even some grassroots organizations now have extensive access to communications possibilities that earlier generations of activists could only fantasize about (Hall, 1994). Camcorders and miniature satellite dishes offer immediate televisual representations of conflict around the world, linking ever larger audiences into worlds of virtual geographies (Wark, 1994). These phenomena are probably best understood as accelerations of media and economic transactions and their impact on how global politics is studied and discussed is already considerable.

But the danger of discussions and celebrations of the end of the Cold War, and of globalization, is that the fate of the poorest people on the planet, of those outside the formal circuits of capital and beyond the reach of cyberspace, populations we might well now call the 'modem-less', will be ignored or forgotten. Where capital is increasingly mobile, labour often is not. These are the people who are refused access to the wealth of the postmodern zones of prosperity, denied transit rights at their borders, and condemned to dangerous refugee camps or political persecution when frontiers are closed (Frelick, 1993). The discourses of globalization and the focus on European transformations after the Cold War often ignore the emergence of what critics are sometimes now calling 'global apartheid' (*Alternatives*, 1994; Richmond, 1994). Clearly any agenda for the critical study of world politics in the era of globalization must take into account the lives of the poorest people if it is to be appropriately comprehensive. Globalization has specific and highly uneven geographies, despite the implicit assumptions of homogenization in most uses of the term (Holm and Sorensen, 1995).

But when the populations of the poor, economic migrants and political refugees *are* taken seriously, they are often represented in the traditional spatial tropes of external threats to the internal order of postmodern prosperity (Kaplan, 1994). The modes of contemporary thinking about global politics are thus also a crucial matter for scholarly investigation, not least because old patterns of thinking may recur to perpetuate the geopolitical practices of the past, albeit now dressed up in the new ideological guises of discourses of globalization.

The disappearance of the cartographic convention of three worlds – 'us', 'them' and 'those in-between' – and its replacement by globalization and North–South definitions, raises many questions about how contemporary global politics should be studied. These questions result from the new post-Cold War dynamics and the not entirely unrelated intellectual ferment in the 'social sciences' as they encounter contemporary social theory (George, 1994).

These debates, and the consequences of the changed geopolitical circumstances, have profound implications for political geography and international relations, the two fields of concern to this chapter. Both have only recently engaged with current social theory with unsettling results for conventional approaches. This chapter looks at the intersection of the fields of international relations and political geography, suggesting that the legacies of empire, geopolitics and realism should not be forgotten in the process of rethinking scholarship in the age of globalization. Drawing on contemporary feminist and poststructuralist theorizing, it argues that disciplines are just that – disciplines – institutional practices of knowledge that constrain as well as facilitate both enquiry and social practice.

Global power and academic disciplines

We need to consider the relationship of institutionalized scholarship to research in the macro-historical context. During the late nineteenth century, geography, as a collection of practices of exploration with all the instrumentation of cartography, if not a formal academic discipline, was a 'sternly practical' pursuit (Livingstone, 1992), instrumental in the expansion, consolidation, administration and ideological justification of the British and other European empires (Godlewska and Smith, 1994). Commercial geography resulted from earlier British economic concerns and provided a basic understanding of the trading patterns of empire and the geographic distribution of raw materials and colonial production. When we consider the institutionalization of the discipline of geography in Britain and its current place in the academic establishment we should not forget its historical part in British practices of hegemony. Disciplinary utility in such practices may partly explain historical patterns of institutionalization. International relations and political geography share many substantive concerns but only a relatively small number of geographers write on these matters. One specialist academic journal caters specifically to political geography, while many serve international relations. When political geography encountered a relatively low point in research activity in the 1950s and 1960s, realist approaches to international relations were thriving, particularly in the USA.

It is not surprising that international relations and strategic studies expanded rapidly if one understands US hegemony in terms of informal imperialism, initially as a power hastening decolonization and subsequently as a powerful state exercising hegemony through the use of diplomacy, military alliances and control over many of the international economic institutions (Hoffman, 1977). Viewed as the management of international political relationships, this process clearly requires a supply of professionals, and political science, with its links to public administration and international relations, is the perfect discipline to provide them.

International relations, and strategic studies in particular, have been described as a predominately Anglo-American academic and policy exercise (Krippendorf, 1987). It has also been a predominately masculine discourse (Sylvester, 1994). The literature on nuclear strategy, and security policy in general, can be understood as part of the processes cementing the Atlantic alliance structure, providing a common discourse for the administration of security policy and the co-ordination of strategic planning (Klein, 1994).

Many political geography practitioners are also Anglo-Americans. Indeed, in the preface to his recent edited collection *The Political Geography of the New World Order*, Colin Williams (1993) notes that all the contributors to that volume are more specifically 'Celtic' in origin. He might have added that they are all men. While geography as a discipline has less direct involvement in the contemporary exercise of international politics, geopolitical themes, albeit usually written by non-geographers, are important to understanding strategy (Dalby, 1990) and the recent global politics of 'development' (Slater, 1993).

Hegemonic scholarly practices and global politics

The political contexts of scholarship raise profound questions about the purpose of both political geography and international relations. Born of hegemony and political power, they produce knowledge, but in whose interests, of what kind and for what purpose? Can enquiry in the positivist mode make useful contributions or does recent social theory lead us to believe that we should abandon scientistic formulations in favour of a conceptualization of scholarly activity as contributing to a global conversation on the fate of the planet in time of crisis? Is the role of the scholar more usefully thought of as a traditional philosopher–critic rather than a ('social') scientist? The issue here is the political function of particular modes of knowledge. If the discourses of political geography and international relations have been complicit in the power relations of empire, and more recently of American hegemony, how then might one proceed to 'do' scholarship in ways that are more self-reflective on the relations of power in disciplinary practices?

One has to ask whether one should operate within the conventional categories and disciplinary boundaries at all. In international relations this point has been forcefully put by Rob Walker (1993) who suggests that the very practices of the bulk of international relations thinking operate to preclude important questions about the possibility of world politics. They do this by ontologizing the territorial state and promptly forgetting this move in the celebration of a variety of empiricist and positivist epistemologies. This 'politics of forgetting' structures research in ways that then operate to perpetuate the political order whose construction and history is lost in tales of the scientific analysis of eternal patterns and returning tragedies. The possibilities of thinking and acting politically are closed off by the practices of statecraft that operate in terms of the self-understandings perpetuated by mainstream international relations thinking.

But if one takes seriously the poststructuralist insistence on looking at how discourses implicate practitioners in making political worlds, rather than in viewing them from some supposedly objective external vantage point, then the political roles of scholarly discourses as both modes of understanding and interpretation, and as disciplines that organize and specify knowledge and the social practices that these set in motion, become important considerations. These matters are relevant to the internal operations of scholarly activity, to matters of who gets published in the disciplinary journals, what perspectives are judged legitimate and scholarly, who gets jobs and promotion. But they also relate to the larger social context of public policy-making because the discursive specifications of social worlds are constitutive of political action; theory is a form of practice (George, 1993). As noted above, in the case of the Cold War, the intellectuals of statecraft, and most obviously the security intellectuals and foreign policy experts, have been influential in empowering particular discursive practices, notably the knowledge practices of strategic studies and related policies of deterrence (Dalby, 1990; Klein, 1994).

The disciplines of international relations and political geography have histories related to the exercise of global power. Both are discourses implicated in one way or another with the Anglo-American political ascendancy of the last two centuries. While participants may not all be guilty of the charges of 'Orientalism' (Said, 1979), or various forms of imperialism, the disciplines' complicity in global power is a factor that has shaped enquiry and is an important theme to consider in trying to think beyond the categories of cold war and towards new political agendas in the face of globalization. As the burgeoning 'post-colonial' literature makes clear, there are no easy answers as to how to 'do' scholarship in ways that avoid the worst pitfalls of ethnocentrism or the operation of power; the point is that one cannot now 'do' it in a manner innocent of these difficulties (Young, 1990; Spivak, 1990). Neither can one 'do' scholarship innocent of the charges made by many feminist writers that both disciplines have been guilty of ignoring, silencing and marginalizing women, their perspectives, their contributions and their presence (Peterson, 1992; Sylvester, 1994). Nor can one easily ignore the vast majority of the world's population living outside the developed world, people whose relative isolation none the less affects matters of global ecology and the functioning of the global economy (Kennedy, 1993).

If globalization is taken seriously as the framework for contemporary discussions of politics, then the global population and the possibility of a world polity become the unavoidable referents for research, a position at odds with traditional practices of geopolitics and international relations, which focused predominantly on the behaviour of economically 'developed' states. Considerations of globalization are in danger of remaining 'incarcerated' within the conventional categories of neorealist international relations thinking (George, 1993), unless the transgression of boundaries, academic and geopolitical, is understood to question the functions of these boundaries and thus open up space to rethink contemporary politics (Rosow, Inayatullah and Rupert, 1994). Useful insights can be gained by crossing the boundaries between international relations and contemporary thinking in political geography.

From political geography to international relations

Both disciplines are concerned with the large-scale global processes of politics and the operation of power, but their approaches are not always similar. Most of the training for international relations scholars is derived from history, sociology, economics and, to a much greater extent, particularly in the USA, political science. Political geography, as a branch of geography, has in the last decade revived a focus on the large picture of global politics in a number of critical ways (Taylor, 1993). Thus, in the post-Cold War era, a number of useful crossfertilizations between the two fields are possible.

First is the territorial theme in geographic writing. As John Agnew (1994a) has made clear, international relations theory has often found itself in a 'territorial trap' where assumptions of states as fixed units of sovereign space, of a polarity between domestic and foreign affairs, and states as the 'containers' of societies, constrain theorizing because of the limits that boundaries are assumed to imply. Most obvious in the operation of 'geo-economic discourse', where national economies are viewed as operating quasi-autonomously in competition in the global economy, these assumptions may be useful to policy-makers interested in using nationalist logic for some purpose, but such reasoning often occludes the globalization of economic activity (Agnew, 1994b). This is not to suggest that all international relations scholars are oblivious to these themes, but to make the point that the literature on territoriality might be taken more seriously, and that implicit assumptions about state boundaries be repeatedly challenged so that political actors other than states are considered in their own right. There is more to global politics than neorealist concerns with international conflict or regime formation.

John Vasquez's (1993) recent comprehensive survey and synthesis of the literature on war between rival states is an important example of some of Agnew's contentions. While Vasquez concludes that territorial conflicts are the primary explanation for the outbreak of war, and its subsequent expansion of conflict through alliance entanglements, he comes to this conclusion citing only a single political geographer and one geographic analysis of this topic (O'Loughlin and Anselm, 1992). At this point one can only speculate on what insights might be gained to elaborate Vasquez's important findings if they were linked with either the geographic literature on boundaries and conflict or, more significantly perhaps, with Sack's (1986) theories of territoriality as a strategy for controlling resources. If territory is but a strategy of power as Sack argues, then the case that Vasquez makes may become very much more interesting. But the transdiscipline link remains to be made.

Second, and related to the first theme, is the overlap between the contemporary concerns in the 'new cultural geography' and the themes of political identity that are an important part of contemporary critical thinking in international relations (Keith and Pile, 1993; Anderson and Gale, 1992). These arguments cut both ways. The geographical arguments point to the complexities of identity formation and the multiple contextually constructed and contested themes of place that are part of the processes of identity formation. With a few noticeable exceptions, the geographic literature on identity formation has not engaged with matters of warfare and state sovereignty and its implications for the construction of identity (O'Tuathail, 1992; Pickles, 1992). The international relations arguments point to the utility of national and state identities in disciplining populations, mobilizing them for war and legitimating the violation of frontiers that are also the symbolic boundaries of political identity (Campbell, 1992, 1993). They also point to related matters of citizenship in respect of militarism and the construction of enemies as the rationale for legitimating masculinist violence. With only a few exceptions, however, the international relations literature has not engaged with the spatial tropes of identity implicit in much of the reasoning of statecraft.

In the case of both these themes, the taken-for-granted nature of the territorial state and stable boundaries is just that, taken for granted. In historical terms, states are social constructions easily viewed as the most powerful of all spatial disciplining practices, and also the most powerful institutions of identity construction (Ruggie, 1993). Can the relative silence on this significance in both disciplines be read as confirmation of just how hegemonic the spatial practices of the modern state are, at least since Halford Mackinder (1904) commented on the significance of closed space ninety years ago? The ontologizing of the territorial state is a very powerful disciplining practice of modernity, one that may facilitate capital accumulation by the constitution of abstract uniform spaces (Smith, 1990), but a practice that has violence as its dark side, the violence of war which has been so significant in the construction of those spaces in the first place (Tilly, 1992).

Furthermore, these matters can also be looked at through 'gendered lenses' (Peterson and Runyan, 1993; see also chapters on gender in this volume). If one extrapolates from the versions of gendered specifications of modernity which distinguish between masculine modes of knowing as 'rational', quantitative, detached, manipulative and powerful in the sense of dominating, and feminine as intuitive, compassionate, involved, participatory and qualitative, then gendered appreciations of space in political

matters are obviously important. The spatial administration of the contemporary polity can be understood as gendered in that it relies on masculine
cartographic practices of precise demarcation and surveillance over ab-
stractly understood territory. A feminine spatiality suggests a more social
understanding of space, one devoid of precise boundaries and more attuned
to the social patterns of spatial activity and the meaning of places (Spain,
1992; Rose, 1993; Massey, 1994). The basic point, that the very organization of territory and the potentials for violent conflict over this organization
is gendered in some way, is a key corrective to the normalization of territory
and states as the natural containers of political community that has sustained both international relations and sociological thinking through much
of this century. Thus the very categories of geopolitical thinking can be
understood as gendered constructions, and hence contestable political constructions rather than the ontological givens for international relations
theory (Dalby, 1994).

From international relations to political geography

At least three obvious themes from the international relations literature are
relevant to the research agenda for political geography in coming years. First
is the question of the global environmental problematique. Matters of
environmental degradation, deforestation, stratospheric ozone depletion,
climate change and renewable resources all fall well within the normal
technical scope of geographic research (White, 1993). All these are having
political effects which transcend the territorial boundaries of states
(Lipschutz and Conca, 1993; Kamieniecki, 1993; Sachs, 1993). It may also
be a valid generalization that anthropogenic environmental changes are in
general making populations more vulnerable to what are, hence, increasingly inaccurately termed 'natural disasters'. Cross-fertilization between
geographic and international relations research on these matters is a useful
avenue but so far, despite much work on global change, only a few
geographers seem to be either involved with scholarly organizations, such as
the International Studies Association environmental section, or publishing
papers on the contemporary evolution of international environmental politics. The explicitly political dimensions of these issues are not a priority
among even those geographers interested in the human dimensions of global
change (but see Seager, 1993).

Second is the question of strategic studies and security policy. Much recent
political geography has ignored strategic considerations. In the case of world
systems theory-influenced approaches, this is not surprising, given the focus
on economic considerations (Taylor, 1993). There have been studies of
'military geography' and of the larger impacts of war and defence prepara-

tions on urban geography and other matters. What has not been taken up to a large extent is the relationships of these themes to state formation itself (Driver, 1991). The broader patterns of historical geography are shaped by military conquest and the construction of empires and colonies. With some exceptions, the explicitly military dimensions of these matters have not been mainstream concerns of political geography. As a result, many geographers have missed the importance of strategic considerations in discussions of territory. By not involving themselves more widely in readings of strategy they have also often ignored the use of geographical ideas in the formulation of strategic policies (Dalby, 1990).

Contemporary commentary on these issues suggests that security policy and strategic discourse have considerable importance in continued militarization and the conduct of American foreign policy in particular. Security policy was part of the practices of American hegemony in the Cold War period – the persistence of large American military budgets and new strategic naval postures of 'from sea to land' suggest that the geopolitical themes of Mahan (1890) and Mackinder (1904) are still relevant to understanding the international politics of the post-Cold War era (Borosage, 1993/4). Dismissing these themes because they are dated, or inadequately formulated social theories relying on outdated and discredited approaches, is to miss the point that they have considerable political purchase in policy-making circles in the military establishments of Western powers. Ignoring them is to make the mistake of assuming that epistemological veracity, rather than political utility is the basis of influence. All this may become even more germane to geographical research if increasingly severe environmental problems become a matter triggering military responses to environmental degradation and the likely resulting migrations (Kakonen, 1994).

This relates to the third theme of importance. In the last decades a 'third debate' on the purposes and methods of international relations has been under way. Drawing from contemporary social and political theory, the more sophisticated parts of this theoretical discussion have much to offer political geography in terms of philosophical introspection and intellectual refinement (Dalby, 1991). This is not least because the 'critical mass' of international relations scholars engaged in this work is so much larger. Questions about the status of the state, the limits of neorealist ontologies and the possibilities of critical interpretative approaches allow for a more penetrating dialogue about the nature of the world system, the global expansion of modernity and the potential for critique (George, 1994). Crucially, decentring the state, focusing on world politics rather than just international relations, and analysing the functions and territorial reach of states as well as other political organizations are issues which can now be addressed.

All these themes have clear implications for the examination of territorial and spatial strategies of rule and sovereignty (Camilleri and Falk, 1992; Weber, 1994). The territorial state is an invention of the European political system, one which so often fails to 'fit' the political situations within which it is imposed as the basic ruling institution of contemporary political life. In addition to the focus on economic globalization, when used as critical categories, both gender and environment problematize territorial claims to autonomy, security and related negative formulations of freedom. Simultaneously they challenge the positivist assumption of neutral detached observers and science beyond society. The interconnectedness of gender relations and ecological linkages provide useful means to evaluate the state as a disciplinary practice. They also indicate the importance of state control of geographical borders and the implications of various responses to attempted migrations.

Globalization calls into question the related matters of citizenship and the constitution of political identity in terms of spatial referents (see the chapter by Icduygu in this volume). While the goal of 'global citizenship' may often be considered unrealistic political idealism, the term necessitates thinking in political terms that transcend both the practical limitations of passports and visas, and the conceptual limits of political community defined solely by states. It also calls into question citizenship premised on (gendered) military service (Enloe, 1993). In so far as citizenship is identified as a resource available to states in time of war, it represents a limited political imagination, one that strains 'liberal' interpretations of the active participant in 'public' affairs. Imagining what citizenship might entail freed from the logic of states and territorial identity is no easy task in a postmodern world, but clearly many human communities have operated without such practices. The possible implications of such reconceptualizations for the growing numbers of international refugees and the mobility of labour are profound (Richmond, 1994).

Future intellectual cartographies?

The aim of these reflections has been to contribute to opening up a dialogue on the fate of the planet and on the mechanisms of rule, epistemological and otherwise, that enmesh us all in a violent and unsustainable world. They also suggest that the related recognition of the inextricability of power from knowledge is crucial to the tasks of reconstituting 'social science' after the Cold War. They imply that the discourses of global politics are part of the problematique for thinking about globalization; the tools of cold war analysis may often be part of the problem to be investigated rather than useful devices for 'making sense' of the world. Finally they also suggest that one of the important tasks for social science after the Cold War is not to limit its focus to the interactions of states, or the finer points of diplomacy and statecraft. Rather, in Bradley Klein's terms,

> we should ask interesting questions that speak to, and that listen to, ongoing social and political struggles. In this sense, the task of social science is to give voice and clarity to the multiple forces and social movements that help constitute world politics. (1992: 166)

Despite the obvious need to encourage the loquacity of subalterns (Spivak, 1988), the difficulties of speaking about 'world politics' in the face of claims to multiple identities remain enormous. The heritage of political geography and international relations offer numerous grounds for concern that some partial claim can easily be universalized as a powerful ideology. The adoption of the rhetoric of the 'global' environment by political élites in the 'North' suggests that local concerns can be rendered universal relatively easily, and in the process can co-opt many local rhetorics of resistance (Shiva, 1994). The politics of discourse are unavoidable in thinking and writing about globalization.

All of this suggests that the new intellectual maps of the world, that Hugh Gusterson (1993) suggests we need to guide our research, must have very different projections from those common in cold war political cartography. While states may no longer be the neat containers of political community that international relations and political geography have for so long assumed, their power cannot be easily discounted. They may not provide the 'security' for their populations that is supposedly their *raison d'être*, but they remain formidable political organizations (see the chapter by Cerny in this volume) even if their frontiers are more permeable than ever before to capital and communications, if not to impoverished refugees and migrants. The discourses of globalization thus demand more nuanced political cartographies from contemporary practitioners trying simultaneously to unravel the legacies of hegemonic academic disciplines and map the new contours of world politics. More specifically, the discursive difficulties of contemporary world politics suggest the need for multiple and overlapping maps, both topological and thematic, which pay less attention to the boundaries of states and more to the flows and fractures that run across those boundaries.

Acknowledgement

Thanks to Spike Peterson for comments on an earlier draft of this chapter.

References

Agnew, J. (1994a) The territorial trap: the geographical assumptions of international relations theory, *Review of International Political Economy*, **1**, 53–80.

Agnew, J. (1994b) Global hegemony versus national economy: the United States in the new world order, in G. J. Demko and W. B. Wood (eds), *Reordering the World: Geopolitical Perspectives on the 21st Century*, Boulder, CO, Westview.

Alternatives (1994) special issue, Against global apartheid: contemporary perspectives on world order and world order studies, **19**(2).

Anderson, K. and Gale, F. (1992) *Inventing Places: Studies in Cultural Geography*, Melbourne, Longman.

Borosage, R. (1993/4) Inventing the threat: Clinton's defence budget, *World Policy Journal*, **10**, 7–15.

Camilleri, J. and Falk, J. (1992) *The End of Sovereignty?* Aldershot, Edward Elgar.

Campbell, D. (1992) *Writing Security: United States Foreign Policy and the Politics of Identity*, Minneapolis, University of Minnesota Press.

Campbell, D. (1993) *Politics Without Principle: Sovereignty, Ethics, and the Narratives of the Gulf War*, Boulder, CO, Lynne Rienner.

Dalby, S. (1990) *Creating the Second Cold War: The Discourse of Politics*, London, Pinter.

Dalby, S. (1991) Critical geopolitics: difference, discourse and dissent, *Environment and Planning D: Society and Space*, **9**, 261–83.

Dalby, S. (1994) Gender and critical geopolitics: reading security discourse in the new world disorder, *Environment and Planning D: Society and Space*, **12**, 595–612.

Driver, F. (1991) Political geography and state formation: disputed territory, *Progress in Human Geography*, **15**, 268–80.

Enloe, C. (1993) *The Morning After: Sexual Politics and the End of the Cold War*, Berkeley, University of California Press.

Frelick, B. (1993) Closing ranks: the north locks arms against new refugees, in P. Bennis and M. Moushabek (eds), *Altered States: A Reader in the New World Order*, New York, Olive Branch.

George, J. (1993) Of incarceration and closure: neo-realism and the new/old world order, *Millennium*, **22**, 197–234.

George, J. (1994) *Discourses of Global Politics: A Critical Re-Introduction to International Relations*, Boulder, CO, Lynne Rienner.

Godlewska, A. and Smith, N. (1994) *Geography and Empire*, Oxford, Basil Blackwell.

Gusterson, H. (1993) Realism and the international order after the Cold War, *Social Research*, **60**, 279–300.

Hall, B. W. (1994) Information technology and global learning for sustainable development: promise and problems, *Alternatives*, **19**(1), 99–132.

Hoffman, S. (1977) An American social science: international relations, *Daedalus*, **51**, 41–59.

Holm, H.-H. and Sorensen, G. (1995) *Whose World Order? Uneven Globalization and the End of the Cold War*, Boulder, CO, Westview.

Kakonen, J. (1994) *Green Security or Militarized Environment*, Aldershot, Dartmouth.

Kamieniecki, S. (1993) *Environmental Politics in the International Arena: Movements, Parties, Organizations and Policy*, Albany, State University of New York Press.

Kaplan, R. D. (1994) The coming anarchy, *Atlantic Monthly*, **273**(2), 44–76.

Keith, M. and Pile, S. (1993) *Place and the Politics of Identity*, London, Routledge.

Kennedy, P. (1993) *Preparing for the Twenty-First Century*, New York, Harper-Collins.

Klein, B. S. (1992) Discourse analysis: teaching world politics through international relations, in L. S. Gonick and E. Weisband (eds), *Teaching World Politics: Contending Pedagogies for a New World Order*, Boulder, CO, Westview.

Klein, B. S. (1994) *Strategic Studies and World Order: The Global Politics of Deterrence*, Cambridge, Cambridge University Press.

Krippendorf, E. (1987) The dominance of American approaches in international relations, *Millennium: Journal of International Studies*, **16**, 207–14.

Lipschutz, R. and Conca, K. (1993) *The State and Social Power in Global Environmental Politics*, New York, Columbia University Press.

Livingstone, D. N. (1992) *The Geographical Tradition*, Oxford, Blackwell.

Mackinder, H. J. (1904) The geographical pivot of history, *Geographical Journal*, **23**, 421–37.

Mahan, A. J. (1890) *The Influence of Seapower on History 1660–1783*, Boston, Little, Brown.

Massey, D. (1994) *Space, Place and Gender*, Cambridge, Polity.

O'Loughlin, J. and Anselm, L. (1992) Geography of international conflict and cooperation: theory and methods, in M. Ward (ed.), *The New Geopolitics*, Philadelphia, Gordon and Breach.

O'Tuathail, G. (1992) Foreign policy and the hyperreal: the Reagan administration and the scripting of 'South Africa', in T. J. Barnes and J. S. Duncan (eds), *Writing Worlds: Discourse, Text and Metaphor in the Representation of Landscape*, London, Routledge.

O'Tuathail, G. and Luke, T. (1994) Present at the (dis)integration: deterritorialization and reterritorialization in the new wor(l)d order, *Annals of the Association of American Geographers*, **84**, 381–98.

Peterson, V. S. (ed.) (1992) *Gendered States: Feminist (Re)Visions of International Relations Theory*, Boulder, CO, Lynne Rienner.

Peterson, V. S. and Runyan, A. S. (1993) *Global Gender Issues*, Boulder, CO, Westview.

Pickles, J. (1992) Texts, hermeneutics and propaganda maps, in T. J. Barnes and J. S. Duncan (eds), *Writing Worlds: Discourse, Text and Metaphor in the Representation of Landscape*, London, Routledge.

Richmond, A. H. (1994) *Global Apartheid: Refugees, Racism and the New World Order*, Toronto, Oxford University Press.

Rose, G. (1993) *Feminism and Geography*, Minneapolis, University of Minnesota Press.

Rosow, S., Inayatullah, N. and Rupert, M. (1994) *The Global Economy as Political Space*, Boulder, CO, Lynne Rienner.

Ruggie, J. (1993) Territoriality and beyond: problematizing modernity in international relations, *International Organization*, **47**, 139–74.

Sachs, W. (1993) *Global Ecology: A New Arena of Political Conflict*, London, Zed.

Sack, R. D. (1986) *Human Territoriality: Its Theory and History*, Cambridge, Cambridge University Press.

Said, E. (1979) *Orientalism*, New York, Vintage.

Seager, J. (1993) *Earth Follies: Coming to Feminist Terms with the Global Environmental Crisis*, New York, Routledge.

Shiva, V. (1994) Conflicts of global ecology: environmental activism in a period of global reach, *Alternatives*, **19**(2), 195–207.

Slater, D. (1993) The geopolitical imagination and the enframing of development theory, *Transactions of the Institute of British Geographers, New Series*, **18**, 419–37.

Smith, N. (1990) *Uneven Development*, Oxford, Basil Blackwell.

Spain, D. (1992) *Gendered Spaces*, Chapel Hill, University of North Carolina Press.

Spivak, G. C. (1988) Can the subaltern speak? in C. Nelson and L. Greenberg (eds), *Marxism and the Interpretation of Culture*, Urbana, IL, University of Illinois Press.

Spivak, G. C. (1990) *The Post-Colonial Critic: Interviews, Strategies, Dialogues*, London, Routledge.

Sylvester, C. (1994) *Feminist Theory and International Relations in a Postmodern Era*, Cambridge, Cambridge University Press.

Taylor, P. J. (1993) *Political Geography of the Twentieth Century: A Global Analysis*, London, Belhaven.

Tilly, C. (1992) *Coercion, Capital, and European States, AD 990–1992*, Oxford, Basil Blackwell.

Vasquez, J. A. (1993) *The War Puzzle*, Cambridge, Cambridge University Press.

Walker, R. B. J. (1993) *Inside/Outside: International Relations as Political Theory*, Cambridge, Cambridge University Press.

Wark, M. (1994) *Virtual Geography: Living with Global Media Events*, Bloomington, Indiana University Press.

Weber, C. (1994) *Simulating Sovereignty: Intervention, the State, and Symbolic Exchange*, Cambridge, Cambridge University Press.

White, R. R. (1993) *North, South and the Environmental Crisis*, Toronto, Toronto University Press.

Williams, C. (1993) *The Political Geography of the New World Order*, London, Belhaven.

Young, R. (1990) *Writing History and the West*, London, Routledge.

3

Beyond the Buzzword: Towards a Critical Theory of Globalization

JAN AART SCHOLTE

On one broad reading, the history of modern social science has been a continual struggle between orthodox and critical knowledge, that is, between understanding that sustains prevailing patterns of social relations and understanding that challenges them with emancipatory intent. Many times critical energy is dissipated and defused, as potentially transformative knowledge becomes marginalized and forgotten, or is neutralized through appropriation by orthodox discourses. Such has been the fate of much (though not all) that has gone under the name of Marxism, feminism, black consciousness, religious revivalism, environmentalism and postmodernism, for example.

Recent years have seen an important reinvigoration of contests between orthodox and critical knowledge around the issue of globalization, i.e., what might be summarily characterized as the process of the world becoming a single place. Yesterday in the lexical shadowlands, today the vocabulary of globality occupies a notable place in the everyday parlance of commerce, governance, academe and entertainment. Debates over globalization relate centrally to questions of social change in the late twentieth century. Discourses of globalization have become a prime site of struggle between, broadly speaking, conservatives who deny such a trend, liberals who celebrate its presumed fruits, and critics who decry its alleged disempowering effects.

Given the inextricability of theory and practice, much is at stake in the formulation of knowledge about globalization. Consciousness does not singly and wholly create the social world, but it does play a significant role in the making of history. Orthodox (i.e., conservative and liberal) paradigms have the effect of containing the concept of globalization and, by extension, the forces for structural disruption and transformation that this trend might encompass and advance. Conservative conceptions tend to defuse global-ization by playing down the extent of the shift or even encouraging a rollback of the process, while liberal views confidently (and sometimes

dogmatically) promote globalization as a means whereby prevailing lines of
social organization (capitalism, rationalism, etc.) will lead to universal
prosperity, peace and freedom. In contrast, critical orientations emphasize
the importance *and the dangers* of the recent accelerated expansion of a
supraterritorial, whole-world dimension of social relations. This reflexive
knowledge enlarges the scope for radically transformative praxes of globalization and aims, in conjunction with well-devised political mobilization, to
reshape social structures so as to enhance possibilities of human dignity,
security, autonomy, justice, equality, tolerance and community.

The consequences of globalization – arguably one of the most wide-
ranging and unsettling systemic trends in contemporary history – remain
quite open and will be considerably influenced by the sorts of knowledge
constructed about, and fed into, the process. To date, orthodox (and especially liberal) discourses have held an upper hand, but ample opportunities
remain to salvage notions of globalization for critical theory and associated
politics of emancipation.

This chapter seeks to embrace and enlarge these possibilities. It first charts
the sudden and rapid spread of a vocabulary of 'global-ness' and then relates
this linguistic development to a major concrete shift in the contours of social
space. In the third step of the argument, cognizance of this new geography
prompts a rejection of long-standing and generally unquestioned social–
analytical premises of methodological nationalism and methodological territorialism. Next, the chapter examines at greater length how different streams
of social thought have engaged with the rise of supraterritorial relations. The
case for critical praxis is elaborated in the final section, which focuses on the
threats posed by the expansion of supraterritoriality to material welfare,
peace, community, the respect of difference, and democracy.

Spread of a buzzword

Innovations in language often intimate that something important is unfolding in the given historical setting. Thus, for example, the appearance of the
word 'international' towards the end of the eighteenth century reflected the
growing importance at that time of modern territorial states in organizing
social relations. By the same token, the striking recent spread of 'global-
speak' deserves close examination.

Until the 1980s notions of globality generally figured little in conceptions
of social life. Such terminology resided at the margins of speech and meaning. In discussing world affairs, speakers nearly always invoked the vocabulary of 'international' rather than 'global' relations and, with isolated
exceptions (e.g. Moore, 1966), the word 'global' was absent from the titles of
publications. As recently as the mid-1980s, concepts of 'global governance',

'global environmental change', 'global gender relations' and 'global political economy' were virtually unknown.

Yet now, just a few years later, ideas of globality pervade the language of journalists, politicians, bankers, advertisers, officials and researchers the world over. In Italian the talk is of *globalizzazione*, in Chinese of *Quan Qui Hua*, in French of *mondialisation*, in Russian of *глобализация*, in German of *Globalisierung*, in Korean of *Gukje Hwa*, and so on. The 'global' prefix is now commonplace, for example, in global markets, global institutions, global communications and the like. Following John Maclean's (1981: 104) early call 'to comprehend and explain the historical process of the increasing globalization of social relations', questions of globalization have become a concern across the academic spectrum in the 1990s. Indeed, the global problematic suggests itself as a focal issue for cross- or even post-disciplinary social enquiry.

To some extent, no doubt, globalization is a buzzword, a term as ambiguous as it is popular. Much discussion of the global circumstance has been conceptually imprecise and empirically thin. References to the global often still merge with ideas of 'international relations' and 'world system' simply to denote the extension of social relations beyond national, state and country confines. But in this loose form ideas of globality say nothing particularly new and could be applied as much to the seventeenth as the twentieth century.

The rise of supraterritoriality

Yet the spread of a new vocabulary of globality may also reflect an inchoate awareness that social relations have in contemporary times acquired an important new character. To invoke Roland Robertson's (1992) felicitous phrase, the world has in many respects become a single place. Not only has the density of contacts between locations worldwide greatly increased on the whole, but also, in a qualitative break with the past, many of those connections have become wellnigh instantaneous.

The latter point warrants elaboration. In pre-global times, world social geography was a matter of scattered places: social relations involved crossing distance, as measured between points fixed in three-dimensional, territorial space. Although developments in transport and communications, such as railways and postal services, had the effect of reducing time–space separations, they never eliminated distance. In contrast, in the globalized world of today people can by various means relate with one another irrespective of their longitudinal and latitudinal position, as it were on a 'supraterritorial' plane. Global events can – via telecommunications, digital computers, audio-visual media, rocketry and the like – occur almost simultaneously anywhere and everywhere in the world. Marshall McLuhan (McLuhan and Fiore, 1967: 63) referred in this respect to conditions of 'allatonceness [where] "time" has ceased, "space" has vanished'. Others have spoken of a new 'space of flows' alongside the old 'space of places', of 'hyperspace' and of a 'nonterritorial region' of world affairs (Castells, 1989: 348; Jameson, 1984: 83; Ruggie, 1993: 172). On these lines, an important distinction can be drawn between *international* and *global* relations. Whereas international circumstances involve crossing considerable distance over more or less extended time intervals, global conditions are situated in a space beyond geometry, where distance is covered in effectively no time.

As the term is understood here, then, globalization refers to the emergence and spread of a supraterritorial dimension of social relations. In institutional terms, the process has unfolded through the proliferation and growth of so-called 'transnational' corporations, popular associations and regulatory agencies (sometimes termed global companies, global civil society and global regimes respectively). Ecologically, globalization has taken place in the shape of planetary climate change, atmospheric ozone depletion, worldwide epidemics and the decline of Earth's biodiversity, among other things. Economically, in what Karl Marx (1857–58: 524) anticipated as capital's 'annihilation of space by time', globality has been realized *inter alia* in twenty-four-hour, round-the-world financial markets, whole-world production lines and a host of global consumption articles. Normatively, globalization has occurred through the expansion of worldwide standards (e.g., common scales of measurement and so-called universal human rights) as well as through non-territorial networks of collective solidarity (e.g., among women, the disabled or indigenous peoples). Psychologically, globalization has developed through growing consciousness of the world as a single place, an awareness reinforced by everyday experiences of diet, music and dress, as well as by photographs from outer space showing planet Earth as one location. In these ways, the rise of supraterritoriality has been comprehensive, in some form and to some degree spanning all aspects of social relations.

Although globalization has been most pronounced and intense in recent years, on a smaller scale and at a slower pace the trend stretches back more than a century. Telegraphic communication appeared in the 1840s and prompted Nathaniel Hawthorne (1851: 273) to exclaim through one of his characters that 'by means of electricity, the world of matter has become a great nerve, vibrating thousands of miles in a breathless point of time'. The first regulatory bodies with a worldwide remit were inaugurated during the third quarter of the nineteenth century, and globally synchronized time was instituted in 1884, in relation to GMT (Whitrow, 1988: 161–5). Telephone calls between countries were initiated a hundred years ago, while airline services and intercontinental short-wave radio programmes multiplied in the 1920s. The first global broadcast was transmitted in January 1930, when the speech of George V opening the London Naval Conference was relayed to 242 radio stations around the world (Huth, 1937: 420). Global influenza killed tens of millions in 1918–19, and multilateral discussions of transboundary pollution were held as early as the 1930s (Rowlands and Greene, 1992: 1). Already at the start of the twentieth century, Leonard Hobhouse (1906: 316) declared that 'humanity is rapidly becoming, phys-ically speaking, a single society', while Martin Heidegger (1950: 165–6) at mid-century proclaimed the advent of 'distancelessness' and an 'abolition of every possibility of remoteness'. Clearly, then, a certain degree of global-ization was in train well before the term itself was invented.

However, it is mainly since the 1960s that globality has figured con-tinually, comprehensively, centrally and intensely in the lives of a large proportion of humanity. Key supraterritorial phenomena such as Euro-currencies, communications satellites, cyberspace, global factories, fibre-optic cables, G7 summits, global newspapers, global thinktanks, mobile telephones, remote sensing and ozone holes are all new to the last few decades. Meanwhile, the number of television receivers worldwide more than quadrupled between 1965 and 1991 to 830 million (UNESCO, 1993: 9–15). The world count of radio sets has increased more than thirty times during the past sixty years, to 1.8 billion, while direct-dial facilities in the mid-1990s link close to 700 million telephone connection points (double the figure fifteen years earlier) across more than 200 countries (Huth, 1937; Ploman, 1984: 34; UNDP, 1994: 161). On one estimate, the rate of plane-tary species loss has risen from some six per year in 1950 to 10,000 annually in 1990 (Myers, 1985: 155). Global companies now account for a major share of world production, while global products figure prominently in world consumption. Marlboros, for instance, are sold and smoked in 155 countries (Mattelart, 1991: 55).

The preceding remarks should not be read to reflect an unbridled global*ism*. It is *not* claimed here that globalization has touched every person, location and sphere of activity on the planet, or each to the same extent; nor that globalization is a linear and irreversible process, even if it has often appeared to have a juggernaut quality; nor, in reductionist fashion, that globalization constitutes the sole or primary motor of contemporary history; nor that territory, place and distance have lost all significance; nor that state and geopolitical boundaries have ceased to be important; nor that everyone enjoys equal access to, an equal voice in, and equal benefits from the supraterritorial realm; nor that globalization entails homogenization and an erasure of cultural differences; nor that it heralds the birth of a world community with perpetual peace. Indeed, in respect of each of these points the contrary has frequently been the case. However, having acknowledged and indeed stressed these qualifications (Scholte, 1993: 32–40), it can still be emphasized that a large-scale, wide-ranging and deeply penetrating shift in the spatial character of social relations has recently been unfolding and that this development warrants the burgeoning research it has attracted.

Towards a new ontology

Rather than exaggerated assertions of the kind just enumerated, what studies of globalization do demand is an abandonment of two pervasive and deeply ingrained premises of conventional social thought, namely, methodological nationalism and methodological territorialism.

The former was a major flaw in modern social enquiry even before the onset of accelerated globalization. This 'common-sense' conception holds that social relations come packaged in national/state/country units that divide the world into neatly distinguishable 'societies'. Social life is thus understood in terms of relatively fixed, territorially bounded, unitary administrative and cultural entities which uniformly absorb all localities within their respective frontiers and are clearly marked off from an 'outside' environment that surrounds them. In view of widely recognized international interdependence, few people today would insist that a national 'society' is, in fact, completely self-contained and self-determining. However, in spite of a number of compelling deconstructions (e.g., Walker, 1993), dichotomies between 'internal' and 'external', 'domestic' and 'foreign', remain a largely unquestioned foundation of most contemporary social analysis.

To privilege national contours of social life in this way is quite unsatisfactory. True, social relations are in many respects and to important extents organized along country lines; yet these 'societies' are – and always have been – concurrently marked by both intra-national divisions and international connections. Household, local, regional and intercontinental circumstances co-exist with national conditions, have relative autonomy from them, and can in some situations have greater importance in social relations. Moreover, the different realms interpenetrate to such an extent that the construction of social knowledge in terms of country units is not only arbitrary but also unhelpful, all the more so in a time of globalization. Appropriately, therefore, a number of theorists have over the past twenty years favoured concepts of 'world system' over notions of 'international relations' (Wallerstein, 1986).

Globalization also calls into question the prevailing territorialist ontology of modern social theory. This entrenched supposition holds that social space is plotted in terms of locations, distances and borders in a three-dimensional geography. Yet globality introduces a new quality of social space, one that is effectively non-territorial and distance-less. World systems involving an interrelation of close-range and long-distance circumstances have existed for centuries, if not millennia (Wheeler, 1954; Abu-Lughod, 1989), but a fully-fledged global aspect is novel in contemporary history. Phenomena such as cyberspace and electronic mass media are not adequately mapped on a territorial grid. Telephony can make a conversation across the ocean as accessible as a chat across the garden fence. Satellite communications are in fact 'cost-distance insensitive', so that transmissions across 8000 kilometres run at the same level as those across 500 kilometres (Ploman, 1984: 63). Ostensibly national-territorial currencies such as the 'US' dollar, the 'Deutsch' mark and the 'Japanese' yen are used in countless transactions that never touch the respective 'home' soils.

Hence globality involves a different kind of location, such that 'directly experienced' social relations need no longer be those of proximity in accordance with conventional euclidean measurements. Global relations are not links *at a distance* across territory but circumstances *without distance* and relatively disconnected from particular location. Globalization has made the identification of boundaries – and associated notions of 'here' and 'there', 'far' and 'near', 'outside' and 'inside', 'home' and 'away', 'them' and 'us' – more problematic than ever. To this extent, a new, non-territorialist cartography of social life is needed.

The question remains whether, in what ways and to what extent contemporary globalization has wrought, or might produce, a fundamental discontinuity in social history. Are there now certain distinctive global forms of social existence which transcend and even supersede circumstances of locality, country and international relations? How, if at all, has globalization encouraged and reflected changes in social structure, and with what consequences for the human condition?

Contending discourses of globalization

As noted in the introduction to this chapter, answers to these questions vary widely, from conservative denials and liberal celebrations to critical perspectives that highlight the disempowering aspects of globalization and seek to overcome them.[1] The resulting debates hold more than academic interest, and indeed are rehearsed in legislatures, boardrooms, the mass media and social movements as well as in lecture theatres. Knowledge is power, and intellectual constructions of globalization help to shape the course of the trend.

Conservative orthodoxy underplays the extent and significance of globalization. In so far as these traditionalist conceptions take cognizance of a rise of supraterritoriality at all, the development is not thought to involve any noteworthy transformation of the world system. Conservative circles also contain reactionaries, such as certain nationalists and religious revivalists who would reverse any globalization that has thus far occurred. For traditionalists, social relations are and/or should be organized in terms of territorial units (be they sovereign national states or smaller localities) with limited interdependence between them and certainly no global fusion. Conservatives tend to reject liberal enthusiasm for globalization as 'utopian' and to ignore critical perspectives altogether.

In academic circles, dismissals of globalization have been especially prevalent among proponents of so-called realist international theory. This analysis holds that the world system is (and by implication always will be) reducible to interstate competition for power. For realists, power politics are today as resilient as ever, and the main contemporary debate about change concerns whether, in the post-Cold War world, this timeless struggle unfolds in a unipolar or multipolar context (e.g., Layne, 1993; Waltz, 1993; Krasner, 1994). From this perspective, notions of globalization are a delusion, indeed one that might detract dangerously from prudent management of the anarchical international society.

Conservative scepticism may have the salutary effect of checking the unrestrained claims made by some of the more ebullient passengers on the bandwagon of globalization studies; however, the denial that anything like globalization has happened is, in the words of one critic, 'baffling and bizarre' (Ruggie, 1993: 142–3). Perhaps realist arrogance belies an intuitive awareness that globalization calls into question crucial underpinnings of traditional knowledge – methodological nationalism and territorialism – and thereby the very discipline of International Relations and the realist vocation itself (Agnew, 1994b). However, recalcitrant conservatism cannot be allowed to block the development of new knowledge and the alternative futures that it might encourage, particularly when far-reaching questions of human and planetary security are at stake.

Another stream of orthodox thinking, liberalism, does acknowledge a reality of globalization, but regards the process uncritically as progressive and benign. This optimistic and frequently complacent discourse reigns among advertisers and management consultants as well as large sections of governing élites and academia. From a liberal perspective, the contemporary emergence of globality is the extension (and perhaps culmination) of a long-term trend of deepening international interdependence. Indeed, in liberal discourse the terms internationalization and globalization are regularly used interchangeably, and cognizance of recent major transformations of social space is often underdeveloped. In liberal eyes, contemporary globalization offers the prospect of at last fully realizing the promise of modernity. Released from the shackles of traditionalism, colonialism and communism – so this account goes – market forces, electoral multiparty democracy, techno-scientific rationality, national self-determination and international co-operation have the opportunity to work their complete magic, and to the benefit of all humanity (Mueller, 1989; Ohmae, 1990; Huntington, 1991; Fukuyama, 1992).

Two broad variants of liberal discourse can be distinguished. Neoliberalism, especially powerful during the 1980s, holds that globalization will yield this 'end of history' more or less automatically. In contrast, reformist liberalism, generally ascendant in the 1990s, prescribes modest initiatives on the part of global governance to correct the 'imperfections' of a 'free' world. In its reformist guises liberalism encompasses certain strains of (self-defined) socialism, feminism and environmentalism.

Liberalist discourse has the merit of recognizing the growing global dimension of social relations, but suffers from a general lack of reflexivity, demonstrated in three principal ways. First, many liberal accounts of globalization are prone to exaggerate the extent of deterritorialization, with references to 'the end of geography', 'the end of sovereignty' and the like (O'Brien, 1992; Camilleri and Falk, 1992). Unmeasured assertions of this kind only feed conservative scepticism and to this extent unhelpfully postpone the day of serious reckoning with globality (Ferguson, 1992). Second, liberal perspectives on globalization tend to presume that the process is inherently beneficial. Like Enlightenment thinkers of the eighteenth century, free traders of the nineteenth century and internationalists of the inter-war period, liberal globalists of the late twentieth century readily fall prey to a naïve optimism, sometimes bordering on the euphoric, that modernity will, almost as a matter of historical inevitability, yield a universal, homogeneous, egalitarian, prosperous and communitarian world society. Yet in practice, globalization has often perpetuated (and in some instances increased) poverty, violence, ecological degradation, estrangement and anomie. Third, liberal accounts of globalization lack a critical examination of their own terms and the social structures that this mind-set bolsters. Tacitly if not explicitly, liberal orthodoxy treats the market, electoral democracy, growth, national solidarity and scientific reason as timeless virtues with universal applicability. The discourse effectively rules out the possibility that capitalism, individualism, industrialism, consumerism, the nationality principle and rationalism might be causes rather than cures of global problems. To this degree, liberalism is ideological, a form of knowledge that obscures disempowerment and thereby serves, often quite unintentionally, to sustain unfreedoms with false promises.

In contrast, critical knowledge has as its primary conscious purpose to identify disempowerment and promote politics of emancipation. Theorists of this bent approach the question of globalization with an awareness that the modern world system has produced widespread violence, arbitrary hierarchies and avoidable deprivation. Critical discourse recognizes that, given this historical record, the rise of supraterritoriality could well involve an extension and reinvigoration – perhaps in new forms – of imperialism, xenophobia, patriarchy, racism, militarism, authoritarianism, fundamentalism, nihilism and other recurrent predicaments of modernity. Globalization's transformation of the space–time dimension of social life should therefore be greeted not with conservative disavowals or liberal confidence, but with vigilance. There are no obvious or unambiguous, let alone necessary, connections between globalization and freedom. Rather, it is the task of critical knowledge to maximize the trend's emancipatory potential by exposing the inadequacies of orthodoxy – conceptually, empirically and ethically – and by imaginatively restructuring the theory and practice of globalization.

Critical accounts of globalization have chiefly developed along two broad methodological lines. On the one hand, historical–materialist analyses have interpreted the rise of supraterritoriality as a particular turn in capitalist development. This work focuses on the implications of globalization for modes of commodification and accumulation, forms of state and regulation, and dynamics of class relations and exploitation (e.g., Lipietz, 1987; Overbeek, 1993). On the other hand, what are broadly termed postmodernist or poststructuralist narratives have highlighted psychological and cultural oppressions that attend globalization. In these writings the establishment of the world as a single place has been linked, *inter alia*, to fragmentations of identity, crises of community and religious resurgence (e.g., Featherstone, 1990; Robertson and Garrett, 1991). The lines between critical political economy and postmodernism often blur in practice. Thus some critical accounts of globalization interlink material and ideational issues (e.g., Harvey, 1989), and critical feminist analyses of globalization may adopt either a poststructuralist or a materialist methodology (Grewal and Kaplan, 1994; Sparr, 1994). Yet there is a common concern among critical theorists with structural oppressions (variously conceived) and a shared premise that the construction of knowledge is a social process with far-reaching practical consequences, such that investigations of globalization should be reflexive and politically alert.

Critical knowledge of globalization is not faultless, of course. Some writings in this vein can exaggerate the extent of globalization and its consequences. Historical materialists often underestimate the significance of ideational forces in globalization, while poststructuralists tend to underplay its economic and ecological aspects. Many critical accounts have given insufficient thought to reconstructing the future following their exposure of present global ills and the ideological character of orthodox conceptions of globalization. However, none of these shortcomings invalidates the under-lying argument for critical knowledge.

Globality and emancipation

On the contrary, the case for critical theory is compelling. To date, glob-alization has often perpetuated poverty, widened material inequalities, increased ecological degradation, sustained militarism, fragmented com-munities, marginalized subordinated groups, fed intolerance and deepened crises of democracy.

This is not to say that there are no grounds for optimism. For example, global trade and finance have played a part in more than trebling world per capita income since 1945, and the proportion of humanity (though not absolute numbers) living in abject poverty has, as measured by the United Nations 'human development index', more than halved between 1960 and 1992 (UNDP, 1994: 1–2). Globalization has helped to increase ecological consciousness and programmes to enhance environmental sustainability. Many of the more globalized parts of the world have witnessed major and quite possibly structural disarmament in recent years, and in so far as war is a struggle for territorial occupation, armed conflict may tend to decline as supraterritorial interests gain greater sway. On certain occasions, global communications have encouraged worldwide humanitarian concern, for example in famine relief and the anti-apartheid movement. Various sub-ordinated groups – including women, the disabled, lesbians and gay men, and indigenous peoples – have grasped possibilities of global organization in expanded campaigns to reverse discrimination. For some, globalization has fostered greater awareness of and respect for the diversity of human cultures. In relation to democracy, recent years have witnessed a spread of multiparty elections to many more countries, often with United Nations oversight, and a proliferation of supraterritorial citizens' action networks (Boutros-Ghali, 1995; Lipschutz, 1992).

However, globalization also shows a far more disturbing face in regard to each of the preceding points. For instance, greatly enhanced capacities for global organization have not been exploited to prevent some 800 million people (one in seven of the world's population) from being undernourished in the early 1990s (UNDP, 1993: 12). In addition, globalization has contrib-uted to a marked increase in world income disparities, both within and between countries South and North (UNDP, 1992: 36; UNDP, 1994: 63; Agnew, 1994a: 270–1; Ghai, 1994: 30–2). Across most of the world, pressures of global capitalism have brought a major deterioration in working conditions and social protection. In spite of the impressive rise of trans-national feminism, women have borne by far the greater brunt of global

restructuring, and global governance has generally been little less patriarchal than sovereign statehood (Peterson and Runyan, 1993; see also the
chapter by Runyan in this volume). In relation to ecology, several of the most
deleterious developments of recent times have unfolded in global space,
including nuclear fallout, ozone holes, reduced biodiversity, depletion of
nonrenewable resources and global warming. Militarism remains alive and
well under conditions of globality, with rocket propulsion and new information technologies introducing unprecedented destructive capacities into
contemporary battle. Eleven major wars broke out in the 'new world order'
of 1991–92 while, much aided by global weapons flows, armed suppression
within countries has increased to the point that, in the 1990s, two-thirds of
the world's states have used their armies against people they claim as citizens
(*Guardian*, 10 November 1993; Nietschmann, 1994: 227, 234). Feeding
other, more subtle forms of violence, the technologies of supraterritoriality
have greatly enlarged capacities (if deployed to such ends) to centralize
decisions, regiment workforces, undermine privacy and extinguish cultures.
In addition, global modes of communication have often tended, by isolating
individuals in their households and workplaces behind television and computer screens, to weaken wider communal bonds. Meanwhile many people
have also reacted to the placeless geography of globality with an ultra-
nationalist, racist, fundamentalist and/or homophobic determination to
reassert territorial identities and suppress alternative forms of collective
solidarity (Scholte, 1996). In these and other ways, globalization has hardly
been a boon for democracy. Not only do democratic institutions continue to
be quite precarious in many countries, but few mechanisms are in place to
ensure participation, representativeness, debate, transparency, constitution-
ality and accountability in the supraterritorial realm itself. Rural Africa
hardly has a voice in global intergovernmental agencies, for example, and
global civil society, inasmuch as one has developed, has tended so far to be
drawn disproportionately from urban, Northern, white, (computer-) literate,
propertied circles (Gill, 1994). On numerous counts, then, globalization has
created situations of heightened vulnerability, and this globality–insecurity
nexus, central to contemporary 'risk society', has figured significantly in
upsurges of fundamentalism and nihilism worldwide (Beck, 1992).

Given these worrying circumstances, it is unconscionable to leave orthodox conceptions of globalization unchallenged. Both the ostrich response of
conservatives and the *laissez-faire* attitude of many liberals are fraught with
danger. Fortunately, these views have become somewhat less prevalent and
entrenched in recent years, although this is not to underestimate their
continuing strength. However, the greater struggle lies between reformist
liberalism, with its claims that the above problems can be solved by institutional adjustments within prevailing social structures, and critical theory

arguments that violence and injustice are embedded in that social order itself. This is the crucial question facing contemporary globalization studies: technical tinkering or radical overhaul? Opting for the former is intellectually less taxing and painful, but the promises of reformist liberalism have been heard before. Students of globalization must surely take seriously the possibility that underlying structures of the modern (now globalized) world order – capitalism, the state, industrialism, nationality, rationalism – as well as the orthodox discourses that sustain them, may be in important respects irreparably destructive.

Globalization has to date mostly been an extension of modernization. At the same time, the rapid rise and wide-ranging reach of this transformation of social space – the transcendence of territoriality – has brought great instability to capitalism, made traditional conceptions of sovereignty unviable, heightened worries about ecological sustainability, injected much confusion into the construction of identity and encouraged reactions against reason. To this extent, globalization has opened space for critical theory and a fundamental rethink of production, governance, ecology and community, as well as the nature and purpose of knowledge itself.

Note

1. This threefold distinction between conservative, liberal and critical views is, of course, somewhat crude. Each category encompasses a diversity of arguments, and some accounts of globalization show a mix of two or three of the broad tendencies.

References

Abu-Lughod, J. L. (1989) *Before European Hegemony: The World System A.D. 1250–1350*, New York, Oxford University Press.

Agnew, J. (1994a) Global hegemony versus national economy: the United States in the new world order, in G. J. Demko and W. B. Wood (eds), *Reordering the World: Geopolitical Perspectives on the Twenty-First Century*, Boulder, CO, Westview.

Agnew, J. (1994b) The territorial trap: the geographical assumptions of international relations theory, *Review of International Political Economy*, **1**(1), 53–80.

Beck, U. (1992) *Risk Society: Towards a New Modernity*, London, Sage.

Boutros-Ghali, B. (1995) Democracy: a newly recognized imperative, *Global Governance*, **1**(1), 3–11.

Camilleri, J. and Falk, J. (1992) *The End of Sovereignty? The Politics of a Shrinking and Fragmented World*, Aldershot, Elgar.

Castells, M. (1989) *The Informational City: Information Technology, Economic Restructuring, and the Urban-Regional Process*, Oxford, Blackwell.

Featherstone, M. (ed.) (1990) *Global Culture: Nationalism, Globalization and Modernity*, London, Sage.

Ferguson, M. (1992) The mythology of globalization, *European Journal of Communication*, **7**, 69–93.

Fukuyama, F. (1992) *The End of History and the Last Man*, London, Hamish Hamilton.

Ghai, D. (1994) Structural adjustment, global integration and social democracy, in R. Prendergast and F. Stewart (eds), *Market Forces and World Development*, New York, St Martin's.

Gill, S. (1994) Opportunities and obstacles to the emergence of a new multilateralism, paper for the International Symposium on Sources of Innovation in Multilateralism, Lausanne, 26–28 May.

Grewal, I. and Kaplan, C. (eds) (1994) *Scattered Hegemonies: Postmodernity and Transnational Feminist Practices*, Minneapolis, University of Minnesota Press.

Harvey, D. (1989) *The Condition of Postmodernity: An Enquiry into the Conditions of Cultural Change*, Oxford, Blackwell.

Hawthorne, N. (1851) *The House of the Seven Gables: A Romance*, Edinburgh, Paterson.

Heidegger, M. (1950) The thing, in *Poetry, Language, Thought*, New York, Harper and Row (1971).

Hobhouse, L. T. (1906) *Morals in Evolution: A Study in Comparative Ethics*, London, Chapman and Hall (1915).

Huntington, S. P. (1991) *The Third Wave: Democratization in the Late Twentieth Century*, Norman, OK, University of Oklahoma Press.

Huth, A. (1937) *La Radiodiffusion: puissance mondiale*, Paris, Gallimard.

Jameson, F. (1984) Postmodernism, or the culture of late capitalism, *New Left Review*, **146**, 53–92.

Krasner, S. D. (1994) International political economy: abiding discord, *Review of International Political Economy*, **1**(1), 13–19.

Layne, C. (1993) The unipolar illusion: why new great powers will rise, *International Security*, **17**(4), 5–51.

Lipietz, A. (1987) *Mirages and Miracles: The Crisis of Global Fordism*, London, Verso.

Lipschutz, R. D. (1992) Reconstructing world politics: the emergence of global civil society, *Millennium*, **21**(3), 389–420.

Maclean, J. S. (1981) Political theory, international theory, and problems of ideology, *Millennium*, **10**(2), 102–25.

McLuhan, M. and Fiore, Q. (1967) *The Medium Is the Massage*, London, Allen Lane.

Mattelart, A. (1991) *Advertising International: The Privatization of Public Space*, London, Routledge.

Marx, K. (1857–58) *Grundrisse: Foundations of the Critique of Political Economy*, Harmondsworth, Penguin (1973).

Moore, W. E. (1966) Global sociology: the world as a singular system, *American Journal of Sociology*, **71**(5), 475–82.

Mueller, J. (1989) *Retreat from Doomsday: The Obsolescence of Major War*, New York, Basic Books.

Myers, N. (1985) *The Gaia Atlas of Planet Management: For Today's Caretakers of Tomorrow's World*, London, Pan.

Nietschmann, B. (1994) The fourth world: nations versus states, in G. J. Demko and W. B. Wood (eds), *Reordering the World: Geopolitical Perspectives on the Twenty-First*

Century, Boulder, CO, Westview.

O'Brien, R. (1992) *Global Financial Integration: The End of Geography*, London, Pinter.

Ohmae, K. (1990) *The Borderless World: Power and Strategy in the Interlinked Economy*, London, Fontana.

Overbeek, H. (ed.) (1993) *Restructuring Hegemony in the Global Political Economy: The Rise of Transnational Neo-Liberalism in the 1980s*, London, Routledge.

Peterson, V. S. and Runyan, A. S. (1993) *Global Gender Issues*, Boulder, CO, Westview.

Ploman, E. W. (1984) *Space, Earth and Communication*, Westport, CT, Quorum.

Robertson, R. (1992) *Globalization: Social Theory and Global Culture*, London, Sage.

Robertson, R. and Garrett, W. R. (eds) (1991) *Religion and Global Order*, New York, Paragon.

Rowlands, I. H. and Greene, M. (eds) (1992) *Global Environmental Change and International Relations*, Basingstoke, Macmillan.

Ruggie, J. G. (1993) Territoriality and beyond: problematizing modernity in international relations, *International Organization*, **47**(1), 139–74.

Scholte, J. A. (1993) *International Relations of Social Change*, Buckingham, Open University Press.

Scholte, J. A. (1996) Globalisation and collective identities, in J. Krause and N. Renwick (eds), *Identities in International Relations*, London, Macmillan.

Sparr, P. (ed.) (1994) *Mortgaging Women's Lives: Feminist Critiques of Structural Adjustment*, London, Zed.

UNESCO (1993) *Statistical Yearbook*, Paris, UNESCO.

UNDP (United Nations Development Programme) (1992) *Human Development Report 1992*, New York, Oxford University Press.

UNDP (1993) *Human Development Report 1993*, New York, Oxford University Press.

UNDP (1994) *Human Development Report 1994*, New York, Oxford University Press.

Walker, R. B. J. (1993) *Inside/Outside: International Relations as Political Theory*, Cambridge, Cambridge University Press.

Wallerstein, I. (1986) Societal development, or development of the world-system? *International Sociology*, **1**(1), 3–17.

Waltz, K. N. (1993) The new world order, *Millennium*, **22**(2), 187–95.

Wheeler, M. (1954) *Rome Beyond the Imperial Frontiers*, London, Bell.

Whitrow, G. J. (1988) *Time in History: The Evolution of Our General Awareness of Time and Temporal Perspective*, Oxford, Oxford University Press.

4

Dangers of Discourse: The Case of Globalization[1]

GILLIAN YOUNGS

Introduction

This chapter sounds a cautionary note about discourses of globalization. Its intention is to offer some contextualization of these discourses and to encourage 'us' to think about what we may be implying or assuming in using them. The 'us' of this statement refers primarily to those broadly defined within the academic discipline of international relations, but the nature of this discipline means that such an 'us' may have a wider application, as will be made clear below. The discussion begins with an explanation of why we need to think in terms of discourses and how they should be understood. The ways in which discourses of international relations have spatially configured the global along specific lines is then considered. Finally, Francis Fukuyama's (1992) 'end of history' thesis will be examined as an illustration of the universalizing disposition of discourses of globalization and the need to be aware of the particularities of their interpretations and messages.

Understanding discourse

The term discourse is used here with a deliberate purpose which it is important to set out as clearly as possible. A growing body of critical work has sought to establish discourse as a central concern of the study of international relations (George, 1994; Der Derian and Shapiro, 1989; Walker, 1993; Der Derian, 1987; Dalby, 1990; Sylvester, 1994; Ashley, 1988, 1991; Peterson, 1992; Campbell, 1992, 1993; Weber, 1994). The fundamental aim of such work is to stress a different way of thinking about theory, one which disrupts ideas about its separateness from practice and explores how theory and practice are intrinsically and problematically interconnected – as Jim George (1994: 3) has put it, the recognition of 'the world-making nature of theory', 'theory *as* everyday political practice'. Perhaps the most important recent collection of material citing discourses as

central issues of concern to students of the theory and practice of international relations was *International/Intertextual Relations* edited by James Der
Derian and Michael Shapiro (1989). As Donna Gregory's helpful foreword to
that volume states:

> Everyday life is ideological in an ontological sense; that which we know and
> which seems true depends on our sense of what is real; through these terms,
> intelligibility becomes possible. But these 'terms' are that 'stock of signs' whose
> meanings have already been designated by the culture. (Gregory, 1989: xx)

And speaking of the authors whose work is contained in the book:

> All these writers share an interest in learning how discourse is related to the
> construction and subjugation of humankind. They provide so rich and com-
> plex a version of international relations that we are better able to see how
> modern simplifications can endanger our future. (ibid.: xxi)

R. B. J. Walker's (1993) arguments concerning theoretical discourses in
international relations and the possibilities for 'political imagination' have
been influential. They have demonstrated the importance of regarding
theories of international relations as dimensions of the practice of world
politics, particularly with regard to the relationship between state sovereignty and political identity. In presenting a deep analysis of the political
meanings integrated into the exercise of state sovereignty, they have given
understanding of this key theoretical concept much more practical substance.[2] They have worked to *locate* the idea of the 'modern' state in its
philosophical and theoretical traditions and have reflected on their meanings
for present-day interpretation. Walker's detailed examination and his declared interest in 'the need for alternative forms of political practice' (Walker,
1993: ix) provide rich roots for exploring theory/practice interconnections
on bases which emphasize a sensitivity to history rather than a predisposi-
tion towards abstraction.

This kind of approach illustrates one of two important linkages which
investigation of discourse prioritizes. This concerns associations between the
terms of understanding and explanation and their interpretations of the past,
the present and the possible. There is emphasis here on the relationship
between thought and action, between understanding of alternative futures
in terms of possible alternative understandings of the present and past. Such
an approach to discourse addresses in a penetrating fashion the historical
background to what may be regarded as limitations to current thinking. It
offers particular perspectives on historical interpretation/analysis and highlights the importance of critical study of inherited discourses of many kinds
including those viewed as theoretical. It suggests that the role of such critical
investigation is vital to our examination of how understandings have
developed over time. It shakes knowledge from its timeless pedestal and

affirms knowledge formation and the production of associated discourses as human activities. The second linkage it thus makes is between knowledge and power or discourse and power (Foucault, 1966, 1969, 1971).

Michel Foucault's work brought together the two linkages, which clearly have an interrelationship. Once discourse and knowledge formation are viewed as influential dimensions of human activity/relations, their relevance to a comprehensive understanding of power is evident. Historical exploration of discourses becomes a part of the drive to understand how ideas or approaches identified with dominant knowledges or social groupings have been established and maintained over time. A Foucaultian approach to discourse denies any unproblematic separation of theory and practice, of thought and action.[3] It also introduces the difficult question of ethics, not as an issue which theorists or commentators need merely to address in connection with their objects of inquiry, but as one which is relevant to their position as subjects engaged in specific forms of discursive practice. Foucault's focus on ethics of the self is most closely identified with his later work, in particular *Le Souci de soi* (1984), Volume 3 of *Histoire de la sexualité*, but it can be traced as a long-term dimension of his philosophical preoccupations. James Bernauer (1988: 72–5) has placed emphasis on this ethical dimension in his discussion of the 'legacy of Foucault's thought'.

> Foucault's ethical perspective was signaled in his concern with the action of the axes: what knowledge does (and not reads), how power constructs (and not represents), how a relationship to the self is invented (and not discovered). Philosophical inquiry becomes substantially ethical, in a Foucaultian sense, when it is concerned with the problematizations which pose themselves to a culture as a result of the interplay of its practices: its types of knowledge, its political strategies, and its styles of personal life. (ibid.: 74)

There are some basic points that can be made here. The nature of discourse matters. Discursive practices matter. When we engage in such practices we need to be aware that they have been formed over time and that they may incorporate assumptions or dispositions which are not immediately evident and that particular kinds of critical work are needed to uncover these (see the chapters by Dalby and Peterson in this volume).

Globalization and international relations as a discipline

Perhaps the most obvious quality of discourses of globalization is their all-encompassing intention or nature, their orientation towards descriptions, explanations or theorizations of the whole, the global. This orientation clearly displays distinctive as well as common characteristics across different areas of substantive and theoretical interest in the field broadly defined as international relations. These areas are numerous and diverse. They include global political economy, global commons and the role of global institutions. They are concerned in a range of ways with change and the particular importance of technology, culture and global structures, processes and patterns of production, marketing and consumption.[4] They renew a debate which has long preoccupied international relations scholars and practitioners concerning the changing capacities and influence of states as key actors.

In developing discourses of globalization, international relationists confront two major challenges, both of which require a self-conscious and self-critical recognition of the nature of their particular realm of thought and its established discursive practices. The first relates to the hybrid nature of international relations as a field of study, and the second concerns the specific, most important dimension of this hybridity. It can be regarded as a strength in the context under discussion here that international relations scholars have always had to recognize the degree to which their subject, as a relatively young discipline, has relied on other long-established areas of thought, e.g. philosophy, political theory, diplomatic history and political economy. The development of the specific academic field of international relations is generally located in this century and identified with efforts to foster international co-operation, and prevent and ultimately cope with the horrors and outcomes of two world wars (Olson and Groom, 1991: 37–78). The two major phases of the discipline frequently identified are the 'idealistic tradition' of the inter-war period and the realist or power politics trend which followed (p. 50). In the latter, the emphasis, as suggested, is on the study of the nature and operation of power. Hans J. Morgenthau's *Politics Among Nations*, first published in 1948, now in its sixth edition (Morgenthau and Thompson, 1985), continues to be seen as the classic realist text. Realist theory is commonly regarded as state-centric in its approach, i.e. concerned principally with the power and relations of states as the prime actors in international relations. Neorealism has represented an important attempt to evolve this state-centric approach although the manner in which this has been done has come under attack.[5]

The enduring state-centric tendencies of the discipline of international relations signal a key dimension of its hybridity; the dependency of its theory – international theory – on political theory. It is crucial to keep this factor to the fore in consideration of the long-standing general theme within the discipline of the changing role, influence and capacities of states (see the chapter in this volume by Cerny). Furthermore, it is necessary to recognize that this defining characteristic of the discipline predates recent debates about globalization.[6] Thus, in important ways it forms the discursive backdrop to such debates and we need to be alive to its actual or potential theoretical influence, overt or otherwise. In the 1950s and 1960s, John

Herz's (1952, 1968) arguments about the 'rise and demise of the territorial state' were particularly influential. His concerns were focused on the challenges presented by the age of nuclear weapons to traditional notions of state security. They urged the rethinking of the 'meaning' of state power and sovereignty, territory and statehood.[7] It could be argued that the nuclear threat remains the most devastating on a global scale although in investigations of globalization it now tends to be considered alongside other 'risks' (Beck, 1992) including those of an environmental nature. With its strong security studies emphasis, international relations as a discipline was by no means a late starter in negotiating threat on a global scale, particularly in relation to the state, security and international politics (see the chapter by Richard Harknett in this volume). Herz's considerations touched on technology and economics, and, in broad terms, it is fair to say that together with the nuclear issue, these factors have represented the other main challenge to state-centric approaches to international relations. Attention to technology has only developed recently (Talalay, Tooze and Farrands, 1996; Kato, 1993; Strange, 1994 (1988); Skolnikoff, 1993; Kennedy, 1993) as, in some senses, a further stage in the broader consideration of economic issues. This consideration has included debates about 'power and interdependence' (Keohane and Nye, 1977) and the preoccupation of neorealists with the extension of theories of power more adequately, in their terms, to include economic dimensions, and, to some degree, the relationship between economic and political influences in the maintenance of power (Keohane, 1984, 1986, 1989; Krasner, 1983).[8] International political economy, increasingly referred to as global political economy (Gill and Law, 1988; Tooze, 1992; Stubbs and Underhill, 1994), as a specialist branch of international relations[9] has focused directly on issues concerning 'states and markets' and international power structures involving state and other interests (Strange, 1994; Cox, 1987). International political economy as a research focus has intrinsically represented a substantial challenge to traditional state-centric perspectives on the international. Whatever its theoretical achievements, and these have been the subject of continuing critique (Murphy and Tooze, 1991), international political economy stresses the need to study the relationship between politics and economics as a means of understanding international relations. The field continues to grapple with this fundamental concern, as the introduction to a recent collection of essays makes clear. Referring to the need for new thinking about the state in relation to international political economy, Geoffrey Underhill (1994: 35) argues:

> We need a link between the state, economic structure, and broader notions of politics. That link is the self-interest of *agents* or *actors*, whether they be individuals, formal or informal groups, or the corporate economic entities known as firms.

An interesting question concerns the practicalities of achieving such new thinking about the state. To what degree and exactly how do the complex and massive traditions of thought about the state/international relationship in international relations influence and delimit the possibilities for developing such new thought, whether along the lines suggested by Geoffrey Underhill or otherwise? This, it seems to this author, is a question yet to be fully considered, let alone answered (see the chapter by Taylor in this volume). It is one which concerns the nature of critical theory building in the historical context of existing theory. It does not reduce the theory problem to the relationship between theory and practice, but takes seriously the material importance of theory as historically constituted and contingent.

Power continues to be a central preoccupation for the field of international relations, but it needs to be considered more forcefully as a dimension of understanding the impact of the discipline's own historical knowledge building processes. The power/knowledge relationship has been recognized in the discipline[10] but explorations of its full implications, certainly in respect of globalization, have barely begun. In simple terms, such a point directs attention to questions of why and how we have come to think as we do, and how such issues affect the possibilities for thinking otherwise, rather than to statements of the need to think otherwise, which too often treat the potential for doing so as unproblematic. These kinds of questions indicate the extent to which theorizing is a practical human activity, distinct but not totally separate from other forms of activity. Theory, therefore, should not be addressed as if it were abstracted from such activity; its history and the influences of that history should be taken into account.

From the standpoint of Marx's theory, John Maclean (1981, 1988) indicated some time ago the importance both of historical awareness of the development of theory, and the connections between apparently differentiated theories. His arguments are of note in the context of this discussion because they emphasize the links between international theory and theories of international political economy, and the problematics of a state-centred theory which claims to theorize the whole, i.e. the international, or the global as we would tend to term it. He convincingly captured the problem in his identification of the 'territorial state' as 'the theoretical boundary for the conception of the whole' (Maclean, 1981: 103).

He signalled his concern over 'the failure in social science to comprehend and explain the historical process of the increasing globalisation of social relations' (p. 104). This involved international relations, which had an apparent 'responsibility for identifying this process', as well as other disciplines which had failed to 'expand upon their localised theory'. His stated intention was to express the broad significance of the arguments that followed. Their immediate context might be international relations but they were viewed as relevant to a much wider audience in the social sciences. Maclean's essay clearly predates a whole wealth of work on globalization across the social sciences,[11] but they still contain a crucial message for those engaged in, or wishing to engage in, global analysis, whether they regard themselves as operating within or outside of the discipline of international relations. It is worth spelling out the message. International relations as a field of study has as its overt focus the examination of the international, or, as it is increasingly referred to, the global,[12] but its own history of conceptualizing and theorizing has featured particular dispositions, notably with regard to the state/international relationship, and these must be taken into account if we are to reach a detailed understanding of international relations' predominant perspectives. This point applies whether one wishes to launch a critique from a Marxist standpoint, as Maclean has, or from any other, or even if one wishes to continue to apply these perspectives. In each case, the need for such detailed understanding is pertinent. Furthermore, it has relevance to other social sciences which have increasingly taken a detailed interest in global analysis.[13]

Our attention is drawn here to the need to be aware of potential sites of cross-disciplinary interest (see the chapters in this volume by Dalby and Taylor), to recognize that the specificities and problematics of attempts by international theory and theories of international political economy to interpret the international/global may represent important resources for other social sciences engaged in parallel tasks. The significance of this point in the light of the present growth in theoretical discourses of globalization, and the notably cross-disciplinary climate for them, cannot be sufficiently underlined. Such theorizing presents enormous challenges. Its universalistic tendencies can so easily mask its particularistic qualities[14] and this problem can be further compounded with uncritical approaches to established patterns of thinking about the international/global.

The universal and the particular in Fukuyama's 'end of history' thesis

Francis Fukuyama's (1992) 'end of history' thesis is illustrative of the supportive environment that the so-called post-Cold War context has provided for discourses of globalization. A key result of the collapse of the bipolar architecture which had dominated understanding of post-1945 world politics has been the new space it has opened up for 'global' thinking (Little, 1995). The Fukuyama thesis, for all its detailed distinctions, is interesting for its demonstration of general characteristics of discourses of globalization. Prime among these is an internal logic which prioritizes the universal over the particular. We need to recognize that this logic characterizes the discourses themselves as much as the phenomena they claim to describe or define. Fukuyama (1992: xvii–xix, 45) has presented a complex argument for the globalization of liberal democracy as a 'universal' ideal in relation to the Hegelian notion of the state as the highest rational form of human organization. The thesis emphasises the universalization of the values associated with 'liberal democracy' and 'economic liberalism' (p. 48). These are portrayed as representing a 'Universal History of mankind', enabling us to think in terms of 'the end of history' (ibid.: 47–51). Furthermore, this process of universalization is directly linked to the claimed capacities of liberal political and economic principles to accommodate the differentiated position of both individuals and societies (ibid.: 201–3). Such principles concern the ideas of growth and progress encompassed within fairly standard notions of development and modernization, and the political as well as economic relationship of individuals to such ideas (ibid.: 131–9).

For Fukuyama, economic development, and the scientific and techno-logical factors, the desire for economic growth and the continuing conquest of nature which are associated with it, represent unifying forces in world history (ibid.: 126).[15] In its combination of political and economic values and its emphasis on the ways in which individual and social inequalities are accommodated via the liberal path, Fukuyama's thesis could be argued to be the ultimate post-Cold War discourse of globalization. It identifies the progressive imperatives and 'homogenizing power' of the liberal capitalist system as an irresistible incorporating influence *both* economically and politically (ibid.: 108). Fukuyama's claims for the 'triumph of capitalism' (Little, 1995), despite their theoretical seriousness, have an almost evangelistic feel to them. This cannot be attributed solely to their precise historical context. It is also associated with universalistic qualities which allow for a sense that questions have been answered, ultimate solutions reached. But, as indicated in this discussion of the thesis, its universalism is highly particularistic. These particularities need to be addressed in spatial and temporal as well as ideological terms (Youngs, 1996). As a discourse of globalization, it is fundamentally state-centric,[16] West-centric, and presents an overtly idealized view of liberal democracy and economic liberalism, especially concerning their interrelationship. Liberal economics and politics are presented as mutually supportive in a positive, unproblematic and cohesive fashion. The 'end of history' is presented as a state-centred celebration of the globalization of the Western capitalist system's capacities to meet economic and political needs. To complement the technical–rational imperative[17] as the objective driving force of economic liberalism, there are the freedoms and satisfaction of recognition which liberal democratic doctrines of rights offer citizens or subjects. This is Fukuyama's broad perspective. It posits that subjective meanings are found through economic opportunity and political recognition, and it declares modernization and democracy as parallel phenomena.

Liberal economics and liberal politics are viewed very much as open frameworks offering seemingly endless opportunities for individual material gain and a social sense of self. Quite simply, they are seen as meeting human needs, 'material' and 'non-material'.[18] This approach to the liberal paradigm avoids critical discussion of causes of persistent inequalities and a detailed interest in the location, exercise and effects of economic and political power. Its overt preoccupation with claiming a universal relevance for liberal values is distinct from an approach which seeks to investigate in detail the differentiated impact of the exercise of such values in practice in varied social contexts, globally and locally. Technological progress is identified as a key globalizing force facilitating the development of a 'global culture' (Fukuyama, 1992: 126; see also Youngs, 1996; A. D. Smith, 1990). An understanding of history is largely reduced to points along the scale of this so-called progress. The main global division identified as of interest in Fukuyama's thesis is between the 'post-historical' part of the world and 'a part that is still stuck in history', in broad respects between the 'developed' and 'underdeveloped' worlds (Fukuyama, 1992: 276, 385).

Concluding comments

Some of the dangers of discourse in relation to globalization have been highlighted here, particularly the tendency to regard theoretical discourses as abstracted from practice rather than as a form of practice. The risks which can result are an ahistorical approach to discourses preventing us from understanding the importance of how they have developed over time, which conceptualizations have come to predominate and how this has happened. Once we begin to address discourses as practice we can consider how their established patterns may affect possibilities for new ways of thinking, whether along complementary or alternative lines. Such discourse analysis is thus a vital part of any critical social journey from the past through the present to the future. Discourses of globalization tend to be futuristic and universalistic in turn. We need to be aware that they nevertheless demonstrate particularities which must be investigated and understood if we are to assess them thoroughly. In doing so, we should not let their forward-looking perspectives mask their associations with existing discourses or standpoints. Finally, in raising the issue of ethics, this chapter has sought to reflect on the role of the theorist. If theory is part of practice, then theorists do not have the luxury of regarding their activities as abstracted from the real world. The abstract dimensions of theorizing should not detract from its practical import. When we engage in theoretical discourses, we are taking part in that so-called real world, albeit in what sometimes seem to be rather detached ways. As many of the chapters in this volume indicate, how we undertake that engagement matters.

Notes

1. Many of the ideas in this chapter were first explored in a paper presented at a conference entitled Knowledges: Production, Distribution, Revision at the University of Minnesota, Minneapolis, 14–17 April 1994. I would like to thank the organizers and the University of Minnesota for the financial support which enabled me to participate in this event.
2. Walker's perspective on state sovereignty stresses its particular definition of the nature of politics in direct relation to time and space. The arguments in this regard are complex and there is not space to explore them fully here. See especially Walker (1993: 50–80, 125–58). See also the chapter on sovereignty by Williams in this volume.
3. My understanding of the thought/action connection in relation to Michel Foucault's work has been significantly aided by Szakolczai (1987).
4. There are a variety of works which have addressed these aspects. Of the more recent, Stubbs and Underhill (1994) is helpfully comprehensive in relation to political economy. See also the chapter by Scholte in this volume, Scholte (1993) and Hurrell and Kingsbury (1992).
5. The founding neorealist text is generally regarded as Waltz (1979). The best volume for understanding debates about the nature of neorealism is Keohane (1986). See also Buzan, Jones and Little (1993), Griffiths (1992), S. Smith (1995) and the chapter by Taylor in this volume.
6. The recent study of globalization and interdependence by R. J. Barry Jones (1995) is important for its contextualization of considerations of globalization within established conceptual developments addressing changing dynamics in international relations. See also Youngs (forthcoming).
7. See John Gerard Ruggie's (1993) recent wide-ranging assessment of the issue of territoriality.
8. The concept of hegemony has been central to neorealist approaches and critiques of them. See in particular Keohane (1984, 1986) and Gilpin (1987). See also Strange (1994), Gill (1993) and Rupert (1995).
9. On the relationship between international political economy and international relations as areas of study, see Tooze (1984, 1991).
10. As already indicated, there are a number of key works which have opened up this area for consideration: Der Derian and Shapiro (1989), Walker (1993) and George (1994). Power/knowledge links have been fundamental to gender analysis. With regard to global processes see, in particular, Peterson and Runyan (1993) and the chapters on gender in this volume.
11. Many examples are quoted and discussed elsewhere in this volume. See, in particular, the chapter by Scholte. Among the most well-known works related to globalization are Giddens (1991), Featherstone (1990), Harvey (1990), Jameson (1991), Robertson (1992) and Dicken (1992).

12. On issues confronted by the discipline of international relations in developing its analysis to that of global relations, see Youngs (forthcoming).
13. Giddens (1991), for example, has drawn on approaches in international relations in his work on globalization.
14. For discussions relating to issues of universalism and particularism, see Walker (1993) and George (1994). See also the chapter by Slater in this volume.
15. See the examination of the Fukuyama thesis in relation to technology and culture in Youngs (1996).
16. Little's (1995) consideration of Fukuyama's critique of realist interpretations of international relations is interesting in this respect.
17. In related contexts, Richard Ashley (1980, 1984) has undertaken extensive critical consideration of the 'commitment to the essential objectivity of technical rationality'.
18. The liberal state in Fukuyama's (1992: 200–2) framework combines 'the freedom to make money' with 'rational recognition', i.e. universal recognition on the basis of rights. See also Little's (1995) discussion of the doubts which intrude on Fukuyama's positive perspective of international relations.

References

Ashley, R. K. (1980) *The Political Economy of War and Peace. The Sino-Soviet-American Triangle and the Modern Security Problematique*, London, Pinter.

Ashley, R. K. (1984) The poverty of neorealism, *International Organization*, **38**(2), 225–86.

Ashley, R. K. (1988) Untying the sovereign state: a double reading of the anarchy problematique, *Millennium: Journal of International Studies*, **17**(2), 227–62.

Ashley, R. K. (1991) The state of the discipline: realism under challenge? in R. Higgott and J. L. Richardson (eds), *International Relations: Global and Australian Perspectives on an Evolving Discipline*, Canberra, Australian National University.

Beck, U. (1992) *Risk Society. Towards a New Modernity*, London, Sage.

Bernauer, J. (1988) Michel Foucault's ecstatic thinking, in J. Bernauer and D. Rasmussen (eds), *The Final Foucault*, Cambridge, MA, MIT Press.

Buzan, B., Jones, C. and Little, R. (1993) *The Logic of Anarchy: Neorealism to Structural Realism*, New York, Columbia University Press.

Campbell, D. (1992) *Writing Security: United States Foreign Policy and the Politics of Identity*, Manchester, Manchester University Press.

Campbell, D. (1993) *Politics Without Principle: Sovereignty, Ethics, and Narratives of the Gulf War*, Boulder, CO, Lynne Rienner.

Cox, R. W. (1987) *Production, Power and World Order*, New York, Columbia University Press.

Dalby, S. (1990) *Creating the Second Cold War: The Discourse of Politics*, London, Pinter.

Der Derian, J. (1987) *On Diplomacy: A Genealogy of Western Estrangement*, Oxford, Basil Blackwell.

Der Derian, J. and Shapiro, M. J. (1989) *International/Intertextual Relations. Postmodern Readings of World Politics*, New York, Lexington Books.

Dicken, P. (1992) *Global Shift: The Internationalization of Economic Activity*, 2nd edn, London, Chapman.

Featherstone, M. (ed.) (1990) *Global Culture, Nationalism, Globalization and Modernity*, London, Sage.

Foucault, M. (1966) *Les Mots et les choses*, Paris, Éditions Gallimard, trans. as *The Order of Things* by A. M. Sheridan Smith, London, Tavistock Publications (1970).

Foucault, M. (1969) *L'Archéologie du savoir*, Paris, Éditions Gallimard, trans. as *The Archaeology of Knowledge* by A. M. Sheridan Smith, London, Tavistock Publications (1970).

Foucault, M. (1971) L'ordre du discours, Paris, Éditions Gallimard, trans. as 'The order of discourse' by I. McLeod, in M. Shapiro (ed.), *Language and Politics*, Oxford, Basil Blackwell (1984).

Foucault, M. (1984) *Le Souci de soi. Histoire de la sexualité, Vol. 3*, Paris, Éditions Gallimard, trans. as *The Care of the Self*, Harmondsworth, Penguin (1990).

Fukuyama, F. (1992) *The End of History and the Last Man*, London, Penguin.

George, J. (1994) *Discourses of Global Politics: A Critical Re-Introduction to International Relations*, Boulder, CO, Lynne Rienner.

Giddens, A. (1991) *The Consequences of Modernity*, Cambridge, Cambridge University Press.

Gill, S. (ed.) (1993) *Gramsci, Historical Materialism and International Relations*, Cambridge, Cambridge University Press.

Gill, S. and Law, D. (1988) *The Global Political Economy: Perspectives, Problems and Policies*, Hemel Hempstead, Harvester Wheatsheaf.

Gilpin, R. with the assistance of Gilpin, J. (1987) *The Political Economy of International Relations*, Princeton, Princeton University Press.

Gregory, D. U. (1989) Foreword, in J. Der Derian and M.J. Shapiro (eds), *International/ Intertextual Relations: Postmodern Readings of World Politics*, New York, Lexington Books.

Griffiths, M. (1992) *Realism, Idealism and International Politics*, London, Routledge.

Harvey, D. (1990) *The Condition of Postmodernity: An Enquiry into the Origins of Social Change*, Oxford, Basil Blackwell.

Herz, J. H. (1952) Rise and demise of the territorial state, *World Politics*, **9**, 473–93.

Herz, J. H. (1968) The territorial state revisited, *Polity*, **1**(1), 11–34.

Hurrell, A. and Kingsbury, B. (eds) (1992) *The International Politics of the Environment*, Oxford, Oxford University Press.

Jameson, F. (1991) *Postmodernism, or, The Cultural Logic of Late Capitalism*, London, Verso.

Jones, R. J. B. (1995) *Globalization and Interdependence in the International Political Economy: Rhetoric and Reality*, London, Pinter.

Kato, M. (1993) Nuclear globalism: traversing rockets, satellites, and nuclear war via the strategic gaze, *Alternatives*, **18**(3), 339–60.

Kennedy, P. (1993) *Preparing for the Twenty-First Century*, New York, Harper Collins.

Keohane, R. O. (1984) *After Hegemony*, Princeton, NJ, Princeton University Press.

Keohane, R. O. (ed.) (1986) *Neorealism and Its Critics*, New York, Columbia University Press.

Keohane, R. O. (1989) *International Institutions and State Power*, Boulder, CO, West-view Press.

Keohane, R. O. and Nye, J. S. (1977) *Power and Interdependence. World Politics in Transition*, Boston, Little, Brown.

Krasner, S. D. (ed.) (1983) *International Regimes*, Ithaca, Cornell University Press.

Little, R. (1995) International relations and the triumph of capitalism, in K. Booth and S. Smith (eds), *International Relations Theory Today*, Cambridge, Polity Press.

Maclean, J. (1981) Political theory, international theory and problems of ideology, *Millennium: Journal of International Studies*, **10**(2), 102–25.

Maclean, J. (1988) Marxism and international relations: a strange case of mutual neglect, *Millennium: Journal of International Studies*, **17**(2), 295–319.

Morgenthau, H. J. and Thompson, K. W. (1985) *Politics among Nations. The Struggle for Power and Peace*, 6th edn, New York, Kopf.

Murphy, C. and Tooze, R. (eds) (1991) *The New International Political Economy*, Boulder, CO, Lynne Rienner.

Olson, W. C. and Groom, A. J. R. (1991) *International Relations Then and Now*, London, HarperCollins.

Peterson, V. S. (1992) Transgressing boundaries: theories of knowledge, gender and international relations, *Millennium: Journal of International Studies*, **21**(2), 183–206.

Peterson, V. S. and Runyan, A. S. (1993) *Global Gender Issues*, Boulder, CO, Westview Press.

Robertson, R. (1992) *Globalization: Social Theory and Global Culture*, London, Sage.

Ruggie, J. G. (1993) Territoriality and beyond: problematizing modernity in inter-national relations, *International Organization*, **47**(1), 139–74.

Rupert, M. (1995) *Producing Hegemony: The Politics of Mass Production and American Global Power*, Cambridge, Cambridge University Press.

Scholte, J. A. (1993) *International Relations of Social Change*, Buckingham, Open University Press.

Skolnikoff, E. B. (1993) *The Elusive Transformation. Science, Technology, and the Evolution of International Politics*, Princeton, NJ, Princeton University Press.

Smith, A. D. (1990) Towards a global culture, in M. Featherstone (ed.), *Global Culture, Nationalism, Globalization and Modernism*, London, Sage.

Smith, S. (1995) The self-images of a discipline: a genealogy of international relations theory, in K. Booth and S. Smith (eds), *International Relations Theory Today*, Cambridge, Polity Press.

Strange, S. (1994) *States and Markets*, 2nd edn (first published 1988), London, Pinter.

Stubbs, R. and Underhill, G. R. D. (eds) (1994) *Political Economy and the Changing Global Order*, London, Macmillan.

Sylvester, C. (1994) *Feminist Theory and International Relations in a Postmodern Era*, Cambridge, Cambridge University Press.

Szakolczai, A. (1987) Concerning the grounds of modern economic society and political economy: an analysis of the writings of Say, Saint-Simon and Sismondi, using the works of Michel Foucault, Ph.D. thesis, The University of Texas at Austin, Texas. Consulted at the Centre Michel Foucault, Bibliothèque du Saul-choir, 43 bis, rue de la Glacière, 75013 Paris, France.

Talalay, M., Tooze, R. and Farrands, C. (eds) (1996) *Technology, Culture and Competitiveness and the World Political Economy*, London, Routledge.

Tooze, R. (1984) Perspectives and theory: a consumers' guide, in S. Strange (ed.), *Paths to International Political Economy*, London, Allen Unwin.

Tooze, R. (1991) International political economy: an interim assessment, in R. Higgott and J. L. Richardson (eds), *International Relations: Global and Australian Perspectives on an Evolving Discipline*, Canberra, Australian National University.

Tooze, R. (1992) Conceptualising the global economy, in A. G. McGrew and P. G. Lewis (eds), *Global Politics: Globalization and the Nation-State*, Cambridge, Polity Press.

Underhill, G. R. D. (1994) Introduction. Conceptualizing the changing global order, in R. Stubbs and G. R. D. Underhill (eds), *Political Economy and the Changing Global Order*, London, Macmillan.

Walker, R. B. J. (1993) *Inside/Outside: International Relations as Political Theory*, Cambridge, Cambridge University Press.

Waltz, K. N. (1979) *Theory of International Politics*, Reading, MA, Addison-Wesley.

Weber, C. (1994) *Simulating Sovereignty: Intervention, the State, and Symbolic Exchange*, Cambridge, Cambridge University Press.

Youngs, G. (1996) Culture and the technological imperative: missing dimensions, in M. Talalay, R. Tooze and C. Farrands (eds), *Technology, Culture and Competitiveness and the World Political Economy*, London, Routledge.

Youngs, G. (forthcoming) *From International Relations to Global Relations. A Conceptual Challenge*, Cambridge, Polity Press.

5

Globalization and Geopolitical World Orders

GEOFFREY PARKER

Since the end of the Cold War, the terms 'globalization' and 'world order' have become an integral part of the discourse on the nature of the international scene. The re-introduction of the term 'world order' was particularly associated with President George Bush, who spoke of the necessity to construct a 'new' order at a time when, in the wake of the Cold War, world order was clearly breaking down. Since then the terms 'international order' (Clark, 1993), 'new international order' (Fisler *et al.*, 1991) and even 'new world order harmony' (Thakur, 1995: 162) have entered the international discourse. The idea of a 'new' order presupposes the existence of a previous 'old' order, and the Cold War is implicitly considered to have fulfilled this role (Taylor, 1989: 68). The additional idea of a new world order as the structure for the implementation of a particular 'vision' of a more satisfactory world is present in Bush's association of the term with what he called 'the vision thing'. There is nothing fundamentally new in such an association. As the nineteenth century drew to a close, the anarchist geographer Elisée Reclus had also looked forward hopefully in much the same way. 'All are awaiting the birth of a new order of things,' he wrote. 'The century which has witnessed so many grand discoveries in the world of science cannot pass away without giving us still greater conquests' (Ishill, 1923: 9). A few years after Reclus, Lord Bryce encapsulated this idea in his Romanes Lecture of 1902, when he spoke of humanity's increased knowledge of the world, the features of which he saw as having 'passed from the chaos of conjecture to the cosmos of science'. This had resulted in 'the completion of the world-process' which he maintained was 'an especially great and fateful event' (Bryce, 1902). The proposition underlying all such thinking is that, despite many evidences to the contrary, it is possible to detect order in world affairs and that this order can be used for the betterment of the human condition.

Just two years after Bryce's Romanes Lecture, the century's first comprehensive geopolitical world view, 'The Geographical Pivot of History', was presented by Halford Mackinder (Mackinder, 1904). For the first time, said

Mackinder, the world had become 'a closed system' the operation of which he referred to as the 'scheme of things entire'. 'Scheme' here can best be understood in the Kantian sense of 'a rule or principle which enables the understanding to unify experience'. The 'scheme' for Mackinder consisted basically of a binary conflictual pattern into which events, however seemingly complex, eventually resolve themselves. This was viewed by him as being less 'order' than 'reality', a term to which he returned and which he later contrasted with 'ideals' (Mackinder, 1919). Although he thus placed the 'ideal' in quite a different category from the 'real', he envisaged the possibility of a synthesis of the two to produce something new and well founded. Reality was governed by its own principles and, in order to be successful, ideals had to take account of them. In other words, they, too, had to be realistic and bounded by those environmental possibilities which Vidal de la Blache had seen as being always present and from which choices had to be made (O'Loughlin, 1994: 232–3). To Mackinder, it was essentially the Anglocentric world expressed politically in the British Empire which fulfilled the role of 'order', a desirable state which needed to be strengthened and perpetuated. On the other hand, the reality, the 'scheme of things entire', was far from being an ideal state of affairs but was a condition containing disorder, danger and confrontation. It was therefore *ipso facto* unsatisfactory and needed to be changed but it actually contained within it alternative world orders functioning as autonomous and competing geopolitical systems. The objectivity of Mackinder's global view can be called into question by the fact that he was himself an advocate of the Anglocentric world order, his underlying purpose being to devise a global scenario which would make it more secure. This he proposed to do by anchoring it more firmly into geopolitical reality as he perceived it. Mackinder's thinking took place against a background of the increasing vulnerability of the order in which Britain held a hegemonic position (Parker, 1985: 19). The assumed 'legitimacy' of this Eurocentric and dominantly Anglocentric world order was contrasted with the 'illegitimate' alternative dominated by Russia.

Mackinder's world view was founded on the proposition that, in one form or another, binary confrontation had been the underlying reality from ancient times to the 'Great Game', which was played in the heart of Asia by those two nineteenth-century superpowers Great Britain and Russia. The idea of the international scene as a game has been used frequently, from Rudyard Kipling's Kim, who played it 'far and far into the North', to Raffestin's use of chess pieces as symbols of world power (Hopkirk, 1990; Raffestin, 1980). The use of games terminology has reinforced the perception of the conflictual nature of the international scene. A challenge to the Great Game came from Germany, and German geopolitical thinking ultimately led to the idea of a *Neue Ordnung* with a different set of rules which appeared to call into question the binary proposition itself by interposing a new geopolitical structure – *Mitteleuropa* – between the players (Naumann, 1916: 179–216). However, to Mackinder Russia had never been more than a 'tenant' of the Heartland, the ultimate centre of land power, and the rise of Germany was seen as the possible replacement of one protagonist or player by another. The same binary thinking subsequently allowed the Soviet Union to be seen as having replaced Russia as the new 'tenant' and even, at some later date, the possibility of China being in a position to replace the Soviet Union. Like its predecessors, the Cold War could thus be interpreted as a binary confrontation of alternative world orders.

A clear distinction can thus be made between the international system as a Kantian 'scheme of things entire' and the existence of particular 'orders' within it. While the former implies something which has an independent existence as a state of affairs, the latter implies purposeful organization and control. In the terminology of the early twentieth century, the 'scheme' is a 'natural' state of affairs and as such it could be violent, destructive and wasteful, while the 'order' implies the overcoming of nature by the human will. Nevertheless, as Bacon observed, 'in order to conquer nature it is necessary to obey her' (Bacon, 1924) and by analogy the successful establishment of an order necessitates 'obeying' the scheme (reality). If the analogy with nature is helpful in distinguishing the concept of 'order' from that of 'reality', the latter can most usefully be viewed as a situation produced by the interaction of a number of centres of power while the former encapsulates the aspiration to an alternative and ideal state of affairs. The main reason for the overlap between the two has been that world views have invariably in the past been influenced by the geographical location of the viewer, and geopolitical world views, while making claims to objectivity, have in fact suffered from a subjectivity produced by this built-in locational factor. Consciously or unconsciously the 'viewpoint' has been transformed into the 'point of view', the centre around which the 'scheme of things entire' functions. Some thirty years before Mackinder's assertion that the geographical pivot of world history lay in the heart of Asia (the Heartland), Charles Dilke, pondering on the changing centre of gravity in the English-speaking world – to which he gave the name 'Greater Britain' – had pointed to the persistence down the ages of subjective and variable world centres. These he collectively named after the *omphalos* (navel) at Delphi, which the ancients had thought of as being the centre of the *oikoumene*, the inhabited world. 'Herodotus held that Greece was the very middle of the world,' said Dilke, 'and that the unhappy Orientals were frozen, and the yet more unfortunate Indians baked every afternoon of their poor lives in order that the sun might shine on Greece at noon' (Dilke, 1868: 70–3). This 'omphalism', according to Dilke, produces world views which are subjective and represent distorted versions of reality. As a result of this distortion, the 'schemes' have taken on many of the characteristics of 'orders'. His wry observation that Fort Riley in Kansas had taken over from Independence in Missouri as 'the centre of the world ... the Hyde Park Corner from which continents are to measure their miles' calls to mind the centrality of the New World in Spykman's map engirdled as it was by the discontinuous and peripheral segments of the Old (Spykman, 1942). While Mackinder had employed geography to justify Britain's 'natural' world pre-eminence by locating the British Isles at the centre of the Land Hemisphere (Mackinder, 1902: 4), Spykman fragmented the World Island so that the centrally located 'Insula Fortunata' of America might remain whole. In such ways those principles underlying the 'scheme of things entire' have actually been employed in the attempt to construct the desired order.

While the Duc de Sully, in the early seventeenth century, was among the first to embark upon the purposeful formulation of a new order as an alternative to an old and ailing one, Sully's *grand dessein*, although firmly rooted in the emerging geopolitical realities of early modern Europe, was far too idealistic to be able to bridge the gap between 'scheme' and 'order'. Two centuries later, the Congress System represented a more realistic attempt to bridge that gap and to tackle the problems arising from the failure to construct a viable order on the basis of those geopolitical realities known collectively as the *ancien régime*. It was predicated on the 'concert' of the great powers and while one of its effects was to institutionalize their dominant role, another was to modify the anarchy of the international system. The simultaneous proposal by the Tsar of Russia for a Holy Alliance was evidence of a fundamentally different approach to international order and of an alternative model for international action.

The aspiration to 'order' on a global scale, the desire to move from the unacceptable reality of the 'scheme' towards the ideal of the 'design', became all the more urgent following the enormous change in the world political map brought about by the decline and fall of the larger units of geopolitical organization, the regional imperial states. These had created 'orders' – organizational structures – over those large stretches of territory which Febvre referred to as *mondes* (worlds) (Febvre, 1935: 314–15). When Marcus Aurelius had talked of Rome, he had meant the World; the *Imperium* was itself the first successful *grand dessein* for a world order. With its fall there was disorder and no successor state was able to hold together the world of the Western ecumene (Parker, 1988: 9 note 3), let alone that wider world which the period of the Great Discoveries was to reveal.

In similar fashion, the contemporary idea of a New World Order has arisen out of the disorder which accompanied the collapse of the Soviet Union, now widely seen as having been, in effect, the Soviet Empire. The fulfilment of the aspiration to order is today, as in the past, contingent upon the production of a design which can successfully replace the contemporary reality with a new order. To be successful, this has to take into account the limits of the possible within the context of contemporary geopolitical reality. As has been observed, the idea of geopolitical reality is not itself some abstract concept but is the creation of the perceptions of those who have a vested interest in that particular system, which will enable the sun to shine on Greece (or Britain, or America, or Europe) at noon. The Omphalos was the imagined centre of the world rather than the real one, but the essential feature of Dilke's omphalism is that it is linked to patterns of behaviour based upon it. From the Peace of Westphalia to the end of the Cold War, the international reality has consisted of a succession of 'schemes', states of affairs which have arisen from the interactions of a number of centres of power. The consequent world political map has been made up less of 'natural' frontiers than a succession of what Le Lannou called 'truce lines' (Le Lannou, 1962). The *grands desseins* – systems, 'concerts', unions, organizations, leagues – have been attempts to introduce some kind of stability into this unstable and untidy reality. Marcus Aurelius's world was viewed and designed from Rome, the world city and the Omphalos of its age, and this enabled a rare coincidence of 'scheme' and 'order' in the first *Imperium*. Subsequent world schemes and orders have overlapped but have never been coextensive. The common factor present in them all has been the failure to produce successful *desseins* which would make the two one. While at the level of the territorial state such structures have been much in evidence, they have remained transient and fragile in the wider cosmos.

With the end of the Cold War, Western civilization has in many ways achieved a global reach similar to that of Hellenic and Roman civilization over the *oikoumene* in the second century AD, when the Roman Empire reached its maximum territorial extent. Globalization can be seen as being both the fulfilment of Bryce's 'world process' and the enlargement of the ancient *oikoumene* into what Mark Jefferson termed the global 'ecumene' (Whittlesey, 1939: 2–3). The Western ecumene has been instrumental in this development and the ideas underlying the concept of the New World Order are essentially Western. In many ways it is a sort of 'Greater West' which is being envisaged. This has led to the conclusion that the closed system is essentially a centre-periphery one in which an enlarged Western ecumene occupies the dominant position as extended *omphalos* of the New World Order. Does this mean that the time is now ripe for a new *grand dessein* to transform scheme into order? The evidence of the past is that design can only become reality when effective geopolitical structures are put in place; the presence or absence of these remains the critical factor in determining whether globalization as scheme can be given the stability of an order.

The relationship of contemporary ideals to reality can be observed in the different 'visions' of the world present in geopolitical discourse. In analysing this, the *Visions de l'Europe* research project uses the *Théorie des Structures Géographiques* (TEGEO) methodology (Jolivet and Nicolas, 1991). While the main purpose of this has been to examine the 'visions of Europe' as revealed in contemporary official discourse, this is set in the wider global context. The survey of German geopolitical discourse on Europe, for example, is also very revealing of the official German world view (Nicolas and Parker, 1995). The 'basic structure' of the German view as revealed by the official discourse is an essentially 'Western' Europe, located mainly to the west of the Baltic-Adriatic isthmus, which is seen as being central to a 'wider structure' including Europe, Northern Asia and Anglo-America. Europe is firmly embedded in a contiguous 'North' stretching latitudinally as a great belt from the American West to the Russian Far East. Both the German and the British world views are revealed as being highly Northern Hemisphere oriented, although, as one might expect, the British view is more global in outlook. This is interpreted as being evidence of binary rather than core–periphery thinking in the official geopolitical discourse of both powers. The overall process within the North is viewed in the German discourse in particular as being one of increasing integration through the extension of institutions, closer economic ties and the spread of common values. The report on the German discourse concludes:

> The German role in this whole process appears to be one in which Germany is seen as acting as the principal link between the former adversaries of West and East in the successful accomplishment of the process of change . . . Germany is seen as occupying a pivotal position. (Nicolas and Parker, 1995: 53–4)

Omphalism would appear to be alive and well and living in Bonn, but the analysis of other national official discourses reveals the presence of the same kind of state-centred world views.

Using the TEGEO methodology, the different visions (designs) of a desired order can thus be extracted from the analysis of the official discourse, and the differences among them can be clearly observed. The incompatibility of many such visions underlies confrontational behaviour patterns, and one of the functions of the European Union has been to attempt to reach an acceptable synthesis among them. If some such synthesis is not achieved, it is left to the realities of global power to determine which particular design is selected for implementation and which New Order, for a time at least, will prevail. In practice the failure of scheme to become order has usually resulted in a state of affairs in which a number of different orders have had to co-exist. Each such situation has then become the latest version of 'the scheme of things entire'. The 'peaceful co-existence' of the Cold War, as a recognition of this reality, constituted a scheme in this sense. Because of the failure of either of the alternative orders to prevail, a confrontational and dangerous reality became a surrogate world order in which the anarchy of Mutually Assured Destruction was transformed through creative tension into the illusion of a force for stability.

The divergence of great power visions of the world has in the past led with grim inevitability towards their being tested by force. Great Games, using the term in a generic sense, have had a way of being transformed into great wars. That *the* Great Game itself did not do so was the result of a massive change in the balance of world power, brought about mainly by the rise of Germany. The Game, rendered increasingly irrelevant, did not so much finish as wind down and end in a stalemate followed by the peaceful resolution of those disputes which had a little while earlier appeared to be so intractable. Hopkirk's Great Game concludes with 'End-game' in which the confrontation was wound down, not because of any change of heart, but because other dangers were looming on the horizon. In 'End-game' the terminology of conflict ('advance', 'attack', 'gain', 'loss', 'forward moves') gives way to that of conflict resolution ('accommodation', 'entente', 'peace', 'agreement', 'convention') (Hopkirk, 1990: 513–24). The conditions for 'problem-solving' were created by the new realities of the world situation (Groom, 1991: 77–8).

With the end of the Cold War, the new world political geography has been far from dominated by the West in some absolute way. The new realities include the signs of a massive change in the centre of gravity of world power away from the West and towards such emerging centres as the Pacific Rim and in particular the Asia–Pacific region. The nature of this 'Global Shift' (Dicken, 1992) needs to be fully understood and acted upon if a successful new global system is to be created. Indeed, the Cold War has developed its own 'End-game' terminology which includes such words as 'shaping', 'redefining', 'orientation', 'creation', 'perception', 'integration', 'transformation' and 'variable geometry' (Miall, 1993, 1994; Wallace, 1992). This is the terminology of 'design' rather than of 'scheme', of purposeful creation rather than acceptance of some natural or inevitable state of affairs. Such terminology stands in marked contrast to the tectonic inevitability implied in Lacoste's (1984: 33) use of the geological analogy 'les grandes plaques' (the great plates) which he saw as being the geopolitical successors to the 'great manichean discourses' of the Cold War.

While the idea of 'designing' the new world appears to have gained the upper hand over natural forces, nevertheless the exercise of free will is still constrained by the possibilities. Successful design must always be dependent upon a knowledge of the materials with which the designer has to work and a recognition of its strengths and weaknesses. In the past, the transformation of design into system was invariably associated with testing in war. Now the analysis and synthesis of the designs on offer can extend the limits of the possible in the creation of international order.

David Silverman, referring to the stages in the development of organization theory, quoted Wittgenstein's analogy of 'throwing away ladders' so as to have the confidence to climb further beyond them. Old propositions, said Wittgenstein, had to be transcended in order to be able to 'see the world aright' (Silverman, 1994: 23). The study of the geopolitics of world views and world orders throughout much of the present century has been hampered by the adherence to old and narrow propositions; at the root of this has been the failure to perceive the distinction between 'schemes' and 'orders'. If, in geopolitical discourse, globalization represents the socio-economic realities of the closed world system, a new 'scheme of things entire', then any successful New World Order has to 'obey' it, in the Baconian sense. It has to spring from an awareness of the great problems involved in translating ideals into realities, and of the historic tendency to blur the distinction between the two. Indeed, the prevalence of Dilke's omphalism has been so persistent that there has often been little recognition of any such distinction. Western geopolitics has, in effect, been trapped in a Ptolemaic system of thought, and for the successors of the ancient Greeks the world order was deemed to be arranged in such a way that the sun should shine upon each of them at noon. The period of the 'Great Discoveries' in geopolitics, coupled with a severing of those old links with state policies which had been epitomized by German *Geopolitik*, has liberated contemporary geopolitics from the constraints of the past. This has at last given it the possibility of finally shaking off the Ptolemaic inheritance and of moving decisively to a Copernican system of thought in which the perception of reality comes less from preconceived notions than from scientific observation. In this way it may be able to join Wittgenstein in kicking away the ladders and thus seeing the world aright.

References

Bacon, F. (1924) *Essays, Civil and Moral*, Letchworth, Temple Press.

Bryce, J. (1902) The relations of the advanced and the backward races of mankind, Romanes Lecture, Oxford, Clarendon Press.

Clark, I. (1993) *The Hierarchy of States: Reform and Resistance in the International Order*, Cambridge, Cambridge University Press.

Dicken, P. (1992) *Global Shift: The Internationalization of Economic Activity*, London, Paul Chapman.

Dilke, C. (1868) *Greater Britain*, London, Macmillan.

Febvre, L. (1935) *A Geographical Introduction to History*, London, Kegan Paul, Trench and Trubner.

Fisler, J., Damrosch, E. and Scheffer, D. J. (1991) *Law and Force in the New International Order*, Boulder, CO, Westview Press.

Groom, A. J. R. (1991) No compromise: problem-solving in a theoretical perspective, *International Social Science Journal*, **127**, 77–86.

Hopkirk, P. (1990) *The Great Game*, Oxford, Oxford University Press.

Ishill, J. (1923) *Peter Kropotkin*, New Jersey, Free Spirit Press.

Jolivet, R. and Nicolas, G. (1991) Signe géographique: chorèmes et tégéos, *Cahiers de Géographie de Québec*, **96**, 535–64.

Lacoste, Y. (1984) Editoriale: les géographes, l'action et la politique, *Hérodote*, **33**, 3–32.

Le Lannou, M. (1962) *L'Europe et le géographe*, Bruges, Sciences Humaines et l'Intégration Européenne.

Mackinder, H. J. (1902) *Britain and the British Seas*, Oxford, Clarendon Press.

Mackinder, H. J. (1904) The geographical pivot of history, *Geographical Journal*, **23**, 421–37.

Mackinder, H. J. (1919) *Democratic Ideals and Reality: A Study in the Politics of Reconstruction*, London, Constable.

Miall, H. (1993) *Shaping the New Europe*, London, RIIA/Pinter.

Miall, H. (1994) *Redefining Europe*, London, RIIA.

Naumann, F. (1916) *Central Europe*, London, King.

Nicolas, G. and Parker G. (1995) *Geovision allemande des Europes*, Lausanne, Eratosthène.

O'Loughlin, J. (ed.) (1994) *Dictionary of Geopolitics*, Westport, CT, Greenwood Press.

Parker, G. (1985) *Western Geopolitical Thought in the Twentieth Century*, London, Croom Helm.

Parker, G. (1988) *The Geopolitics of Dominance*, London, Routledge.

Raffestin, C. (1980) *Pour une géographie du pouvoir*, Paris, Librairies Techniques.

Silverman, D. (1994) On throwing away ladders: re-writing the theory of organisations, in J. Hassard and M. Parker (eds), *Towards a New Theory of Organisations*, London, Routledge.

Spykman, N. (1942) *America's Strategy in World Politics: The United States and the Balance of Power*, New York, Harcourt, Brace.

Taylor, P. (1989) *Political Geography: World Economy, Nation-State and Locality*, London, Longman.

Thakur, R. (1995) The United Nations in a new world order, in K. P. Bajpai and H. C. Shukul (eds), *Interpreting World Politics*, New Delhi, Sage.

Wallace, W. (1992) *Dynamics of European Integration*, London, RIIA/Pinter.

Whittlesey, D. (1939) *The Earth and the State*, New York, Holt.

6

Global Restructuring and International Migration: Consequences for the Globalization of Politics

HÉLÈNE PELLERIN

The question of international migration has received renewed interest in the last ten years, from about the time globalization became a popular concept. This coincidence is often interpreted causally: global restructuring generates or amplifies migration and, in turn, the movement of people across borders is an indication of the globalization of societies, and of the obsolescence of national boundaries.

Migration is not a new phenomenon, nor a feature specific to the global era of social relations. But the processes of spatial redefinition involved in global restructuring concern migrants in two related ways: as objects of structural change and as participants in global restructuring. In the case of the former, international migration is characterized by growing numbers of people forced to move, and by deterioration in the conditions of their movement. As agents of change, migrants participate in the process of transforming social organization. Their movement, and the conditions surrounding it, imply change in the organization of production, in the territoriality of societies, as well as in the social production of ideas and identities, both in regions of origin and destination.

For some, contemporary international migration reflects the internationalization of civil society, that is, into a society of state-transcending social groupings (Smith, 1993). Such an interpretation, however, ignores the limits imposed on the constitution of extra-national but territorially bounded social organizations by global restructuring, existing forms of social organization and emerging power relations.

The following analysis examines developments in international migration in the context of global restructuring. Such socio-historical analysis helps in assessing the significance and impact of migration on the restructuring of social relations.

World order, international migration and global change

What impact does globalization have on international migration, and what role does the latter play in the process of globalization? These are interconnected questions which should be considered in the context of the under-theorization of migration in recent decades. The phenomenon requires methodological and ontological re-examination. In fact, most theoretical and methodological tools for analysing international migration were inherited from the immediate post-World War II period, reflecting the main characteristics of the movement of people and of the emerging world order of that time. In order to understand the current complex reality of migration, one needs to locate both the phenomenon and the method of understanding it in their historical contexts.

The fact that international migration cannot be understood outside the context in which it unfolds does not indicate that it is simply a reaction to whatever historical change is taking place. It suggests instead that migration always takes place within structures and social practices. In other words, migrants are not a social category isolated from class, gender or ethnic group. The term 'migrant' cannot meaningfully be used in a generic sense. What migrants do and do not do is the result of a series of conditions that emanate from circumstances immediately surrounding them or associated with their position and roles in social structures. These circumstances and structures, as well as impacting on migration, also determine, to a large extent, the social significance of the phenomenon in a given historical context.

International migration can be considered as a specific set of historically located social practices. Migrants should not be considered methodologically as a social category abstracted from their social context. A psychological analysis of the individual preferences of migrants is insufficient to understand the conditions shaping migration flows. Individual migrants are not simply or mostly rational actors calculating cost benefits.

Structural factors are important in shaping the decisions of individual migrants, and in constraining the possibilities and alternatives offered to them.[1] International migration results from decisions – proactive or reactive (Richmond, 1994) – of migrant individuals or groups conditioned by a variety of historical constraints related to both zones of origin and destination. We need, therefore, to work towards defining the structures and circumstances that shape international migration.

'Push' and 'pull' factors, specifying the variety of conditions inciting emigration and immigration, are important in this respect. These factors can be economic, political, environmental or ideological. The push–pull model of analysis locates migration processes historically. But this conceptual framework tends to be limited due to its reliance on quantitative or tangible variables in regions of origin and reception. Such analysis identifies typical influences in emigration as lack of employment or food, violence and military conflict, and in immigration as higher wages, greater employment opportunities and attractive social benefits. The problem with the logic of this approach is that it is too individualistic and rationalistic. Migrants are portrayed primarily as rational actors subjected to structural forces. At its worst, the logic suggests that migration is shaped by the market law of supply and demand for migrants; at its best, it focuses on structures of authority and power in the world, in recent years particularly in receiving states.[2] There is little sense of the historical nature of the push and pull factors of migration and their respective impact, or of the role of migrants themselves, or migration processes more generally, in shaping changes.[3]

Two dimensions are missing from mainstream analyses. The first alerts us to the holistic explanatory basis for migration which may not, however, be internally coherent. The notion of world order developed by Robert Cox (1987) can fill this gap. A world order as a set of historical structures combines and shapes interactions across the economic, political and ideological levels of social practice. One can investigate these interactions as they affect the terms and directions of migratory flows at both local and global levels. The second missing dimension is dialectical. It represents a failure to recognize that migrants, individually and collectively, are agents participating in structural change as well as subjects of dynamics they do not control. The concept of world order contains a dialectical view of the agent–structure dimension of social practices, as well as of the material and ideological sources and manifestations of power. Hence, relations of production and authority rest partly on normative and legal frameworks in which decisions and actions are constructed and legitimized. Moreover, both agents and structures are involved in the making of world order, but often in different time frames.[4] According to Marx, individuals or collective agents act in circumstances not of their own choosing which are often constituted by traditions and the regularity of social practices.

The nature of production, considered in a broad sense of social and power relations, is a fundamental aspect of any world order because it relates to a particular territoriality, a concrete space of social relations. And this territoriality is directly impacting on international migration. In fact, the latter has traditionally been understood in the material context in which it occurs (Petras, 1981), but these material conditions should not only be looked at in quantitative terms; the organization of production involves social, political and ideological dimensions as well. Global restructuring reflects this, involving changes in decisions about what, when and where to produce, and how production should be organized and distributed. Transformations in the territoriality of production are central. The resulting shift in the configuration of power between capital and labour is an important conditioning dynamic of international migration. To these material changes, one should also add the social and ideological dimensions that condition migration. Traditions, legal codes and 'societal paradigms'[5] are important features of a world order. They determine the 'relevant' basic social categories, their interaction and their respective integration. Various forms of integration of diverse social forces and agents condition the existence and patterns of migration. Varying resources, regulations and support for migrants shape their practices and limit the scope of their impact.

Oppenheimer wrote that 'all world history is basically the history of migrations'.[6] Yet the significance of migration has varied across time and place in accordance with its dynamics and its forms of integration in world order. The migration of the Huns in the fourth and fifth centuries was different in dynamic, form and impact from the movement of African slaves to the American continent in the eighteenth and nineteenth centuries, or from the migration of Europeans to North America in the nineteenth century. Contrasts are also evident between post-1945 migration patterns and those of the more recent period of global restructuring. In each case, different economic dynamics and political and ideological structures determine the general conditions of migration flows, from the zones and categories of migrants involved, through the direction of migration flows, to the form of integration in receiving zones. And in each case, migrants have played a significantly different role in the making of a world order.

The post-war world order: Pax Americana, Fordism and integrated forms of migration

We need to investigate the main developments and structures of the post-1945 world order because of their influence on current interpretations of migration. This period is often referred to as Pax Americana, a more or less coherent system where political, ideological and economic structures were interconnected to provide stability at the world level (Cox, 1987). Politically, American hegemony was founded on military superiority and on political–diplomatic activity in various regions of the world. Ideologically, the liberal democratic model of society, defined as participatory democracy based on individualism, was gaining influence in the world. In the economic realm, a particular form of organization of production, Fordism,[7] became dominant.

Under Pax Americana, migration tended to follow the contours of existing structures of production and politics. Within this context migrants tended to come either from regions of the world integrated into economic spaces of production, such as former or neocolonial empires, or from countries involved in the East–West ideological struggle. As a result, the Mediterranean basin and some Asian and East European countries were the largest regions of emigration. Whatever their origin, most migrants of the 1960s and early 1970s were either directly recruited or integrated into managed structures that monitored their movement and settlement. In the case of migrant workers from the Mediterranean going to Western Europe, the contracts and agreements monitoring their functions were concluded between workers and employers, or between sending states and employers and/or receiving states. Through such agreements a guest-worker system was institutionalized, at least in most of Western Europe. A similar mechanism existed in the USA with the Bracero programme for Mexican workers in the agricultural sector (Portes, 1977). Other sources of immigrants to North America were sustained by the international community and the international agency involved with migrants, the International Migration Office. In Australia, a similar pattern of migration was unfolding that responded to the needs of the nationally managed economy, and there, too, newcomers were scrutinized and assessed according to their skills and correspondence to economic needs (Quinlan and Lever-Tracy, 1988).

A system of refugee selection and determination was established to deal with migrants associated with the military and ideological structures of Pax Americana. The Geneva Convention of 1951 and the 1967 protocol that enlarged the definition of refugee to non-communist states' nationals all concurred to regulate the flows of refugees, both in terms of their skills, the quotas, and the direction of the people forcibly displaced. Under this system, refugees were to be located in specific geographically circumscribed camps, and were managed and monitored by the United Nations High Commissioner for Refugees along with receiving states (Meissner *et al.*, 1993).

This model of migration corresponds to two features of the economic organization of the time: the highly integrated level of national economic management, and the central place occupied by the migrant workforce in the economies of both sending and receiving countries. The Fordist mode of regulation linked social and political conditions directly to the production process. In this system, strategies of capital accumulation and organization of production were centrally and nationally constructed and managed, even in cases when firms were expanding internationally. A large segment of the labour force was involved in negotiated arrangements with employers and states.[8] This organized group of protected workers was participating in a project of economic recovery and growth through 'corporatist' structures that shaped and channelled their demands (Cox, 1977). However, economic growth depended significantly on the flexibility provided largely by a migrant workforce. The dynamic of the corporatist welfare system itself was thus relying on the marginalization of a large segment of the workforce.[9]

Concentrations of emigration followed the development of peripheral forms of Fordism in the early 1960s (Lipietz, 1987). At this time, firms' international expansion and the attempt by host governments to adopt mass production and consumption strategies led to important changes in the organization of production. Labour surplus, often the product of urbanization, industrialization and mechanization of work, led to strategies of emigration, often managed by states themselves. Many sending states were relying on regulated outflows of people to alleviate social tensions and earn foreign currencies through a system of remittances (World Bank, 1981), and many were also able to negotiate propitious conditions for the migration of labour in exchange for investments, trade agreements or military aid, thus feeding the economic dynamic of Pax Americana based on labour-intensive production strategies and mass consumption of goods, including military.

In receiving regions, migrants originally constituted a reserve army of labour (Castles and Kosack, 1973), but later became a structural element of the economy. They were involved in the monopolistic, Fordist sectors and firms of France, Belgium and Germany, in the service sector in, for example, Britain, and in 'soft' manufacturing industries (e.g., textiles, footwear and, more recently, electronics) in countries such as the USA, Australia and Canada. But despite their central role in these countries, migrants were not a significant force socially or politically. They were identified as an economic factor of production whose mobility was monitored by states, in conjunction with firms' needs, and the issue of migrants' rights was limited largely to specific labour markets and regulations. A crucial example of this is the guest-worker system where the geographical destination of migrants, the duration of contracts, the sector and sometimes even the firm where the labour force was to be hired, and finally the duties and skills required from migrants were determined by either firms or state departments. The situation of migrants thus contrasted strikingly with that of nationals. Sending regions projected an equally limited view of emigrants, who were considered mostly as an asset in an export strategy of growth. As representatives of a particular form of labour, migrants were uneasily integrated, in so far as labour unions denied their specificity.

Pax Americana started to collapse with the erosion of the economic, military and financial power of the USA, but the absence of any serious contender prevented its replacement.[10] This collapse was characterized by important changes in the political and economic realms of social practices. Fordism became exhausted, its profitability being undermined by overproduction and underconsumption trends. With the fiscal crisis of the state, Fordism could no longer integrate, if it ever did, social forces and particularly migrants. In the late 1960s, migrants' behaviour became rigidified (Marie, 1988), and the disposable workforce became ethnic groups which intended to stay for a longer time (Castles *et al.*, 1984).

Global restructuring and international migration: the emergence of a new pattern of migration

Globalization is often understood in terms of the reconfiguration of space–time dimensions of social organization (Rosenau, 1992; Harvey, 1990). New post-Westphalian structures of power and social organization are emerging, less centred on national territories or models of production (Cox, 1992). The locus of power in the world, and within societies, escapes any single state management, as new processes and agents gain power and influence over many significant dynamics of world order, from financial activities to the organization of production (Strange, 1994). The ideological realm of social activity of the emerging world order must be understood in the context of a diminishment of states as pillars of social cohesion and integration, and of economic management. The dominant norms focus on the self-regulated market, and encourage the commodification of every social activity and process.

The term post-Fordism adequately reflects the uncertainties and complexities of the current transformation of Fordism as a dominant mode of regulation and organization of production (Amin, 1994). Unlike its predecessor, post-Fordism does not rely on a territoriality defined by the nation-state, nor on a social structure that is limited to or centred on national social forces. Post-Fordist global restructuring of social relations of production is constituted on the basis of transnational, or international, strategies of expansion of firms and the disruption of nationally integrated economic spaces. This is particularly evident from the vantage point of large firms, with strategies of decentralization, diversification and expansion (Ruigrok and Van Tulder, 1993), and new production processes and subcontracting practices which alter relations between firms or plants across the world. The transnational production process varies in form: it encourages the creation of cross-border networks of firms that are hierarchically organized, but which in many cases also require geographical proximity (Bernard, 1994: 222). Firms, large and small, have participated in this new phase of restructuring. Many have developed alliances and merged functions, while others have diversified their sources of supply and their markets.

The emerging world order has significantly affected social structures and relations, creating new conditions for international migration. Less structured and state-controlled flows of migrants have resulted. A new international division of labour is unfolding involving new forms of integration of various regions. Many parts of Africa, Asia and Latin America are now intensifying their specialization in the extraction and production of primary goods, from particular categories of food crop to oil and minerals (Verhaeren, 1986; McMichael and Myhre, 1991). This leads to renewed economic interests in some regions, and greater integration, but at the periphery of the world economy.

New waves of migration are being generated from regions where the modernization and the mechanization of traditional industries pushes people to urban centres or abroad. Foreign investment in these areas encourages the trend towards rural exodus and emigration (Pastor, 1989/90). Other conditions for emigration stem from the collapse of the development-state (Elsenhans, 1994). Sources of credit have been reduced, capital has been flowing out constantly (OECD, 1992) and new conditions have been imposed on future credit. With the assistance of foreign private or multilateral institutions, many regions have planned and implemented privatization programmes and austerity measures, and modernized traditional sectors such as agriculture in order to increase their competitiveness. These measures have disrupted social organizations and in some cases (e.g., the Philippines and Mozambique in the latter half of the 1980s) caused violent struggles, leading to increased domestic and cross-border migration for economic and asylum purposes.[11]

In some regions higher levels of industrialization and integration in post-Fordist industrial forms have produced incentives for emigration linked specifically to corporatist transnational strategies. The migrants emerging from these conditions are mostly highly skilled people. Currently, these migrants are comparatively few in number, but their significance may increase if they trigger a chain of migration of less skilled people (Sassen, 1988; Lim, 1992).

In host countries, traditional and new pull conditions for migration co-exist and adjust to labour market restructuring. Reforms have been the result in a variety of sectors and specializations. Each country or region has developed specific labour market needs related to the characteristics of their economy, e.g. the service economies of the USA, Canada and Britain, the information–industrial models of Japan and Germany, and the more traditional manufacturing emphasis of other countries (Castells and Aoyama, 1994).

In general, restructuring of production has led to a greater flexibilization of labour markets, with sustained efforts by employers and states to reduce labour rigidities and costs. One aspect of this restructuring is the increasing flexibilization of the work process and hence of the workforce (Boyer, 1988). Another dimension is the extension of the labour process beyond the workplace and the reach of labour legislation. With possibilities of subcontracting and dividing tasks and products into a variety of steps, the production process can now extend well beyond the factory, and can include various sets of social relations, from a region to a specific community, or to household units (Sabel, 1991). In play here are efforts to reduce production costs by the externalization and decentralization of processes. Practices of subcontracting and contracting out, of encouraging workers to become self-employed, and of informalizing many activities are examples of these efforts.

Labour is at the forefront of the restructuring of production through practices of deregulation of work. Women have been particularly vulnerable to this trend in a range of complex ways (Standing, 1992; see also the chapter in this volume by Anne Sisson Runyan). Migrants have also suffered, because of their legal status, their presence in those sectors accounting for most change, and new definitions of the economy's needs. The reliance on households and communities for subsistence and reproductive functions has grown throughout Western Europe and North America in the last twenty years. Such a situation has been even more widespread among migrants, particularly among newer waves. It is interesting to note in this respect that, despite an increase in the categories of migrants not traditionally connected with labour markets (notably through family reunion), the proportion of migrant workers in the total working population has not substantially decreased.[12] The growing number of female migrants, notably in Western Europe, is an adjustment to labour market demands (Morokvasic, 1991). Some studies have indicated that self-employment is increasing in ethnic communities in Western Europe and North America (Palidda, 1992; Waldinger *et al.*, 1990). Links between these communities and international firms and networks of partnership and subcontracting might partly explain their growth, as demonstrated in the garment and electronic industries (McLean Petras, 1992; Sassen, 1984).

Labour power is central to restructuring, and states have been involved in the associated transformation of corporatist structures in the name of greater competitiveness on a global scale. While supporting capital's needs for greater mobility and spatial flexibility, states have worked to deregulate labour markets and social contracts. There has been a shift from state-controlled emigration to more transnational forms of emigration, where migrants themselves manage their movement. Increased capital flows, changes in the organization of production and the fiscal crisis of the welfare system have reduced the importance of the movement of labour as a strategy for capital accumulation. States pay more attention to capital's mobility. The decision of the US administration to interrupt the Bracero programme of contractual labour migration with Mexico in 1965, and to replace it with the Maquiladoras arrangement whereby US capital could move to some regions of Mexico and benefit from propitious conditions of production and accumulation, is an obvious example of this shift (Revel-Mouroz, 1979). The reduction in the number of migrants accepted in receiving societies since the first half of the 1970s also confirms this new priority.[13] At the same time, however, new waves of migrants have been accepted or tolerated, but in increasingly precarious conditions: workers on a short-term, temporary or seasonal basis, asylum claimants, refugees recognized as such by the UN convention, and undocumented travellers. These categories of migrants will constitute the main flow into Western Europe in the next decade, more important than the flow of highly skilled migrants (SOPEMI, 1992; ETUI, 1993).[14]

Neoliberal restructuring has deregulated labour markets, and made vulnerable many social movements, old and new. Women, migrants, ethnic minorities and labour have been seriously affected by changes in economic and political structures. Processes of regional integration have reinforced this tendency, since they prioritize capital mobility and greater policing of social activities. Take Western Europe as an example; following the TREVI group on monitoring terrorists, the Schengen agreement and the Dublin Accord have enhanced the ability of states to harmonize their controls over the circulation of migrants and particularly of asylum seekers (Bunyan, 1993), while advocating greater competitiveness and tight police controls for managing social exclusion (Balibar, 1993).

While migrants have been central to restructuring, they have been increasingly marginalized politically and socially. If in the immediate post-1945 period their condition was limited by an economic reading of their function, the contemporary context depicts them as either criminal or victim.[15] Such an interpretation neglects the dialectics of migration, according to which migrants have been instrumental in restructuring and the politics of organization. Migrants' experiences arguably demonstrated the limits of the system of protected work and negotiated corporatism. Post-Fordist processes of production have generated a long-term deterioration of labour practices, and a greater reliance on social units for social reproduction. The conditions of migrants, who rely heavily on personal and community networks, are similar to other social groups resisting marginalization in the era of neoliberal restructuring.

Contemporary international migration is simply one dimension of the greater general precariousness of individuals and collectivities. At the same time, migrants have contributed to the 'spatial disarticulation' of societies (Lipietz, 1994). Ethnic tensions and various forms of identity revivalism are an indication of both the loss of social cohesion and the attempt to reconstruct collective identities on new grounds. The practices of most migrants play a role in both: the rigidification of their presence on foreign soil, their reliance on ethnic or community networks, and their relative vulnerability in societies they have left and those which receive them have contributed to social disarticulation. Simultaneously, they are participating in the reorganization of social and political movements, which is part of the redefinition of the politics of organization of social relations.

Conclusion

One does not need to be overly pessimistic intellectually to see that the emerging world order has served the expansion of capitalism in a significant way (Ross and Trachte, 1990). The collapse of nationally oriented economic programmes around the world and the growing commodification of social relations indicate the increasing power of capital over societies. International migration, not unlike other social practices, has been constrained by concrete limits to social mobility.

Forms of resistance to this expansion have varied in scope and strategy, but they all seem to be rather weak. The relative powerlessness of resistance stems largely from changes in the territoriality of production and of societies. The changes generated by post-Fordist strategies and global restructuring make traditional and universalizing forms of organization and mobilization obsolete. Indeed, deregulation and shifts in state forms have privatized and diversified social relations of production. Post-Fordism involves a territoriality that is neither state-centric nor homogeneously unfolding and structured. Traditional parameters of organization based on workplace mobilization or on negotiated agreements with states have become less effective both in mobilizing forces (Jenson, 1989) and in resisting capitalist expansion. By contrast, ethnicity and other forms of representation based on individual experiences are gaining greater attention, as the rise of new social movements suggests.

Migrants in receiving societies often emphasize their identity and origin. Yet this approach can have limited success if it is structured around strategies of inclusiveness and recognition based on an integrative and interventionist model of state regulation. The current trends towards reduced state power of intervention in social integration schemes limits the effectiveness of such approaches. The activities of the EC migrant forum, and of local second-generation migrants' initiatives such as France-Plus in France, are cases in point – successfully mobilizing but achieving little in terms of concrete improvements (EC Migrants Forum, 1993; Wihtol de Wenden, 1992). Considering their particular place in the production process, migrants could and should focus also on the material conditions characterizing and limiting their possibilities.

Such seems to be the strategy pursued by a collective of migrant workers in Western Europe, the Commission for Filipino Migrant Workers.[16] By focusing on the reality of deregulated work practices and social relations of production generated by post-Fordism, this movement has been successful in improving work-related conditions. The strategy adopted can be extended to other movements in societies also experiencing greater social and economic precariousness.

While the 'globalization of politics' has been unfolding at a steady pace for twenty years, creating a 'space in itself' with specific social relations of production, conscious efforts will be required for understanding the possibilities of a 'politics of globalization' in the new territorialities emerging, that is, the creation of a 'space for itself' (Lipietz, 1994), with a constructed consciousness of the new social relations of production. As suggested here, international migration is wrongly perceived as a marginal issue in this context. It has been and continues to be influential. Indeed its role may be significant in the future formulation of a politics of globalization.

Notes

1. For an account of the theoretical debate on the causes of migration, see the short overview by Gardezi (1995: ch. 2).
2. Borrowing from a demographer who, after studying migration flows over a few centuries, stated that 'whether migration is controlled by those who send, by those who go, or by those who receive, it mirrors the world as it is at the time', Zolberg indicated that since the post-1945 period, the locus of decision and determination of migration flows lies essentially within the receiving countries, mainly of the OECD (Zolberg, 1990).
3. For an opposing view, see Bach and Schraml (1982).
4. As Cox (1987: 4) wrote: 'Historical structures are persistent social practices, made by collective human activity and transformed through collective human activity.'
5. A societal paradigm can be defined as a 'mode of structuring legitimate identities within the universe of political discourses' (Lipietz, 1991: 20).
6. *System der Soziologie* (1923), quoted in Thränhardt (1992).
7. Regulation school terminology has been useful for associating a particular form of organization of production to an historical context. Fordism was the term introduced and largely used in the literature to refer to the post-war economic order. See, among several others, Lipietz (1991) and Jessop (1990).
8. These arrangements were related to job classification schemes, employment security, incremental wages and social benefits, and general upward mobility. As Bernard (1994: 219) correctly pointed out, organized labour was not involved in work-related managerial decision-making.
9. Many labour organizations adopted a rather contradictory attitude towards this reality. They accepted the temporary use of foreign labour for the logic of economic growth while refusing to recognize any difference between migrants and national workers (Bastenier and Targosz, 1991).
10. On the issue of declining hegemony, I refer to Strange (1989).
11. The violence constitutive of the refugee experience stems from such conditions

(Zolberg *et al.*, 1989).

12. The activity rate in Western Europe is higher or equal for foreigners when compared with that of nationals: in 1991 it was 55.4 per cent for nationals of the European Union and 58.6 per cent for foreigners, with some variations according to the country of origin and gender. Foreign employment has either increased faster proportionately than national employment, or it has slowed down at a lesser pace (SOPEMI, 1993).

13. Notable exceptions to border closing are the oil-producing countries, where migration flows have been maintained or increased since the 1970s, except for the Gulf war interruption (Gardezi, 1995).

14. According to UNHCR figures, the number of asylum seekers in the European Union has gone up, from 70,950 in 1982 to 559,829 in 1992 (ETUI, 1993).

15. The Trilateral Commission is calling for the development of effective policies to stem the movement of people considered, alongside 'environmental degradation, drugs and terrorism, and weapon proliferations', as threatening stability and welfare (Meissner *et al.*, 1993).

16. Information provided by M. Ledesma, the executive director of the Commission for Filipino Migrant Workers, in an interview in Amsterdam, 31 May 1994.

References

Amin, A. (ed.) (1994) *Post-Fordism: A Reader*, Cambridge, Blackwell.

Appleyard, R. T. (1992) *International Migration: Challenge for the Nineties*, Geneva, International Organization for Migration.

Bach, R. L. and Schraml, L. A. (1982) Migration, crisis and theoretical conflict, *International Migration Review*, **16**(2), 329–41.

Balibar, E. (1993) L'Europe des citoyens, in O. Le Cour Grandmaison and C. Wihtol de Wenden (eds), *Les Étrangers dans la cité: expériences européennes*, Paris, La Découverte.

Bastenier, A. and Targosz, P. (1991) *Les Organisations syndicales et l'immigration en Europe*, Louvain-la-Neuve, Academia.

Bernard, M. (1994) Post-Fordism, transnational production and the changing political economy, in R. Stubbs and G. R. Underhill (eds), *Political Economy and the Changing Global Order*, Toronto, McClelland and Stewart.

Boyer, R. (1988) Division or unity? Decline or recovery? in R. Boyer (ed.), *The Search for Labour Market Flexibility*, Oxford, Clarendon Press.

Bunyan, T. (ed.) (1993) *Statewatching the New Europe. A Handbook on the European State*, Nottingham, Russell Press.

Campbell, D. (1994) Foreign investment, labour immobility and the quality of employment, *International Labour Review*, **133**(2), 185–204.

Castells, M. and Aoyama, Y. (1994) Paths towards the informational society: employment structures in G-7 countries, 1920–90, *International Labour Review*, **133**(1), 5–33.

Castles, S. and Kosack, G. (1973) *Immigrant Workers and Class Structure in Western Europe*, London, Oxford University Press.

Castles, S., Booth, H. and Wallace, T. (1984) *Here for Good. Western Europe's New Ethnic Minorities*, London, Pluto Press.

Cox, R. W. (1977) Labor and hegemony, *International Organization*, **31**(3), 385–424.

Cox, R. W. (1987) *Production, Power and World Order*, New York, Columbia University Press.

Cox, R. W. (1992) Global perestroika, *Socialist Register*, London, Merlin Press, pp. 26–43.

EC Migrants Forum (1993) *For a Joint Action for Tolerance in Europe (Pact)*, report presented at the conference of 11–12 March 1993 at the European Parliament, Strasbourg.

Elsenhans, H. (1994) Third world development state in crisis and the crisis of mainstream development theory, paper presented at the Department of Political Science, York University (Canada), 22 Sepember.

ETUI (1993) *Immigration in Western Europe: Development, Situation, Outlook*, Brussels, European Trade Union Institute.

Eurostat (1992, 1981, 1977) *Basic Statistics of the Community*, Brussels.

Eurostat (1994) *Eurostatistics: Data for Short-Term Economic Analysis*, General Statistics Series 1B(4).

Gardezi, H. N. (1995) *The Political Economy of International Labour Migration*, Montreal, New York, London, Black Rose Books.

Gill, S. (1992) The emerging world order and European change, in R. Miliband and L. Panitch (eds), *Socialist Register*, New World Order, London, Merlin Press.

Grahl, J. and Teague, P. (1989) The cost of neo-liberal Europe, *New Left Review*, **174**, 33–50.

Gramsci, A. (1971) *Selections from the Prison Notebooks*, ed. by Q. Hoare and G. N. Smith, New York, International Publishers.

Harvey, D. (1990) *The Condition of Post-Modernity*, Oxford, Blackwell.

Hettne, B. (1992) The double movement: global market versus regionalism, paper presented at the UNU symposium 'Multilateralism and Images of World Order', Florence, 30 September–13 October.

ILO (1990) *The Promotion of Self-Employment*, Report VII of the ILO Conference, 77th session, Geneva.

Jenson, J. (1989) Paradigms and political discourse: protective legislation in France and the US before 1914, *Canadian Journal of Political Science*, **22**(2), 235–58.

Jessop, R. (1990) Regulation theories in retrospect and prospect, *Economy and Society*, **19**(2), 153–216.

Lim, L. L. (1992) International labour movements: a perspective on economic exchanges and flows, in M. M. Kritz, L. L. Lim and H. Zlotnik (eds), *International Migration Systems. A Global Approach*, Oxford, Clarendon Press.

Lipietz, A. (1987) The globalization of the general crisis of Fordism 1967–1984, in J. Holmes and C. Leys (eds), *Frontyard Backyard*, Toronto, Between the Lines.

Lipietz, A. (1991) Governing the economy in the face of international challenge: from national developmentalism to national crisis, in J. F. Hollifield and G. Ross (eds), *Searching for the New France*, New York, Routledge.

Lipietz, A. (1994) The national and the regional: their autonomy *vis-à-vis* the capitalist world crisis, in R. Palan and B. Gills (eds), *Transcending the State–Global Divide. A Neostructuralist Agenda in International Relations*, Boulder, CO, and London, Lynne Rienner.

McLean Petras, E. (1992) The shirt on your back: immigrant workers and the reorganization of the garment industry, *Social Justice*, **19**(1), 76–114.

McMichael, P. and Myhre, D. (1991) Global regulation vs. the nation-state: agro-food systems and the new politics of capital, *Capital & Class*, **43**, 83–105.

Mahon, R. (1987) From Fordism to ? New technology, labour markets and unions, *Economic and Industrial Democracy*, **8**, 5–60.

Marie, C.-V. (1988) Entre économie et politique: le 'clandestin', une figure sociale géométrie variable, *Pouvoirs*, **47**, 75–92.

Meissner, D. M., Hormats, R. D., Garrigues Walker, A. and Ogata, S. (1993) *International Migration Challenges in a New Era*, report to the Trilateral Commission, **44**, New York, Trilateral Commission.

Morokvasic, M. (1991) Roads to independence: self-employed immigrants and minority women in five European states, *International Migration*, **29**(3), 407–17.

OECD (1992) *International Direct Investment. Policies and Trends in the 1980s*, Paris, OECD.

Palidda, S. (1992) Le développement des activités indépendantes des immigrés en Europe et en France, *Revue Européenne des Migrations Internationales*, **8**(1), 83–95.

Pastor, R. A. (1989/90) Migration and development: implications and recommendations for policy, *Studies in Comparative International Development*, **24**(4), 46–64.

Petras, E. M. (1981) The global labor market in the modern world economy, in M. M. Kritz, C. B. Keely and S. M. Tomasi (eds), *Global Trends in Migration*, New York, Center for Migration Studies.

Picchio, A. (1992) *Social Reproduction: The Political Economy of the Labour Market*, Cambridge, Cambridge University Press.

Portes, A. (1977) Labor functions of illegal aliens, *Society*, **14**(6), 31–7.

Quinlan, M. and Lever-Tracy, C. (1988) Immigrant workers, trade unions and industrial struggle: an overview of the Australian experience, 1945–1985, *Economic and Industrial Democracy: An International Journal*, **9**(1), 7–41.

Revel-Mouroz, J. (1979) Coopération et conflits dans les zones frontalières en Amérique latine, *Notes et Études Documentaires*, **4533–4**, 31–44.

Richmond, A. (1994) *Global Apartheid: Refugees, Racism and the New World Order*, Oxford, Oxford University Press.

Rosenau, J. N. (1992) Citizenship in a changing global order, in J. N. Rosenau and E.-O. Czempiel (eds), *Governance Without Government: Order and Changes in World Politics*, Cambridge, Cambridge University Press.

Ross, G. (1993) Post-Fordist politics: social democracy, labour and the left in Europe, in J. Jenson, R. Mahon and M. Bienefeld (eds), *Production, Space, Identity*, Toronto, Canadian Scholars' Press.

Ross, J. S. and Trachte, K. C. (1990) *Global Capitalism: The New Leviathan*, Albany, State University of New York Press.

Ruigrok, W. and Van Tulder, R. (1993) The elusive concept of globalization and rival internationalization strategies, paper presented at 'Emerging World Order' seminar, University of Amsterdam.

Sabel, C. (1991) Moebius-strip organization and open labor market: some consequences of the reintegration of conception and execution in a volatile economy, in P. Bourdieu and J. S. Coleman (eds), *Social Theory for a Changing Society*, New York, Westview Press.

Salt, J. (1993) *Migration and Population Change in Europe*, United Nations Institute for Disarmament Research, Research Paper 19, New York.

Sassen, S. (1984) The new labor demand in global cities, in M. Smith (ed.), *Cities in Transformation*, Beverly Hills, Sage.

Sassen, S. (1988) *The Mobility of Labor and Capital: A Study in International Investment and Labor Flow*, New York, Cambridge University Press.

Smith, M. P. (1993) Can you imagine? Transnational migration and the globalization of grassroots politics, paper presented at 'World Cities in a World System' conference, Sterling, VA, 1–3 April.

SOPEMI (1992 and 1993) *Trends in International Migration*, Paris, OECD.

Standing, G. (1992) Global feminization through flexible labor, in C. K. Wilber and K. P. Jameson (eds), *The Political Economy of Development and Underdevelopment*, New York, McGraw-Hill.

Strange, S. (1989) Toward a theory of transnational empire, in E.-O. Czempiel and J. N. Rosenau (eds), *Global Changes and Theoretical Challenges: Approaches to World Politics for the 1990s*, New York, Lexington Books.

Strange, S. (1994) Rethinking structural change in the international political economy: states, firms, and diplomacy, in R. Stubbs and G. R. D. Underhill (eds), *Political Economy and the Changing Global Order*, Basingstoke, Macmillan.

Thränhardt, D. (ed.) (1992) *Europe: A New Immigration Continent. Policies and Politics in Comparative Perspective*, Münster, Lit Verlag.

Tienda, M. and Booth, K. (1991) Migration, gender and social change, *International Sociology*, **6**(1), 51–72.

Verhaeren, R. (1986) Les répercussions de la crise, in Politiques d'immigration en Europe: France, RFA, Grande-Bretagne, Suisse, Suède, *Problèmes Politiques et Sociaux*, **530**, 9–11.

Waldinger, R., Aldrich, H. and Ward, R. (1990) *Ethnic Entrepreneurs: Immigrant Business in Industrial Societies*, London and Newbury Park, Sage.

Wihtol de Wenden, C. (1992) Les associations 'beur' et immigrés, leur leaders, leurs stratégies, *Regards sur l'Actualité*, **179**, 31–44.

World Bank (1981) International migrant workers' remittances: issues and prospects, Staff Working Paper 481.

Zolberg, A. (1990) *The Future of International Migration*, Working Paper 19, Brussels, Commission for the Study of International Migration and Cooperative Economic Development.

Zolberg, A., Suhrke, A. and Aguayo, S. (1989) *Escape from Violence: Conflict and the Refugee Crisis in the Developing World*, New York and Oxford, Oxford University Press.

Part 2

Territorial Logics

7

The Modern Multiplicity of States

PETER J. TAYLOR

It is the very nature of the modern state that there should be many states.
(Poggi, 1978: 13)

Social science has been endemically state-centric (Taylor, 1996). Conceived in a world academy dominated by states, the various social sciences have obediently followed agendas in which the 'society' they aspire to understand is defined politically by state boundaries. This is usually implicit in theoretical writing but quite explicit in empirical studies when the abstraction is stripped away. The result is a body of knowledge structured around states as the primary units of analysis. For instance, economic transactions across the world are usually studied through state-generated statistics about 'international' trade rather than as commodity chains in the multiple production process that generates trade. Similarly in political studies, focus on the state distorts what is viewed as 'political' and thus neglects the study of many power relations, such as those within households or firms. All this is commonplace: the poverty of state-centric thinking produces narrowly selective social sciences that omit or neglect much that is social. In this chapter I wish to take this argument a stage further. The claim I make is that *state-centric thinking severely disables our capacity for understanding the states themselves.*

This may seem an odd, even absurd, claim. How can a focus on a particular social institution be detrimental to its perceived meaning? Well, of course, it all depends on how the subject is perceived and how the social theory is conceived. In the study of states, the simple fact of their multiplicity is omitted or neglected to the severe detriment of our understanding of them. This has operated in two main ways. First, theories of the state are just that – arguments about the state in the singular. The theories focus upon the relationship of the state to its civil society with no or minimal recognition of the existence of other states. Second, the discipline of international relations has been dominated by its 'realist school', which acknowledges the multiplicity of states but with an extremely limited view of the meaning of the states. These studies treat states as interacting 'black boxes', ignoring the relationship with civil societies so well covered in the singular state theory. There have, of course, been many calls to remedy these deficiencies by combining what each does best, but with only limited success. Such a 'dual' theory concerns simultaneous analysis of the state 'looking in' on its civil society and 'looking out' to other states. But 'looking both ways' does not address the question of multiplicity *per se*. It remains a dual theory of the state only, rather than a theory of multiple states.

The failure of the combination strategy to treat multiplicity adequately is an indictment of the international relations half of the sum. The 'realist' acceptance of the multiplicity of states has been at a very superficial level: as merely the context within which an individual state has to operate. The outcome is, therefore, that although we have a relatively sophisticated concept of stateness from theories of the state, we have a wholly inadequate understanding of inter-stateness from international relations studies. But since multiplicity is an inherent feature of modern states, this deficiency undermines our understanding of them whatever the degree of state-centricity in our work. This chapter confronts the poverty of our thinking on inter-stateness by returning to the basics of international relations, in particular the concept of state sovereignty and its relationship to nation and territory. There are three main steps to the argument. First the modern theory of multiple sovereignties is distinguished from premodern universal sovereignty. This leads to the differentiation of the modern inter-state system from other states systems, and in the second section this is explored through the concept of inter-stateness. Finally, the utility of this analysis for current debates on the demise of the state(s) is considered.

Political organization of world-systems

The discussion that follows treats world-systems as largely autonomous units of social change which exhibit a social organization larger than the local. That is to say, there are crucial political and economic processes that integrate the reproduction of a number of localities over a geographical area. The modern world-system is just such a social organization with a hierarchical spatial division of labour and an inter-state system that integrates localities globally. Concentrating on the political processes, we can investigate how the modern inter-state system is different from political organization in other earlier world-systems.

The first point to make is that there is nothing unique about a world-system whose politics is organized through a multiplicity of states. Adam Watson (1992) has suggested a model of alternative political organizations in world-systems in which states systems of independent polities represent one end of a spectrum. He also identifies hegemony and dominion as increasing degrees of centralization towards the other end of the spectrum, universal empire. From this perspective, the modern inter-state system is just the latest of several examples of states systems. Although it has lasted a relatively long time, approximately half a millennium, it is unusual but not unique in this respect. Hence we can treat the inter-state system as just another competitive political arena. This is the realist assumption underlying much international relations theory, which considers modern states to be no different from predatory states of the past. But there is more to the political organization of world-systems than a scale from decentralization to centralization.

There is another, more historical, way of viewing past, premodern states systems. Rather than treating them as the opposite of empires, they can be viewed as interludes between empires. In the rise and fall of empires, states systems are an essentially *temporary* political organization existing only while imperial control cannot be exercised. This can be shown in two ways. First, in terms of political practice, recognition of states is based solely on ability to defend territory in a predatory political world. In such 'eras of warring states' the eventual outcome is the elimination of the weak until one state emerges as a new universal empire. David Wilkinson (1984) has labelled this process a 'duck shoot' as the eventual winner picks off its rivals one by one. Second, in terms of political theory, universal empire is viewed as a normal and proper organization whatever the contemporary reality. In states systems the previous empire is viewed as a 'golden age' of stability; Confucius, for instance, looked back to a largely mythical Zhou imperial age when writing in China's era of warring states. This imperial presumption in premodern politics is encapsulated by the traditional concept of sovereignty. The distinctiveness of the modern inter-state system is based upon a total reversal in the geographical meaning of sovereignty.

The traditional concept of sovereignty is fundamentally singular in nature. There is only one sovereign, the emperor, whose realm is universal. That is to say, all other political leaders are deemed politically inferior and subject to the emperor's ultimate authority. For instance, the Roman Emperor was *dominus mundi*, lord of all the world. Such a definition meant that there could be no 'recognition' of any other polity as autonomous. If in practice some peoples were outside imperial political control, this was a wrong to be righted, since all owed allegiance to the universal lord. For instance, when a British delegation visited China in 1793, they were treated as vassals of the emperor, resulting in their country being added to the list of 'kingdoms of the western ocean' pledging allegiance to China (Peyrefitte, 1992: 231). In an imperial system, it can be no other way; all polities have to be fitted into a slot below the emperor who occupies the apex of the political hierarchy.

Despite the decentralized nature of society in feudal Europe, this theory of sovereignty was inherited through Roman Law (Yates, 1975). The social fragmentation and associated political decentralization should not be interpreted as multiple sovereignties, therefore. Rather, an unusual joint sovereignty was accepted with Bishop of Rome and Holy Roman Emperor at the political apex of Christendom, having authority over spiritual and temporal affairs respectively. Although this arrangement prevented the creation of a centralized empire, it still meant that there was only one empire and one emperor recognized within the system. For instance, the historian's labelling of sixteenth-century Spanish possessions in the Americas as the 'Spanish Empire' was not how contemporaries interpreted the conquests (Elliot, 1989). In their world there could be only one emperor and he was the Holy Roman Emperor who resided in Germany. Territorial expansion across the Atlantic did not alter this simple fact. The abnormal notion of there being several 'emperors' with their 'empires' in a single world-system is a product of the nineteenth century, after the formal end of the Holy Roman Empire. The Austrian Hapsburgs kept an imperial title and later the Germans and then the British redesignated their sovereigns as emperor and empress respectively, but this had nothing to do with Roman Law or any other traditional concept of sovereignty. These were political moves within an inter-state system in which a completely different notion of sovereignty prevailed.

In early modern Europe, the concept of sovereignty was utterly changed. From being universal it became bounded. Sovereignty became associated with territory. Previously the concept of territory meant merely the land surrounding and dependent upon a city and had no link with sovereignty (Gottmann, 1973). By bringing these two concepts together in the modern world-system, a very different type of states system was created: an inter-state system based upon multiple sovereignties. With the gradual acceptance of territorial sovereignty between the Treaties of Augsberg (1555) and Westphalia (1648), an inter-stateness was created in which states recognized each other's existence on a formal basis of equality. As Rosenburg (1990: 256) has stated: 'Recognising the historical novelty of this circumstance is quite crucial.' Sovereignty became a matter of both control of territory with authority over the people therein, sometimes referred to as 'internal sovereignty', *and mutual recognition among members of the states system,* which has been called 'external sovereignty' (James, 1984). It is the latter consequence of bounding sovereignty that makes modern states and their inter-state system unique. In contrast to an imperial hierarchy, inter-stateness assumes a reciprocity based upon mutual recognition of many sovereignties.

Hence the political organization of the modern world-system is different from that of premodern world-systems. Very obviously different from centralized empires, it can also be distinguished from decentralized states systems which were a temporary political organization retaining the traditional concept of a singular sovereignty. Unique among world-systems, our system is not premised upon the normality of universal political authority but operates through an assumption of multiple sovereignties, an inter-state system based upon a mutuality of political recognitions.

Exhaustive multiplicity

Without a dominating concept of universal political organization, the systemness of the modern inter-state system has been expressed through its exhaustive multiplicity. Every member of humanity is expected to be a citizen or subject of a state. There is a category of stateless person but this is a severe political disability, usually refugee status dependent upon the goodwill of sympathetic states. But not only people are given state identities. All commodities that cross state boundaries are considered in terms of their country of origin. Even electronic mail, which is often viewed as beyond the state, is identified by country codes within the electronic addresses. In short, the state covers all; you cannot get 'outside' the state system. There is currently an instructive illustration of this. Several African states in the 1990s have effectively ceased to function. For instance, neither Somalia nor Liberia has a government that controls its sovereign territory. Nevertheless this lack of 'internal sovereignty' has not been deemed reason to change the 'external sovereignty'. These states still officially exist and are members of the United Nations. It seems that while we cannot guarantee African people's basic subsistence, we do insist they conform to norms of inter-stateness.

This exhaustive multiplicity is physically denoted by the world political map of state boundaries. This most familiar of all maps defines the mosaic of multiple sovereignties at a given point in time. It is the product of territorial behaviours that have created (largely) mutually accepted boundaries. The collective presumption that world politics will be so demarcated we can term inter-territoriality. This first emerged in Europe in the early modern period when medieval juridical arrangements incorporating interpenetrating patterns of lordship were converted into modern boundaries. The latter separated communities between different sovereign territories in a way quite alien to previous political organization. The change can be followed in early modern cartography: at the beginning of the sixteenth century, maps were full of towns and rivers, but by its end European maps had become dominated by political boundaries. This modern obsession with boundaries was extended to the rest of the world as Europeans incorporated non-European peoples into their world-system. In the words of Jean Gottmann (1952: 512), 'all the vast globe was partitioned as it was discovered and mapped'. Frontiers were forever moving and replaced by boundaries because in the modern world-system there can be no empty political spaces.

For the last two hundred years, inter-stateness and inter-territoriality have been joined by an inter-nationality as the prime legitimation of a decentralized political organization. Jonathan Ree (1992) has coined this term to convey the idea that every nation exists within a multiplicity of nations. Once again, this is exhaustive. It is difficult to conceive of a 'nationless' person. Every member of humanity is assumed to have a cultural identity that is their nationality. Particular definitions of nationalities may be contested – is the Protestant community in Northern Ireland British, Irish or Ulsterish? – but there is a common presumption of nationality. This makes nationalism a very distinctive political ideology. Unlike other ideologies, oppositions are not contrary but alike. Thus whereas the opponents of socialism are anti-socialists, the opponents of liberalism anti-liberals, and so on, the opponents of nationalists are typically other nationalists.

We began this section by relating exhaustive multiplicity to the universalism of premodern systems. We can see now their functional similarity: universalism orders humanity through a singular ideal, the modern states system is equally comprehensive but through a multiple ideal. No world-system can operate with a political vacuum in its midst. These exhaustive multiplicities in the politics described above serve to prevent such a vacuum within the modern world-system.

Inter-stateness and trans-stateness

How are inter-stateness and its associated concepts important for political analysis? A simple example will illustrate its utility. It is often assumed that in a Marxist political analysis communism supersedes socialism through a 'withering away of the state'. But this is impossible. It may have been just credible to build socialism in one country but this was never the case for communism. Stateless communist communities in the territory of the former socialist state would be easy prey to still-existing other states. We need to understand that the theory addresses a withering away of the states (plural) (Wallerstein, 1984: 47). Our analysis of the nature of exhaustive multiplicity demonstrates that a withering away of inter-stateness is required, and nothing less.

Inter-stateness is a particularly fruitful concept for dealing with the contemporary concern for the future of the state. This literature faces a very difficult conundrum. On the one hand, we live in an ever-changing world-system to which states adapt by modifying their functions in sometimes quite fundamental ways. On the other, we have no reason to think that modern states are eternal so that it is quite reasonable to search for signs of their demise. The conundrum is: how can we tell the difference between 'ordinary' change in states and the 'extraordinary' change that signals their imminent end? I think it helps greatly if we reconceive the demise argument as demise of inter-stateness. This raises the question of what replaces inter-stateness and the idea of trans-stateness directly presents itself. We can consider inter-stateness as the medium of ordinary change and trans-stateness as the medium of extraordinary change.

By using the prefix 'inter' to describe the multiplicity of states I have intended to convey much more than simply the notion of 'between'; the additional meanings of mutuality and reciprocity have been central to my discussion. Hence inter-stateness is not just about relations between states. It signals that multiplicity is part of their nature as modern states. Moving on to the prefix 'trans', we can develop a much richer meaning than the simple notion of 'across' by emphasizing the stronger sense of 'beyond'. In this way trans-stateness implies an opposite form of world politics to inter-stateness: whereas inter-stateness is implicated in the reproduction of modern politics, trans-stateness consists of processes which undermine it.

In terms of our original conundrum, therefore, this analysis suggests a research programme in which inter-stateness is investigated as adaptive change and trans-stateness as demising change. Of course, political processes do not always divide easily between these two opposites. Nevertheless, this framework provides a focus for state demise questions that takes into account the fundamental multiplicity of modern states. In particular we can use these concepts to link such study of states to world-systems ideas on hegemonic cycles. In this model the nature of the world-system alters with the rise and fall of hegemonic states. At their peak, during periods of 'high hegemony', the hegemons promote economic and political freedoms which facilitate an unusual degree of trans-stateness. For most of the time, however, inter-stateness dominates in a competitive political world in which any 'cosmopolitan internationalism' is only a dimly perceived ideal.

The main advantage of linking the inter-stateness/trans-stateness balance to the world hegemony model is in treating the changing nature of the modern multiplicity of states. Thus far inter-stateness has been considered a constant of the modern world-system, but that does not mean it has been unchanging. We can recognize three stages in the development of the modern inter-state system. The one that emerged out of the Dutch hegemonic cycle was the closest in nature to premodern states systems. The Treaty of Westphalia produced what Gross (1968: 65) has termed the era of the 'liberty of states', in which predatory behaviour was the norm in a manner not unlike the realist depiction of international relations. Nevertheless, a systemness was created through the emergence of international law in which the universalist pretensions of papacy and empire were eliminated. This was Voltaire's 'commonwealth divided into several states' and Burke's 'diplomatic republic of Europe' (Bull and Watson, 1984: 1). A stronger systemness was to evolve during British hegemony in what Hinsley (1982) calls 'the modern international system'. The 'liberty of states' was curtailed by the Concert of Europe through which the great powers attempted to control political change. With US hegemony, a further change has occurred as political boundaries become effectively frozen. Coplin (1968: 31) writes of a 'profound and historic shift' with the international outlawing of aggression through the United Nations. In the government-less states of Africa referred to earlier, for instance, there are no outside predators ready to partition the uncontrolled sovereign territory, as occurred to weak states in eighteenth-century Europe. Hence we can see that modern multiplicity has taken three main forms of inter-stateness in the reproduction of the inter-state system.

In addition, trans-stateness has developed with each successive hegemony. At Westphalia in the Treaty of Osnabruck, the rights of religious minorities were recognized. This extrapolation of Dutch religious tolerance was only a weak expression of trans-stateness but its importance should not be underestimated (Walzer 1992). In the nineteenth century Britain pursued an anti-slavery policy in which it proclaimed a moral right to interfere with other countries' sovereignty. These two examples illustrate a hegemonic trans-stateness that can be said to culminate in the United Nations Declaration of Human Rights, which all states affirm on joining that organization. But this latter trans-stateness is part of a much more comprehensive pattern during American hegemony which Hopkins (1990: 410) sees as 'state-subversive'. In his interpretation, this third hegemonic cycle (the first two being the Dutch and British respectively) has been characterized by 'trans-statal institutions', denoting a fundamental alteration in the balance between inter-stateness and trans-stateness. This is, of course, the context within which the wide-ranging concern for the demise of the state has arisen. The demise is in inter-stateness, the rise is in trans-stateness.

Conclusion

I began this short discussion with a lament about state-centric social science and its inability to properly understand that which lies at the heart of its own bias. I have argued elsewhere that this is partly a problem of our impoverished political lexicon (Taylor, 1995). We seem to be pre-eminently concerned, as social scientists, with an abstracted absurdity: 'the state'. Even where states are recognized in their plurality, focus remains on the state in the singular. For instance, the widely used Open University text *States and Societies* (Held *et al.*, 1984: ix) begins by informing the reader that 'this book focuses on the modern state' before the editor introduces the readings with an essay entitled 'Central perspectives on the modern state'. From the perspective of the arguments above, such language is more applicable to premodern worlds than the modern world-system. The multiplicity of states is integral to the meaning of modern states, and in this chapter I have provided some hints, and only hints, about how political analysis can incorporate modern multiplicity. But let me leave the last thought to Rosenburg's (1990: 258) pertinent simile: 'A modern state out of the state system is like a fish out of water; it literally cannot breathe; it cannot even secure its domestic sovereignty.'

Social scientists have for too long been studying states as if they existed only like fish on a fishmonger's slab.

References

Bull, H. and Watson, A. (1984) *The Expansion of International Society*, Oxford, Clarendon.

Coplin, W. D. (1968) International law and assumptions about the state system, in R. Falk and W. F. Hanreider (eds), *International Law and Organization*, Philadelphia, Lippincott.

Elliot, J. H. (1989) *Spain and Its Empire, 1500–1700*, New Haven, Yale University Press.

Falk, R. and Hanreider, W. F. (eds) (1968) *International Law and Organization*, Philadelphia, Lippincott.

Gottmann, J. (1952) The political partitioning of our world, *World Politics*, **4**, 512–19.

Gottmann, J. (1973) *The Significance of Territory*, Charlottesville, University Press of Virginia.

Gross, L. (1968) The Peace of Westphalia, 1648–1948, in R. Falk and W. F. Hanreider (eds), *International Law and Organization*, Philadelphia, Lippincott.

Held, D. *et al.* (1984) *States and Societies*, Oxford, Robertson.

Hinsley, F. H. (1982) The rise and fall of the modern international system, *Review of International Studies*, **8**, 1–8.

Hopkins, T. K. (1990) A note on the concept of hegemony, *Review*, **13**, 409–12.

James, A. (1984) Sovereignty: ground rule or gibberish? *Review of International Studies*, **10**, 1–18.

Peyrefitte, A. (1992) *The Immobile Empire*, New York, Knopf.

Poggi, G. (1978) *The Development of the Modern State*, London, Hutchinson.

Ree, J. (1992) Internationality, *Radical Philosophy*, **60**, 3–11.

Rosenburg, J. (1990) A non-realist theory of sovereignty? Giddens' 'The nation-state and violence', *Millennium*, **19**, 249–59.

Taylor, P. J. (1995) Beyond containers: internationality, interstateness, interterritoriality, *Progress in Human Geography*, **19**, 1–15.

Taylor, P. J. (1996) Embedded statism and the social sciences: opening up new spaces, *Environment and Planning A*, **28**(11).

Wallerstein, I. (1984) *The Politics of the World-Economy*, Cambridge, Cambridge University Press.

Walzer, M. (1992) The new tribalism, *Dissent*, Spring, 164–71.

Watson, A. (1992) *The Evolution of International Society*, London, Routledge.

Wilkinson, D. (1984) Kinematics of world systems, mimeo, Los Angeles, Department of Politics, UCLA.

Yates, F. A. (1975) *Astrea. The Imperial Theme in the Sixteenth Century*, London, Routledge and Kegan Paul.

8

Rethinking Sovereignty

MARC WILLIAMS

Introduction

Sovereignty is one of the central concepts in the study and practice of international relations. Recently, major changes in world politics, and new theoretical approaches to the discipline of international relations have once more brought the concept of sovereignty to the fore. A number of writers have begun the task of rethinking sovereignty, notably, Held (1989, 1991), Ashley (1988), Walker (1991, 1993), Campbell (1993), Camilleri and Falk (1992) and Weber (1992). To some extent, of course, concern about the adequacy of the term sovereignty to capture the essence of world politics is neither novel nor startling. What, we may therefore ask, is different about the current historical conjuncture and hence the reason for contemporary unease? One answer may be that since no concept is fixed in an ahistorical manner, periodic rethinking is inevitable. The ebb and flow of world history will lead both practitioners and academics to reclassify, recategorize and rethink existing concepts. Thus a period of intellectual renewal and ferment is a normal part of any academic discipline. This answer need not be at odds with our second answer, which stresses the particularities of the current historical moment. We live, we are told, in an age of globalization, and the onset of globalization should lead us to discard old and tired concepts. We cannot, therefore, operate with a jaded and worn view of sovereignty in the face of these new realities. A rethinking is in order. If it is accepted that sovereignty is one of the principal organizing concepts of international relations (James, 1986: 267), and globalization marks a new epoch in the development of world politics, it becomes necessary for students of international relations and practitioners of foreign policy to examine the doctrine of sovereignty, to test its changing meanings and continued usefulness in the context of contemporary transformations.

This chapter interrogates the concept of sovereignty in the light of recent doubts about its applicability. Like all major concepts in political usage, sovereignty is an inherently problematical term. First I examine the concept in terms of its origins, and demonstrate that many key questions posed for contemporary analysis can be traced to its earliest usage. Following this, the chapter will examine what can be termed the conventional critique of sovereignty. As an idea and political practice, sovereignty has long held a dominant position in political discourse, but a persistent critique and refutation of its main tenets has accompanied conventional usage. The defenders of the idea of sovereignty accuse the critics of misunderstanding the real meaning of the term, and the chapter assesses the extent to which the criticisms of sovereignty are well founded or based on error. This should produce a precise understanding of the current orthodox use of the term. We will come to recognize that like almost all important concepts in the political lexicon, sovereignty is ambiguous, disputed and frequently misunderstood and misapplied. This brief historical excursion and the uncovering of the tensions, contradictions and difficulties surrounding its usage prepare the way for a discussion of the extent to which globalization poses a challenge to conventional notions of sovereignty.

The next section of the argument focuses on globalization and its implications for thinking about sovereignty. It takes globalization as a starting point for an exploration of the continued centrality of the state and sovereignty in international relations discourse. I am particularly interested in the extent to which the phenomenon of globalization and globalizing practices presents a new and different political landscape. I argue that only to the extent that globalization represents significant change should we be concerned with reinterpreting sovereignty. In other words, if globalization does not call into question the main features of the Westphalian concept of international society, the rebuttal of the critique of sovereignty stands. In the concluding section I address the continued relevance of sovereignty in a world marked by difference, turbulence and uncertainty. Are we at the end of international relations, understood as inter-state relations, or is the inter-state system still the most accurate depiction of contemporary world politics?

The concept of sovereignty

Sovereignty, like all ideas, is both a product of history and a creator of history. Ideas do not exist outside of the history of women and men, nor do they arrive fully formed. Sovereignty has played a key role in shaping the modern world and material changes have affected the ways in which scholars and practitioners have thought about it. Thus it should be viewed as both a norm and a practice (Conca, 1994).

The modern doctrine of sovereignty arose in Western Europe during what has been termed the long sixteenth century. It was closely linked to the rise of capitalism as a form of social organization (Inayatullah and Blaney, 1995) and the development of the state as a political association. As an idea and an institution, sovereignty is at the heart of the modern state and is linked to key political concepts such as power, order, legitimacy and authority. If today sovereignty has global application, it must be recognized that the concept expresses neither a timeless nor universal truth. The successful transplantation of the European states system to Africa, Asia and Latin America entailed the triumph of the doctrine of sovereignty on an international scale. With the granting of independence to political units in Africa, Asia and the Caribbean, sovereignty was diffused to a wider public. The new states were modelled on the European ideal and sovereignty became the cornerstone of their identity. If sovereignty is the requirement for membership of international society, these new states were duty bound to accept what, in terms of their own traditions, was an alien concept. It may have been novel in the political lexicon of Third World élites but sovereignty soon became an important and vital tool in their attempts to assert their independence. This very European concept is now fervently supported by the ruling Third World élites. Indeed, sovereignty, it can be argued, has been crucial in maintaining and perpetuating the new states. Lacking the requirements for the effective exercise of sovereign power, they have been able to use the juridical shell to receive support from the international community crucial to the continued existence of these quasi-states (Jackson, 1990). The expansion of Western international society to other parts of the world tends to mask the particularities of time and place surrounding the origins of the concept of sovereignty.

Others have traced these origins in great detail (Hinsley, 1986; Camilleri and Falk, 1992; James, 1986). The story is well known and can be reproduced succinctly. The modern concept was developed in Western Europe between the fifteenth and sixteenth centuries. It is difficult to date precisely when sovereignty became accepted and established. The Treaty of Westphalia (1648) is normally taken as the starting point of the European states system, i.e. a system of sovereign states owing allegiance to no superior. The Peace of Westphalia should properly be viewed as the culmination rather than the onset of this process. Its importance is that it marks conclusively the end of one era and the beginning of another.

The development of sovereignty and its applicability rests on the separation of powers between the state and the community.

> The concept of sovereignty originated in the closer association of the developing state and the developing community which became inevitable when it was discovered that power had to be shared between them. The function of the concept was to provide the only formula which could ensure the effective exercise of power once this division of power or collaboration of forces had become inescapable. (Hinsley, 1986: 222)

The doctrine of sovereignty is central to the authority of the ruler, the nature of political obligation and the organization of political power in territorial space. The theory of sovereignty attempts to answer three interrelated questions (Camilleri and Falk, 1992: 18) and the discourse on sovereignty has centred on the answers given to these questions. First, where is sovereignty located? In other words, where do we find the ultimate source of power in a political community? Secondly, what is the relationship between state sovereignty and the wider political community? Thirdly, what are the limits, if any, practical or normative, to the exercise of sovereignty?

The modern theory of sovereignty, despite its nuances and ambiguities, can be said to consist of two key features. First, a distinction is made between internal and external sovereignty. Second, in both its internal and external dimensions, sovereignty refers to the existence of a supreme law-making authority. As Hinsley (1986, 26) puts it, sovereignty is the 'idea that there is a final and absolute political authority in the political community ... and no final and absolute authority exists elsewhere'. Sovereignty in this view is an essentially legal concept. Moreover, it is absolute and not relative. An entity cannot be more or less sovereign. It either possesses sovereignty or not. Sovereignty, then, refers to the existence of a specified holder of supreme coercive power within a legally defined (territorial) community. Internally, the state is supreme and has command over its subjects. Externally, sovereignty is taken to mean that states are subject to no higher authority. States may voluntarily submit to international law or the decisions of an international organization, but they recognize no authority higher than themselves. From this conception of sovereignty flows the equality of all members of international society, in so far as it is conceived to be constituted by sovereign states. The doctrine of sovereign equality means not equal capability but equal rights (James, 1991).

This definition and defence of sovereignty is not unchallenged. The conventional critique can be classified in three categories: moral, analytical and empirical. For some writers, sovereignty is a dangerous notion since it appears to give untrammelled power to an individual or a group and in so doing ignores other individual and group rights. To vest any individual or group with supreme coercive power, the critics claim, is fundamentally undemocratic and opens the way for the abuse of power (James, 1986: 257–65). Defenders of sovereignty have conceded the possibility of conflict between sovereignty and democracy (Stankiewicz, 1969: 6–7), but tend to argue that the exercise of power is not unlimited. The sovereign has to maintain order, and in fulfilling this function the norms and values of a society are taken into consideration. Some critics (Benn, 1969) have argued that since the term is so imprecise and ambiguous it should be abandoned. But if we were to abandon all essentially contested terms in political science the field would be severely impoverished. The existence of competing definitions and contrary usages would not in itself lead one to reject the concept. In this it is no different from other key terms, e.g. power, authority and legitimacy. Furthermore, the defenders of sovereignty argue that abandoning the term would not achieve the goal sought by the critics.

The most powerful objections to the concept are those which I have termed empirical but in fact combine normative and analytical elements. The argument that sovereignty is increasingly irrelevant in the modern world takes a number of forms. First, it is claimed that it is no longer possible to pinpoint a single source of power in complex political systems (Camilleri and Falk, 1992: 31–2). Authority in the modern state apparatus is fragmented, with a number of bodies responsible for collective decision-making. If a sole sovereign ever existed, one certainly does not exist now. This critique does not rest only on the formal separation of powers in modern states but also recognizes the growth of governmental organizations, quasi-governmental institutions and non-governmental associations in the modern body politic. Law-making and observance of rules cannot be confined to some mythic sovereign power. In response, sovereignty theorists accept that the locus of sovereignty has shifted historically and that the relationship between the sovereign state and the wider political community is not static (Hinsley, 1986: 219–21). The existence of non-sovereign bases of authority is, however, not deemed sufficient to weaken the theory. Sovereignty is the justification for the maintenance of order in society, the doctrine that a final source of authority and site of supreme coercive power exists in the state.

By far the most developed critique of sovereignty has been made by writers who stress its irrelevance to the day-to-day workings of the state (Held, 1989: 229–37). Put another way, critics expose the gaps between the claims of supremacy and the ability of states to exercise control over their territory in an effective manner. Thus, in this line of reasoning sovereignty is outmoded because although states may possess *de jure* rights, *de facto* they are unable to use them meaningfully. In so far as it can be demonstrated that the gap between the possession of sovereignty (formal sovereignty) and the capacity to exercise those rights (effective sovereignty) is so wide that it no longer makes sense to say that states possess supreme authority, the concept of sovereignty should be abandoned.

The twin forces of interdependence and transnationalism, it is alleged, have eroded the capacity of the state to make domestic policy and to act independently in international relations. Developments in technology and the global economy, it is argued, have acted to constrain national policy. Technological change has created a shrinking world. This is most marked in the field of communications, where the flows of information across national boundaries can no longer be controlled by national governments. In reduc-

portation costs, technology has increased the movement of people and migration), the movement of goods (manufactures and raw), and the movement of services (capital and finance). Growing interdependence brought about partly by these technological changes has made it increasingly difficult for governments to manage national economic policy. As a foremost student of interdependence put it: 'To the extent that integration of money and capital markets does occur, national monetary and credit policies are weakened' (Cooper, 1968: 14).

Theorists of sovereignty have countered these claims on two grounds. They do not dispute the evidence produced by those analysts who challenge the primacy of the state in world politics. One part of the rebuttal asserts that interdependence theorists confuse autonomy with sovereignty. At no time in history were states able to exercise all the rights that they claimed – absolute power is a myth. In any event, diminution of the state's control over aspects of domestic policy merely reveals a loss of autonomy, not sovereignty (Hinsley, 1986; James, 1986). Some writers within the state-centric paradigm contest the claim that the state is losing its authority. Sullivan (1989: 165) notes that although interdependence does exist, 'current levels in some dimensions are not necessarily higher than in other eras'. His review of the evidence leads him to conclude that interdependence may be less significant than the proponents would have us believe (ibid.: 274). In a similar vein, Thomson and Krasner (1989: 198–206) argue that an historical perspective shows that both international and domestic transaction costs have been reduced and that at no time did states exercise the type of control posited by the interdependence theorists. Moreover, they point out that a concentration on economic interdependence ignores military and security concerns. In this issue-area, states have increased their ability to control micro-processes (ibid.: 197, 208–12). Far from seeing a reduction of state activity, they maintain that in the modern economy some transactions, e.g. the maintenance and transfer of property rights, require the consolidation of sovereignty (ibid.: 214–16).

The growth of international organizations and the development of international law are sometimes adduced as explanations for the contemporary irrelevance of state sovereignty. How, it is asked, can states claim to be sovereign when they exist in a world of increased international organizational activity? The proliferation of international organizations and the development of international regimes poses a problem for analysis based on state sovereignty. On the one hand, these organizations and regimes provide competing authority structures, and on the other the development of majoritarianism and consensus in international organizations frequently leads to outcomes at odds with state policy. But the proliferation of international organizations, even the growth of regional integration, can be held to be firmly in keeping with the exercise of sovereignty. States consent to be members of such organizations and can withdraw at any time. Indeed, it has been argued (in the context of British membership of the European Union) that such enmeshment enhances rather than reduces sovereignty (Taylor, 1991). International law has expanded to include individuals and non-governmental organizations within its regulatory systems. In the light of such developments, it is claimed, the idea of membership of a national community, subject to a specific sovereign authority, begins to lose force (Held, 1989: 235). But traditional theorists maintain that international law is a law between states rather than one above them. States are not subject to compulsory jurisdiction, most international law still concerns states and international law is predominantly made by states or the representatives of states (James, 1986: 196–224).

This survey of the concept of sovereignty provides an important preliminary to a discussion of sovereignty in the age of globalization. I have demonstrated the robustness of the concept and the ability of theorists of sovereignty to rebut the arguments of their critics. It now remains to question the extent to which globalization offers a distinct challenge to the tenets of sovereignty. In this respect, globalization must result in system transformation different from interdependence and integration. In essence, increased transactions will not in themselves pose a problem to sovereignty unless it can be demonstrated that new authority patterns have emerged or are nascent in this process.

Globalization and sovereignty

The previous section examined the defining characteristics of sovereignty and concluded that many attempts to prove sovereignty outmoded were effectively rebutted by theorists of sovereignty. This section is concerned with the construction of sovereignty in an age of globalization. To what extent does globalization erode sovereignty? Or is the endlesslessly shifting concept of sovereignty reconstituted and reformulated in a manner likely to maintain its centrality in international relations?

An investigation of the impact of globalization on sovereignty necessitates an enquiry into the impact of globalizing forces on the state. The death of the state has often been reported in international relations. Globalization is the latest in a long line of assassins. We are told that it marks the end of a system of independent sovereign states and hence the irrelevance of sovereignty. It has been argued that 'in a world of regional and global interconnectedness, there are major questions to be put about the coherence, viability and accountability of national decision-making entities themselves' (Held, 1993: 4). This kind of questioning is echoed by Rosenau (1989), McGrew (1992) and Ruggie (1993) among others. In a recent article, Saurin (1995) contends that the age of globalization marks the end of international relations, with the latter seen as a state-centric discipline. He argues that 'only by rejecting the *a priori* analytical primacy accredited to the state can one begin to approximate a credible explanation of global social change' (ibid.: 258).

These observations lead immediately to two further questions: what is meant by globalization and how does it affect the nation-state and its claims to sovereignty? Embedded in both questions is an interrogation of the historical relevance of globalization. It is by no means clear whether it refers to a new era in human relations or whether it is the current manifestation of a set of processes with a long historical time-span (Scholte, 1993a).

Globalization has been variously defined, and no consensus exists on the causes of this phenomenon. For the purposes of this chapter, I will use McGrew's (1992) general definition. He claims that globalization is

> the multiplicity of linkages and interconnections that transcend the nation-state (and by implication the societies) which make up the modern world system. It defines a process through which events, decisions, and activities in one part of the world can come to have significant consequences for individuals and communities in quite distant parts of the globe. (ibid.: 13–14)

In what sense then is globalization different from interdependence? I argued in the previous section that realist scholars have, if not successfully rebutted the claim that interdependence poses a threat to sovereignty, at least cast serious doubt on the validity of such an assertion. Both interdependence theorists and proponents of globalization speak of interconnectedness, but globalization must signify more than interdependence. One way of thinking about this difference is to define interdependence as interconnectedness which erodes the effectiveness of national policy and threatens national autonomy. Keohane and Nye's (1977) classic distinction between sensitivity interdependence and vulnerability interdependence becomes crucial in this context. A key feature of globalization as already outlined is interconnectedness, but unlike interdependence, which stresses mutuality, globalization also refers to the possibility of dependence (McGrew, 1992: 94). Crucially, the conceptualization of globalization refers to the reordering of time and space. Interdependence theorists have focused on the internationalization of international relations whereas writers within the paradigm of globalization argue for a move to a global society (Lipschutz, 1992; Shaw, 1992; Scholte, 1993b). Those who posit increased interdependence concentrate on detailing the ways in which national societies have become more interconnected, whereas a stress on global society emphasizes the transcendence of the national base and the creation of (genuinely) global structures.

In the context of sovereignty and statehood, it has been argued that

The 'international' and 'internationalization' refer to an attempt to say that social order is a state bounded order, and constitute world order on the basis of statehood but they are *not* synonymous with world order *per se*. Both the concepts of 'international' and 'internationalization' rest upon particularist claims to exclusive authority. 'Globalization' by contrast, admits of the fact that exclusivity is neither an actuality nor a historical possibility. (Saurin, 1995: 257)

I will return to this theme later.

In short, 'globalization as a concept refers both to the compression of the world and the intensification of the consciousness of the world' (Robertson, 1992: 8). This compression is normally accounted for through the rapid advances in technology and the increased intensification of economic activities. It is this interpenetration of national societies which subverts the competence of national authorities and erodes their autonomy. Moreover, the development of transnational networks and global authority structures dislocates and fractures national decision-making. Accompanying this physical shrinking of the world, as it were, and the idea of a global village, is a changing conception of time and space. Giddens (1990: 14) uses the concept of time–space distanciation to refer to the 'conditions under which time and space are organised so as to connect presence and absence'. Globalization increases the processes whereby networks of communication and systems of production link the local and global levels so that social relations can no longer be conceived solely in local terms. Our everyday life is structured in such a way that social interactions are embedded in global networks. In this formulation, globalization is defined as the 'intensification of worldwide social relations which link distant localities in such a way that local happenings are shaped by events occurring many miles away and vice versa' (Giddens, 1990: 64).

In a similar vein, Harvey (1989: 284) contends that globalization has led to 'an intense phase of time-space compression that has had a disorienting and disruptive impact upon political-economic practices, the balance of class power, as well as upon cultural and social life'. Although Harvey does not use the term globalization, his depiction of time–space compression in the postmodern condition is applicable to the discourse of globalization. He claims:

> The intensity of time-space compression in Western capitalism since the 1960s with all its congruent features of excessive ephemerality and fragmentation in the political and private realm does seem to indicate an experiential context that makes the condition of postmodernity somewhat special. (ibid.: 306)

Following from the above, it can be observed that globalization has two broad implications for the discourse on sovereignty. First, political, social and economic activities are becoming global in scope and dissolving the internal/

external distinction crucial to the orthodox definition of sovereignty. If the line between internal supremacy and external equality can no longer be maintained, sovereignty must be reformulated. If globalization has blurred the distinction between national and international, transformed the conditions of national decision-making, altered the legal framework and administrative practices of states, obscured lines of responsibility and changed the institutional and organizational content of national politics (Held, 1993: 238), then sovereignty as a doctrine is of limited relevance. In this sense, globalization refers to more than the erosion of autonomy. It highlights a change in the political landscape and requires an adaptation of political practice. The internal/external distinction is no longer helpful because, to paraphrase Richard Cooper (1968), domestic policy is now foreign policy and foreign policy is now domestic policy.

Globalization posits an emerging world society and global social structure, one in which cross-border transactions are significant not quantitatively but qualitatively. These interactions help to define and shape the contours of daily life. Local, national and regional authorities are involved in the making of decisions, and transnational coalitions of state and non-state actors crucially determine economic and political outcomes. According to this view, it makes little sense to speak of distinct national economies, polities and, by extension, cultures. International co-operation and policy co-ordination, e.g. the Group of Seven or the Group of 77, are manifestations of this process but do not exhaust the possibilities. Across many domains, for example financial, trade, health/disease, travel, communications, sport and religion, discrete national policies are no longer available.

The causes of environmental degradation and attempts to address these problems provide an important example of the inapplicability of the internal/external distinction in an era of globalization. Environmental problems arise not from discrete acts in individual states but 'are fundamentally rooted in the process of globalisation which has rendered the territorial state incapable of fulfilling its traditional functions' (Thomas, 1993: 3). The environmental problematique touches on issues pertaining to human rights, democracy, accountability, gender, ideology and power. These issues, of course, have local manifestations, and there are different degrees of relative autonomy in the manner in which national societies can respond to them. But they are simultaneously local, national *and* global issues. The internal/external dichotomy is increasingly redundant in the face of these developments.

Second, globalization, in representing a reordering of time and space, ruptures the territoriality of conventional international relations. Sovereignty is inextricably linked with the nation-state as a fixity in time and space. Globalization presents a different articulation of time and space. Authority structures need no longer be fixed to territorial actors, thus making the state increasingly problematic in an international relations discourse enmeshed in a territorial vision of the world. Instead we should visualize a range of loci of decision-making, legitimacy and authority in the contemporary world. So far analysts have done little more than point to the importance of international regimes and organizations. But even if the exact nature of these 'postmodern international political forms' (Ruggie, 1993: 140) cannot be specified with any certainty, given the absence of the necessary theoretical tools, we should not be constrained from moving beyond an international relations discourse so reliant on the state and sovereignty. Ruggie (1993: 143) has warned of the dangers of an 'extra-ordinarily impoverished mind-set . . . able to visualise long-term challenges to the system of states only in terms of entities substitutable for the state'.

Moreover, conventional accounts of sovereignty, stressing a juridical definition of the state, subordinate and marginalize sociological accounts of it. Attention to the phenomenon of globalization forces us to rethink the concept of the state. It is far from clear that the nation-state effectively acts as a repository for all the sentiments normally attached to it, or fulfils the needs of its citizens. Traditionally the state is taken as a site of authority and legitimacy. As citizens, we project our values outwards from the state, with internal conflicts already settled and finalized within the terrain of the nation-state. This account is, at best, a convenient fiction. The complex sets of questions surrounding issues such as identity, nationality and nation-alism, and culture cannot be settled on the basis of pre-existent, unwavering national units. National identity and values are formed in interaction with people and structures across the globe. No single, uncontested repository of value resides within the territory of the state. National identity and national culture are the products of transnational networks created through the process of globalization. Globalization effectively ruptures the territoriality of the nation-state.

The foregoing has suggested that not only is globalization distinct from interdependence but it poses a challenge to sovereignty which cannot be met through a restatement of the distinction between sovereignty and auton-omy, a reassertion of the necessity to identify an ultimate source of authority in the conflict between state and community, or a return to the claim that sovereignty signifies constitutional independence. Nevertheless, it remains unclear whether sovereignty is completely redundant. Globalization carries with it both integrating and disintegrating tendencies. The eruption of nationalism and ethnic claims can be seen as a response to the globalizing ethic. And it is certainly true that the possession of sovereignty still appears to be of value in the contemporary world. The Kurds, Palestinians, Basques and others struggling to create their own national states still attach value to the possession of sovereignty. It may be that these groups are mistaken, but the force of their belief will not be countered by some logical demonstration of their 'error'. Third World states may possess negative sovereignty rather than positive sovereignty, and it may be in the best interests of most Third World citizens if their leaders relinquished national sovereignty (Jackson, 1990), but this is wishful thinking. In this sense sovereignty will continue to be important in global politics.

Moreover, realist writers continue to emphasize the dominance of the state in many areas of social life. The state is not a passive victim of globalizing forces but an active participant in the process. It is also important to recognize the variety of states in international affairs. These changes do not affect all states equally and in some respects some states are strengthened by some of the processes at work (Giddens, 1990: 73–4; McGrew, 1992: 92–4).

Conclusion

I have argued that sovereignty is a robust concept. It is flexible and has withstood a number of challenges since it first became an organizing principle of the international system. The plasticity of the concept is indicated, for example, by the debates on the location of sovereignty. Theoretical arguments concerning the source of sovereignty have mirrored shifts in domestic and international politics.

Theorization of globalization limited to interconnectedness between national societies is not sufficient to render sovereignty redundant as an explanatory concept. However, the primacy given to territoriality and the importance of the internal/external distinction are undermined by the process of globalization. Political, social, cultural and economic activities are becoming increasingly global in scope and the definitive separation of the domestic from the international is no longer possible. Considerations of the impact of globalization on perceptions of time and space provide a strong challenge to conventional notions of sovereignty. The proliferation of authority structures and the rupture between territoriality and order, legitimacy and the exercise of power, as far as they have occurred, do call for a rethinking of sovereignty. Though theorists of globalization have yet to demonstrate convincingly the existence of competing non-territorial sites of authority, the orthodox conception of sovereignty is nevertheless under strain. Globalization is a multi-faceted process and, as such, not all tendencies point to the growing irrelevance of the state. Sovereignty provides a perspective on the world but has never been a fixed concept. It will remain important as territorial actors seek to enhance their capabilities.

References

Ashley, R. K. (1988) Untying the sovereign state: a double reading of the anarchy problematique, *Millennium*, **17**, 227–62.

Benn, S. I. (1969) The uses of 'sovereignty', in W. J. Stankiewicz (ed.), *In Defense of Sovereignty*, New York, Oxford University Press.

Camilleri, J. A. and Falk, J. (1992) *The End of Sovereignty?* Aldershot, Edward Elgar.

Campbell, D. (1993) *Sovereignty, Ethics, and the Narratives of the Gulf War*, Boulder, CO, Lynne Rienner.

Conca, K. (1994) Rethinking the ecology-sovereignty debate, *Millennium*, **23**, 701–11.

Cooper, R. N. (1968) *The Economics of Interdependence*, New York, McGraw Hill.

Giddens, A. (1990) *The Consequences of Modernity*, Cambridge, Polity Press.

Harvey, D. (1989) *The Condition of Postmodernity*, Oxford, Basil Blackwell.

Held, D. (1989) *Political Theory and the Modern State*, Cambridge, Polity Press.

Held, D. (1991) Democracy, the nation-state and the global system in D. Held (ed.) *Political Theory Today*, Cambridge, Polity Press.

Held, D. (1993) *Democracy and the New International Order*, London, Institute of Public Policy Research.

Hinsley, F. H. (1986) *Sovereignty*, 2nd edn, Cambridge, Cambridge University Press.

Inayatullah, N. and Blaney, D. (1995) Realizing sovereignty, *Review of International Studies*, **21**, 3–20.

Jackson, R. (1990) *Quasi-States: Sovereignty, International Relations and the Third World*, Cambridge, Cambridge University Press.

James, A. (1986) *Sovereign Statehood*, London, Allen and Unwin.

James, A. (1991) Sovereignty in Eastern Europe, *Millennium*, **20**, 81–9.

Keohane, R. O. and Nye, J. S. (1977) *Power and Interdependence*, Boston, Little, Brown and Co.

Lipschutz, A. (1992) Reconstructing world politics: the emergence of global civil society, *Millennium*, **21**, 389–420.

McGrew, T. (1992) A global society, in S. Hall, D. Held and T. McGrew (eds), *Modernity and Its Futures*, Cambridge, Polity Press.

Robertson, R. (1992) *Globalization: Social Theory and Global Culture*, London, Sage.

Rosenau, J. N. (1989) Global changes and theoretical challenges: toward a post-international politics for the 1990s, in E.-O. Czempiel and J. N. Rosenau (eds), *Global Changes and Theoretical Challenges*, Lexington, MA, Lexington Books.

Ruggie, J. G. (1993) Territoriality and beyond: problematizing modernity in inter-national relations, *International Organization*, **47**, 139–74.

Saurin, J. (1995) The end of international relations? The state and international relations theory in the age of globalization, in J. Macmillan and A. Linklater (eds), *Boundaries in Question: New Directions in International Relations*, London, Pinter.

Scholte, J. A. (1993a) *The International Relations of Social Change*, Buckingham, Open University Press.

Scholte, J. A. (1993b) From power politics to social change: an alternative focus for international studies, *Review of International Studies*, **19**, 3–21.

Shaw, M. (1992) Global society and global responsibility: the theoretical, historical and political limits of international society, *Millennium*, **21**, 421–34.

Stankiewicz, W. J. (1969) In defense of sovereignty: a critique and an interpretation, in W. J. Stankiewicz (ed.), *In Defense of Sovereignty*, New York, Oxford University Press.

Sullivan, M. P. (1989) Transnationalism, power politics and the realities of the present system, in M. Williams (ed.), *International Relations in the Twentieth Century: A Reader*, London, Macmillan.

Taylor, P. (1991) British sovereignty and the European community: what is at risk? *Millennium*, **20**, 73–80.

Thomas, C. (1993) Beyond UNCED: an introduction, *Environmental Politics*, **2**, 1–27.

Thomson, J. E. and Krasner, S. D. (1989) Global transactions and the consolidation of sovereignty, in E.-O. Czempiel and J. N. Rosenau (eds), *Global Changes and Theoretical Challenges*, Lexington, MA, Lexington Books.

Walker, R. B. J. (1991) State sovereignty and the articulation of political space/time, *Millennium*, **20**, 445–62.

Walker, R. B. J. (1993) *Inside/Outside: International Relations as Political Theory*, Cambridge, Cambridge University Press.

Weber, C. (1992) Reconsidering statehood: examining the sovereignty/intervention boundary, *Review of International Studies*, **18**, 199–216.

9

What Next for the State?

PHILIP G. CERNY

Introduction

The essence of the state – and the main practical condition for its viability – lies in the fact that sovereign and autonomous political institutions are capable of deriving legitimacy from a distinct citizenry located in a defined territory. The international system did not present a fundamental challenge to the state so long as that system was based on states as the basic units or agents – in other words, when the international system was also a 'states system'. Indeed, in such a context, the international system constituted a bulwark of the state and the ultimate proof of its sovereignty and autonomy. However, increasing transnational interpenetration has the potential to transform the international system from a true states system into one in which this external bulwark is eroded and eventually undermined. This process, which is at the heart of globalization, is not homogeneous. It is a multilayered phenomenon which incorporates the state – and sustains some of its ostensible functions – while at the same time altering its very essence and undermining its constitutional foundations. In particular, by altering the basic structural conditions for the provision of *public* (as well *private*) goods, globalization profoundly challenges our understanding of such central concerns as security, collective choice, political obligation, citizenship, legality, democracy and justice. Although this chapter focuses on advanced industrial states, these developments impact on all states and involve deep structural change in the international system itself.

The classical Western concept of the state is found in the first paragraph of Aristotle's *Politics*:

> Observation shows us, first, that every polis (or state) is a species of association, and, secondly, that all associations are instituted for the purpose of attaining some good – for all men do all their acts with a view to achieving something which is, in their view, a good. We may therefore hold that all associations aim at some good; and we may also hold that the particular association which is the most sovereign of all, and includes all the rest, will pursue this aim most, and will thus be directed to the most sovereign of all goods. This most sovereign

and inclusive association is the polis, as it is called, or the political association. (Aristotle, 1962: 1)

Oakeshott described the state (or at least the version found in the Western constitutional tradition) as a 'civil association' the sole purpose of which was to enable other more circumscribed social, political and economic activities to take place, and which must continue to exist as long as people wished to pursue those other activities. This form is seen as distinct from an 'enterprise association' – which has particular ends and which can be dissolved when those ends are no longer, or unsatisfactorily, pursued (Auspitz, 1976; Oakeshott, 1976). The state encompasses the political system within which agents interact, constituting the very playing field for the game of 'politics', as well as forming a potentially autonomous collective agent within that field. However, a critical threshold may potentially be crossed when the *cumulative* effect of globalization in strategically decisive issue-areas undermines the *general* capacity of the state to pursue the 'most sovereign of all goods', i.e. the 'common good', or the capacity of the state to be a true 'civil association'. Even if this threshold is not crossed, however, it is arguable that the state does not remain what it was before.

The key to the new role of the state lies in the way that economic competition is changing in the world. On one level, the way the state itself works is changing. The main task or function of the contemporary state is the promotion of economic activities, whether at home or abroad, which make firms and sectors located within the territory of the state competitive in international markets – what I have called the 'competition state' (Cerny, 1990). This goes beyond the idea of the 'strategic state' or the 'developmental state' of the 1980s. The difference is that, while the state has always been to some extent a promoter of market forces, state structures today are being transformed into more and more market-oriented and even market-based organizations themselves, fundamentally altering the way that public and private goods are provided. Indeed, states are transforming – marketizing – *themselves* in the search for competitiveness in an increasingly economically interpenetrated world. On another level, states have promoted the formation of a web of transnational regimes and other linkages which have increasingly been developing the capacity to operate autonomously of those states. However, the authority of such institutions is inherently problematic, making it virtually impossible to establish clear or even operationalizable lines of political (especially democratic) accountability. As a result of this twofold movement, we may be witnessing the transmutation of the state from a civil association into a more limited form of enterprise association, or perhaps some more complex combination of the two, operating within a wider market and institutional environment. This is not merely a change in degree, but a change in kind. Uneven globalization is thus leading to the emergence of a still-embryonic 'residual state', which may be vulnerable to crises of legitimacy.

Globalization, structural differentiation and the state

The significance of globalization lies in the way that it has altered the relationship between different kinds of goods and assets. (For a more extended treatment of this argument, see Cerny, 1995.) Many of what constituted 'public goods' in the Second Industrial Revolution (which was characterized by the 'American system' of mass production) are no longer controllable by the state because they have become transnational in structure and/or constitute private goods in a wider world marketplace. The Third Industrial Revolution (currently involving restructuring and adaptation to new technology and global markets) has also profoundly altered the structure of both public and private goods through a process of differentiation within production processes and through the segmentation of markets. The globalization of finance has increasingly divorced finance capital from the state (Cerny, 1994). In this context, political control, stabilization, regulation, promotion and facilitation of economic activities have become increasingly fragmented. From international regimes (Krasner, 1983) to local pressures and subaltern forms of resistance (Sathyamurthy, 1990), new 'circuits of power' (Foucault, 1980) are emerging not so much to challenge the state as to overlap with it, cut across it and fragment it.

In the Second Industrial Revolution state, public goods were perceived by all interested parties as national-level phenomena, even by Marxist–Leninists. Those public goods are essentially of three kinds. (I am here borrowing freely from Theodore Lowi's three categories of public policy: distributive, regulatory and redistributive (Lowi, 1964, 1969).) The first involves the establishment of a workable market framework for the operation of the system as a whole, or *regulatory* goods. This includes the establishment and protection of private (and public) property rights, a stable currency system, the abolition of internal barriers to production and exchange within the national market, the standardization of a range of facilitating structures such as a system of weights and measures, a legal system to sanction and enforce contracts and to adjudicate disputes, a regulatory system to stabilize and co-ordinate economic activities, a system of trade protection, and various facilities which can be mobilized to counteract system-threatening market failures (such as 'lender of last resort' facilities, emergency powers, etc.).

The second kind involves various specific (direct or indirect) state-controlled or state-sponsored activities of production and distribution:

productive/distributive public goods. This includes full or partial public owner-ship of certain industries, provision of infrastructure and public services from sewerage and urban planning to military and diplomatic support for firms operating overseas, direct or indirect involvement in finance capital (includ-ing publicly owned or state-sponsored long-term credit banks), and, most obviously, a variety of public subsidies. The third kind of public goods are *redistributive*, especially those developed in response to the expanding polit-ical and public policy demands of emerging social classes, economic interests and political parties. Redistributive goods have included direct health and welfare services, employment policies, systems for corporatist bargaining and environmental protection – indeed, the main apparatus of the national welfare state. The development of the provision of all three kinds of goods was intertwined with the converging structures of the national economy and the nation-state and rested on the merging of large-scale specific assets across structures of bureaucracy and capital. The supply or fostering, directly or indirectly, of all three categories in a globalizing world has, however, become problematic for states.

Regulatory goods are an obvious case. In a world of relatively open trade, financial deregulation and the increasing impact of information technology, property rights are increasingly difficult for the state to establish and maintain. Cross-border industrial espionage, counterfeiting of products, copyright violations and the like have made the multilateral protection of 'intellectual property rights' a focal point of international disputes and a controversial cornerstone of the Uruguay Round negotiations. International capital flows, the proliferation of 'offshore' financial centres and tax havens, etc. have made the ownership of firms and their ability to allocate resources internally through transfer pricing and other means increasingly opaque to national tax and regulatory authorities. Traditional forms of trade protec-tionism are both easily bypassed and counterproductive. Currency exchange rates and interest rates are set in rapidly globalizing marketplaces, and governments attempt to manipulate them, often at their peril. Legal rules are increasingly evaded, and attempts to extend the legal reach of the national state through the development of 'extraterritoriality' are ineffective and hotly disputed.

Finally, the ability of firms, market actors and *competing parts of the national state apparatus itself* to defend and expand their economic *and political* turf through activities such as transnational policy networking and 'regulatory arbitrage' – the capacity of industrial and financial sectors to 'whipsaw' the state apparatus by pushing state agencies into a process of competitive deregulation – has both undermined the control span of the state from without and fragmented it from within (Cerny, 1993b: chs 3–4; Cerny, 1994). This is what economists call 'competition in laxity'. Real or potential inefficiencies in the provision of regulatory public goods can have exceptionally wide ramifications, because such goods also constitute the framework within which *private* goods as well as *other* public goods are produced and supplied. Regulatory public goods are fundamental to the capitalist state.

Perhaps a more familiar theme in the public goods literature, however, has been the impact of globalization on productive/distributive public goods. The most visible aspect has been the crisis of public ownership of major industries and the wave of privatization which has characterized the 1980s and 1990s. Such core industries were once perceived as 'strategic': without national control over them, a country would become both structurally and, indeed, militarily weak. The steel, chemicals, railroad, motor vehicle, aircraft, shipbuilding and basic energy industries were once seen as fundamental to the national interest itself. But in the world of the 'competition state', international competitiveness counts for far more than maintaining an integrated and autonomous national economy. The internationalization of these industries – with foreign investment in both directions – has even included high-technology production of components for weaponry (Graham and Krugman, 1989: ch. 5).

Furthermore, the state is increasingly regarded as structurally inappropriate for providing productive/distributive goods. Public ownership is often seen today as so inefficient economically – the 'lame duck syndrome' – as to render counterproductive its once-perceived benefits of national planning, providing employment or increasing social justice. Third World countries, too, have increasingly rejected 'delinkage' and Import Substitution Industrialization and embraced Export Promotion Industrialization – thereby imbricating their economies even more closely with the global economic order (Harris, 1986; Haggard, 1990). And even where public ownership has been expanded or maintained, its ostensible rationale has been as part of a drive for international competitiveness and not an exercise in national exclusiveness – as in France in the early 1980s (Cerny, 1985). The same can be said of more traditional forms of industrial policy, such as state subsidies to industry, public procurement of nationally produced goods and services, and trade protectionism. Monetarist and private-sector supply-side economists, of course, deny that the state has ever been in a position to intervene in these matters in an economically efficient way, and argue that the possibility of playing such a role at all in today's globalized world has utterly evaporated in the era of 'quicksilver capital' flowing across borders (McKenzie and Lee, 1991). However, even social liberal economists nowadays regard the battle to retain the idea of the 'national economy' as lost, and see states as condemned to tinkering around the edges (Reich, 1991).

The outer limits of effective action by the state in this environment are usually said to comprise its capacity to promote a relatively favourable investment climate for transnational capital by providing a circumscribed range of public goods or specific assets, described as 'immobile factors of capital'. Such potentially manipulable factors are often thought to include: 'human capital' (the skills, experience, education and training of the workforce); infrastructure (from public transportation to high-tech 'information highways'); support for a critical mass of research and development activities; the basic public services necessary for a good 'quality of life' for those working in middle-to-high-level positions in otherwise footloose (transnationally mobile) firms and sectors; and the maintenance of a public policy environment favourable to investment and profit-making by such companies, whether domestic or foreign-owned.

Finally, globalization has had a severe impact on the potential for the state to provide redistributive public goods efficiently. Corporatist bargaining and employment policies are challenged everywhere by international pressures for wage restraint and flexible working practices. Although the developed states have generally not found it possible to reduce the overall weight of the welfare state as a proportion of GDP, there has been a significant transformation in the balance of how welfare funds are spent, from the maintenance of free-standing social and public services to the provision of unemployment compensation and other 'entitlement' programmes. The latter have ballooned as a consequence of industrial 'downsizing', increasing inequalities of wealth, the ageing of the population in industrial societies, etc., tending to crowd out funding for other services. Finally, the most salient new sector of redistributive public goods, environmental protection, is particularly transnational in character; pollution and the rape of natural resources do not respect borders.

Therefore, in all three of the principal categories of traditional public goods – regulatory, productive/distributive and redistributive – globalization has undercut the structural capacity of the national state. Central to this transformation, however, has been the changing technological and institutional context in which *all* goods are increasingly being produced and exchanged. The Third Industrial Revolution has been central to the globalization of economic structures. Five inextricably linked trends are significant here. The first is the development of flexible manufacturing systems, and their spread not only to new industries but to older ones as well. The second is the changing hierarchical form of firms (and bureaucracies) to what has been called 'lean management'. The third is the capacity of decision-making structures to monitor the actions of all levels of management and of the labour force far more closely through the use of information technology, and thereby to increase the use of such methods as performance indicators. The fourth is the segmentation of markets in a more complex consumer society. Finally, the Third Industrial Revolution has itself been shaped by increasingly autonomous and globalizing financial markets and institutions. The rapid development of 'post-Fordism', characterized by a wider process of 'flexibilization', has been analysed extensively across the social sciences (see Amin, 1994).

At the heart of flexibilization in both production processes and firms themselves has been the explosive development of information technology. Olson (1971) argued that one of the key factors making collective action difficult in large groups was their inability to *monitor* the behaviour of members who might be tempted (or determined) to 'free-ride', that is to use public goods without paying their share of the costs. The rapid development of electronic computer and communications technology has transformed this problem, bridging one of the oldest institutional conundrums in history and theory, that between centralization and decentralization. This monitoring capability also leaps national borders and brings firms, markets and consumers into a single, global production process in an increasing number of sectors.

But these aspects of the Third Industrial Revolution – flexibilization of production, firm structure and monitoring – only represent the 'supply side' of the equation. The 'demand side' involves the development of ever more complex consumer societies and the resulting *segmentation of markets*. The technological capacity to produce flexibly – the ability of business to produce at the appropriate scale – has combined with an increasing differentiation of the class system in advanced capitalist societies. Much of the Long Boom grew out of burgeoning first-time markets for such products as cars, so-called 'white goods' (refrigerators, washing machines, etc.) and television sets. Customers subsequently looking to buy new models, however, demanded higher specifications and greater choice. Differentiating demand and flexible supply, then, converged on market segmentation, producing a wider range of variations of a particular product or set of products, with each variation aimed at a particular subset of consumers. This process has also created consumer demand for foreign-produced goods and has forced firms to internationalize. These pressures now also apply to the provision by governments of public goods, with 'choice' replacing standardized collective provision.

The final characteristic of the Third Industrial Revolution is the growing significance of global financial markets. In product terms, finance has become the exemplar of a flexible industry, trading in notional and infinitely variable financial instruments. Furthermore, product innovation has been matched by process innovation, principally through communications and information technology as well as advanced mathematics (Chorofas, 1992). Market demand for financial services products is continually segmenting, too. But probably the most important consequence of the globalization of financial markets is their increasing structural hegemony. In a more open world, financial balances and flows are increasingly dominant, while exchange rates and interest rates, essential to business decision-making as well as to public policy-making, are increasingly set in world markets. In addition, as the trade and production structures of the Third Industrial Revolution go through the kinds of changes outlined earlier, they will be increasingly co-ordinated through the application of complex financial controls, notably rapidly evolving accounting techniques and financial performance indicators. Such strictures apply equally to government bureaucracies and other organizations.

Thus globalization entails *the undermining of the public character of public goods and of the specific character of specific assets,* i.e. the *privatization and marketization* of economic and political structures. States are pulled between structural pressures and organizational levels they cannot control. Economic globalization contributes not so much to the supersession of the state by a homogeneous global order as to the splintering of the existing political order. Indeed, globalization leads to a growing disjunction between the democratic, constitutional and social aspirations of people – which are still shaped by and understood through the frame of the territorial state – on the one hand, and the dissipating possibilities of genuine and effective collective action through constitutional political processes on the other. Certain possibilities for collective action through multilateral regimes may increase, but these operate at least one remove from democratic or constitutional control and accountability; they are also vulnerable to being undermined by the anarchic nature of the international system.

The residual state in a segmented world economy

We have for so long been accustomed to telling the story of how the modern state gradually expanded its social and economic functions that it is cognitively dissonant to describe how those functions are being increasingly constrained in the contemporary world. Governments, mired in embedded financial orthodoxy, are constantly straining to do more for less. Nevertheless, in spite of the globalization of economic structures, the national state retains great political, social and psychological significance for its citizens. States also retain vital political and economic functions at both domestic and international levels – and some of these have actually been strengthened by globalization. In this context, 'policy wonks' (enthusiasts) everywhere are seeking to 'reinvent government', that is to restructure the state so that it can play *new* roles in the future (Osborne and Gaebler, 1992). However, while the state retains a crucial structural role in a globalizing world, its holistic and overarching character has been deeply compromised. A growing plurality of structures and processes is emerging to provide different sorts of public goods and to perform a range of what were once state functions. Nevertheless, states retain both a certain legitimacy and a range of residual functions, some of which have actually been reinforced by globalization. The state today is therefore a potentially unstable mix of civil association and enterprise association – of constitutional state, pressure group and firm – with state actors, no longer so 'autonomous', feeling their way uneasily in an unfamiliar world.

The primary significance of the state as a social structure lies not merely in its role as a provider of goods (public and private) or manager of assets. It also has a more symbolic social function, embodying the sense which people have of belonging to a particular social unit (see the chapter by Williams in this volume). In the terms used by Ferdinand Tönnies (1957), the strength of any such unit derives from its particular mix of *Gesellschaft* and *Gemeinschaft*, the former representing the practical functions and the latter being a form of organic emotional/psychological bonding similar to that found in extended families and village societies. The modern nation-state became the central structure of modern society not only because of the Second Industrial Revolution, but also because it embodied what Florian Znaniecki (1973) has called a 'national culture society'. In this context, the challenge of globalization affects a range of classical issues, including political obligation, the nature of community, the viability of constitutions and the democratic accountability of state actors not merely for their own actions but for the 'state of the nation'.

If it is suggested that this sort of socio-psychological function is a necessary part of human existence, as is the case in much social and political philosophy, then the issue can be addressed in two parts. First, can the residual state maintain this *gemeinschaftlich* bond in spite of the circumscription of its *gesellschaftlich* functions? Second, might there be some *alternative* structural form which could evolve into a repository for this feeling of social belonging? As the state is likely to retain a range of key political and economic functions despite (and partly because of) globalization, the decay of *gemeinschaftlich* loyalty will be uneven, proceeding more rapidly in economically weaker states. For example, if Reich (1991) is correct in his analysis in *The Work of Nations*, economic globalization is likely to lead to two kinds of socio-economic stratification: (a) between a relatively large class of 'symbolic analysts' (managers, technicians, researchers, intellectuals, etc.) consisting of about 20 to 40 per cent of the population in advanced societies, and a low-paid service sector covering most of the rest (advanced societies having lost much of their labour-intensive production to the Third World); and (b) between countries with differential capacities for providing 'immobile factors of capital'. Some, because of their infrastructure, education systems, workforce skills and quality-of-life amenities, are able to attract mobile, footloose capital of a highly sophisticated kind (employing many symbolic analysts engaging in 'high value-added activities'); others have to depend upon low-wage, low-cost manufacturing or agricultural production.

If the developed 'trilateral' states of the USA, Europe and Japan (along with perhaps some others) are able to provide these advanced facilities better, then *gemeinschaftlich* loyalty in those states may be eroded more slowly or perhaps even stabilize. On the other hand, mobile international capital may well destabilize less favoured states, whose already fragile governmental systems will be torn by groups attempting to recast those *gemeinschaftlich* bonds through claims for the ascendancy of religious, ethnic or other grassroots loyalties. Today's revival of 'nationalism' is not of the state-bound, nineteenth-century variety; it is more elemental, and leads to the breakup of states rather than to their maintenance. Max Singer and Aaron Wildavsky (1993) have characterized this bifurcation of the world as leading to the differentiation of 'zones of peace' and 'zones of turmoil'. But it is unclear whether the zones of peace will expand or contract. A linked scenario might be the emergence of an uneven patchwork – sometimes called the 'new medievalism'. However, the outcome may depend far more on how the residual state adapts to carrying out its new, circumscribed range of political and economic functions than on science fiction-like attempts to relocate *gemeinschaftlich* loyalties on new but more problematic levels.

If we want to find an alternative way of conceiving the residual state, probably the best places to look are American state governments. These governments can claim only a partial loyalty from their inhabitants, and their power over internal economic and social structures and forces has been limited indeed. However, they have been required to operate over the course of the past two centuries in an increasingly open continental market, without there being such a thing as state 'citizenship' (only residence, alongside the free movement of people within the USA as a whole). Nevertheless, they do – like counties, provinces and regions in other countries – foster a sense of identity and belonging that can be quite strong. In economic policy matters they represent the essence of the 'competition state'. Their taxing and regulating power has been seriously constrained in many spheres by the expansion of the weight and the legal prerogatives of the federal government. However, at the same time, their ability to control development planning, to collect and use the tax revenues they do impose (as well as offering tax incentives and subsidies), to build infrastructure, to run educa-tion and training systems and to enforce law and order gives these subna-tional states a capacity to influence the provision of immobile factors of capital in significant ways.

The main focus of the competition state in the world – in a way that is partly analogous to the focus of American state governments – is the promotion of economic activities, whether at home or abroad, which will make firms and sectors located within the territory of the state *competitive in international markets*. In this process, however, the state to some extent becomes an agent of its own transformation from civil association to enterprise association. Rather than providing public goods or other services which cannot be efficiently provided by the market – in other words, rather than acting as a 'decommodifying' agent where market efficiency fails – the state is drawn into promoting the commodification or marketization of its *own* activities and structures (including the internal fragmentation of the state itself). The state has always to some extent been a promoter of market forces rather than a purely hierarchical or 'public' organization; this market-izing quality is especially inherent in the concept of 'regulatory public goods' explained earlier. But there is a difference between the state promoting market activities as a general public good and being itself transformed into a market-based organization *per se*. In effect, it is the *transformation of the mix of goods from public-dominated to private-dominated* which in turn transforms the state from a primarily hierarchical, decommodifying agent into a primarily market-based, commodifying agent. By increasingly both promoting the transnational expansion and competitiveness of its industries and services abroad, and competing for inward investment, the state becomes a critical agent, perhaps *the* most critical agent, in the process of globalization itself.

This paradox, in which the competition state at one and the same time maintains itself *and* undermines itself by focusing on one central public role – promoting competitiveness – while downgrading or shedding many of its other traditional public roles, is paralleled by developments at the multilateral level. In order to pursue policy goals which are beyond the control span of the state, of course, a network of international and transnational regimes has grown up, some with more general and some with more circumscribed jurisdictions (Krasner, 1983; Kratochwil and Mansfield, 1994). Such regimes, where they are successful in fulfilling their tasks – and even if they are sometimes essentially intergovernmental bodies – have increasingly been developing the capacity to operate more autonomously of the states which have established and maintained them (Ruggie *et al.*, 1992). However, the authority of such regimes is inherently problematic, given the anarchical character of the international system. In effect, it becomes virtually impossible to establish clear or even operationalizable lines of democratic accountability, leading to something like an international 'quangocracy'.

The shift of decision-making power in a globalizing world is differentiating along several dimensions – not merely downward to domestic firms and markets or into different corners of the splintered state, but also upward to international markets and firms and to a range of more or less functionally specialized international bodies. In this world of constitutional decay and fragmentation, no single structure or closely interwoven set of structures is actually hegemonic in a traditional political sense. Strategic issues are difficult to resolve, and conflicts can undermine the cohesion of distinct decision arenas. However, classical pluralist theory suggests that cross-cutting conflicts and overlapping webs of affiliations may prove better at stabilizing global society in the long run than any attempt to resolve them authoritatively. Pluralists have argued in the past that the stability and viability of constitutional democracy depends less upon formal democratic accountability and more upon the peaceful competition of a plurality of groups with overlapping memberships. Resituating this problematic at a global or transnational level, the residual state would not simply decay, but could remain a key building block (among others) in this 'plurilateral' web – its role would be increased and reinforced, rather than undermined, by the process of globalization (Cerny, 1993a).

At the same time that the state faces these changes, there is a search for new ways for it to function and new roles for it to play. The most important changes have been analogous to the changing structures of production and distribution in the Third Industrial Revolution, as described above. The attempt to make the state more 'flexible' has moved a long way over the past decade or so, not only in the USA and Britain – where deregulation, privatization and liberalization have evolved most – but also in a wide range of other countries in the First and Third Worlds (and more recently in the Second World, too). Some of these changes have become controversial not only because they have challenged tried-and-tested ways of making and implementing public policy or confronted important cultural values, but also because their prescriptions can only be tested at the risk of failure.

Privatization and deregulation are particularly important because they involve the increasing interweaving of the domestic economy and the global economy. In particular, they expand the possibilities for regulatory arbitrage or 'competition in laxity'. This is where the state's response to economic pressures – especially external pressures – increasingly becomes one of adjusting levels of regulation and intervention *downward* so as not to lose competitive advantage *vis-à-vis* states which have looser regulation or greater market freedom for businesses. This is especially true for footloose, mobile transnational capital. The 'ratchet effect' – the term used by Mrs Thatcher's guru Sir Keith Joseph for what was once called 'creeping social-ism', i.e. that each attempt to use the state to achieve a new discrete policy goal ratchets up the size and unwieldiness of the state as a whole – has been turned on its head. In a globalizing world, the competition state is more likely to be involved in a process of competitive deregulation and creeping liberalization.

Beyond privatization and deregulation, probably the most extensive experiment in the USA and Britain has been the subcontracting-out of public and social services. Whether it is garbage collection, prisons or the running of state-financed schools, the state has attempted to replace hierarchical systems with recurrent contracting. As with private firms, too, what has seemed to make such innovations realistic has been the possibility of vigilant performance-monitoring (especially using new information technology) and the application of highly targeted financial controls. Closely linked to subcontracting is the attempt to introduce 'internal markets' into previously hierarchical organizations. In Britain, it is being made possible for recently privatized electricity suppliers – thought by many economists to be as near as you can get to a technological 'natural monopoly', given the expense of laying parallel cables and so on – to compete on price *in each other's geographical areas* by requiring each of them to sell a certain amount of the electricity they produce to industries (and eventually to private consumers) at prices set by their competitors. The structural division of Britain's National Health Service into suppliers and purchasers of services has been even more politically controversial given the salience of the NHS to the *gemeinschaftlich* ideology of the post-war welfare state and of the Labour Party; nevertheless, the Labour Party has recently announced it would only attempt to reverse some, and not all, of these changes should it come to power.

Some of the packages of proposals to 'reinvent government' go much further, of course, calling for a new entrepreneurialism (and intrapreneurialism?) in the far reaches of government and the public sector. Although some leading American advocates of the process (especially those close to the Clinton administration) believe that these reforms can be consistent with centre–left, social–liberal principles (Osborne and Gaebler, 1992), the most extensive experimentation has been carried out by recent Conservative governments in Britain. Policy innovation on both left and right is thus enmeshed in the global structural changes addressed here.

Conclusions: state viability in a globalizing world

This chapter has argued that globalization has undermined the sovereign and inclusive character of the national-level political association (Aristotle, 1962) and the character of the national state as a civil association (Oakeshott, 1976). Rather than globalization leading to the emergence of a more clearly defined and homogeneous global order, it has instead been characterized by the increasing differentiation of both economic and political structures. Globalization is an inherently heterogeneous and fuzzy phenomenon. Against this background, the state is increasingly being transformed into a complex mix of civil and enterprise association – the 'residual state' rooted in the competition state. The state retains a certain hold over national consciousness and constitutional legitimacy, and its residual functions (the 'competition state') are still central both to the globalization process and to carrying out a range of crucial political, economic and social tasks.

Just how far state structures will be transformed is not clear. However, it is evident that this transformation is one of kind, not merely of degree – indeed, incremental changes in particular issue-areas can be misleading. The 'commodified' state is developing into an enterprise association, with key civic, public and constitutional functions either increasingly subordinate to the imperatives of the global marketplace or even vestigial. Whether such a new role will prove stable and durable, and whether the world order within which it evolves will be one of peace or turmoil, cannot be conclusively predicted. Will the state, despite its changing role, remain a key element in a stabilizing, 'plurilateral' web of levels and institutions, or will its decay exacerbate wider trends toward instability? These are questions of paradigmatic significance, and the answers to them will be crucial for understanding the future. We are only now in the first stages of a complex, worldwide evolutionary process which is transforming the state and will affect the viability not merely of state capacity or policy effectiveness, but also of legitimacy, constitutionalism and democracy, for a long time to come.

References

Amin, A. (ed.) (1994) *Post-Fordism: A Reader*, Oxford and New York, Basil Blackwell.

Aristotle (1962) *The Politics of Aristotle*, ed. and trans. by Ernest Barker, New York, Oxford University Press.

Auspitz, J. L. (1976) Individuality, civility, and theory: the philosophical imagination of Michael Oakeshott, *Political Theory*, **4**(3), 261–352.

Cerny, P. G. (1985) State capitalism in France and Britain and the international economic order, in P. G. Cerny and M. A. Schain (eds), *Socialism, the State, and Public Policy in France*, London and New York, Pinter and Methuen, pp. 202–23.

Cerny, P. G. (1990) *The Changing Architecture of Politics: Structure, Agency, and the Future of the State*, London and Newbury Park, CA, Sage.

Cerny, P. G. (1993a) Plurilateralism: structural differentiation and functional conflict in the post-Cold War world order, *Millennium: Journal of International Studies*, **22**(1), 27–51.

Cerny, P. G. (ed.) (1993b) *Finance and World Politics: Markets, Regimes, and States in the Post-Hegemonic Era*, Cheltenham, Glos. and Brookfield, VT, Edward Elgar.

Cerny, P. G. (1994) The dynamics of financial globalization: technology, market structure, and policy response, *Policy Sciences*, **27**(4), 319–42.

Cerny, P. G. (1995) Globalization and the changing logic of collective action,

International Organization, **49**(4), 595–625.

Chorofas, D. N. (1992) *The New Technology of Financial Management*, New York, John Wiley and Sons.

Foucault, M. (1980) *Power/Knowledge: Selected Interviews and Other Writings 1972–1977*, ed. by Colin Gordon, New York, Pantheon Books.

Graham, E. M. and Krugman P. R. (1989) *Foreign Direct Investment in the United States*, Washington, DC, Institute for International Economics.

Haggard, S. (1990) *Pathways from the Periphery: The Politics of Growth in the Newly Industrializing Countries*, Ithaca, NY, Cornell University Press.

Harris, N. (1986) *The End of the Third World*, Harmondsworth, Penguin.

Krasner, S. (ed.) (1983) *International Regimes*, Ithaca, NY, Cornell University Press.

Kratochwil, F. and Mansfield, E. D. (eds) (1994) *International Organization: A Reader*, New York, HarperCollins.

Lowi, T. J. (1964) American business, public policy, case studies, and political theory, *World Politics*, **16**(4), 677–715.

Lowi, T. J. (1969) *The End of Liberalism: Ideology, Policy, and the Crisis of Public Authority*, New York, Norton.

McKenzie, R. B. and Lee, D. R. (1991) *Quicksilver Capital: How the Rapid Movement of Wealth Has Changed the World*, New York, Free Press.

Oakeshott, M. (1976) On misunderstanding human conduct: a reply to my critics, *Political Theory*, **4**(3), 353–67.

Olson, M. (1971) *The Logic of Collective Action*, Cambridge, MA, Harvard University Press.

Osborne, D. and Gaebler, T. (1992) *Reinventing Government: How the Entrepreneurial Spirit Is Transforming the Public Sector, from Schoolhouse to Statehouse, City Hall to the Pentagon*, Reading, MA, Addison-Wesley.

Reich, R. B. (1991) *The Work of Nations: Preparing Ourselves for 21st-Century Capitalism*, New York, Knopf.

Ruggie, J. G., Caparoso, J. R., Weber, S. and Kahler, M. (1992) *Symposium: Multilateralism*, special issue of *International Organization*, **46**(3), 561–708.

Sathyamurthy, T. V. (1990) Indian peasant historiography: a critical perspective on Ranajit Guha's work, *Journal of Peasant Studies*, **18**(1), 90–144.

Singer, M. and Wildavsky, A. (1993) *The Real World Order: Zones of Peace/Zones of Turmoil*, Chatham, NJ, Chatham House Publishers.

Tönnies, F. (1957) *Community and Association*, East Lansing, MI, Michigan State University Press (originally published as *Gemeinschaft and Gesellschaft* (1887)).

Znaniecki, F. (1973) *Modern Nationalities: A Sociological Study*, Westport, CT, Greenwood Press (originally published 1952).

10

Territoriality in the Nuclear Era

RICHARD J. HARKNETT

The end of the Cold War has brought renewed scholarly attention on those forces in international politics that can be associated with change. Two broad sets of dynamics – one set producing greater integration of global affairs; the other creating increased fragmentation – have come into fuller focus since the collapse of the bipolar US–Soviet structure (Gaddis, 1991). Although present throughout the post-World War II period, many of these forces became so intertwined with the superpower competition that they became indistinguishable from it. Freed from the conceptual boundaries of the Cold War, analysis of these international forces can begin anew.

The destructive potential of nuclear weapons represents one such force requiring renewed conceptualization. The impact of nuclear weapons on international security relations more than most twentieth-century developments was inexorably tied to the Cold War superpower competition. The emergence of nuclear weapons paralleled the post-1945 distribution of power and helped reify Cold War bipolarity in both scholarship and policy. The end of the Cold War and its international structure, however, did not bring the elimination of nuclear weapons. This chapter assesses the impact nuclear weapons may have on international security relations divorced from their Cold War framework. Specifically, attention is focused on the relationship between nuclear weapons and the fundamental rationale for the territorial state – that is, its ability to afford protection to its population. I argue that the nuclear era requires a reconceptualization of territoriality in which state territorial integrity is supported through reliance on deterrence rather than by organizing for defence.

The second phase of the nuclear era

The emergence of the modern international system, defined by the central status accorded the territorial state, is typically dated by the Treaty of Westphalia. It is an international system that has been dominated by the dynamics and logic of power politics (Vasquez, 1993).

The basic unit of the current international system is the territorially defined, mutually exclusive state (Mellor, 1989; Gottmann, 1973). It is this system of rule that, in modern times, has been considered best for fulfilling the twin objectives of physical protection and promotion of a general population's welfare (Ruggie, 1993). The essence of the territorial state is its territoriality – that is, its defensibility against hostile outside forces. Although the stability of the state rests on other factors, such as internal and external legitimacy (Herz, 1973: 31) as well as relations with other states (Gulick, 1955; Morgenthau, 1985), the fundamental rationale for organizing within the territorial state unit is its potential ability to protect a specific population. The establishment of a basic level of security serves as the foundation for all other political–social activities.

In the context of international relations, territoriality consists of the set of state policies and organizations constructed to deny the extension of direct political control over, and to ameliorate indirect political influence of one's territory from, hostile external forces. In this sense, territoriality supports the modern manifestation of sovereignty in which political authority structures are territorially bounded (Hinsley, 1986). The undermining of territoriality, therefore, would strike at the foundations of national sovereignty as we conceive of it today. To the extent that the protective power of the state is enhanced, it can be argued that territorially bounded authority structures are supported. Since the sovereign territorial state is the central unit of the international system, the state's enhancement or detraction directly affects the potential for systemic change.

Whether the territorial state will continue to be considered the most efficacious political–social structure has been a central topic of debate in the literature on international economics and research into the technological revolutions in communications and transportation (Krasner and Thomson, 1992). Globalization debates over issues such as population growth, pollution, ozone depletion, migration and health have centred on questions concerning the appropriateness and limitations of the territorially bounded state international system (Wijkman, 1992; Matthews, 1992; Simon, 1992). Interestingly, the debate over the future of the state has not been taken up by traditional security studies specialists. Although the emergence and history of the modern state has been tied closely in security studies literature to the development of military capabilities and organizations that have enhanced territorial defence (McNeill, 1982), little attention has been directed towards the relationship between recent advancements in military capabilities (i.e., nuclear weapons) and the modern state structure. This chapter thus focuses on the impact of the advent of the nuclear era on the function and power of the state to afford protection to its populace.

In examining the relationship between state territoriality and nuclear weapons, it becomes clear that the Cold War may be understood best as a transition period in which state approaches to security lagged behind strategic reality. Mutual superpower possession of nuclear weapons eliminated military assault against their respective homelands and major allies as a rational option for challenging the *status quo*. Objectively, such a move would have led to catastrophic costs that would have outweighed any potential benefit. Yet both main Cold War protagonists remained mired in their focus on the ability to project and use military power to advance national interests. The Cold War followed the pattern of traditional power politics which assumes, given anarchy, the constant potential for conflict and thus promotes a self-help approach to security (Vasquez, 1993). Both the USA and the Soviet Union pursued nuclear strategies that, at times, included the possibility of limited use, counter-force first strikes and pre-emption (Freedman, 1989), all of which seem absurd in the face of a strategic environment dominated by assured destruction capabilities. In retrospect, it is a testament to the robust nature of MAD (mutual assured destruction) that despite heavy investment in modernization and war planning neither superpower could find a sustainable escape from the condition (and implications) of assured destruction.

This is not the first time in modern history that state approaches to security seem to have been at odds with new strategic conditions brought about by technological innovation. In the early 1900s, prior to World War I, the political and military doctrines of all the great powers placed great emphasis on maintaining the military offensive. This focus on offensive capability and tactics endured despite available evidence, which included the recently fought American Civil War and the Russo-Japanese conflict, suggesting that defensive innovations had made such offensively-oriented doctrines problematic (Miller *et al.*, 1991). This strategic reality, in which the advantage had shifted from offence to defence, did not come into full view until fighting began. It was a reality confirmed by the devastating losses incurred on both sides of the Great War.

Not unlike the generals and military analysts of the early twentieth century, post-World War II strategists noted the potential impact of technological and military innovation, but hesitated to conclude that it required a fundamental alteration in state security behaviour. However, simply because change is not acted upon does not mean that in reality it has not occurred. In historical terms, therefore, the Cold War might be considered the first phase of a broader and novel international context that also began in 1945 – what might be differentiated as the nuclear era. The severe competition (Cold War) between the USA and the Soviet Union overshadowed a more subtle and underlying change in the method by which states should organize themselves for protection (nuclear era). A shift in strategic reality – this time from a defence to a deterrence-dominated territorial security environment – may be occurring in the nuclear era. This may be the case despite the superpowers' hesitancy to change fully their military doctrines during the first phase of the nuclear era to reflect the shift (Mlyn, 1994). Fortunately, to date the world has avoided the type of confirmatory experience felt by the strategists of the early twentieth century.

The changes wrought in state security relations by the emergence of nuclear weapons have been relatively obscured from vision, first by the Cold War edifice and then by the reconstruction efforts that followed its collapse. Critical to reconceptualizing the territorial state in the nuclear era is recognizing that the mass-destruction potential of nuclear weapons holds out the prospect of altering in significant ways how states perceive their security interests. It is the impact of nuclear weapons on territoriality that is the key.

Territoriality and the universalist solution

John Gerard Ruggie has concluded that the work of John Herz in the 1950s and 1960s can be considered the only 'serious' attempt by an international security specialist to address territoriality in the context of the nuclear era (Ruggie, 1993: 143). In a series of articles, John Herz argued that the basic rationale behind the organization of state policies and structures was to provide for protection against external aggression. The maintenance of a state's territorial integrity was a prerequisite for the establishment of internal social order and the promotion of a population's general welfare. The state, according to Herz, attempted to fulfil its protective function through the construction of a relatively impermeable territorially demarcated hard-shell of defence. This hard-shell could be enhanced, of course, through appropriate application of military strategies, which would guide the technical development, the tactical use and the operational deployment of military capabilities. In some cases, offensively oriented doctrines that advocated holding the initiative to put at risk the assets of opposing states were perceived as the best defence. However fulfilled, the protective function of the state became a central issue for all modern states. The degree to which states differed in their ability to carry out this function was reflected in the distribution of power across the international system. The major states of the international system tended to be those with the base capabilities to protect themselves against external interference. John Herz argued that the advent of nuclear weapons called the protective function of the territorial state into question. Because of nuclear weapons, the most powerful units in the international system had become vulnerable to utter devastation in an instant. The hard-shell of defence had been overwhelmed by a technical advance which had ushered in, according to Herz, a new 'condition of permeability' (Herz, 1973: 121).

The possession of a relatively small number of these weapons can put at risk an entire society. Possession of an assured destruction capability by all parties involved in a dispute creates a unique strategic environment. Continued survival depends not on one's own actions, but on the continued sanity of one's opponents. The protective function of the state no longer rests in the set of state strategies and organizations dedicated to protection. State territoriality in a nuclear context becomes a misnomer. For Herz, the destructive potential of nuclear weapons means that states no longer have principal control over their own protection. This new condition of absolute permeability means a loss of protective power at the state level.

According to Herz, this loss of protective power creates incentives and pressures to move away from the modern state system. The desire and need for protection continues to exist even if the territorial state can no longer provide it. Some new authority structures must be created to fulfil this function. The pressure will only increase as nuclear weapons spread to more countries. As more states acquire the destructive potential associated with these weapons, more state security relations will have to function under a condition of permeability. Hard-shell territoriality will begin to disappear on a broader scale. In a proliferated world, the continued survival of individual societies will be linked and connected on a daily basis. Herz concludes that since security in the nuclear era may no longer rest at the state level, it must become a global concern. The pressures on territoriality created by nuclear weapons creates the incentive to move towards an alternative universalist system of global order. The universalist solution to a nuclear world flows from a theoretical analysis of the impact nuclear weapons have had on state territoriality. Herz sees this analysis flowing from a realistic assessment of the security problems facing states in the nuclear era.

Post-Cold War policy debates, however, have moved in the opposite direction. The pressures created by nuclear weapons on state territoriality have led to policies which essentially hope to restore pre-nuclear territoriality. The universalist solution of Herz rests on a recognition of the current security reality, accepts it, and suggests that it must be dealt with under new structures.

The basic desire for security is the driving force. What might be distinguished as the restorative solution posits an ideal situation in which, through greater trust, both the technology and knowledge associated with nuclear weapons can be forsaken and we can return to the days in which conventional capabilities held sway.

Territoriality and the restorative alternative

The superpowers and their great power allies made nuclear weapons central to their state security during the Cold War. They also pursued a co-ordinated policy, which breached ideological lines, to stop the spread of nuclear weaponry to other states in the system. With the end of the Cold War, the spread of nuclear weapons became recognized as a primary international security threat. Major efforts were begun to strengthen and broaden the trade practices, technology transfer agreements and international treaties that encompass the nuclear non-proliferation regime. The conventional wisdom supporting nuclear non-proliferation policy promoted a simultaneous reduction in the role to be played by nuclear weapons in great power politics (Harknett, 1994). The disarmament begun under the Strategic Arms Reduction Treaties (Start I and Start II) was heralded by the USA and Russia as fulfilment of pledges made in the Non-Proliferation Treaty to link non-nuclear-weapons states' rejection of nuclear weapons with reductions by the nuclear weapon states. Thus, non-proliferation in the early 1990s became intertwined with a broader consensus on moving away from a nuclear weapon-dominated international security environment (Nye, 1992). In terms of territoriality, non-proliferation and nuclear disarmament policies can be viewed as responses to the loss of protective power at the state level that seek to restore a form of pre-nuclear-era defensibility to the state. Taking the lead in 1993, the Clinton administration initiated a national security strategy that it hoped would: reverse the spread of nuclear weapons to rogue countries (identified at the time as Iran, Iraq, Libya and North Korea) through counter-proliferation; strengthen existing denial tools through non-proliferation; and reduce the role of nuclear weapons through disarmament and greater reliance on extended conventional deterrence (Clinton, 1994). What is so intriguing about this approach is that it accepts the Herz analysis of the impact of nuclear weapons on state territoriality. Non-proliferation and disarmament policies are driven by an underlying recognition that protective power has been lost at the state level. But rather than advocate a global transformation of political organization and authority to deal with the condition of permeability, non-proliferation and disarmament policies taken to their logical end promise to reverse that condition. In a nuclear disarmed world, defensibility is attainable again; the hard-shell is relevant. With territoriality restored, the rationale for the state system remains secure.

The reasons for the USA and other great powers to seek this solution to the nuclear era are clear. A return to an international system of relatively impermeable territorial states would mean that varying abilities to provide protection would again be a basis for distinguishing state power internationally. Where the traditional relationship between military capabilities and defensibility exists, basic power politics dominates. The restoration of such a system obviously favours those states possessing heavy concentrations of traditional measures of power and, not surprisingly, these same states take the lead in non-proliferation efforts.

Both universalist and restorative solutions to the nuclear era assume the following: that the protective function of the state has been overwhelmed by nuclear weapons; that the loss of protective power undermines state territorial integrity; and that the undermining of state territoriality threatens the stability of the territorial state system. The universalist solution assumes that the new condition of permeability produced by nuclear weapons is permanent and thus requires systemic change. The restorative solution sees this condition as reversible, requiring only state behavioural change.

The universalist solution has typically been critiqued as a utopian vision. The restorative solution, however, also rests on a set of idealistic principles (Carr, 1946). Successful non-proliferation and eventual disarmament requires a high degree of state co-ordination and trust. The movement to reduce the role played by nuclear weapons short of disarmament runs against traditional balance of power dynamics in which existing capabilities rather than professed intentions drive state assessments of one another. Giving conventional forces an enhanced role in one's defence posture does not change the fact that nuclear weapons exist. For example, imagine a regional crisis in which an ally of the USA is threatened by a state possessing a small nuclear arsenal. In order to deter potential aggression against the ally, the USA might threaten the regional adversary with retaliation by precision-guided conventional weaponry. Because of the USA dominance in high-tech conventional weapons, it might be believed that the punishment that could be inflicted might be of such a high level as to make an attack on the American ally worthless. However, relying on conventional deterrents to dissuade a nuclear-armed regional actor does not transform the environment into a pure conventional military situation. Would the USA have attacked Iraq on 17 January 1991 with a conventional air assault if Saddam Hussein had possessed a nuclear weapon? Would the crisis dynamics have been different had Baghdad attempted to deter a USA offensive with the threat of nuclear retaliation on Israel and Saudi Arabia? A great power like the USA simply saying nuclear weapons are irrelevant does not make them so. Therefore, while greater emphasis on conventional weapons might support non-proliferation efforts, in the end hard-shell territoriality can only be restored through total nuclear disarmament. This, of course, would require not only the dismantling of existing arsenals, but intensive verification regimes as well. One of the paradoxical twists associated with nuclear weapons is that the likelihood of their use increases as their numbers decrease. Nuclear use becomes 'thinkable' again below the assured destruction level of possession. As unlikely as moving beyond the current state system may seem to many, such a solution is at least based on a more realistic assessment of the contemporary security environment and how self-preservation drives people to organize politically than the restorative angle taken by current non-proliferation policy.

Soft-shell territoriality

Although a number of questions can be raised regarding the two solutions to the nuclear era offered above, it is the basic analysis concerning the impact of nuclear weapons on territoriality that is critical. Both conclude that nuclear weapons have overwhelmed the protective function of the state and thus promise to undermine the integrity of each territorial unit and the territorial state system. The brief history of the nuclear era, however, suggests that such an assessment is inaccurate (or at least debatable). Although the time period is too short and the number of relevant states too small to support a sophisticated correlative analysis, the empirical record to date is clear. Nuclear weapon states have not gone to war with each other. When military crises between nuclear states have arisen, in every case the direction of the confrontation has been toward de-escalation and a non-military solution. Although the empirical record is constrained by the above-mentioned limitations, it is of some significance. During the first fifty years of the nuclear era, wars have been fought between states when at least one side did not possess nuclear weapons (US–PRC in Korea, India–Pakistan, India–PRC) but not after mutual possession. The absence of war between nuclear powers cannot be explained away by a lack of dispute. During the Cold War, the two superpowers engaged in a number of military crises that in every instance led to de-escalation rather than war. The same is true with the 1969 Sino-Soviet border confrontation and the several post-1987 Pakistani–Indian crises. Although the cause of a non-event is difficult to establish, the unmistakable trend in security relations between nuclear-weapon states has been towards war avoidance.

One possible explanation for this trend can be drawn from a third look at the relationship between nuclear weapons and territoriality. Rather than viewing the impact of nuclear weapons as stripping away the protective function of the state, it is possible to conceptualize their impact as an enhancement to territorial integrity. It is true that the destructive potential of nuclear weapons has made every country vulnerable to rapid annihilation. The pre-nuclear conceptualization of territoriality as a hard-shell of defence in which protection was achieved by planning to repulse an offensive attack has indeed been undermined by nuclear weapons. The traditional relationship between offensive and defensive strategies no longer makes sense in the nuclear context. However, Herz made a fundamental error in his otherwise thoughtful analysis (the same is true of restorative analysis that accepts the Herzian view of territoriality). Herz narrowly defined the means of protection that can be associated with the function of protection. Conceptually, he made no distinction between defensibility (that is the ability to defend oneself) and the role of the state as protector. Prior to the end of World War II, protection of state territorial integrity rested on the ability to repel an attack. That this was the primary manner by which states fulfilled their protective function should not mean that it is the only way to fulfil that function. The undermining of a particular means does not necessarily imply abandonment of the function.

In the nuclear era, the protective function is fulfilled by the ability to dissuade an attacker. Rather than attempt to resist attacking forces physically, protection rests on the attempt to convince a potential opponent not to initiate an offensive in the first place. Territoriality in the nuclear era can be conceptualized not as a hard-shell of defence, but rather as a *soft-shell of deterrence*. The territorial state retains its protective function in the nuclear era through the dissuasive power of nuclear possession.

What is the consequence of soft-shell territoriality on international security relations? In a security environment dominated by conventional weapons, the ability to project and use force depends on a variety of factors: the size of a military force, the sophistication of the weapons, industrial base, soldier training, geography and weather. Traditionally this ability has been used to measure how power is distributed across the international system. Great powers are distinguished by their military prowess, particularly in their relations with smaller powers. The variation in defensibility impacts significantly on great-power/small-power dynamics and on the range of behaviour in which each type of state can engage. The classic case of the Melian dialogue as told by Thucydides captures this relationship well. As the generals of ancient Athens prepared to invade the tiny island of Melos, they explained away their actions by noting that 'the strong do what they have the power to do and the weak accept what they have to accept' (Thucydides, 1985: 402). In a world of hard-shell territoriality in which offence and defence are highly relevant, differences in military capability (even subtle ones) will impact on state security relations.

The world of soft-shell territoriality, however, potentially alters the dynamics associated with traditional power politics. This alteration holds not only for great power relations constrained by a condition of mutual assured destruction, but, given further proliferation, for great-power/weak-state relations as well (Preston, 1994). The traditional realist view has held that the independence of small or weak states depends on the balance of power, a great power benefactor, and/or 'their lack of attractiveness for imperialistic' exploitation (Morgenthau, 1985: 196). According to this view, the independence of small powers is exogenously dependent. This is what differentiates them from great powers, which, on a rising scale, possess the internal ability to protect themselves. Soft-shell territoriality supported by nuclear possession challenges this fundamental distinction. In the world of soft-shell territoriality all states become dependent, to a certain degree, on decisions made outside their borders. Ultimate security rests on restructuring the decision-making of potential opponents so that war is no longer considered an option. While that dissuasive influence requires possession of a particular capability, whether security is actually gained is more directly tied to the decision-making of the opponent.

The lack of an effective hard-shell, which is critical in distinguishing states in a conventionally dominated security environment, may become less consequential if a robust soft-shell is in place. Since nuclear weapons simplify greatly a state's ability to inflict destruction on an opponent at a relatively low level of nuclear possession, differences in conventional force structures will become less relevant. The weakness in defensive power typical of small states may be compensated by the possession of nuclear deterrent power. While small nuclear-armed states will remain defensively weak, and thus permeable, the soft-shell of deterrence may be effective in constraining the willingness of great powers to project military capability abroad. Although *able*, great power states may be *unwilling* to use force when faced with the risk of nuclear retaliation. This may hold even if the levels of retaliation between the great and weak powers are disproportionate. Would the USA use conventional force in the Middle East/Persian Gulf against a country that threatened to retaliate with nuclear weapons against Israel and one American city? Can the USA in such an instance assume that the country attempting to deter its action would be 'self-deterred' because of the larger US nuclear arsenal? Why should a leadership facing defeat differentiate between loss of leadership as a result of conventional military victory or nuclear bombing when, in either event, it loses? The mere fact that these questions would have to be answered implies that such a context for dispute is already different from one in which conventional military might is the defining factor. Although the USA in the above example would be capable of producing a conventional military victory, the question becomes whether it would be willing to make the attempt in an environment of heightened risk.

In this sense, the impact of nuclear weapons on territoriality may be to enhance individual state territorial integrity despite continued variance in the traditional sources of power. Rather than undermine the territorial state system as Herz suggested, deterrence power may stabilize it. While conflicts of interest will still exist, a world of soft-shell territoriality increases the incentives for states to co-operate in avoiding war even while they try to gain advantages over one another.

This last point is important. Organizing state territoriality around the soft-shell of nuclear deterrence does not mean an elimination of competition in the pursuit of power and influence, but rather a redirection of that competition away from direct military challenges to state territorial integrity. The distribution of power would remain significant. It would, however, be measured through greater attention to such variables as economic disparities, natural resource endowment and political stability. The ability to affect state behaviour beyond one's borders would have to emphasize these non-military sources of power. The struggle for power and the contest over influence would increasingly take place in a realm in which direct military challenge of territorial integrity would no longer serve as arbiter.

The promise of soft-shell territoriality

The end of the Cold War signalled the cessation of a particular competition, not the conclusion of an era. The superpower rivalry overshadowed the true transformation in state security relations begun in 1945. The change wrought by the nuclear era is one of adaptation in the means by which states protect themselves. Territoriality – the ability to protect and support a state's territorial integrity – had traditionally been perceived in terms of defence. The level of vulnerability produced by the threat of nuclear attack is such that territoriality must be rethought. Rather than promote a forward movement beyond state sovereignty or a reversal of the vulnerability altogether, the possession of nuclear weapons by more countries may support the territorial integrity of states across the distribution of traditional power. The territorial state and its system may remain alive and well behind a soft-shell of deterrence. In contemplating the future of state relations, the dynamics that can be associated with such a re-conceptualization of territoriality need to be considered.

Acknowledgement

The author wishes to thank the Charles Phelps Taft Foundation for its generous support.

References

Art, R. and Jervis, R. (eds) (1992) *International Politics: Enduring Concepts and Contemporary Issues*, 3rd edn, New York, HarperCollins.

Carr, E. H. (1946) *The Twenty Years' Crisis, 1919–1939*, New York, Harper Torchbooks.

Clinton, W. (1994) *A National Security Strategy of Engagement and Enlargement*, July, Washington, DC, Government Printing Office.

Freedman, L. (1989) *The Evolution of Nuclear Strategy*, New York, St Martin's Press.

Gaddis, J. L. (1991) Toward the post-Cold War world, *Foreign Affairs*, **70**(2), 102–22.

Gottmann, J. (1973) *The Significance of Territory*, Charlottesville, VA, University Press of Virginia.

Gulick, E. (1955) *Europe's Classical Balance of Power*, New York, Norton and Co.

Harknett, R. (1994) The logic of conventional deterrence and the end of the Cold War, *Security Studies*, **4**, 86–114.

Herz, J. (1973) *The Nation-State and the Crisis of World Politics*, New York, David McKay Co.

Hinsley, F. H. (1986) *Sovereignty*, 2nd edn, Cambridge, Cambridge University Press.

Krasner, S. and Thomson, J. (1992) Global transactions and the consolidation of sovereignty, in R. Art and R. Jervis (eds), *International Politics: Enduring Concepts and Contemporary Issues*, 3rd edn, New York, HarperCollins.

McNeill, W. (1982) *The Pursuit of Power*, Chicago, University of Chicago Press.

Matthews, J. T. (1992) Redefining security, in R. Art and R. Jervis (eds), *International Politics: Enduring Concepts and Contemporary Issues*, 3rd edn, New York, Harper-Collins.

Mellor, R. (1989) *Nation, State, and Territory*, London, Routledge.

Miller, S., Lynn-Jones, S. and Van Evera, S. (eds) (1991) *Military Strategy and the Origins of the First World War*, Princeton, Princeton University Press.

Mlyn, E. (1994) *The State, Society, and Limited Nuclear War*, New York, State University of New York Press.

Morgenthau, H. (1985) *Politics among Nations*, 6th edn, New York, Knopf.

Nye, J. S. (1992) New approaches to proliferation policy, *Science*, **256**(5061), 1293–7.

Preston, T. (1994) The challenge of nuclear proliferation in the post-Cold War era, unpublished manuscript, Department of Political Science, Washington State University.

Ruggie, J. G. (1993) Territoriality and beyond: problematizing modernity in international relations, *International Organization*, **47**, Winter, 139–74.

Simon, J. (1992) The infinite supply of natural resources, in R. Art and R. Jervis (eds), *International Politics: Enduring Concepts and Contemporary Issues*, 3rd edn, New York, HarperCollins.

Thucydides (1985) *The Peloponnesian War*, New York, Penguin Classics.

Vasquez, J. (1993) *The War Puzzle*, Cambridge, Cambridge University Press.

Wijkman, P. M. (1992) Managing the global commons, in R. Art and R. Jervis (eds), *International Politics: Enduring Concepts and Contemporary Issues*, 3rd edn, New York, HarperCollins.

11

Citizenship at the Crossroads: Immigration and the Nation-State

AHMET ICDUYGU

Introduction

While nearly all advanced industrial countries are losing their 'comfortable certainties concerning the nation-state' (Young, 1993: 3), two particular forces seem to be shaping the contours of this global question. The end of the Cold War, the emergence of 'New World Order' and the rise of globalization have paved the way for a wide questioning of both 'nation' and 'state' (Dunn, 1994; Hont, 1994; Brecher *et al.*, 1993; Featherstone, 1990), and the consequences of international migration and the presence of millions of immigrants in search of access to citizenship and citizenship rights in the receiving nation-states have posed a fundamental challenge to both the theory and practice of governance in contemporary societies (Yang, 1994; Hintjens, 1992; Silverman, 1991, 1992; Baubock, 1991; Hammar, 1990; Brubaker, 1989, 1990; Miller, M. J., 1989). These two forces contribute, from different perspectives, to a central question of the changed meanings of nation, state, nation-state, citizenship, multiculturalism, residence, nationality, community, identity and social relationships resulting from globalization. The main aim of this chapter is to examine the new and emerging context of citizenship and immigration issues which has become a key topic on the political agendas of migrant-sending and receiving countries as well as in the eyes of international migrants.

The consequences of international migration policies and practices of citizenship are experienced at three levels: that of migrants themselves, that of the country they enter, and that of the country they leave.[1] The main perspective of many studies of citizenship and immigration has been at the second level.[2] Little attention has been paid to the first and third levels.[3] Considering the recent reactivation of the politics of immigration, citizenship and nationhood, and the consequent complex configuration of those politics in any one state, the citizenship issue is no longer a simple internal matter for a single government or movement across a single border. It impacts on the governments of both migrant-sending and migrant-receiving countries, the migrants and their families, and the international community and its representative bodies.[4] This chapter aims to shed light on the interrelationship of the three levels outlined above and the way they are incorporated into the citizenship and immigration debate.

The chapter is in four parts. The first provides a brief evaluation of the challenge posed by immigration to the nation-state. This examines such questions as the meaning of citizenship to nation-states and why states employ differing strategies in relation to immigrants, granting citizenship to some and not others. Drawing on evidence from the cases of Turkish immigrants in Australia and Sweden, the second part investigates why immigrants do or do not change their citizenship. The third part considers the role of citizenship policies and practices in migrant-sending countries, referring particularly to the Turkish case and the contribution to the immigration and citizenship debate made by the notion of dual nationality. The concluding section comments on policy implications and future developments.

The meaning of citizenship for migrant-receiving countries

Since World War II, millions of foreign citizens in search of work and a better life, and sometimes of political freedom and protection from persecution, have left their homes and been admitted as legal residents of so-called Western democracies. However, most do not, or cannot, become citizens of the country they now live in, and few are granted all civil, political and social rights.[5] Many immigrants have lived in these states for several decades, paid taxes and been affected by political decisions, but never had full political rights. In some cases, even civil and social rights have been limited, such as refusal of employment in the public sector or denial of welfare and economic security. The anomalous status of immigrants contradicts the abstract assumption basic to democracy: that legal residents of a state are, with few exceptions, members of its society and must therefore meet all obligations and enjoy full civil, political and social rights (Hammar, 1986: 738). It is clear that international migration creates political imperatives for new forms of citizenship, related to residence rather than nationality, based on these democratic principles (Silverman, 1991: 333).

The relationship between the concept of citizenship, defined as the legally acknowledged membership of a state, and the concept of nationality, defined as the socially acknowledged membership of a nation, is the core context in which the status of immigrants and the processes of access to citizenship and citizenship rights are discussed. Before addressing this core issue, one should emphasize the difference between state and nation. Having defined state as a legal and political organization, with the power to require the obedience and loyalty of its citizens, and nation as a community whose members are bound together by a sense of solidarity, a common culture, a national conscious-ness, it is possible to argue that 'while state is a legal and political concept, nation is a cultural one' (Ma, 1992: 294). In the light of this distinction, it can also be argued that the notion of a homogeneous nation-state, which is based on the ideal of 'one nation in one state', is more fiction than reality. Conflicting with the theoretical construction of an ideal nation-state, inter-national migration makes an important contribution to the increasing ethnic and cultural diversity of migrant-receiving countries, which implies the rise firstly of multicultural (or multiethnic) societies, and secondly of kinds of multinational states. The term multinational state highlights the co-existence of many national groups in one state organization (Ma, 1992: 295–6). In the context of immigration and citizenship, the act of receiving immigrants could be seen as a step towards the formation of a multicultural society, and granting full citizenship rights as another stage in the emer-gence of a multinational state.[6] Concerns associated with the concept of multinational states relate to the possibility of fundamental challenges to governance in a society which appears increasingly fragmented into a multitude of immigrant groups, each having its own distinct national identity and making social and political demands based on that identity (Miller, D., 1993: 1003).

We need to consider the implications of the two models of the nation, contractual and ethnic (Silverman, 1992: 19–27), and the two major principles of existing citizenship policies, *jus sanguinis* (the blood principle) and *jus soli* (the soil principle) (Hammar, 1990: 72–5). Based on the distinction between the universalist approaches of the French Enlight-enment and the particularist approaches of German Romanticism, it has been suggested that there are two general models of the nation. In the first – the contractual model of the French tradition – the nation is seen as a voluntary association or contract between free individuals. In the second – the ethnic model of the German tradition – the term nation refers to the concept of a predetermined community bound by blood and heredity. Paralleling these two models are two principles of citizenship policies applied by states. While a number, mainly traditional migrant-receiving lands such as the USA, Canada and Australia, adhere to the soil principle and grant citizenship to all people born in their territory, others, mainly West and North European countries, adopt the blood principle, in which people inherit their parents' citizenship.[7] Although most states apply a mixture of these two principles, this dichotomy, which corresponds in certain respects to the distinction between the contractual and ethnic models of the nation, is often at the heart of the debate about citizenship rights.

Another dimension of this debate is the contrast between the permanent settlement of immigrants in traditional receiving countries and the temporary stay of so-called guestworkers in Europe. This is often seen as a reflection of the polarity of the two types of citizenship principle (Kadioglu, 1992: 199–202; Hammar, 1990: 72–5). For instance, traditional immigration countries, where nation is understood in the contractual model, prefer that permanent immigrants become citizens as soon as possible. They apply the soil principle of citizenship and grant it through a much more liberal system. However, most countries in Europe, which are exposed to immigration transformed from temporary to *de facto* permanent settlement, and in which nation is partly understood in the ethnic model, avoid *de jure* permanence, adhering to the blood principle and offering a very restricted admission to membership.

The dynamics and characteristics of policies of citizenship are complex and varied but there is a common framework to the debate. Four basic points are at issue. The first is that immigration has significantly affected nation-states in the post-World War II period. The increasing cultural and ethnic diversity of populations in the migrant-receiving states is the demographic legacy of mass post-war immigration. Second, these states have started to recognize the reality and implications of that cultural diversity. Third, there is a greater awareness of the need for policy initiatives to help states manage the consequences of cultural diversity in the interests of the individual and society as a whole. Fourth, there is a recognition of the importance of citizenship policies in integrating immigrants into receiving societies.

There is evidence that the notion of citizenship has meaning for states beyond a purely legal definition of membership and embracing issues of social transformation. In practice, understanding of citizenship as membership of the state or nation is often confused by the actors involved. Opponents of liberal citizenship policies, for example, argue that naturalization will not result in integration of immigrants because of enduring barriers to their becoming members of the nation, bound by a sense of solidarity, common culture and national consciousness (Miller, M. J., 1989: 947–9). Many proponents of these liberal policies, however, do emphasize citizenship as a means of conferring a sense of 'belonging to, and identification with the nation, its people, its values and its institutions' (MacPhee, 1982: 1), and encourage relaxed naturalization criteria and dual citizenship.

If it is true that 'the development of the concept of membership in a national polity went hand in hand with the nation-states in the West' (Kadioglu, 1992: 200), then the situation today in migrant-receiving countries tells us that there has been a major transformation since World War II. As Silverman (1992: 35) has pointed out:

The link between the nation and the state has become visibly dislocated and
the gap is likely to grow even more . . . the dislocation of these elements today,
the breakdown in blood and soil definitions of community and the reformulation of the notion of citizenship are all factors in the contemporary crisis of the
nation-state.

While acknowledging the difficulties of coping with the diversity of established policy, practice and outlook with regard to immigration and citizenship admission among nation-states, liberalizing naturalization and dual
citizenship rights seems to be a practical solution (Hammar, 1986: 745–6,
1990: 191–219; Miller, M. J., 1989: 949–50). Of course, this liberalization
cannot fully encompass the emotional identification of immigrant groups
with their origin and nation, but it is an important signal that 'you
[immigrants] are welcome here [in the host country], but you must be
willing to integrate' (*Turkish Daily News*, 1993), as newspapers reported the
German government's view on naturalization in the case of the millions of
Turkish migrants in the country. If citizenship is formal legal membership of
a state implying loyalty to state rather than nation, it is important for both
symbolic and practical reasons, with the emphasis on the latter. Referring to
this practical significance for both receiving states and immigrants, the
following statement was made in a Council of Europe document (1991:
19):

> Seen from the point of view of States it is not in a country's national interest
> that a large section of its population should remain from generation to
> generation without the nationality of the country which has become its home.
> Seen from the viewpoint of long time immigrants, who in practically all
> respects are acknowledged in the host country, the absence of full participation
> in the political life there can only be felt as deplorable.

The meaning of citizenship for international migrants

Central to considerations of citizenship and nationhood in migrant-receiving
societies are immigrants' related perceptions and attitudes. The significance
to immigrants of adopting citizenship in the host country, and the reasons
some do while others do not, are issues which must be addressed. The term
'life strategies' helps us negotiate the meaning of the citizenship process for
immigrants.[8] Indeed, each major event in an immigrant's life, such as
gaining access to citizenship, involves individual or collective adaptation in
relation to economic and social conditions and expectations. Successive
significant events can be seen in terms of sequential plans and actions,
constituting a life strategy. The main question guiding this analysis is: what
are the strategic implications of changing citizenship within the larger
context of the migration and settlement process?

There are a number of influences in play here: whether the receiving society is permanent- or temporary-settlement oriented, the documented or undocumented status of the migrants, their qualifications and positions in the labour market, the duration of stay, and the kinship or informal ties maintained in their host and origin countries. The following discussion, focusing on the particular cases of the naturalization process of Turkish immigrants living in Australia and Sweden, is useful in illustrating the kinds of meanings, costs and benefits affecting their decisions.

Information about the changing citizenship strategies of immigrants was drawn from two extensive surveys of the migration, settlement and integration experiences of Turkish migrants in Melbourne, Australia, and Stockholm, Sweden.[9] The surveys indicated that although Australian immigration policy emphasizes permanent settlement and the soil principle of naturalization,[10] and Swedish immigration policy accepts both permanent and temporary settlement and grants citizenship mainly according to the blood principle,[11] the majority of Turkish migrants in both cases had, on arrival, no intention of permanent settlement. Although most regarded their stay as temporary, only a few actually returned to Turkey. This reveals that while migrants retain a willingness to return to Turkey, settlement has been characterized by a transition from temporary sojourn to unplanned settlement (Icduygu, 1993: 76, 1994: 82). There is no doubt that the issue of becoming a citizen in the host country plays an important strategic role in this transition. The Melbourne survey indicates that among the interviewed Turkish immigrants who were eligible to become Australian citizens, 63 per cent had taken out citizenship at the time of their interview in 1987.[12] The Stockholm survey revealed that the proportion of Turkish-born people with Swedish citizenship was 39 per cent in 1991.[13] Despite the time gap between these two surveys, the disparity in the figures was due mainly to differences between the immigration, settlement and consequent citizenship policies in Australia and Sweden. One could expect that those exposed to the pronounced permanent characteristics of Australian immigration would adopt the idea of permanent settlement and naturalization more readily than those subject to Swedish immigration and settlement policies, with their unclear indication of whether immigration should be permanent and whether immigrants should be encouraged to adopt Swedish citizenship.

The surveys show that when immigrants were asked why they had become citizens or intended to do so, mostly pragmatic considerations were important factors. For instance, with the exception of only 3 per cent of respondents in Stockholm and 10 per cent in Melbourne, who cited the advantages of travelling on the passports of host states, more than a third of the sampled immigrants in Stockholm and nearly a quarter of those in Melbourne said that becoming a citizen gave them a chance to live in both host and home countries without visa and residence permit problems. With citizenship rights and the right to seek permanent positions in public and government services, many immigrants believed that job opportunities would be more abundant, not only for themselves but, most importantly, for their children. While a quarter in Stockholm and 13 per cent in Melbourne gave 'making the future for their children easier and more comfortable in the receiving society' as their reason for choosing to be an Australian or Swedish citizen, among them were many who said that because of their decision they expected their children, as citizens, to be able to find permanent government jobs.

A fifth of respondents in Stockholm and over two-fifths in Melbourne were motivated by normative and moral factors as well as pragmatic considerations. For instance, in Australia, 21 per cent felt that citizenship was a proper step to take after achieving permanent residency, while another 21 per cent cited the importance of the various rights of citizenship, such as voting. In Sweden, the corresponding figures were 5 and 15 per cent respectively. Respondents often pointed out that Turkey's 1981 decision to allow dual citizenship was a stimulus for their decision.

Practical imperatives also played an important part in the attitudes of those who indicated that they had no intention of becoming citizens in their receiving states. A third in Melbourne and a quarter in Stockholm believed that they would gain no benefit from naturalization, and 23 per cent in Melbourne and 21 per cent in Stockholm feared losing rights in Turkey, such as ownership of property. Some complained that the dual citizenship regulations in Turkey were unclear, and said there had been rumours of property confiscation by the Turkish government as a result of dual citizenship. More than a fifth of respondents in Australia and nearly a third in Sweden said they were unwilling to become citizens because they intended to return to Turkey. A fifth of both the Melbourne and Stockholm samples based their refusal to pursue citizenship in the host country on psychological and moral concerns: they considered themselves Turkish rather than Australian or Swedish.

Whether distinctions between the results of the two surveys reflect differences in historical, social and economic contexts of migratory processes to the two countries, or the different characteristics of the Turkish immigrant populations, or a combination of these, is a complex issue beyond the scope of this chapter. Although distinctions between the two cases are apparent, there are similarities in respect of immigrants' perceptions of and attitudes to their own position in the processes of settlement and access to citizenship. A feeling of temporariness is more notable among Turks in Sweden than those in Australia, but for the vast majority in both countries, the issue of access to citizenship is mostly a matter of pragmatism rather than normative and moral commitment.

The meaning of citizenship for migrant-sending countries

The cases of Turkish immigrants in Australia and Sweden demonstrates the importance of Turkey's introduction of dual citizenship in 1981. Until then, the only option was forfeiting substantial citizenship rights in Turkey. The surveys cited above show the resultant increase in Turkish immigrants adopting citizenship in receiving states (Icduygu, 1991: 329). In Melbourne, 20 per cent of sampled immigrants were Australian citizens in 1981, and this proportion had increased to 63 per cent by 1987. In Stockholm, 5 per cent held Swedish citizenship in 1981, but the figure was 39 per cent by 1991.

It is recognized that most migrant-sending states today prefer the blood principle of citizenship. Based on national practical interests, these states wish to maintain close contacts with their citizens abroad and tend to encourage emigrants to retain their citizenship and transfer it to their children (Hammar, 1990: 73). Migrant-sending states are unlikely to view favourably the naturalization policies and practices of receiving states under which hundreds of thousands of their citizens will be lost to them. However, in acknowledgement of the realities of permanent residence abroad, and the process of access to citizenship rights in receiving states, many migrant-sending states today tend to stress the importance of legal regulations which permit immigrants to qualify for naturalization without surrendering their original citizenship. Sending states increasingly view dual citizenship as an important and practical tool of integration.

It provides an opportunity for migrant-sending states to overcome the negative consequences of the permanent migration of their citizens while offering some practical solutions to the naturalization difficulties of migrant-receiving states and immigrants themselves. Since the renunciation of native citizenship is often considered an enormous psychological and practical barrier to naturalization, the acceptance of dual nationality by receiving and sending states will increase the proclivity of immigrants to seek naturalization (Brubaker, 1989: 115–16; Miller, M. J., 1989: 948). Although there is a basic consensus on the advantage of dual citizenship in helping to resolve the anomaly of immigrants' status, the negative aspects have received much more attention. For example, it is argued that dual citizenship creates a complex situation that does not conform with egalitarian democratic norms, such as dual military obligations, dual loyalties and dual political rights.

However, as pointed out by many proponents of dual citizenship, these problems can be limited by bilateral and international agreement. The nature of dual citizenship, which is always on the international agenda, reveals that the process of acquiring the citizenship of another country without surrendering original citizenship involves consequences for governments of both sending and receiving states and the international community as a whole. Since the early 1980s, there has been increasing support for a reconsideration of the Council of Europe Convention of 1963, ratified by only eleven states, emphasizing single citizenship. The convention's stance was seen to discourage moves towards dual citizenship, but now international co-operation has been proposed with the intention of liberalizing dual citizenship arrangements around the world (Hammar, 1990: 119–24; Miller, M. J., 1989: 949).

Concluding remarks

In the light of massive international migration, the issue of access to citizenship and citizenship rights is of increasing global importance. Arguments in favour of facilitating access to citizenship by alien residents have been challenged on ideological and structural grounds. The former has brought into focus the relationship between the symbolic and normative implications of citizenship and its practical consequences, including the question of whether citizenship is membership of a state, a nation or both. The latter implies an extension of the citizenship debate to, and a new emphasis on, the triple structure of the migratory process – sending state, receiving state and migrants – in an international context. The triple structure and the international context are intricately linked in international migration, nation-state and naturalization issues.

If citizenship is considered important both symbolically and practically, if it amounts to membership of the state and is the foundation of democratic society, and if an active and cautious citizenry is essential to the reasonable functioning of democracy, we can conclude that there is a crucial need for more liberal naturalization policies. In achieving this liberalization, it is important to understand that naturalization is mostly a matter of pragmatic choice rather than a normative, moral and psychological commitment process. If pragmatism directs the three main actors of the naturalization process – sending and receiving states, and migrants – there are promising solutions to the dilemma of naturalization. Dual citizenship appears to offer the most pragmatic way forward in circumstances where the naturalization issue challenges concepts such as nation, state and citizenship. As stressed throughout this chapter, whatever the answer, there are consequences and responsibilities for the governments of both sending and receiving countries, for the migrants and their families, and for the international community and its representative bodies.

Notes

1. For an analytical approach to the consequences of migration, see Day (1985).
2. See Hintjens (1992); Silverman (1991, 1992); Brubaker (1989, 1990); Miller, M. J. (1989); Hammar (1985, 1986, 1990); Tung (1985).
3. See Yang (1994); Icduygu (1991); Evans (1988); Seitz and Foster (1985).
4. As the world and nation-states in the international system approach the turn of the century, various implications of the immigration and citizenship debate have arisen. For instance, as economic and political integration continues within the European Union, the concept of European citizenship is becoming a subject of growing debate. See Meehan (1993); Van Steenbergen (1990).
5. For instance, about 18 million people in Western Europe in the early 1990s were not entitled to citizen status in the countries in which they lived because of their immigrant status. More than two-fifths of the three million-plus overseas-born residents of Australia eligible to become Australian citizens have not done so. These figures and others have led researchers and policy-makers to focus on the politics of citizenship in the modern nation-state.
6. This kind of multinational state, which is a product of the more recent mass international migration, differs from the historically determined and long-established multinational state in which there often exists a type of federalism – a form of shared rule based on the notion that sovereignty is vested in national or ethnic groups of people who delegate powers to federal and provincial governments. Ma (1992: 298) suggests that real examples of multinational states are Canada, the former Soviet Union and Switzerland.
7. An informative note might be added here with regard to some European countries: although a number of states in Europe, such as Britain, France, Belgium and The Netherlands, have traditionally applied the soil principle, this has recently changed to include elements of the blood principle.
8. The concept of life strategies, which is more often used in sociological and demographic literature, implies adaptations of one's life and lifestyle to different environmental conditions (Crow, 1989; Morgan, 1989).
9. The Australian data were collected by the author in 1987 from interviews with 276 immigrants in Melbourne. The choice of Melbourne as the research site was not arbitrary: this city has served as the primary destination point for more than half of Turkish migrants to Australia. The respondents were selected on a multi-stage sampling basis through the 1981 census maps. All were migrants born in Turkey, of Turkish ethnic origin and aged 18 or over on arrival in Australia. The Stockholm data were obtained in 1991 from interviews with 297 immigrants in Stockholm where almost three-fifths of Sweden's Turkish community live. Interviews covered migration, settlement and integration processes. The sampling procedure utilized information from the Register of the Total Population maintained by Statistics Sweden. The sample was built up using the web technique, taking into consideration the distribution of age, sex, length of residence, and area of residence demonstrated in the 1990 registration figures. For reasons similar to the Melbourne survey, respondents were selected from migrants born in Turkey, of Turkish ethnic origin and aged 18 or over on arrival in Sweden.

10. Australia prefers that permanent immigrants become citizens without delay, and children born on its territory should therefore automatically become citizens according to the soil principle. Current regulations stipulate that an overseas-born person in Australia on a permanent resident visa for at least two years is eligible for citizenship. Based on a liberal policy, naturalization requirements in Australia are relaxed, the procedures simple and the costs low. Almost all immigrants considered of good conduct and with the residence requirement of two years are granted citizenship.

11. Swedish immigration policy has been ambivalent on the issue of permanence (Hammar, 1985: 48–9). Sweden grants citizenship mainly according to the blood principle, and it does not encourage immigrants to become citizens. Although in Australia naturalization is mostly considered a matter of right for an immigrant, in Sweden it is an issue of state discretion. Compared with other European countries, Swedish policies can be considered liberal, but they appear protectionist when compared with those of Australia. In Sweden immigrants are required to have five years' residence before applying for citizenship. Naturalization requirements are much more demanding, including that the applicant is an able person deserving of citizenship and that he or she prove a willingness to integrate into the nation's language and culture.

12. This figure reflects the proportion within the median period of residence of fourteen years.

13. This figure reflects the proportion within the median period of residence of sixteen years.

References

Baubock, R. (1991) *Immigration and the Boundaries of Citizenship*, Vienna, Institute for Advanced Studies.

Brecher, J., Brown, J. and Cutler, J. (1993) *Global Visions: Beyond the New World Order*, Boston, South End Press.

Brubaker, W. R. (1989) *Immigration and the Politics of Citizenship in Europe and North America*, Lanham, MD, German Marshall Fund of the United States.

Brubaker, W. R. (1990) Immigration, citizenship, and the nation-state in France and Germany, *International Sociology*, **5**(4), 379–407.

Council of Europe (1991) *Report on Political Participation*, Strasbourg, Council of Europe.

Crow, G. (1989) The use of the concept of strategy in recent sociological literature, *Sociology*, **23**, 1–24.

Day, H. L. (1985) Consequences of international migration for those who remain in the countries of immigration, paper presented at Emerging Issues in International Migration seminar, International Union for the Scientific Study of Population, 22–26 April, Bellagio, Italy.

Dunn, J. (1994) Introduction: crisis of the nation state, *Political Studies*, **42**, special issue, 3–15.

Evans, M. D. R. (1988) Choosing to be a citizen, *International Migration Review*, **22**(2), 243–63.

Featherstone, M. (1990) *Global Culture: Nationalism, Globalization and Modernity*,

London, Sage.

Hammar, T. (1985) *European Immigration Policy*, Cambridge, Cambridge University Press.

Hammar, T. (1986) Citizenship: membership of a nation and of a state, *International Migration*, **24**(4), 735–48.

Hammar, T. (1990) *Democracy and the Nation State*, Aldershot, Avebury.

Hintjens, H. M. (1992) Immigration and citizenship debates: reflections on ten common themes, *International Migration*, **30**(1), 5–16.

Hont, I. (1994) The permanent crisis of a divided mankind: 'contemporary crisis of the nation state' in historical perspective, *Political Studies*, **42**, special issue, 166–231.

Icduygu, A. (1991) Migrant as a transitional category: Turkish migrants in Melbourne, Australia, unpublished Ph.D. thesis, Demography Department, Australian National University, Canberra.

Icduygu, A. (1993) Temporariness versus permanence: changing nature of the Turkish immigrant settlements in Australia and Sweden, paper presented at the 22nd General Conference of the International Union for the Scientific Study of Population, 24 August–1 September, Montreal.

Icduygu, A. (1994) Facing changes and making choices: unintended Turkish immigrant settlement in Australia, *International Migration*, **32**(1), 71–93.

Kadioglu, A. (1992) Citizenship, immigration and racism in a unified Germany with special reference to the Turkish guestworkers, *Journal of Economics and Administrative Studies*, **6**(1–2), 199–211.

Ma, S. Y. (1992) Nationalism: state-building or state-destroying? *The Social Science Journal*, **29**(3), 293–305.

MacPhee, I. M. (1982) Australian citizenship, *Parliamentary Debates*, Canberra.

Meehan, E. (1993) *Citizenship and the European Community*, London, Sage.

Miller, D. (1993) Book review of *Dimensions of Radical Democracy: Pluralism, Citizenship, Community* by Chantal Mouffe, *American Political Science Review*, **87**(4), 1003–4.

Miller, M. J. (1989) Dual citizenship: a European norm? *International Migration Review*, **23**(4), 945–50.

Morgan, D. (1989) Strategies and sociologists: a comment on Crow, *Sociology*, **23**, 25–9.

Seitz, A. and Foster, L. (1985) Dilemmas of immigration – Australian expectations, migrant responses: Germans in Melbourne, *Australian and New Zealand Journal of Sociology*, **21**(3), 414–30.

Silverman, M. (1991) Citizenship and the nation-state in France, *Ethnic and Racial Studies*, **14**(3), 333–49.

Silverman, M. (1992) *Deconstructing the Nation*, London, Routledge.

Tung, R. K. (1985) Voting rights for alien residents – who wants it? *International Migration Review*, **19**(3), 451–7.

Turkish Daily News (1993) Turks should be made first-class citizens, Ankara, 15 June, p. 8.

Van Steenbergen, B. (1990) Scenarios for Europe in the 1990s: the role of citizenship and participation, *Futures*, **22**(9), 961–9.

Yang, P. Q. (1994) Explaining immigration naturalization, *International Migration Review*, **28**(3), 449–77.

Young, C. (1993) The dialectics of cultural pluralism: concept and reality, in C. Young (ed.), *The Rising Tide of Cultural Pluralism*, Wisconsin, University of Wisconsin Press.

12

The Globalization of Telecommunications and the Issue of Regulatory Reform

GERHARD FUCHS AND ANDREW M. KOCH

Introduction

In the not-so-distant past, telecommunications technology and markets were largely directed and regulated by nation-states. Infrastructure and telecommunications policies, even if not perceived as such, were usually formulated in virtually closed actor networks – featuring state agencies such as postal administrations, and their preferred suppliers. A telecommunications regime was developed and maintained under technological constraints and state directives.

Today, this stable technical and political framework is breaking down, and in some respects much of it has already vanished. Telecommunications decisions are being politicized, as new actors enter and compete in the telecommunications arena, and liberalized, as new markets are opening the arena for competition. The globalization of the telecommunications industry has altered the traditional relationship between state actors and the industry. In the process, the legitimating structures for telecommunications policy have been eroded. The old regulatory regime is collapsing.

The type of new regime that will emerge in its place is still uncertain. It will require a reconceptualization of the relationship between market and state. As the emerging trends in technology, production and transportation suggest, this reconceptualization must occur on a global scale. These trends have dramatically challenged existing regulatory authorities and generated a perceived need for new regulatory agencies within nation-states, of which the Office of Telecommunications (Oftel) in Britain is one example. However, nation-state actors increasingly find themselves in a paradox. While the regulation of telecommunications is still largely the domain of nation-state authority, the actors, services and production of telecommunications technologies transcend nation-state boundaries. There is a growing discrepancy between the states' desire to regulate telecommunications activity in the pursuit of security and economic stability and the ability of the states to generate the power necessary for such ends.

This chapter 'takes stock' of the current situation, the actors and the dynamics of globalizing trends in the telecommunications sector. Such analysis is necessary because some of the more theoretical studies focus on narrow aspects of production or are working with rather reductionist assumptions about the effects of globalization. The focus on production tends to ignore the large service-oriented activity of telecommunications. A strictly 'business-oriented' approach, on the other hand, tends to treat national public policy only as an obstacle to be overcome. Both of these ignore the political dimension of telecommunications.

After surveying recent trends, this chapter concludes with a discussion of the regulatory challenges resulting from globalization. Marketization has dominated much of the global dimension of telecommunications activity over the last decade, but it is fair to ask whether or not such a trend will continue to dominate the telecommunications sector. Even if it does, the influence of the various actors may steer the telecommunications sector in subtle, yet important, new directions.

Dimensions of globalization

What does globalization represent? Is it an activity carried out by nation-states or is it a result of economic enterprises? Is it a term relevant only to the leading industrial economies or is it truly global in its scope? Finally, what are the effects that this trend is likely to produce for both politics and economics?

The term globalization seems superficially to indicate the universalization of economic or political phenomena. However, in practice it is more complex. At its core, globalization indicates that the traditional inward-looking role of the nation-state has changed. On this basic level, globalization has transformed the national economy from a domain characterized by clearly identifiable rules, trade policy and national economic self-sufficiency. Essentially, globalization seems to presuppose a process in which traditional notions of national sovereignty are disintegrating (see the chapters in this volume by Cerny and Williams).

Nation-states have responded by forming trading blocs, organizing themselves into cohesive structures which take on the economic roles once considered the exclusive domain of their individual members. Economic policy, trade and investment strategies, and institutional structures are established on a regional basis. In outward appearance, the three major blocs (European, North American and East Asian) appear to be fortresses against the intrusion of outside competitors. They aim to maintain regional growth and stability and protect domestic markets through a regional strategy.

It should be noted, however, that such a strategy represents a political response to economic globalization. If we focus on economic activities, a very different picture emerges. As Ohmae (1985) has remarked, in the information–communications technology sector, leading multinational corporations strive to achieve a global presence in each of the major industrial trading blocs. In Europe especially, this trend is accelerating due to rising research and development costs, which make it unreasonable to expect that the investments pay for themselves in small national markets (Van Tulder and Junne, 1988) or even within the trading blocs themselves. In response, multinational corporations attempt to establish a presence throughout the triad and to construct triad-wide consortia.

Resulting competition is not between regions but between globally active consortia, which can also bear a transnationally institutionalized form of technology development cutting across the trading blocs themselves. Investment, research and development, and, ultimately, trade and employment activities occur not as a result of a bloc's political imperatives, but according to the market imperatives in which the multinational corporations operate.

Telecommunications and globalization

Information technologies have an interesting dual function in the process of globalization. On the one hand, the telecommunications sector is being extensively globalized; on the other hand, telecommunications networks are an important precondition for globalization in the world economy (Schneider, 1994; Strange, 1994).

> The emergence of the phenomenon of globalization, the emergence of the global option, would have been inconceivable without the development of information technologies, and particularly telecommunications. These technologies have been a necessary critical material condition for the emergence of the global option in as far as they have enabled particular labour processes, or sometimes entire production facilities, to be dispersed across the globe, while allowing managerial control (and in the case of industrial production, often the most advanced design functions) to remain centralized in the 'world cities' of the core societies. So central have been these new microelectronic technologies to the recent development of the international economy, that elsewhere Castells and others have suggested that global restructuring at root, must be considered as a 'techno-economic' process. (Henderson, 1989: 3)

As Chandler (1990) has pointed out, organizational differentiation, the growth of corporate hierarchies, and the spread of technical communications and transport systems are highly interdependent. The division of labour and the expansion of markets and hierarchies have been inseparable from the parallel growth of global communications infrastructures. Furthermore, the new decentralized organizational forms of multinational corporations could be designed only on the basis of advanced global communications structures. Communications technologies are, in this sense, important enabling conditions to differentiation and institutional integration. The relationship between the spread of multinational corporations and communications revolutions can be pictured as shown in Table 12.1.

Table 12.1 Multinational corporations and communications revolutions

Era	Invention
Fifteenth and sixteenth centuries	Diffusion of paper production
	Invention of double entry book-keeping
	Emergence of the first postal system in continental Europe
Nineteenth century	Emergence of the railroad and steamship
Twentieth century	International telephony
	Commercial air travel
	Satellite communications
	International computer networks

Each one of these communication developments made a new form of organizational structure possible. Looking specifically at the technological changes from the nineteenth to the twentieth centuries, railroad, steamship and telegraphs have limiting characteristics in either speed or capacity to transmit large and diverse amounts of data across vast areas. In the late twentieth century such limitations have broken down. Computer and satellite technology make the transmission of complex design information, manufacturing orders and even capital flows almost instantaneous. The technical limitations to true globalized production have disintegrated, leaving only political and organizational impediments.

Actors in telecommunications

The question of who are the current actors within the telecommunications sector is not easy to answer. The issue is best approached by defining exactly what telecommunications was and what it has become in the late twentieth century.

In general, telecommunications comprises all aspects of voice and data transmission by radio, television, wire, microwave and satellite. However, people in the industry make a further distinction between telecommunications (two-way services such as telephone and data traffic) and broadcast (such as radio and television) (Savage, 1989). While this distinction is being eroded by new technologies, this difference is still important. However, this chapter concentrates on the general meaning of telecommunications.

In the recent past, the number of relevant actors in the telecommunications sector was limited. There were the national network operators, and their preferred suppliers and government representatives who closely co-operated without much public control or user participation. International aspects of telecommunications were of secondary importance. International matters were handled within organizations like the International Tele-communications Union (ITU) and in bilateral or multilateral agreements worked out between national delegations. Trade was limited and multi-national corporations could extend their reach primarily by buying local production units creating strictly national products.

Over the last two decades the number of actors in telecommunications has increased steadily. The result has been a growing differentiation among them. To assess the resulting divergence of interests and to assist in identify-ing the different regulatory problems that might arise, the following distinc-tions are useful. Taken as a whole, these categories might also be useful in highlighting the conflicts among the various actor groups in the creation of a new regulatory regime.

a) *Information carriers*: These corporations basically offer transmission ca-pacities, the infrastructure over which data are being sent. This includes the old network operators, like British Telecom or German Telekom, but also new actors like the public utilities or the railways.

b) *Service providers*: This group offers specific products over the networks. In some cases it may include the old network operators, but also new specialized actors or diversifying actors like the public utilities (Bayern-werke AG in Germany) or manufacturing companies (like Mercedes Benz).

c) *Content providers*: These actors produce and provide the content of services to be offered over the networks, primarily in the area of information-oriented services (e.g., from telelearning to local weather information).

d) *Equipment producers*: This group includes the old telecommunications equipment producers, the computer manufacturers and, increasingly, companies in the field of consumer electronics.

e) *Regulatory and political authorities*: In the past, network operators were usually either part of the public administration or quasi-public institu-tions. At present, nearly everywhere new independent regulatory in-stitutions are being established, whose prime purpose is no longer to run the telecommunications sector but to control it.

f) *Users*: This groups includes both corporate and private users of tele-communications services. Telecommunications technology has in-creased the centralization of corporate planning and production strate-gies even while actual manufacturing may occur in diverse areas.

Private use of network services has also expanded greatly over the last decade.

There are clear overlaps among the various groups of actors, and differences in the dimensions of their activity. For example, some actors like AT&T or Alcatel are active in four areas (a–d), others concentrate on one speciality (e.g., many of the specific service providers). In addition, some content services may be available from a variety of network providers. International Value Added Network Services (IVANS) are offered by the old network operators but also by a variety of other organizations like EDS, IBM, DEC, Philips, GEIS and Andersen Consulting. In addition, some multinational corporations are simultaneously users of the network, as they co-ordinate their production and marketing strategies, and network operators (or even re-sellers of transmission capacity), if they are building their own corporate networks (see Table 12.2).

Table 12.2 Actors and interests

	Content or substance (information)	Process (handling and transmitting information)	Format (hard copy, record, display, etc.)
Information carriers	XX	XXX	XX
Service providers	X	XXX	XX
Content providers	XXX	X	XX
Equipment producers	X	XX	XXX
Information users	XXX	X	XX
Regulatory and political authorities	XX	XXX	X

X = minor, XX = medium, XXX = major

The rest of this chapter focuses primarily on the information carriers (especially the old network operators), although in the formation of any new regulatory regime, the other actor groups are equally important. In the pursuit of globalization, three different strategies can be distinguished for this group of actors: transnationalization, international alliances and the harmonization of telecommunications policies.

Transnationalization is a strategy used by large and advanced telecommunications operators (TOs) to expand beyond national markets by offering new service options within the context of existing international telecommunications services and/or by foreign direct investment (FDI). There are a number of examples for new service options: the simple resale of licences, various options in billing procedures and set-up times, credit card and calling card services and third party calling services.

Reliable data on FDI by TOs are difficult to generate but, according to our calculations, the annual foreign investment by the TOs of the OECD countries varies between 2 per cent and 8 per cent of each firm's total capital investment. The trend is clear: the volume and proportion of FDI is increasing. Two developments are marked: a cross-penetration of markets within the OECD area and a flow of investment from OECD countries to developing countries (Bauer, 1992: 2).

FDI takes various forms:

- Purchase of shares of other TOs
- Establishment of joint ventures
- Acquisition of a franchise for the operation of telecommunications services
- Mergers and acquisitions

Recent examples of these activities are numerous. In 1990, shares of the PTO of New Zealand were purchased by a consortium of Ameritech and Bell Atlantic (both from the USA). In 1991, 49 per cent of the shares (with voting rights) of the Mexican PTO, Telefonos de Mexico (Telmes), were bought by a consortium including South Western Bell (a regional holding company in the USA) and France Telecom.

International alliances and packaging of services offer other means to expand markets. Offshore services are being provided by alliances of network operators. Recent examples include:

- Eunetcom (France Telecom and German Telekom)
- Unisource (PTT Netherlands, PTT Sweden, Swiss PTT, etc.)
- The agreement reached with CEPT to establish METRAN in 1990 (a transmission network independent of specific services, comprising digital cross-border transmission links)
- An announced 34 Mbps fibre backbone called GEN (General European Network) among British Telecom, STET, France Telecom, German Telekom and Telefonica
- The Hermes consortium which consists of 14 railways, Mercedes Benz and Compagnie de Suez

The first two offer services to international customers such as virtual private networks, private lines, messaging and calling card facilities. METRAN and GEN offer a harmonized broad band infrastructure covering a variety of European countries. Hermes is an initiative aimed at developing a new telecommunications infrastructure which also offers services.

Harmonization is the co-ordination of telecommunications policies among countries. This has meant the creation of common standards and/or the development of common policies for the provision of services. Both on the regional as well as on the global level, the number of standardization institutions of a public, semi-public and private character has increased exponentially (Genschel and Werle, 1992).

Regulatory challenges

The regulatory structure that has been based on the national interest of individual states has broken down. Attempts by national regulatory authorities to influence national producers and markets have declined in direct proportion to the level of globalization in the telecommunications sector. The asymmetry among states in the regulation of telecommunications has also affected the strategic decisions of the TOs (Bauer, 1992). Figure 12.1 illustrates that while policy continues to be made in relation to domestic contexts, services are increasingly provided on a domestic-foreign and foreign-foreign basis.

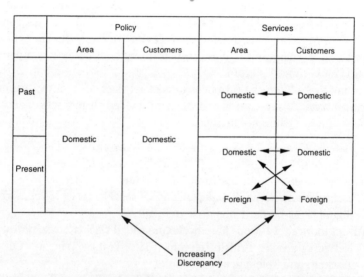

Figure 12.1 National regulation and internationalization of markets

We need to consider whether a direct replacement of the nation-state regulatory scheme of the past is necessary to a globalized telecommunications environment. The answer hinges on matters in two distinct areas. First, are there technical questions that can be managed only on a global level? Secondly, are there questions that relate to issues of power, performance and the distribution of economic rewards (what can generally be called 'political questions') that can be addressed only within a regulatory context? The answer to both questions is 'yes'.

There are strong imperatives for the co-ordination of technical matters in the establishment and maintenance of a global telecommunications network. They relate to the allocation of frequencies, geostationary positioning of satellites and the regulation of international networks, access conditions and intellectual property rights. The task for policy-makers is to formulate a framework in which these matters can be addressed. Policy, however, has lagged behind the hectic pace of globalization, making the co-ordination of these efforts time-consuming and subject to competing interests and pressures. Existing structures within the telecommunications sector are only partly capable of addressing these matters as they impact on the pace and character of continued expansion. The dominant institution dealing with matters of international telecommunications policy is the ITU. However, it has already expressed the view that it does not see itself as fit to cope with the complexity of these challenges (Hamelink, 1994). The ITU is currently undergoing an internal restructuring aimed at reducing the dominance of national governments' regulators and seeking to give more influence to business organizations and transnational actors. This is a trend also observed in a number of other international telecommunications organizations. Given increasing deregulation and liberalization, this is an understandable move, but the repercussions are also dramatic. While the old organizations had a good chance of their agreements being implemented at the national level (because of the procedural rule requiring consensus among national delegations), the new bodies can issue recommendations but with absolutely no guarantee that the agreements will be implemented by all participants. This holds true even for the European Union, which is largely supportive of transnational policy formulation efforts.

Globalization seems to require the destruction of existing institutions. Some new structure is needed, however, to co-ordinate the policy issues generated by globalization. This means that any new institutional structure would have to merge considerations of technical issues with trade, competition, international capital movements and issues of national sovereignty. Thus any type of new regulatory regime cannot escape political considerations.

It is a cliché of public policy that every policy creates winners and losers. It can also be said, however, that the lack of a regulatory policy creates outcomes that benefit some over others. Yet the problems of constructing such a regime are manifold. Not only are interests of the nation-state participants in any such regime diverse, but the interests of the other actors will probably vary greatly. As a result, there is likely to be much difficulty in finding a policy consensus among the TOs, the states and the users.

For any international regime to appear legitimate, all states must see a benefit from the outcome (Keohane and Nye, 1977: 235). Already, Third

World states are complaining about their access to satellites and other communications technologies. This is just one of a range of complications in attempts to reach a comprehensive agreement.

The legitimacy of any new regime will, at least in part, depend on its ability to address the concerns of users, both multinational corporations and the public. Regarding the public interest in the EU, Mansell (1993: 215) correctly asks:

> Are European institutions strong enough to ensure that the public interest in telecommunications embraces the concerns of smaller firms and residential consumers in the face of strong pressures to redefine that interest more narrowly in terms of the strategic priorities of a relatively small number of multinational suppliers and users?

This is a problem that any new regulatory regime must address on a global basis. But today, even the future of European regulation is unclear.

> A European regulatory authority for telecommunications is way ahead of reality. Even if it did happen, it would have to rely on local and national independent regulatory authorities to do most of the work. Put another way, unless there are proper independent national regulatory authorities, there will be no enforcement and implementation. (Analysis, 1992: 106)

The main political issue underlying these concerns is access, which will define who is able to use global networks and under what conditions. This is important at the national as well as the international level. Global network providers aim to combine their offer of transmission capacities with available services. Specific services are channelled through specific networks, with the network operator determining access conditions. Parts of the residential population as well as whole countries might be thus deprived of the use of essential services. With international markets and international competitiveness increasingly tied to 'information age' technologies, the issue of access has a strongly political component. Tensions are bound to increase, particularly between the First and Third Worlds.

International organizations like the ITU at least provided a forum for the Third World to discuss its problems and, in some cases, to fight effectively (given the consensus rule). With the demise of the ITU (Werle and Genschel, 1993) and the emergence of new international bodies based on market power, the interests of less developed countries threaten to be overlooked. Furthermore, telecommunications in the past still provided a flow of income for these countries, especially in the field of long-distance traffic. But due to new technologies, countries which demand (excessive) fees for through-coming or outgoing traffic might simply be bypassed and even forced into a situation in which they have to pay compensation to the leading network operators of the world.

It seems obvious that a global market requires a global regulatory authority, but none seems to be on the horizon. Without establishing more effective regulatory institutions, telecommunications networks will be tailored to the benefit and needs of a small club of globally operating, oligopolistic firms. Their conception of the public interest will be more narrowly defined than that of the old monopoly TOs.

To acquire and maintain legitimacy, any new regulatory regime must account for the diverse interests of the TOs, the nation-states, the users and the producers. Given the diversity of interests, the problems of constructing such a regime are monumental. The globalization of telecommunications will nevertheless continue, and users who can afford to will benefit from this process. But this falls well short of the fulfilment of the potential of the telecommunications revolution.

References

Analysis (1992) *Performance of the Telecommunications Sector up to 2010 under Different Regulatory and Market Options*, Cambridge, Analysis.

Bauer, J. M. (1992) Globalization of telecommunications operators under asymmetric national regulatory policies, Ninth International Telecommunications Society Conference, 14–17 June, Sophia Antipolis.

Chandler, A. D. (1990) *Scale and Scope: The Dynamics of Industrial Capitalism*, Cambridge, Belknap.

Genschel, P. and Werle, R. (1992) *From National Hierarchies to International Standardization: Historical and Modal Changes in the Coordination of Telecommunications*, Cologne, Max Planck Institut für Gesellschaftsforschung.

Hamelink, C. J. (1994) *The Politics of World Communication*, London, Sage.

Henderson, J. (1989) *The Globalization of High Technology Production: Society, Space, and Semiconductors in the Restructuring of the Modern World*, London and New York, Routledge.

Keohane, R. O. and Nye, J. S. (1977) *Power and Interdependence*, Boston, Little, Brown.

Mansell, R. (1993) *The New Telecommunications: A Political Economy of Network Evolution*, London, Sage.

Ohmae, K. (1985) *Triad Power*, New York, Free Press.

Savage, J. G. (1989) *The Politics of International Telecommunications Regulation*, Boulder, CO, Westview Press.

Schneider, V. (1994) Multinationals in transition: global technical integration and the role of corporate telecommunications networks, in J. Summerton (ed.) *Changing Large Technical Systems*, Boulder, CO, Westview Press.

Strange, S. (1994) Rethinking structural change in the international political economy: states, firms, and diplomacy, in R. Stubbs and G. R. D. Underhill (eds), *Political Economy and the Changing Global Order*, London, Macmillan.

Van Tulder, R. and Junne, G. (1988) *European Multinationals in Core Technologies*, Chichester, John Wiley and Sons.

Werle, R. and Genschel, P. (1993) From national hierarchies to international standardization. Modal changes in the governance of telecommunications, *Journal of Public Policy*, **13**(3), 203–25.

13

The Globalization of Knowledge and the Politics of Global Intellectual Property: Power, Governance and Technology

CHRIS FARRANDS

This chapter explores the ways in which changes in technology have reshaped political space. It does so by examining the politics of intellectual property regimes (IPRs). Extensions of technology have helped to extend IPRs in a form of international enclosure analogous to the enclosure of common land in England in the eighteenth century. It also argues that as knowledge is an increasingly important power structure, the apparently peripheral or technical issues of intellectual property represent an important arena of conflict through which we can identify issues, agendas, structures and processes which characterize emerging global politics.

Territory, space and international relations

If international relations are moving from some apparently stable structure based on nation states, it does not follow, for all the rhetoric about globalization, that there is some single, rational, stable outcome towards which they are moving (Farrands and Talalay, 1994). There is good evidence that the structures of international relations are becoming more diverse. Markets, economic actors, regional, cultural, religious or pan-nationalist movements all make significant claims on power and authority, eroding without clearly replacing the established structures of international society. All of these possibilities are covered by the label 'globalization' in some sense or other. One possible outcome of these changes is a global system modelled by liberal universalism; but there is little evidence that this is actually emerging. A different outcome would be an integrated world system dominated by the still-powerful centres of late capitalism. A further model for the direction of the international system would be one of regionalization: global forces in the international system collapsing one pattern of differentiation (nation-states) to replace it with another, where Europe, America and Japan each compete for hegemony through powerful regional or trade and finance-based blocs. These models imply some sort of deterritorialization of politics, a move away from fixed, recognizable territorial units (states, superpowers, major alliance blocs, etc.) towards something much more amorphous where political power is not identified closely with specific territorial claims. The regional blocs model, however, suggests not a deterritorialization of politics but a shift in boundaries and a reconstitution of what are seen as legitimate bases for boundary construction, where race, religious affiliation, economic interests and ethnicity compete with nationalism. Regional blocs are certainly key actors in the negotiation of intellectual property rules, and, as this chapter will argue, regional blocs are often the arena where rules are managed and enforced by firms or groups of firms, rather than by either the nation-state or an all-embracing globalized system. But there is no one exclusive system of IPRs. This diversity is useful to the most powerful, providing a framework within which interests can compete effectively on some agendas while exercising a largely unquestioned control in others.

One starting-point for this analysis, in the spirit of exploring points of contact between political geography and international relations, is to consider the way in which relations between concepts of space and of territory are constructed. Schatzki (1991) has proposed an individualist interpretation of spatiality, while Harvey (1990), for example, has explored the argument that space and time are essentially socially constructed: 'attachment to a certain conception of space and time is a (collective) political decision' (ibid.: 432). Political geography relates imagined realities to economic and social conditions including especially the capitalist system which make certain kinds of realities probable or possible. Space may be territorial, and it may well have some links to territory – not the same thing. But space may also in common usage (among academics) be a looser idea than this, and not tied to three-dimensional physical space. Space implies relative distance or proximity, but it also implies a structure which embodies political relationships, by which is understood power relations. Thus writers on the European Community have talked of a common social space or a common industrial space, a conception which excludes certain people in the first case or certain firms in the second. European Union policies on innovative technologies have focused around the idea of the creation of unique spaces for particular purposes, as many examples show in official policy proposals (see Commission of the European Community, 1990). This idea of space focuses on particular policy arenas, but it implies a set of cultural claims which have evolved in a particular history. They are linked to a territory – the Twelve or whatever – but they are not boundaried only by that territory. The 'Common European Home' and the 'European Economic Space' imply in their respective ways not only a territory, but also an interior mental space and propose a form of privileged space beyond the limits of the formally constituted political territory of the EU. This may be seen as an assertion of a traditional European identity or as a project to reassert European colonial dominance (or perhaps as both); but it is not a deterritorialization of politics. The project for the creation of a European Union itself is mapped out in the Maastricht Treaty in terms of three parallel but separate areas of activity which create jurisdiction and legal competence, the European Community, the Common Foreign and Security Policy, and intergovernmental co-operation in domestic policy and intelligence-related activities. These are linked to territory but are not purely territorial. In each case political power is distributed in certain ways among the main EU institutions and between the EU institutions and its citizens, companies, networks, private institutions and member states.

There may be a problem here not so much between political geographers and international relationists as between the ways in which the word 'space' and 'espace' are used in English and French. For there has been an inter-change between English and French discourse which has involved an importing of French usage into English. Many of the more abstract, deterri-torialized uses of 'space' in English owe much to a borrowing from French, where the noun is used at a different level of abstraction, as a careful reading of the relevant entry in Larousse suggests. French political scientists have talked about intellectual space or industrial space, etc. with a freedom which Anglo-American writers have borrowed. This usage has clearly shaped the language of EC/EU policy. It also shapes the language of political geography. Harvey (1990), for example, is clearly influenced in part by this possibility of the deterritorialization of space, or at least by the idea that the relationship between space and territory is a key problematic for political geographers. This idea is explored in much greater depth and with much greater sophisti-cation by Lefebvre (1991) in an influential text published originally in French and translated into English only recently:

> We are confronted not by one social space but by many – indeed by an unlimited multiplicity or uncountable set of social spaces which we refer to generically as 'social space'. No space disappears in the course of growth and development: *the worldwide does not abolish the local*. This is not a consequence of the law of uneven development, but a law of its own right. The inter-twinement of social spaces is also a law. Considered in isolation, such spaces are mere abstractions. As concrete abstractions, however, they attain 'real' existence by virtue of networks and pathways, by virtue of bunches or clusters of relationships. Instances of this are the worldwide networks of communica-tions, exchange and knowledge ... thus social space ... emerged in all its diversity – and with a structure far more reminiscent of flaky *mille-feuille* pastry than of homogenous and isotropic space of classical (Euclidean/Cartesian) geometry. (Lefebvre, 1991: 86)

He goes on to argue that an understanding of the social distribution of power, knowledge and ideology requires a critique of space, which is to say a critique of the production of space over time and in diverse particular contexts (ibid.: 92ff.). This sense of the possibility of political power being invested in diverse non-linear spatial forms has shaped the questions which this paper tries to ask (cf. also Walker, 1993, on territory, sovereignty and authority).

Two specific examples develop this. Langdale (1989) has looked at the way in which technological innovation in networked communications recreates the space in which business activity takes place, arguing that technology creates new opportunities for firms to collaborate and to compete at the same time. Electronic media do not merely appear to change space and time; they actually do change it radically in a way which redistributes advantages and opportunities, and which over time is built into people's unspoken operating assumptions. The Italian scholars Belandi and Romagnoli (1991), looking at the changing nature of industrial organization in a major textile city in the 1990s, argue that changed economic relations create changed structures of political networks and so transform the spatial reality within which everyone in the city lives and works. The city (in their case Prato) has an economic and political existence as a whole in the imagination of its inhabitants which they articulate and reproduce through their daily lives. But changes in external conditions and in available technologies will transform aspects of the economy so as to transform the nature of the city as an industrial district. For Belandi and Romagnoli, as for Lefebvre in his more abstract study, space is created and recreated by people, and in consequence there is no one space, but a series of overlapping and interleaving spaces. This is equally, it can be argued, the case where intellectual property rules reproduce, reflect but also create structures of space which have a deep political resonance to which all actors in the global political economy must respond. The relationship between space, territory and power is central to the working of intellectual property rules: thus IPRs create a differentiated space in the global economy.

Knowledge as power in political space

Susan Strange (1988) has argued that the international political economy is characterized by a knowledge structure which is increasingly important. The initial insight that knowledge in international relations is distributed unevenly, that it structures whole areas of relationships, and that it is constitutive of a global political economy, is important. Strange sees knowledge as broadly defined. Technology (as know-how, as technique, as culture, as institutionally embedded capacity to reshape the environment) is a part of the knowledge structure, while technology (in the sense of information systems) gives some actors the ability to access this technology not only to use it and exploit its potential, but also to deny it to others. In the same way, intellectual property rules are a control of knowledge, of who gets it and how they can use it. This control is only possible because certain technologies (i.e. expert systems, telecommunications satellites and EDI) facilitate the necessary management of information at a global level.

Intellectual property rules create a structure of political space which is of the greatest importance in advanced technology industries. They create private property rights within a defined area over a defined category of ideas. It follows from this that the reconstitution of intellectual property rules recreates political space. It both recreates a structure of power and at the same time gives power to certain actors or institutions in the form of capabilities and structural position at the expense of other actors. IPRs have been traditionally understood as territorial. For one thing, they reflect the jurisdiction of state courts, and jurisdiction, to be clear, must apply in a defined territory where enforcement or other remedies are available. IPRs have traditionally depended on the state for enforcement and for precise definition through the legal process. But they have more recently been increasingly detached from the individual state through international agreements including those which create extra-territorial rights, and are now largely policed by corporations and their lawyers or by international institutions. These detailed patterns of social relations are most often the subject of inter-corporate negotiations backed up by the possibility of court action (and the potential threat of enormous legal expenses). They control the definition as well as the management of major cultural and legal spaces, which may overlap and often now focus on products or core technologies rather than on particular territories (i.e., biotechnology). This is an aspect of the phenomenon that has come to be called globalization.

Globalization is a central but contested concept in the emerging international relations agenda. If there is a shift from the 'international' to the 'global' in international relations, it may involve a changing structure of political space, an obsolescence of established territorialities, or a compression of political space (Schott, 1993; Smith, 1993). Although globalization may sometimes be taken to indicate a homogenization of international relations – and perhaps there are occasions when cultural homogenization genuinely takes place – globalization processes in international relations are some form of reconstitution of difference rather than a homogenization. Whatever form they take, they shift or reupholster existing power relations much more often than they make any radical change in them (the point is developed in Farrands and Talalay, 1994). Globalization changes relationships. Multinational business provides a principal agent of globalization and becomes the object of globalizing forces as innovation changes the structure of company activity (Dunning, 1994). As Lefebvre suggests, the 'new' spatial

patterns overlay older ones without necessarily destroying them (1991: 84). Stopford and Strange (1991: 34ff., 71ff.) emphasize the importance of technological change as a force for change in the global economy producing impacts which in turn shape political change. If we see technology as more than just a series of techniques, then the processes which accompany technological change form part of an intricate process of interaction in which culture and beliefs as well as past practices, know-how and formal knowledge combine.

Intellectual property as a form of power

We tend to see intellectual property as a boringly technical, specialized area. But if critical social theory teaches anything at all, it is that we should start to be interested in areas which are represented in general as boring, technical and therefore not for us, when they are also arenas of very considerable power. We have to ask how this power is constituted, who uses it and benefits from it, and who is excluded from it, how and why. An underpinning of this argument is the common assumption of any capitalist economy, that private ownership is a core principal and that it can and should be extended into any possible area of life. IPRs can be seen as a liberalizing influence, but historically they have also been a mercantilist influence. Patenting systems are supposed to open a market for ideas, but they were originally intended to be restrictive. National patent offices in countries such as Britain and France were created to protect the national body of knowledge (under protest from liberals) only when German science took a dominant position in the nineteenth century. Liberal writers such as Parrinder (1993) continue today to maintain that IPRs can restrict trade and provide a covert form of protection. At one level, IPRs establish a balance between the individual rights of property holders and their users. Their purpose is not to protect secrecy. If firms or inventors wish to keep their discoveries secret, they do not publicize their nature or, often, even their existence by patenting them. Secret military inventions have very rarely been patented. This was, for example, for a long time the case with microwave communications, and as a result of the failure to patent discoveries made by government researchers at the Malvern radar and radio research centre, British firms were unable to capitalize on the civil applications of a large publicly funded investment. At this level, IPRs reflect a view of a balance of interests between the diffusion of a technology, which is generally held to benefit the national economy as a whole, and the rights to recover profits from an investment which provides an incentive to invest and innovate on the part of individuals and companies (Olleros, 1984).

At a second level, IPRs organize relations between the rival states and rival firms which compete in world markets. The major innovators are large firms and large government-funded institutions. It is generally the case that large firms control the setting of standards in their industry, as is certainly the case in computing, biotechnology and pharmaceuticals, for example. Technological competition is a basic tool of corporate strategy, and technological advantages are to be sought through the deployment of technologies (Porter, 1983). These may create defensive barriers to entry directed against other firms, or they may be means of gaining high ground in competition. They may also provide an issue around which collaborative interests between companies cluster: there has been a steady growth of inter-firm collaboration since the 1980s for reasons connected with technology sharing and the creation of intellectual property managing blocs. Some government agencies appear to be directly involved, but for the most part collaborative groupings are managed by companies, which are often able to gain exclusions from anti-trust or anti-monopoly controls where they are promoting technological advantage. Here, too, key actors in the global political economy are reconstituting space through their choices and behaviour, and often on a strictly non-territorial basis. The setting of common standards in these frameworks is often dependent on technical advice from trade associations. This process is relatively transparent in the USA, where both the ITC and the Office of Technology Assessment are highly porous to industrial influence, but more opaque elsewhere, including in the European Union, where a host of technical committees dominate agenda setting, common standards negotiations, trade regulation, and the management of derogations from competition rules. These technical committees represent in almost all cases a combination of bureaucratic and industrial interests whose 'technical' expertise goes substantially unchallenged in the political arena. Technical committees in the EU are dominated by the small number of major global players, and tend to exclude the interests of smaller firms as well as consumers or environmental interests.

Although there are tendencies to merge IPRs into a single framework, and although liberal argument tends towards a unification of IPRs, they remain diverse. There are different, partially overlapping IPRs. Foray (1993) has considered the possibility of an integration of intellectual property regimes. He points out that IPRs serve particular interests in the various states that participate in them, and reflect the level of development of key companies and their strategic position in the world economy. In consequence, he argues, an integration of IPRs into a single structure is implausible politically. It would be against the interest of key players. However much leading companies and their client governments claim to want a more integrated system in some respects, they are not seeking the total integration of a global system. The rhetoric of integration can be used to suppress opposition from outside the domain of the established players without any serious attempt to follow it consistently. Kendall (1991) and Mill (1993) suggest that a more integrated system of IPRs is necessary within the European economic space if the Single Market is to work, but this does not argue for a genuinely global single IPR, and a careful reading suggests that they are looking for more integration – but by no means 'total' integration – in the EU itself.

At a third level, one which legal analysis neglects, IPRs distribute power between cultures and forms of societies. They disadvantage groups which do not have access to lawyers and techniques for asserting rights much as other technical–rational systems do. They give legitimacy to groups and interests which can sustain certain kinds of arguments in certain privileged kinds of language. The US company which learned traditional Indian clothing manufacturing techniques, took them home and perfected them in an industrial system, patenting them in the USA, illustrates this. They then went back to India, where the techniques were established as so much a part of tradition that they were unpatented (and in Indian national law, un-patentable because inalienable by any individual or firm). The firm appealed to the Indian national courts to enforce international law, because the US patent was enforceable in international law. They argued that the Indian government had conceded this right in agreeing to the GATT treaty, a step which led to rioting and violent outbursts against the Indian government as well as against the USA and the GATT treaty. Comparable issues over biodiversity and the Rio Summit have also brought conflict between tradi-tional peoples and established powers. The overall point here is that the extension of IPRs in the GATT is a devastating political change which increases inequalities in the international system quite markedly. It is analogous to the ending of traditional rights of hunting, wood-gathering and grazing involved in the enclosures of common land in eighteenth-century England which led to a wave of rural violence which was characterized as criminal by those who controlled the definition of crime, but which was more a popular resistance, as Thompson (1975) has shown.

The new intellectual property agenda

There is therefore no single intellectual property regime in the international political system. Different rules cover different areas – patents and copyright, licensing, and so on – and have their origins in different national jurisdic-tions and international agreements. Together, they constitute a system of governance in which a wide variety of stakeholders have some interest in stable management. That is to say that control, legitimation and regulation are managed by a variety of interests only some of which are governments. Because US patent law has been reputed to be more effectively enforced than any other in the last fifty years, firms and research institutions have learned to patent discoveries in the USA (Pavitt, 1982). The US legal and political system allows for strong forms of extraterritorial intervention in these questions. But this system of governance is regulated and controlled by firms to an extent not generally recognized. IPRs are the outcome of interactions within networks of firms. The pursuit of common standards is a process where firms stake out the grounds for the alliances they would like to create. The 'technical' rationality involved in this way of thinking has been the subject of strong criticism in analyses of issues such as global warming, deforestation and the environment, but, except for the issues surrounding biodiversity (Acharya, 1991), it has been little explored in the context of IPRs.

Among the changes in international relations in the last decade has been a new emphasis on IPRs in the agenda (Litman, 1989; Dhanjee and de Chazournes, 1993). This puts an important emphasis on the consequences of technological change. The development of rapid copying systems calls into question the established rules. Electronic data transmission, satellite broadcasting and rapid broadband telecommunications systems reshape the agenda. But other changes have a more problematic impact. Copyright applies to computer software, patenting to hardware. But software has been increasingly embedded in chips as their capacity has grown. The changing technology of computer chips and of chip manufacturing systems has undermined what used to be seen as a relatively solid boundary between what could be copyrighted and what could be patented. It has produced a confusion which international law and international institutions find difficult to resolve. Copyright applies for fifty years from the death of the author; patents last for between eight and twenty years depending on what is patented and where. There is a continuing focus on fraud in the new agenda because it enables the dominant countries to penetrate and control aspects of developing country domestic economies – and their domestic space. Key centres of software copyright fraud include the well-educated but poor societies of India, Thailand and Taiwan. What is not on the 'new agenda' – conventionally, at least – is the question of how the handling of these problems might restructure power and redistribute access to knowledge (Smith, 1993). The new agenda is an extension of the already considerable influence of dominant powers in the global knowledge structure.

A focus on IPRs had scarcely figured in GATT talks before 1986 (Winham, 1986). The USA initiated a further round of GATT talks through the Punta del Este meeting which started the Uruguay Round in 1986. Why did the USA move to restart trade talks so quickly and why did they put intellectual property as a priority when it was outside the traditionally established GATT agenda? Meessen (1987) presents an unconvincing argument that technical change alone created the piracy threat. These were, and are, real problems, but they do not explain the urgency and importance which these issues assumed. It is perhaps more plausible to argue that US interests changed. US trade policy, always dependent on corporate and political coalitions, has become increasingly protectionist as the USA has lost its dominant world position. The rhetoric of the end of the Cold War, including the language of 'economic security' and 'strategic industrial policy', has been directed towards this end, and the focus on IPRs has been a specific instrument to achieve it.

Intellectual property rights in biotechnology

IPRs occupy a particular place in the development of biotechnology which helps one to focus on many of the issues raised in this paper (Turner, 1994). There are now a number of partially overlapping regimes for the control of knowledge in pharmaceuticals, genetic engineering, animal and human biotechnology and fermentation. These regimes constitute structures of political and legal space, separately for the USA and the EU. Licensing agreements create their own space. But regardless of where licences are held, what is often key to understanding their effect is to ask in which courts they may be enforced, often in US courts. US patent holders (including non-US firms) retain the majority of genetic engineering patents. Their influence extends outside the territorial space of the United States. Acharya (1991) shows how this tends to exclude many interests with the effect of reducing the ecological resources of disadvantaged peoples. Bizley (1991) suggests that the development of animal biotechnology in Europe is disadvantaged as a result of a relatively weak IPR which discourages investment, although Gugerell (1994) has defended the economic efficiency of European patent legislation. What is clear is that there are distinctive legal and political economy spaces delineated by the IPRs. As important as the theoretical content of rules about IPRs is the context in which they are implemented. Testing rules for biotechnology products have limited the capacity of firms to exploit discoveries, especially because of public concern. This has been most marked in Northern Europe and in particular states in the USA (Kendall, 1994). The lack of a common global structure of IPRs creates spatial patterns whereby gains, risks and costs are distributed across the developed economies and between the developed and developing economies. The detailed, everyday interaction in the market (cf. Wheale and McNally, 1986; Gallois, 1991) reproduces these spaces and in the process confirms or reconfigures the distribution of power and capability which they embody. Companies plan strategies to take account of these patterns (Kendall, 1991; Scott-Ram, 1994). Individual state territories do not alone control their destinies, and regional bodies are growing in power, but to suggest that there has been a wholesale deterritorialization of power and control in biotechnology would be wrong.

Conclusions

Intellectual property rules create and reproduce political space and provide an arena in which important conflicts emerge between states, companies and technologies and between regional bloc interests. The impact on those excluded from the status of major stakeholder is also, in a different way, likely to be considerable. To operate such a system requires a very high level of co-operation, and the systems of governance which have evolved to manage and maintain this co-operation provide a compelling locus of power and authority. But this co-operation is neither global nor harmonious. It embodies a set of very specific interests. These interests are not those either of states or of firms alone; but the boundaries between the state and the firm are as problematic as the boundaries among states or between firms. The study of IPRs also points to the conclusion that there is a new diversity within the emerging international system which much prevailing theory can cope with at best only with great difficulty. Emergent regional blocs are important here. National governments retain the capacity to move resources and define agendas powerfully, but are at the same time channels for other interests. There is very little evidence that the politics of IPRs has shifted wholly away from a territorial basis. But the territorial bases around which IPRs are constituted are uncertain and overlapping, highly contentious in law and quite different both from that which one would anticipate working from the 'Westphalia' model of uniquely sovereign territorial states and from that one would expect if one believed the rhetoric of 'globalization' as a uniform process of homogenization. International relations is both more difficult and more interesting than those models would suggest. But it requires at the least a greater sensibility to spatial and territorial issues than is usual amongst international relationists. And it demands a greater awareness not just of power structures but also of how they are articulated and managed through the interaction of institutional and legal frameworks than political geography often achieves. Linking international relations and geography does not offer an academic marriage made in heaven, but it does at least propose a useful mutually critical cohabitation.

References

Acharya, R. (1991) Patenting of biotechnology: GATT and the erosion of the world's biodiversity, *Journal of World Trade Law*, **25**(3), 71–87.

Belandi, M. and Romagnoli, M. (1991) Le città tessili e le sfide del cambiamento, unpublished paper, Istituto di Ricerche e Interventi Sociali (IRIS), Prato, Convegno Internazionale di Studi, conference organized by the Economics and Business Faculty, University of Florence, 22–23 November 1991.

Bizley, R. E. (1991) Animal patents in Europe, *Chemistry and Industry*, 15 July 1991, 505–7.

Commission of the European Community (CEC) (1990) *Eurotecnet Information Package*, action programme to promote innovation in the field of vocational training resulting from technological change in the European Community, Brussels, Commission of the European Community.

Dhanjee, R. and de Chazournes, L. B. (1993) Trade related aspects of intellectual property rights: objectives, approaches and basic principles of the GATT and of intellectual property conventions, *Journal of World Trade*, **24**, 3–15.

Dunning, J. (1994) Multinational enterprises and the globalization of innovatory capacity, *Research Policy*, **23**, 67–88.

Farrands, C. and Talalay, M. (1994) Globalization, technological change and international political economy, unpublished paper delivered to the Annual ISA Convention, Washington, DC, March/April.

Foray, D. (1993) Feasibility of a single regime of intellectual property rights, in M. Humbert (ed.), *The Impact of Globalization on Europe's Firms and Industries*, London, Pinter, pp. 85–96.

Gallois, D. (1991) Le choix européen: les stratégies agroalimentaires, *Le Monde*, 27 September.

Gugerell, C. (1994) Is European patent law suitable to provide effective protection for future products?, in V. Kendall (ed.), *Biotechnology Products*, EPLC Pharma Law Report no. 9, March.

Harvey, D. (1990) Between space and time: reflections on the geographical imagination, *Annals of the Association of American Geographers*, **80**(3), 418–34.

Kendall, V. (1991) Protecting intellectual property in a single market, *European Trends*, **4**, 43–7.

Kendall, V. (1994) *Biotechnology Products*, EPLC Pharma Law Report no. 9, March, London, EPLC Ltd.

Langdale, J. V. (1989) The geography of international business telecommunications: the role of leased networks, *Annals of the Association of American Geographers*, **79**(4), 501–22.

Lefebvre, H. (1991) *The Production of Space*, Oxford, Blackwell.

Litman, J. (1989) Copyright legislation and technological change, *Oregon Law Review*, **68**(275), 423–509.

Meessen, K. M. (1987) Intellectual property rights in international trade, *Journal of World Trade Law*, **21**(1), 67–74.

Mill, J. (1993) Knowledge sans frontières, *New Scientist*, 6 November.

Olleros, F.-J. (1984) *The Process Life Cycle and the Technological and Competitive Evolution of Industries*, Les Cahiers du CETAI, no. 84–12, November, Montreal, Université du Montréal.

Parrinder, P. (1993) The dead hand of European copyright, *European Intellectual Property Review*, **11**, 391–3.

Pavitt, K. (1982) R & D, patenting and innovative activities: a statistical exploration, *Research Policy*, **11**, 33–51.

Porter, M. (1983) The technological dimension of competitive strategy, in R. S. Rosenbloom (ed.), *Research on Technological Innovation, Management and Policy*, vol. 1, Greenwich, CT, JAI Press, pp. 1–34.

Ray, G. F. (1979) Research policy and industrial materials, *Research Policy*, **8**, 80–92.

Reddy, N. M. and Zhao, L. (1990) International technology transfer: a review, *Research Policy*, **19**, 285–307.

Schatzki, T. R. (1991) Spatial ontology and explanation, *Annals of the Association of American Geographers*, **81**(4), 650–70.

Schott, T. (1993) World science: globalization of institutions and participation, *Science, Technology and Human Values*, **18**(2), Spring, 196–208.

Scott-Ram, N. (1994) Biotechnology and intellectual property, in V. Kendall (ed.), *Biotechnology Products*, EPLC Pharma Law Report no. 9, March.

Seyoum, B. (1993) Property rights versus public welfare in the protection of trade secrets in developing countries, *International Trade Journal*, **7**(3), Spring, 341–59.

Smith, D. A. (1993) Technology and the modern world system: some reflections, *Science, Technology and Society*, **18**(2), Spring, 186–95.

Stone, P. (1987) Patent and knowhow licensing, *European Trends*, **4**, 60–5.

Stone, P. (1989) Block exemption for knowhow licences, *European Trends*, **2**, 58–61.

Stopford, J. and Strange, S. (1991) *Rival States, Rival Firms*, Cambridge, Cambridge University Press.

Strange, S. (1988) *States and Markets*, London, Pinter.

Strange, S. (1994) Rethinking structural change in the international political economy: states, firms and diplomacy, in R. Stubbs and G. Underhill (eds), *Political Economy and the Changing Global Order*, London, Macmillan.

Thompson, E. P. (1975) *Whigs and Hunters: The Origin of the Black Act*, London, Allen Lane.

Turner, M. (1994) Legal protection for biotechnological inventions, in V. Kendall (ed.), *Biotechnology Products*, EPLC Pharma Law Report no. 9, March.

US National Research Council, *Global Dimensions of Intellectual Property Rights in Science and Technology*, Washington, DC, National Academy Press.

Walker, R. J. B. (1993) *Inside/Outside: International Relations as Political Theory*, Cambridge, Cambridge University Press.

Waltz, K. N. (1993) The emerging structure of international politics, *International Security*, **18**(2), Fall, 44–79.

Wheale, P. R. and McNally, R. M. (1986) Patent trend analysis: the case of microgenetic engineering, *Futures*, October, 638–57.

Winham, G. R. (1986) *International Trade and the Tokyo Round*, Princeton, Princeton University Press.

Part 3

Trading Places or Gendering the Global

14

An International Political Economy of Sex?[1]

JAN JINDY PETTMAN

This chapter addresses the implications of women as bearers of sex, of women's bodies being sexualized (and presumed available for men's sex and service) and the dangers facing women in an international context. These dangers are especially threatening when women are away from their own countries, or otherwise 'out of place'. They are more likely to be thus viewed in the face of the current intensified globalization and restructuring of the international political economy, including, for example, migrant labour in internationalized/racialized domestic service, mail-order brides, sex tourism and militarized prostitution. This chapter explores the dangers in these contemporary forms of international traffic, and asks whether this analysis supports the notion of an international political economy of sex.

Women 'out of place'

The domestication of women and their containment in the private sphere writes them out of the public–political sphere, such that women's appearance and performance in public space can itself be seen as a transgression, and so 'invite' sexual approach or attack. Security may be sought through the protection of a man, though the cost of protection may be possession and control. Moreover, a woman may even be threatened by her protector – there is not necessarily safety at home.

There is a close, though by no means fixed or uncontested, connection between the social control of women and violence against them, and between these and the wider structures of gender/ed power. Women are kept resourceless or in their place at least in part through the threat or act of violence (Hanmer, 1989; Kelkar, 1992). Violence is a part of the domestication of women, whereby they learn to live with their oppression, and so guarantee men's access to their bodies, and to their labour.

The domestication of women naturalizes men's sex right to women's bodies, labour and children. This 'right' is related in different ways to the construction of women/women's bodies as the bearers of sex: women are, and are for (heterosexual) sex (Brown, 1987). Women are there to service men, providing domestic and sexual labour, which is assumed to be a labour of love. The close associations of women, bodies, sex and service to men means that women are seen as sexed beings, and that women's labour, too, is frequently sexualized.

Women are vulnerable to body policing and to violence if they trangress the public/private boundary or appear unruly or out of (men's) control. They are also vulnerable in terms of their association with another kind of boundary, that drawn around different political collectivities for the purposes of inclusion or exclusion (Yuval-Davis and Anthias, 1989: Pettman, forthcoming a). They are frequently constructed as markers of difference, and as reproducers, both physically and culturally, of political collectivities. Consequently their sexuality, fertility and relations with others, especially with other group men, are guarded, especially in times of mobilization or conflict along the boundary lines. As family, community or national 'mothers', women may be treated as their men's and community's possessions or property, and so be punished for any suspected boundary transgressions or for 'inappropriate' or culturally inauthentic behaviour (Hendessi, 1990; Bhabha, 1993).

Rape and sexual intimidation and harassment are regularly used against women, not only in identity conflicts, but because those women are where they are not supposed to be. This may be read as availability, or as transgression of men's social space. Stepping out of place or out of line may be taken as having provoked the violence, as having 'asked for it'. Here we note the apparent contradiction in the routine invisibility and yet at times hypervisibility of women (and of gay and/or racialized men) who may then experience harassment and violence in public places. This suggests that public space is male, heterosexual and, in First World states, white. Violence demonstrates the boundaries of belonging, as well as who owns the territory.

Many women in very different cultures and social spaces curtail their own movements, clothing, relations, in attempts to protect themselves (Pain, 1991; Carillo, 1993). There is a political geography of gender which is universal, although it takes specific socio-cultural form in different times and spaces. Some feminist geographers map a 'geography of women's fear' in Western states (Pain, 1991). Daphne Spain (1993) argues that there is a direct correlation between women's spatial segregation and their status in different places, and feminist anthropologists and others test these associations. So ideologies of control, seclusion, honour and shame determine women's mobility and access to resources and opportunities (Afshar and Agarwal, 1989). Class is a crucial component in these configurations. For example, upper-caste Indian women and upper-class Bangladeshi women are more tightly controlled and contained than other women; the poorest women may be the most free to move and work outside their home, under urgent economic compulsion. But these women are seen as outside protection, and so again made vulnerable (Ram in Afshar and Agarwal, 1989; Rozario, 1992). Male kin may project resentment and suspicion especially at women's contacts with non-kin men. Webs of connection between marriage, kin, community and control recur here, explored early on by Gayle Rubin (1975), as a political economy of the sex/gender system (but see Rubin's rethinking, 1993). Seclusion, chaperonage and segregation are part of the surveillance of women and the disciplining of women's sexuality. They relate to the maintenance of family and community honour and status, and competition for resources. Patriarchal policing joins with the border patrols of the nation/race/community, marked on the bodies of women.

Women on the move

Many women and girls are no longer where they are supposed to be, forced or pressured or choosing to move, in some cases doing so to get away from home. Many are displaced by wars, communal or political, including state, violence. Women and children make up the vast majority of refugees. Other women move, more or less freely, subject to and acting upon a range of pushes and pulls which constitute another aspect of the international political economy of gender, the changing sexual division of labour. In some of its more dangerous forms it is not only gender but sex that informs and inflames this division.

The globalization that witnesses the rapid mobility of capital and transnational corporations also relies upon cheap labour, including labour migrants (see Pellerin, this volume). Labour migration over the last decade especially has been increasingly female. Many women are on the move, from countryside to town, town to city or capital or military base, to export-processing zone. Thus labour migrants go from poorer states like Sri Lanka and the Philippines to oil-rich Middle East states, to Japan, Hong Kong and Singapore (Heyzer *et al.*, 1994). Many still go from poorer Asian and North African states to Europe; and many others to the USA from other states of the Americas. These movements reflect the contemporary international hierarchy of states and regions. They also reflect the impact of international processes and relations, from development to international debt and structural adjustment policies (Afshar and Dennis, 1992). Class and region compound the effects of economic dislocation, poverty and changing patterns in the sexual division of labour and the nature of women's work.

Women's labour is also mediated by age and stage in the lifecycle, such that the changing international division of labour exploits many very young women, 'ill-educated teenagers' (Standing, 1992: 368). Girls labour in homes, subsistence and other types of farming, provide child care and nursing. There is in some countries extensive illicit trade in children for factory, domestic and sex work. Recruitment procedures include buying children from impoverished parents or those unable to repay debts, making them bonded labour, working to pay off the debt, in a trade in bodies that is painful for both the labourers and relinquishing parents. Girl children's vulnerability in these exchanges is intensified through widespread, though regionally and culturally specific devaluation, which also manifests itself in high rates of female foeticide and infanticide, and in higher rates of girl child mortality through systematic lack of care and unequal access to food and health care (Batou, 1991; Carillo, 1993; Oldenburg, 1992).

The changing international division of labour is also racialized, and women's and children's nationality, ethnicity and citizenship become part of the equation, often placing them at further risk. This is so for older and, more recently, minority workers in First and Third World states, and for recent labour migrants in many different parts of the globe. Women labour migrants may travel alone, or as part of a recruitment package. They often find themselves in situations where women abroad are again beyond the bounds of protection. This is frequently compounded by racialized or culturalized minority status, and insecure residence and employment rights. This is particularly the case where they are engaged in two of the most significant sectors of women's foreign work: 'domestic service' and 'entertainment'.

Internationalized domestic service and politics

Domestic service is a problematic arena for feminists, happening as it does within (other people's) homes, where the employer or daily superviser is often another woman. The 'domestic' is usually from another class and often from a different racialized or culturalized nationality from the woman in whose service she works. In situations of unequal power relations and of highly personalized and intimate relations, the question arises whether 'servants [are] ever sisters' (Gaitskell, 1982).

Domestic service has long been the site for 'close encounters' between colonizing and colonizer women. Colonized women have provided domestic labour and child care in white households, despite the common characterization of them as unclean, unfit and irresponsible mothers. In Australia, for example, many Aboriginal 'half-caste' girls have been seized from their families, institutionalized and trained as domestic servants (Tucker, 1987; Ward, 1988; Huggins, 1987). Other examples of racialized domestic service include the stereotyped mammy of the slave and post-slavery US South (Rollins, 1985), the black maids of white madams in South Africa (Cock,

1989), and the African–American maids and now the Central or South American nannies in contemporary USA (Tinsman, 1992). Their labour makes them party to others' family secrets, and thus vulnerable to sexual and other abuse and exploitation. These relations saturate politics among women, as other women's domestic labour permit some women, including some feminists, to go out to work and to pursue other interests and causes. This is a reminder that much feminist writing on 'care' assumes that domestic and reproductive labour is provided by women of the family working for love, so erasing the widespread provision of care and labour in dominant group or wealthier homes by poorer and/or racialized women (Graham, 1991). White First World/black Third World dichotomies are misleading here, as, for example, poor Asian country domestics allow élite countrywomen and some East Asian and Middle East women certain domestic freedoms.

Nowadays a significant part of international labour migration is in the form of those going to domestic service – largely unnoticed by most IR and IPE commentators until the Iraqi invasion of Kuwait drew international media attention to their plight (Enloe, 1990b). Shifts in international politics and the international political economy are evident in the ebb and flow of this trade. Thus Filipina maids go to Hong Kong, Japan, Jordan, Syria and Saudi Arabia in large numbers as part of an international trade estimated to involve between 1 and 1.7 million Asian women domestic workers. Here distinctions need to be made between those states and households where home state women can take up paid work outside the home while 'foreign' domestic workers do family and household labour and those households in some Gulf states, for example, where local women remain at home, and the use of foreign domestic labour adds to family prestige, as well as supporting local women in their reproductive labour. In both cases, cheap foreign 'maid' labour has the effect of reinforcing the gendered division of domestic labour and relieving the pressure on states to take responsibility for child care and social welfare (Heyzer and Wee in Heyzer, 1994: 44).

Domestic service is not a marginal or occasional economic category. In 1986, paid household service in Latin American countries accounted for between 30 and 70 per cent of non-agricultural women workers. In the 1980s in the USA it was the fastest-growing employment sector for immigrant women. We were reminded of this trade in the recent 'nanny wars' story surrounding the Clinton administration (*New Republic*, 15 February 1993, p. 13) where undocumented workers became an issue between different racialized groups when it was suggested that some African and Hispanic Americans were fearful of losing work to 'aliens'. These incidents also point to the growing significance of a globalized underground economy and of a racialized underclass whose illegal or temporary status places them in particular dependence on their employers, without union or advocacy support and fearful of state agent attention (Sivanandan, 1989; Abella, 1991: 73).

In an increasingly regional and globalized market, many women cross state borders in search of work that is simply not available or even more poorly paid at home. But the international traffic in women's labour and bodies is also often sponsored or at least condoned by their home states (Palma-Beltran, 1992). The 'export of women' from states like the Philippines, Indonesia and Sri Lanka is part of the international politics of debt, and of poorer states' search for hard currency in the form of remittances, as well as reflecting lack of employment opportunities at home. The Philippines receives an estimated US$3 billion in remittances from overseas workers; Bangladeshi workers sent US$771 million home in 1989, accounting for 60 per cent of the year's merchandise crop (Heyzer, 1994: 13). Poor state dependence on remittances compounds domestic workers' vulnerability through lack of protection from their embassies, whose responsibility to safeguard their nationals' interests is compromised by concern to maintain the wider trade and aid from these richer states (Humphrey, 1991). It also affects the status and image of the sending states, and underlines the growing power and wealth differences between states internationally and in the region. This is dramatically illustrated in relative income per head in 1992 of US$680 for sending countries and US$10,376 for receiving countries of those engaged in the international trade in Asian domestic workers (Heyzer, 1994: xxiii).

Domestic service is internationalized/racialized not only in the origins and different backgrounds of the 'serving' women, but in the construction of different racialized gender stereotypes of women from different countries. Hence preferences in the USA for maids from Central and South American states rather than African–American and local Hispanic communities; and in Jordan for the lighter-skinned and (more likely) English-speaking Filipinas as against Sri Lankan maids (Humphrey, 1991). Women from sending countries are associated with servant status, and are locked dangerously into racialized stereotypes as passive, accommodating or exotic, aggravating the already sexualized nature and associations of domestic work.

'Domestic service' is frequently sexualized, even before one adds the compounding effects of racism. Here arise questions about women's bodies, of pollution, sex and danger. Heidi Tinsman (1992) explores the assumed connections between domestic service and sexual availability, where the domestic labourer is seen to have sold her body and not just her labour, and where male domination asserts authority over dependants and servants, especially women. The result is 'sorry tales and strange moralizing' (p. 50), where any kind of privacy, respect or care is capriciously dependent on the good will of the man and, often, the woman of the house. Racialized gender stereotypes which construct women as promiscuous or exotic heighten the danger and are mobilized to blame the victim. Tensions may be caused between the worker and a jealous or fearful wife, who may be a complicit or active policer of race-related sexual boundaries.

The boundaries between different categories of female labour migration and women's position within them are not necessarily clear. 'Entertainers' is often a transit category to or euphemism for prostitution. Some 286,000 Filipinas and some 50,000 Thai women entered Japan as entertainers between 1988 and 1992. They are particularly vulnerable as young women, in jobs that are sex-related, who frequently become overstayers, in a country which is both largely unknown to them and where they are subjected to gendered racialized stereotyping and treatment (David, 1992). This in turn affects labour migrants in more 'respectable' jobs, as, for example, Filipina maids who avoid contact with or the appearance of being 'entertainers'.

'Mail-order brides'

Much has been written about domestic labour in general, about the marriage contract as a work contract (Oakley, 1974), and about the frequent assumption that women's work in the care and servicing of men and children is a labour of love. While many, including a fair number of feminists, might wish to retain notions of marriage or households based on love and fair work practices, marriage's dubious sexual politics and the common choice of wives who are younger, smaller and with less power and status do little to encourage this optimism. This is especially so when marriages are not only across racialized/nationality lines, but deliberately sought there by men looking for 'other' women as better wives.

There is now a significant international trade in wives, another part of the international traffic in women, captured in the phrase 'mail-order brides'. Here again women become tradeable commodities, as evidenced by an Australian man's book which offered men advice on 'How to marry a female ... virgin, Where to find them, How to meet them and How much it will cost to bring them to Australia' from the Philippines (Morgan, 1993). Some who have acquired brides assume rights that may stifle any rights or choices for those women. Here the international context is introduced whereby women are brought from outside the man's state across international borders. This affects women's citizenship status if they enter as fiancées or recent wives, for example, as they may be threatened with deportation if they are 'ungrateful' (and lack of knowledge of immigration rules and resources and support available to them, without trusted kin or women's networks, means this threat can be effective regardless of the legal niceties).

We find the international, too, in the ways that some countries become acquirers of brides and others supply them, roughly reflecting their relative positioning in the international political economy.[2] In Australia, for example, 'mail-order bride' meant Filipina, but the trade now extends to Thai and Malaysian women. Lately personal and agency advertisements for Russian and East European 'wives' have appeared in local papers. Mail-ordering husbands are stereotyped as older white, often rural, men, presumed to be 'purchasing' a wife because no Australian woman would have them, or because they fear and reject Australian women as too feminist. But a significant part of the trade involves migrant and minority men, including those whose rural or remote working place does not encourage meeting local women, or who lack a community or social network of their own.

Many Filipinas married to Australian men bitterly resent those who see them as 'mail-order brides', a stereotype that encourages their treatment as exotic/available Asian women, or passive victims. Filipina women, indeed non-refugee Third World women generally in Australia, are on average better educated and with higher-level occupations than many Australian-born women (Price, 1990); and it is Filipinas who have the highest proportion of parents residing with them. Some women did enter Australia as part of the trade, seeking an Australian husband for better opportunities for themselves and their children, and resources for family at home, including sponsorship of others to migrate. In this they were acting as agents and making what they could of arrangements that turned out to be quite satisfactory according to many of them (Cahill, 1990). Nevertheless, the compounding of male domestic power with their absence from their own country and consequent isolation can make these marriages difficult for some women and deadly for others.

The trade can mean danger to women who come into Australia under its terms and in a state of acute dependence on their new husband. Violence against these women has recently attracted media attention. Since 1980 eighteen Filipina women and four children have died at the hands of their husbands, and four women and a child have disappeared (Centre for Philippines Concerns, Australia, 1995).

As in the different but similarly sexualized/racialized situation of international child prostitution, this has led to pressure on the Australian government to take some responsibility, to deny serial sponsors and those with a history of domestic violence permission to sponsor again, and to counsel and advise prospective migrants/brides on both domestic violence and the provision and support available against it. These moves are part of new international exchanges and alliances between white Australian and migrant, including Filipina Australian and Filipina, feminists (Marginson, 1992).

International services: sex tourism and militarized prostitution

In one of the first feminist IR texts, Cynthia Enloe prompted us to ask how Asian women's sexuality is being packaged and sold internationally, and how this feeds off and into representations of colonial and Third World women as passive/exotic (Enloe, 1990a). In these backlash times, they can come to stand for essential femininity, the essence of service and sex. Media images, tourist brochures and airline advertising like the 'Singapore girl' associate the Asian woman with male adventure and female availability. These kinds of images are used to sell tourism and make 'other' women available to the tourist/predatory sexed gaze. They join the colonial/Third World scenery as unspoiled and part of the natural resources, there for the taking (Mies, 1986).

Sex tourism is part of a huge international hospitality and service trade that combines domestic service in its dangerous associations with women/femininity/sex/service. Internationalized/racialized domestic service and mail-order brides are examples of traffic across state or collectivity borders whereby the woman leaves home by choice or in response to various kinds of family, political and/or economic coercion. But the international traffic in women also manifests itself in men from wealthy states crossing borders to purchase or otherwise use 'other' women's bodies. Here we may ask why they are so often men, who may use women or boy or girl children.[3] Eighty-five per cent of tourists to the Philippines are men. We ask, too, why some countries, richer and more powerful in the international political economy (IPE), send the men; and why poorer countries and regions sell women, young men and children to these men. Why do some states become sex tourist destinations, and why do others supply those tourists (Enloe, 1990a)? There is an international political economy of sex here, as sex tourism and the relations between clients and prostitutes mirror relations of domination, subordination and exploitation between First and Third Worlds (and between men and women internationally?) (Ong, 1987; Hall, 1992: 74).

The film *The Good Woman of Bangkok* caused a stir when released in Australia in 1992. The Australian film-maker begins the film with the declaration that, on his marriage break-up, he headed for Bangkok in search of prostitutes for sex and a script (Souter, 1992). The film constructs a sexualized relationship that mirrors First World–Third World colonial and contemporary power relations (Martin, 1992). In the film, several young Australian men discuss both the sexual/servicing attractions of Thai women, and a political economy that represents the bar girls as victims of poverty who were 'being helped out' by the men's trade. Certainly there is a political economy in sex here, as so many young women and some young men go to the cities and often into hospitality, entertainment and prostitution work.

Their movement is shaped by relations of colonialism, development, urbanization, industrialization, the growing internationalization of state economies, indebtedness and the conditionality and structural adjustment policies of IMF- and World-Bank-propelled policies. These materialize in the growing impoverishment of rural and urban poor in many Third World states and regions, and in increasing numbers of women who head households and/or are the only family income earner. There is trade, too, in the 'purchase' of young women and children from parents, who are paid a bond which their children must pay off (Kempton, 1992). Once in the trade it may be very hard to go home, through fear and shame, unmarriageability when there are few options, and now AIDS. Alternatively, those who do go home may become part of an AIDS track, in the circulatory traffic between urban and rural areas (Ford and Koetsawang, 1991).

Here, then, is an international political economy of sex, with the demand in terms of militarized prostitution and sex tourism, and supply factors including the impact of development and restructuring, rural impoverishment and urban unemployment, the low status of women, and the search by poor states for foreign exchange (Hill, 1993). This is a tale of our times. Thailand's sex tourism can be traced back through local forms of prostitution and concubinage, and colonial sex trading. Its scope and numbers dramatically changed in the face of another international process, militarization, linked especially to the use of Bangkok for R&R (Rest & Recreation) in the Vietnam War (with some 700,000 US military personnel involved between 1962 and 1976), and more recently in the Gulf War. It has been compounded by the enormous growth in sex tourism, often supported or overlooked in Thailand's search for foreign currency in the face of the debt crisis. A class and racialized hierarchy reveals special dangers and devastation for poorer prostitutes, including those who come across the Thai/Burma border, displaced and impoverished through military action and discrimination on both sides of the border.

The lethal combination of poverty, powerlessness and poor health is evident in the figures. Many prostitutes know little or nothing of AIDS, but even if they did they would be in no position to demand that their clients use condoms. Indeed, their clients' fear of AIDS has had the apparent effect of sending them in search of younger and younger girls and boys, in the hope that they are newer and therefore cleaner. A recent report suggested that in Chiang Mai 72 per cent of prostitutes tested HIV positive among those charging 30–50 baht (about $2), 30 per cent charging 50–100 baht, and 16 per cent among those charging over 100 baht. The incidence was especially high among those who had been working for more than a year, and among young women from the hill tribes and from across the Burmese border (Eddy and Walden, 1992: 18).

What sex tourism requires is women economically desperate, men affluent to travel and willing to pay for it, local governments in search of foreign currency, and foreign businessmen (and women?) selling sexualized travel (Enloe, 1990a). The industry is propelled by local business owners, bar managers and pimps. Much of the local trade is actually dominated by men from the client states. US men stayed or came back to Thailand after the Vietnam War and own many of the bars in Patpong and Pattaya. Australian men own many of the bars in the Philippines, reflected along with the targeted clients in names like Ned Kelly and Crocodile Dundee (Hall, 1992: 73).

Much of the foreign sex is not so much individual or group sex tourism as militarized prostitution, which has developed especially around the huge foreign military bases like those until recently in the Philippines. Militarized prostitution is seen as providing for the (hetero)sexual needs of the (male) soldier, rationalized in different ways such as 'boys will be boys', maintaining morale and rewarding long overseas service, and (less explicitly) defusing the intense and intimate homosocial living of the base by providing a 'safe' outlet. There is often a racialized as well as sexualized subtext here. The soldiers' use of foreign (i.e., local) women may also play a role in the elaboration of their own identities as American, so consolidating the very boundary of national difference that they are crossing for sex (Baustad, 1994: 13).

From colonial times to the present, there has been a long, now well-documented, history of international politics surrounding military prostitution, with colonial authorities and more recently commanders from the foreign military negotiating with local government officials to procure sex for soldiers while at the same time attempting to cause the least local political impact and disruption (Enloe, 1990a; 1993). Managing a military base is a foreign policy issue, a community relations issue and a law and order issue. It is also a public health issue, with familiar antecedents in terms of earlier troublesome STDs, from the Indian Contagious Diseases Act to the present, and especially since AIDS appeared as a threat to 'our men' and military security itself (Bonacci and Luce, 1992).

AIDS itself is very much a part of this international political economy of sex, demonstrating how permeable state borders and people's bodies are to certain kinds of international traffic. It is also internationalized in its construction in terms of sex/body/danger and of particular kinds of racialized and otherwise differently marked bodies. A rather different reading of AIDS as a threat to national security is made by Filipina feminist members of GABRIELA, who see American military men and foreign sex tourists as infecting the Philippines body politic, and invading national sovereignty. Their politicization of prostitution and violence against women locates the analysis with the international political economy, within relations both dependent and militarized. The impact of a politics of unequal trade and debt, World Bank conditionality, restructuring and the government's search for hard currency is linked with a feminist analysis of patriarchy and the eroticization of women's bodies (Enloe, 1990a: 38).

Women in action and international coalitions

While the focus of this chapter on women's bodies and international boundary-drawing and transgression may give the impression that women are objects, constructed, used and abused in men's and states' competitions and conflicts, women in many of these relations do act, though within a range of constraints. Many women have sought to make sense of and to resist the uses made of them, symbolically and materially, and some of those struggles are now being theorized and are informing theorizing in feminist IR (e.g., Sylvester, 1993).

Women's and feminist organizations like GABRIELA in the Philippines, the Third World Movement Against the Exploitation of Women (TWMAEW), EMPOWER and the Campaign to End Child Prostitution in Asia work politically in support of women and children caught up in the current powerful international and sexual politics. Their analyses frequently link feminist and international political economy knowledge, creating theory from women's own experiences, and developing strategies for change (Sen and Grown, 1987; Heyzer, 1994). In the process, connections and networks are built internationally through women's non-governmental organizations and international women's conferences (Krause, this volume) in recognition of both the impact of the international on all women's lives, and of the gendered power of international political relations and processes generally. Part of the work here is addressing differences among women, including power relations between women; for there is no automatic or transparent interest or identity among women, despite their many common experiences.

Towards a research agenda

Women are now becoming visible internationally, and they have entered the changing international agenda whose 'new items' now include some of the issues raised in this chapter. There is growing recognition of the international in the everyday lives of women and men. We are coming to recognize women's different positioning within international relations and processes. Here I argue further that women's bodies are frequently sexualized, marking them out in particular and often dangerous ways, including, and sometimes especially, in the international. A more inclusive and there-fore gendered notion of security thus demands the admission of both women's experiences and women's bodies into the account.

Thinking and writing about these dangers leave me with difficult ques-tions, which include:

1. Rethinking sexual difference and gender power in international rela-tions requires 'rethinking the body' (Grosz, 1994), recognizing women and men as gendered, sexed and embodied. Fierce contests within and against feminism, and around the new men's studies, need addressing here (for example, Flax, 1987; Gatens, 1991; Hearn and Morgan, 1990; Connell and Dowsett, 1992).

2. Here and in other writings, 'women' often mean very young women, and girl children. On other occasions, in sex tourism, for example, young men and boy and girl children are involved. While this says something about the masculinism of domination practices (Peterson, 1992), it needs more careful thought. While 'women' are still marginal in IR, 'children' (half? of the world's population, and crucially involved in labour, war, prostitution ...) are still almost entirely absent.

3. I am deploying notions like international political economy, state bor-ders, the North–South, while the processes of globalization, uneven development within states and regions and migrations across states and regions make a mockery of a mainstream understanding of space and territory in IR. With super rich élites in some poorer states, and poorer radicalized, migrant and minority women in First World heartlands, the old IR dichotomies are no longer tenable. At the same time, intensified globalization makes 'the international' a part of each place and life. The international/internal state distinction becomes ever more problematic – is everything now part of the international? What is the difference between sex tourism that takes Australian and Japanese men to Thai-land and the Philippines and that which takes poor radicalized women from Southeast Asia to the brothels of Amsterdam or Sydney? Might it make more sense to talk of globalization and localization, to relate these stories?

4. Even so, the state is not withering away. Its roll-back, often associated with IMF/World Bank conditionality and global restructuring to facili-tate the free movement of capital, makes both state and people more accessible to exploitation, undermines women's employment oppor-tunities in state, especially welfare, sectors, and further burdens the work of women as carers and compensators for inadequate state provision. At the same time most states, especially richer ones, are reinforcing their regulation of migration, settlement and citizenship

rights, and many states are increasingly militarized and coercive in the exercise of their prerogative powers so closely associated with the IR state (Pettman, 1996).

5. Class, we are told, has lost its salience, and older industrial/labour politics no longer make sense. Yet the contemporary globalized political economy strategically determines people's choices and changes, and locates individuals as well as states in complex and highly unequal relations with each other. It enormously complicates any analysis of nationalism, citizenship or sovereignty. Is it that class really is now a global phenomenon? Yet its infinite specificity and formative interrelations with other dimensions of domination require careful reading.

6. Within this globalized political economy, and its characteristic 'forced march' of women (Grewal, 1994; Runyan, this volume), what are the possibilities of a more internationalized and multilayered feminist politics, all the stronger for the criss-crossing of ideas, networks and moving women themselves? The recent growing visibility of women's rights issues and alliances have been fed into the Vienna Human Rights Conference, the Universal Declaration against Violence against Women, campaigns to make war rape a war crime, and in a revived and somewhat wider definition of the international traffic against women, including women's rights as migrant labourers and sex workers, for example. Some states, including Australia, are now legislating against 'their' men who abuse children in other states or acquire child pornography from overseas. The international exploitation of women's and children's bodies, labour and sex, and their vulnerability to sexual abuse and violence are often the motive force and shared experience behind international coalitions that challenge conventional readings of sovereignty, and deny the inside/outside and international/domestic separations so long used to organize both academic and political international relations. This encourages us to pursue readings of the international as personal, and the personal as international (Enloe, 1990a), to extend the everyday of feminist politics strongly into the international.

7. Within the contexts of these understandings and campaigns and the kinds of international traffic in women which inform them, when considering the concept of the international political economy of sex, how useful is it to focus on the sexualization of women's bodies and sexploitation at the same time as on the changing international sexual division of labour and the global political economy?

Notes

1 This chapter draws on writings towards my forthcoming book *Worldling Women*. An earlier version was given at the 1993 International Studies Association Conference in Washington. My thanks to those who contributed to its reworking, especially to Lester Ruiz, Marysia Zalewski, Nedra Weerakoon and the editors of this collection.
2 There is another kind of international trade that threatens women, with significantly higher numbers of male children as a result of female foeticide in India and Pakistan and East Asian states and the one-child policy in China, and reports already of buying and raiding across borders, including from China into Vietnam. There is a chilling edge to this (beyond the onslaught against girls which it speaks to) in suggestions that more girl children might survive as their value increases through comparative scarcity, though this value is as a commodity, and not as rights-bearer (Oldenburg, 1992; *Weekend Australian*, 26–27 June 1994).
3 A recent estimate suggested 800,000 child prostitutes in Thailand, and 2 million 'others' (*Bangkok Post*, 28 May 1993); another estimates 200,000 child prostitutes (Kempton, 1992, noting that 'the new colonialism pillages Asia for children'). Age grading confuses the already murky waters, some girlfriends or waitresses may move in and out of prostitution, and its officially illegal status discourages measurement.

References

Abella, M. (1991) Recent trends in Asian labour migration: a review of major issues, *Asian Migrant*, **4**(3), 72–7.

Afshar, H. and Agarwal, B. (1989) *Women, Poverty and Ideology in Asia*, London, Macmillan.

Afshar, H. and Dennis, C. (1992) *Women and Structural Adjustment Policies in the Third World*, London, Macmillan.

Batou, J. (1991) 100 million women are missing, *International Viewpoint*, no. 206, 13 May, 26–8.

Baustad, S. (1994) Sex and empire building: prostitution in the making and resisting of global orders, paper for the Citizenship, Identity, Community Conference, York University, Ontario.

Bhabha, J. (1993) Legal problems of refugees, *Women: A Cultural Review*, **4**(3). 240–9.

Bonacci, M. and Luce (1992) The AIDS threat to South East Asians and US military personnel, *Bulletin of Concerned Asian Scholars*, **24**(3), 48–9.

Brown, W. (1987) Where is the sex in political theory? *Women and Politics*, **7**(1), 3–23.

Bush, D. (1992) Women's movements and state policy reform aimed at domestic violence against women ... US and India, *Gender and Society*, **6**(4), 587–608.

Cahill, D. (1990) *Intermarriages in International Contexts: Study of Filipina Women Married to Australian, Japanese and Swiss Men*, Quezon City, Scalabrini Migration Center.

Carillo, R. (1993) Violence against women: an obstacle to development, in M. Turshen and B. Halcomb (eds), *Women's Lives and Public Policy*, Westport, CT Greenwood Press.

Cock, J. (1989) *Maids and Madams*, London, The Women's Press.

Connell, R.W. and Dowsett, G. (1992) *Rethinking Sex: Social Theory and Sexuality Research*, Carlton, Melbourne University Press.

David, R. (1992) Filipino workers in Japan: vulnerability and survival, *Kasarinlan*, **6**(3), 9–23.

Eddy, P. and Walden, S. (1992) Deadly business, *The Australian Magazine*, 19–20 September, pp. 12–18.

Enloe, C. (1990a) *Bananas, Bases and Beaches: Making Feminist Sense of International Politics*, London, Pandora.

Enloe, C. (1990b) The Gulf crisis: making feminist sense of it, *Pacific Research*, November 3–5.

Enloe, C. (1993) *The Morning After: Sexual Politics at the End of the Cold War*, Berkeley, University of California Press.

Flax, J. (1987) Post-modernism and gender relations in feminist theory, *Signs*, **12**(4), 621–43.

Ford, N. and Koetsawang, S. (1991) The socio-cultural context of the transmission of HIV in Thailand, *Social Science and Medicine*, **33**(4), 405–14.

Gaitskell, D. (1982) Are servants ever sisters? *Hecate*, **7**(1), 102–12.

Gatens, M. (1991) Representation in/and the body politic, in R. Diprose and R. Ferrell (eds), *Cartographies: Poststructuralism and the Mapping of Bodies and Spaces*, Sydney, Allen and Unwin.

Graham, H. (1991) The concept of caring in feminist research: the case of domestic service, *Sociology*, **25**(1), 61–78.

Grewal, I. (1994) Autobiographic subjects and diasporic location, in I. Grewal and C. Kaplan (eds), *Scattered Hegemonies: Postmodernity and Transnational Feminist Practices*, Minneapolis, University of Minneapolis Press.

Grewal, I. and Kaplan, C. (eds) (1994) *Scattered Hegemonies: Postmodernity and Transnational Feminist Practices*, Minneapolis, University of Minnesota Press.

Grosz, E. (1994) *Volatile Bodies: Towards a Corporal Feminism*, Sydney, Allen and Unwin.

Hall, C. M. (1992) Sex tourism in South-East Asia, in D. Harrison (ed), *Tourism and the Less Developed Countries*, London, Belhaven Press.

Hanmer, J. (1989) *Women, Policing and Male Violence: International Perspectives*, London, Routledge.

Hearn, J. and Morgan, D. (1990) *Men, Masculinities and Social Theory*, London, Unwin Hyman.

Hendessi, M. (1990) *Armed Angels*, London, Change International Reports.

Heyzer, N., Lycklama a Nijeholt, G. and Weerakoon, N. (eds) (1994) *The Trade in Domestic Workers: Causes, Mechanisms and Consequences and International Migration*, Kuala Lumpur, Asian and Pacific Development Centre, and London, Zed Books.

Hill, C. (1993) Planning for prostitution: an analysis of Thailand's sex industry, in M. Turshed and B. Halcomb, *Women's Lives and Public Policy*, Westport, CT, Greenwood Press.

Huggins, J. (1987) Aboriginal domestic servants in the interwar years, *Hecate*, **13**(1), 77–82.

Humphrey, M. (1991) Asian women workers in the Middle East: domestic servants in Jordan, *Asian Migrant*, **4**(2), 53–60.

Kelkar, G. (1992) Violence against women in India, Gender Studies Paper, Bangkok, Asian Institute of Technology.

Kempton, M. (1992) A new colonialism, *New York Review of Books*, 19 November, p. 39.

Marginson, M. (1992) Filipina migration and organisation in Australia, *Lilith*, no. 7, 11–24.

Martin, J. (1992) Missionary positions, *Australian Left Review*, May, 35–6.

Mies, M. (1986) *Patriarchy and Accumulation on a World Scale*, London, Zed Books.

Mitter, S. (1986) *Common Fate, Common Bond: Women in the Global Economy*, London, Pluto.

Morgan, K. (1992) *War of the Sexes*, Victoria Park, Western Australia, Fivestar Books.

Oakley, A. (1974) *The Sociology of Housework*, London, Robertson.

Oldenburg, P. (1992) Sex ratio, son preference and violence in India, *Economic and Political Weekly*, 5–12 December, 2657–62.

Ong, A. (1987) *Spirits of Resistance and Capitalist Discipline: Factory Women in Malaysia*, Albany, State University of New York Press.

Pain, R. (1991) Space, sexual violence and social control, *Progress in Human Geography*, **115**(4), 415–31.

Palma-Beltran, R. (1992) Filipino domestic helpers overseas, *Asian Migrant*, **4**(2), 37–59.

Peterson, V. S. (1992) Introduction to S. Peterson (ed.), *Gendered States*, Boulder, CO, Lynne Reinner.

Pettman, J. J. (1993) Gendering international relations, *Australian Journal of International Affairs*, **47**(1), 47–62.

Pettman, J. J. (1996) Border crossings/shifting identities: minorities, gender and the state in international perspective, in M. Shapiro and H. Alker (eds), *Boundary Challenges: Territorial Identities and Global Flows*, Minneapolis, Minnesota University Press.

Pettman, J. J. (forthcoming a) Women, nationalism and danger, in J. Purvis and M. Maynard, *Women's Studies in National and International Contexts*, London, Falmer Press.

Pettman, J. J. (forthcoming b) *Worlding Women: A Feminist International Politics*, Sydney, Allen & Unwin.

Price, C. (1990) *Ethnic Groups in Australia*, Canberra, Australian Immigration Research Centre.

Rollins, J. (1985) *Between Women: Domestics and Their Employers*, Philadelphia, Temple University Press.

Rozario, S. (1992) *Purity and Communal Boundaries: Women and Social Change in a Bangladeshi Village*, London, Zed Books.

Rubin, G. (1975) The traffic in women: notes on the 'political economy' of sex, in R. Reiter (ed.), *Toward an Anthropology of Women*, New York, Monthly Review Press.

Rubin, G. (1993) Thinking sex: notes towards a radical theory of the politics of sexuality, in L. Kauffman (ed.), *American Feminist Thought at Century's End: A Reader*, Cambridge, MA, Blackwell.

Sen, G. and Grown, C. (1987) *Development, Crises and Alternative Visions: Third World Women's Perspectives*, New York, Monthly Review Press.

Sivanandan, A. (1989) New circuits of imperialism, *Race and Class*, **15**(2), 1–12.

Souter, F. (1992) The bad man of Bangkok?, *HQ*, Autumn, 110–14.

Spain, D. (1993) Gendered spaces and women's status, *Sociological Theory*, **11**(2), 137–49.

Standing, G. (1992) Global feminisation through flexible labour, in C. Murphy and R. Tooze (eds), *The New International Political Economy*, Boulder, CO, Lynne Rienner.

Sylvester, C. (1993) Feminists write international relations, *Alternatives*, **18**(1), 1–4.

Truong, T.-D. (1990) *Sex, Money and Morality: Prostitution and Tourism in South-east Asia*, London, Zed Books.

Tinsman, H. (1992) 'The indispensable service of sisters': considering domestic service in Latin America and United States Studies, *Journal of Women's History*, **4**(1), 37–59.

Tucker, M. (1987) *If Everyone Cared: An Autobiography*, Melbourne, Grosvenor.

Ward, G. (1988) *Wandering Girl*, Broome, Western Australia, Magabala Books.

Yuval-Davis, N. and Anthias, F. (eds) (1989) *Woman/Nation/State*, London, Macmillan.

15

Feminism, Gender Relations and Geopolitics: Problematic Closures and Opening Strategies

ELEONORE KOFMAN

Gender and geopolitics, the twain have not yet met beyond a few brief exchanges. Traditional geopolitics was hegemonically masculine (Connell, 1990), i.e. strong masculinity presented as the dominant form and dependent on subordinate female identities, though this was usually not explicitly enunciated. Although it provides an easy target, I am not going to discuss classic geopolitics (see Dalby, 1990a; Parker, 1985) and examine how it has ignored gender issues, while predicating its analyses on patriarchal assumptions and sexist and racist images. To some extent this is being done indirectly by those writing the history of geography and its close association with exploration, conquest and imperialism (Domosh, 1991; Driver, 1992; Godlewska and Smith, 1994; Livingstone, 1993). What is more interesting is the degree to which the recent revival of geopolitics has confronted gender divisions and issues. Critical geopolitics in particular has suggested that feminist debates have much to offer in the rethinking of the field (Dalby, 1991; Dodds and Sidaway, 1994; O'Tuathail, 1994a,b). Yet only in relation to security discourses has the medium been used to unravel the contemporary operation of gender and geopolitics (Dalby, 1994), although the geopolitical economy approach has also indicated ways in which gender inequalities are part of the global system. In this chapter I shall firstly address very briefly the relationship of feminist geography to global issues, and secondly the extent to which the newer approaches have integrated an understanding of gender divisions and relations in the world. I conclude that these perspectives still face a number of problematic closures and remain wary of a revival of a sub-discipline called geopolitics.

Feminist geography, geopolitics and the global

The lack of interest by feminist geographers in geopolitics fits in more broadly, though in a more acute fashion, with a generally low profile in political geography. Most edited texts in political geography contain few female, and even fewer feminist, contributions, although this has begun to change in the journal *Political Geography*, where in special issues (edited by Kofman and Peake, 1990; Staeheli, 1994) the multiplicity of scales or themes where gender issues have obvious insights to offer in shaping the way we study issues such as the state, local politics and citizenship were emphasized. In the 1980s feminist geographers were on the whole more interested in subverting the meaning of the political and the boundaries between the private and the public than in reconstructing the field of political geography. This fitted in with a politicized human geography, especially in the cultural and social fields (Jackson, 1987; Smith, 1989). If this was the case then geopolitics, with its continuing Mackinderian feel of statescraft and male-dominated agents and institutions, was an even less attainable and worthy object of reconstruction.

An insular stance was not only shared by other feminisms but was also characteristic of broader trends in British geography. Feminist geography, especially in Britain, continues to focus on its own society, or at most on the Anglo-American realm, which shares its theoretical preoccupations. Horizons across the Channel have barely received a glimpse (but see Kofman and Sales, 1992, 1996).

The international dimension was pursued by feminists in development geography who tended to approach the political with a small 'p' (Momsen and Kinnaird, 1993), although recently the political has come more to the fore (Radcliffe and Westwood, 1993). Whilst venturing outside the core states in the world economy, feminist development geography has tended to undertake studies on communities, individual states or comparisons between them, but to a much lesser extent on the global system. A major area of work by geographers has been on the family, household and community, the distribution of resources within it, and its mediation and strategies in the face of structural adjustment.

Nor should we forget that feminist approaches and gendered analyses in international relations, which might have provided insights and resources, have lagged behind other social science disciplines. When Linda Peake and I edited the special issue on gender of *Political Geography Quarterly*, *Bananas, Beaches and Bases* (Enloe, 1989) had just been published and feminist analyses had not yet ventured out of specialist journals. Today this literature (Grant and Newland, 1991; Peterson, 1992; Peterson and Runyan, 1993; Sylvester, 1993, 1994; Tickner, 1992) is rapidly expanding. It shows how much feminist geographers and international relations scholars share in terms of our preoccupations about the categories and procedures of analysis, about what is important in the understanding of a changing world, the implications for the production of knowledge in the experience of non-dominant groups and how to challenge existing perspectives.

New geopolitical approaches

The revival of geopolitics in the 1980s remained fairly traditional in its interpretation of geopolitics as a popular term for global rivalries in world politics (Taylor, 1989: 43); it has sought to understand the history of the subdiscipline in this century (Hepple, 1986; Parker, 1985) and individual geopoliticians (O'Tuathail, 1994c; Smith, 1984). This revival is by no means confined to Anglo geography, having been prominent in France as well (Moreau Defargues, 1994). Here the geopolitical implied action, movement and, above all, the strategic as an integral element of political life at all scales (Girot and Kofman, 1986; Lacoste 1986, 1993). Geographical knowledge is political and originally served to wage war, as Lacoste demonstrated in his path-breaking book *La Géographie, ça sert d'abord à faire la guerre* (1976). States do not have the monopoly of geopolitics; indeed the renewal of interest was initially related to its potential use by oppositional and resistance movements. Geopolitics refers to a type of practice and reasoning in which geographical knowledge is used by rivals to increase and maintain different forms and degrees of power for the control of territory which ranges from the urban to the international (Lacoste, 1986: xiii–xiv). We all have a need to deploy strategic thinking to fix, limit and control others once we move out of familiar spaces.

Charnay (1992) develops the concept of generative strategy which traces the extension of this type of action and system of legitimation from the anthropological or adaptation of the species to the geopolitical or the strategic organization of space:

> Ideologically and ethnically, beyond its operational aspects, strategy consists in the consideration of variations in the negation of the Other, and tactics of reification through systems of violence and constraint, subversion and persuasion. ... Geopolitics is globalizing and anthropomorphic; it considers as a whole ... everything in its presence: essentially the State. And it is relational and situational: that is it considers the possibilities of respective influences of each one of these entities. (p. 297)

It is this emphasis on the strategic which we also find in Foucault's conceptualization of space and exercise of power (1980, 1984). Foucault (1980), in an interview in 1977 with geographers from the journal *Hérodote*,[1] commented that

> the formation of discourses and genealogy of knowledge need to be analysed. ... in terms of tactics and strategies of power ... deployed through implantations, distributions, demarcations, control of territories and organizations of domains which could well make up a sort of geopolitics where my preoccupations link up with your methods. (p. 77)

Significantly geopolitics[2] in this sense does not necessarily constitute a

subdiscipline but rather a form of reasoning and practice applicable at different scales, spatially and temporally variable in its intensity. It is not confined to the state although the way it is used by different agents and institutional arrangements will depend on how we define its logic and objectives.

Although classic geopolitics was avowedly state-centric in its premises (Taylor, 1993b: 36), newer approaches no longer treat the state as unchanging, decontextualized or without strains or stresses from above and below. Hence (Ward, 1992) the state is simultaneously brought back in and thrown out; nation-states operate in a thick context of time and space. State-centric and comparative perspectives and structurationism *á la* Giddens are invoked here. It is also a means of bringing geography back in (Starr, 1992), an objective espoused by what has been termed critical geopolitics as well (Dalby, 1990a, 1991, 1994; Dodds and Sidaway, 1994; O'Tuathail and Agnew, 1992). A diminished role is also accorded the state in approaches derived from international political economy (Agnew and Corbridge, 1989, 1995)[3] and world systems (Taylor, 1993a,b).

My intention in this chapter is not to give an inventory of the burgeoning field but rather to ask to what extent it has embraced aspects of gender divisions and relations. So I shall restrict my analysis to critical geopolitics and global political economy as the two general frameworks to be examined in greater depth, although it should be noted that these may be blended in different ways (Dodds and Sidaway, 1994) and interwoven through the conjoining of a geopolitical imagination with development studies (Slater, 1993, this volume).

Critical geopolitics, which some have suggested should be written as geo-politics to indicate the cross-cutting of the two elements (O'Tuathail, 1994a), is concerned with how geopolitical reasoning is integrated into political discourse to maintain social and political relations of dominance within contemporary international politics (Reynolds, 1992). It has been heavily influenced by poststructuralist theory, Foucauldian conceptualization of the relationship between knowledge and power and the third debate in international relations (Dalby, 1991). Whilst it rejects the grand narratives and absolute conceptions of space upon which classic geopolitics is premised, the deconstructing of discourses, which legitimate particular institutional and political arrangements, is still firmly located within the spatialization of international politics by core powers and hegemonic states. Geopolitics is a discursive practice by which intellectuals of statescraft 'spatialize' international politics in such a way as to represent it as a 'world' characterized by particular types of places, peoples, dramas (O'Tuathail and Agnew, 1992). It is clear that the intellectuals of statescraft (state bureaucrats, foreign policy experts and advisers) occupy the male-dominated bastions of the coercive and infrastructural apparatuses of the state (see classification by Franzway *et al.*, 1989). Reynolds (1993) has commented that it 'tends to neglect, but not ignore, the material side of politics focusing instead on understanding the power of symbolism, images and representation'.

Whilst critical geopolitics has been aware of gender issues and feminist epistemologies, the studies of dominant discourses present women as the passive object of analysis. The world is divided into masculine and feminine categories; orientalism and sexual metaphors of containment and rape serve to describe 'the Other', in particular the USSR (O'Tuathail and Agnew, 1992). Psychoanalytic readings, especially post-Lacanian feminist psychoanalysis, are invoked in our understanding of processes of normalization and the insatiable will to control 'the Other' (O'Tuathail, 1994a). A few daunting questions remain for me. How might women occupy other positions in this narrative, how might they become subjects, even in subordinate positions, or are they doomed to remain forever prisoners of the text? What can we say about the real women who choose, or more frequently are forced, in varying degrees, to trade places (Sisson Runyan, this volume)?

Other themes in critical geopolitics involving militarization and security concur with themes on the feminist international studies agenda (Enloe, 1989, 1993; Tickner, 1992) in which women do exist as subjects of political practices. Social movements have attempted to reformulate the notion of security away from the idea of the state as being the sole guarantor of security (Dalby, 1990b, 1994) and expand different aspects of what security means so as to encompass economic and social dimensions. This raises issues of security, for and from whom, and links up with feminist thinking on oppression, insecurity, structural violence and protection; it is seen as a step to reconceptualizing world security (Peterson, 1992). Feminist geographers (Pain, 1991; Valentine, 1992) have restricted their studies to danger at local levels, how familial ideology and gender divisions of space have created awareness of insecurity in public places, and thus the need to turn to the protection of a man in the family. The military, too, as the 'protector of national security', agent of violence and bearer of socio-sexual order (Benton, 1993), exemplifies the pertinence of bringing together representations of hegemonic masculinity and femininity, the control of women as symbols, consumers, workers and emotional comforters, and the international political economy of defence (Enloe, 1989, 1993). Comparisons can be made between the local and domestic/global security (Pettman, this volume), including the gendered metaphors of the nation as family.

In approaches derived from international political economy (Agnew and Corbridge, 1989; Corbridge and Agnew, 1991) and world systems perspectives (Taylor, 1990, 1993b), there is a far greater emphasis on the material conditions of global inequalities and its maintenance through geopolitical orders and codes. Both stress the historical development of different forms of geopolitical discourse, especially its origins in the encounter between Europeans and others in the emergence of the world economy (Agnew and Corbridge, 1995: 49). They argue that we are now witnessing a tentative globalization of modern life and the construction of overlapping sovereignties and networks of power that are associated with a new hegemony of transnational liberalism and market-access economics (ch. 7). Their hope is for a counter-hegemonic project which, rather than mastering space, seeks the empowerment of subaltern men and women through associational socialism, i.e. market socialism and pluralist states (p. 225). Women appear to be a group that have fared badly from globalization and are providing, along with environmentalists, indigenous peoples, peace groups, etc., new social forces, representational spaces and forms of organization. Beyond this vague internationalism, there is little examination of how such groups might achieve a voice and a place in a less exploitative global system, and to what extent markets may bring disadvantages or opportunities for women.

Gender inequalities are now figuring in the geography of world systems (Taylor, 1993b). For Wallerstein (1991, 1992), racism[4] and sexism make up one of the three elements of geoculture, the underside of geopolitics or the cultural framework within which the world system operates. These systems are a necessary component of the structures of the world system due to the ideology of universalism and are the means of addressing the contradictions of capitalist accumulation and legitimating the real inequalities in a world consisting of a single division of labour (Wallerstein, 1991: 171–3). Oddly, there is no mention of patriarchy (Mies, 1986), whilst sexism is located in the household where it maintains a sexual division of labour, ensuring that non-waged activities subsidize waged work. Housewives do not work and therefore do not contribute to surplus value (Wallerstein, 1992). There seems little awareness of the connection between the two previous statements. In the end this analysis cordons off gender inequalities and hierarchies into the private sphere of the household and reduces gender inequality and identity to a single dimension.

Whither geopolitics?

I have so far sketched out some of the ways in which new approaches have tried to engage with women and gender relations. It might seem that attending to some of the problematic aspects might make it worth feminists investing energy in rethinking geopolitics. However, I would like to suggest that the closures practised in delimiting the field, and deciding what we consider significant and worth explaining in trying to understand the nature of the international system, continue to pose major barriers. Just as in international relations, so too in geopolitics and international politics, what we look for depends on how we make sense of, or 'order' our experience (Peterson and Runyan, 1993). And that in turn involves what counts as valid and relevant experiences. How should the state be conceptualized and what types of commodification, exchanges and modes of circulation are relevant in the making of the global system? Who are the actors in this system? It may well be that by the time we have opened up and democratized geopolitics, it will have ceased to exist as it is currently presented.

Closures and openings

Whether in theory or in empirical studies, one of the most noticeable closures in critical geopolitics is the tendency to concentrate almost entirely on the geopolitics of hegemonic and core powers, although papers on popular geopolitics are appearing (Popke, 1994; Sharp, 1993). Given the influence of Foucauldian notions of the relationship between knowledge and power, it is surprising that geopolitical critique does not pursue more fully his broader vision of geopolitics as an integral aspect of tactics and strategies throughout economic, social and political life (O'Tuathail, 1994a: 515). Situating geo-politics among dominant states tends to reproduce a model of geopolitics which reinforces the exclusion of internal structures and those who are not unambiguously dominant in the world. For example, Japan (O'Tuathail, 1993) receives little attention since it does not conform to the model of other economically hegemonic powers. Even more so, the geopolitics of non-dominant states are marginalized, or highlighted, merely because of their interest to hegemonic powers (Dodds, 1994b, on Argentina), making it rather difficult to envisage how any geographical dialogue (Taylor, 1993b) or empowering, counter-hegemonic geopolitics are likely to occur by the next century.

A second related aspect which has been privileged in critical geopolitics is foreign policy (Dodds, 1994a). Again this sits oddly with a desire for opening up the boundaries which classic geopolitics and realist IR have imposed upon the domestic and international. It serves to confirm the idea that foreign policy is bipartisan and insulated from democratic politics (Taylor, 1993a on Britain). The emergence of new regional blocs, especially the European Union, has increasingly undermined the divide between national and foreign policies, inside and outside (Walker, 1993). It has already begun to modify the relationship between state apparatuses, their competencies and expert-ise, and brought new actors on to the scene, as in the case of social policy. Other policy issues, such as immigration have always demonstrated an interaction between internal structures and international arrangements.

Anglocentricism, let alone Eurocentrism (Kofman, 1994; Slater, 1993, 1994), typifies our view of the world. The geopolitical concerns of non-Anglo states in particular are translated into the models and issues elaborated by the intellectuals of core states (Taylor, 1993a). This of course goes well beyond geopolitics and characterizes much of Western social sciences which impose their intellectual paradigms on societies that often have other pre-occupations. It is more than the cultural side of economic hegemony; the reverse is the downgrading of the non-dominant society and culture. Slater calls this the problem of worlding, whereby the West becomes the primary referent for theory and the periphery is viewed through the lenses of a simplified heterogeneity, in which the Third World is interesting for its culture of violence and traditions. Postmodernism, though postulating difference, has remained largely fixed in the West and has not taken an interest in the realities of the South and the imposition of universalizing ideas and practices of neoliberalism and structural adjustment (Mohan and Slater, this volume). In the core states, it is inevitably the voices of the male élites, occupying positions in the most insulated, coercive and infrastructural state apparatuses, that are heard. So should we not be calling for the democratization of geopolitics in terms of who elaborates it and whose geopolitics it is?

Another significant closure, pertaining primarily to approaches derived from global political economy, concerns the make-up of the international system and the most significant objects that are commodified, circulated and exchanged. Geographers have concentrated on production, exchanges of goods and flows of money and communications, and have paid less attention to the movement of people, especially its international politics. To some extent this can be attributed to a division of labour within geography where the economic was split off from the political, and the local from the global. In feminist geography connecting up separate agendas would involve, for example, colonization and 'housewifization' (Mies, 1986); gender, sexuality and migration (Kofman, 1996); and structures of violence, labour and resources (Peterson and Runyan, 1993). The concept of work has also received considerable scrutiny so as to cover sexual, domestic, informal and factory, and to reveal the financial savings of labours of love in caring for those not in work. Women participate in the various forms of circulation in the global economy and contribute to the balance of payments of debtor states (Pettman, this volume). Similarly, political economy perspectives should take account of social and political movements organized around these issues (Krause, this volume).

As has been noted previously, the state as the pillar of traditional geopolitics has been subjected to criticism, particularly in relation to global flows transcending boundaries, and the territorial sovereign state. We are fortunately nuancing the simplistic death pronouncements for the state

(Taylor, 1994) and exploring more considered and differential evaluations. But in order to prise open the state more fully and articulate the internal with the international, the wider debates in social and political theory cannot be ignored as they have previously been in geopolitics, nor the realist tradition in international relations. The problem is not merely the state-centred nature of the analyses, but the tendency to leave the state untheorized and the international autonomous from the internal. Problematizing the state and recognizing the significance of internal structures (Dalby, 1990a: 40–1) needs to be pursued further. Security and the military are integral elements of the assumed and taken-for-granted constructions of territorial states 'which render women vulnerable in different ways in different places' (Dalby, 1994: 596).

The literature on state theorization is abundant, but for our purposes the most interesting developments are the relaxing of the dichotomy between state-centric and society-centric theories tending towards more strategic accounts (Jessop, 1990), a dynamic reading of the interplay between state forms operating at different levels (Balibar, 1991), the institutional forms of state, power and territory (Driver, 1991), the reshaping as opposed to the retreat of the state (*West European Politics*, 1994), and the gendered state. Whilst the debate on the latter has produced a copious literature, and some fundamental re-evaluations about the state (Connell, 1990; Cooper, 1993; Franzway *et al.*, 1989; MacKinnon, 1989; Peterson, 1992; Watson, 1990), this has hardly percolated into geographical awareness (Johnston, 1993).

The state remains important in socio-sexual and cultural relations and policies. We should not misconstrue the impact of the state to regulate, mediate and shape social relations simply because it has been opened up economically. It is not accidental that there has been a proliferation of states in Eastern Europe and the former Soviet Union since 1989. Nationalist movements have never clamoured for the end of the state, but only for their own state with its accompanying landscapes and territory. Similarly, in relation to pressures from above, the integration and loss of sovereign powers to a higher level is not getting rid of the state as a process. Balibar (1991: 16–17) captures this well when he speaks of 'statism defined as a combination of administrative/repressive practices and contingent arbitration of particular interests, including those of each nation or the dominant classes of each nation. The state today in Europe is neither *national nor supranational*'. Changing forms of the state should not be equated with the demise of the state.

The state, constituted within gender relations and as a central institution of gendered power encompassing multiple agencies and levels, has influence both in shaping and mediating gender identities and in what is at stake in the social struggle surrounding sexual politics (Franzway *et al.*, 1989). It is no monolithic power but differentiated, at times contradictory, complex and confused (Kofman, 1993). Connell's concept of a gender regime (1990: 523–6) is particularly helpful as a first step towards understanding the different and changing forms of the gendered state in space and time and the type of socio-sexual order it generates (Benton, 1993). A gender regime implies 'the precipitate of social struggles and is linked to – though not a simple reflection of – the wider gender order of society'.

The gender regime comprises three main structures: a gendered division of labour within the state apparatus; a gendered structure of power in the state apparatus; and a gendered structure of cathexis (emotional attachments). Connell's analysis is confined to individual states but it could be extended to the relationship between different states and the gender regimes produced through new forms of regionalization, for example the European Union and NAFTA (Sisson Runyan, this volume). On what basis are new gender regimes constructed, and how does one regime relate to and affect others? The new states of Eastern Europe have demonstrated the role of the state in overturning the previous socio-sexual order and the struggles generated by and against these changes (Einhorn, 1993; Funk and Mueller, 1993). Despite earlier hostility to the state in the 1970s, European feminists in general are learning to live with it and to appreciate some of its interventions (Dahlerup, 1994). The rapidly changing political situation in Western Europe has drawn increasing interest in the gender implications of welfare regimes covering work, family and social policy (Lewis, 1993; Kofman and Sales, 1996) and the implications of the increasing harmonization within the European Union. The shift in the meaning and practices of what used to be called domestic and foreign policy has made gender issues, such as employment and related measures, child care, abortion and sexuality, more clearly apparent. NAFTA, too, raises a multiplicity of gender issues, although, as Marianne Marchand (1994, this volume) points out, there has been virtually no analysis of the gender implications, which are not straightforward.

Conclusions

The most successful incorporation of feminist insights and gender issues into geopolitics would dismantle and democratize geopolitics such that it no longer involved the personnel of statescraft located within the most repressive echelons of the state. Real groups would then begin to figure in the landscapes and maps of the global economy and power relations. Geopolitics would open out into a broader context which we could call global political geography, in which comparative analyses and the local, however that is defined, would also be included. This does not mean that geopolitics would simply disappear or be dissolved. It might still be retained as a form of reasoning and strategy commonly deployed in maintaining power and situating institutions in relation to others (broadly defined). It is therefore necessary to understand how and why the intensity and geographical and historical specificities of this form of geopolitics vary, and what uses could be made of it. Opening it up would in effect be a process of democratization, but it would also entail a questioning of its status within political geography and more broadly its role in regulating and structuring economic, social and political life. However, even if we were to democratize it, I would argue against locating it within a subdiscipline, where it is all too easy to lose sight of the material and symbolic practices which link people and places in the world. Feminist thinking in international political economy precisely indicates how we might combine the trading of people and places beyond existing borders in the changing forms of global economy together with representations and divisions of spaces and places.

Equally, we have to go beyond the statement that the demarcation between the ordered sphere of the domestic and the dangerous, anarchic sphere of the international is breaking down, especially in relation to new forms of regionalization such as the European Union and NAFTA, and to examine the exact nature of the strong articulation between the two. To proclaim or cajole the dismantling and/or lowering of state boundaries is not enough. Given the role of the state, and its continuing significance in practising closures and openings in the global system, further explorations of the state would be a much needed, though by no means sufficient, step in incorporating feminist insights and gender relations into our understanding of global political geography.

Furthermore, without reference to other factors, such as households and localities where women are more visible, there is also a tendency to pay lip-service to women's presence or paradigmatic progressive organizations. It is, as we have seen, far easier either to lock them into the gendered metaphors of textual analysis or to focus critiques on the all too visible hegemonic masculinity of global institutions and inter-state power.

Notes

1. *Hérodote* was launched in 1976 by a group of geographers around Yves Lacoste who adopted a polemical stance, criticizing establishment geography and the refusal to confront geography as political. It did much to open up geography to debates in the social sciences; its first issues contained an interview with Michel Foucault, reviews of books by Bourdieu and Virilio, articles on the relevance of Hegel to geography, and popular and official discourses and spatial metaphors. The initial subtitle 'Strategies, géographie, idéologies', was changed in 1982 to 'Revue de géographie et de géopolitique', which reflected a more narrowly

geopolitical focus and concentration on topical places and issues in the world. Raffestin (1994: 295) argues that from a despair with the failure of Third World movements, Lacoste has since the 1980s taken a nationalistic turn in his interpretation of geopolitics.

2. Ashley (1987) derives the geopolitics of geopolitical space from a Foucauldian perspective to argue that the realist conception of international relations is, despite its pretensions to universalism and timelessness, a profoundly historical conjuncture, an interpretation of interpretations. Although Foucault's interviews on space are not referred to, the geopolitical outlook is compared with a genealogical attitude in that it is 'preoccupied with motion, space, strategy, and power' (p. 411).

   In O'Tuathail's recent writing (1994b), it is Foucault's concept of governmentality or ensemble of rationalities concerned with the governing of territories and populations which is applied to geopolitics as the twentieth-century form concerned with the task of hegemonic management.

3. Agnew and Corbridge (1995) develop a far more elaborate conceptualization than I am able to present in this chapter. However, for my purposes, I hope I have not unduly simplified their formulation.

4. The racism of geopolitics, though not developed as much as it should be, is nevertheless recognized, for example in principles of biological imperialism (Mackinder) and scientific selection (Hobson) (Kearns (1993).

References

Agnew, J. and Corbridge, S. (1989) The new geopolitics: the dynamics of geopolitical disorder, in R. J. Johnston and P. J. Taylor (eds), *A World in Crisis*, Oxford, Basil Blackwell, 2nd edn, pp. 266–88.

Agnew, J. and Corbridge, S. (1995) *Mastering Space: Hegemony, Territory and International Political Economy*, London, Routledge.

Anthias, F. and Yuval-Davis, N. (1992) *Racialized Boundaries*, London, Routledge.

Ashley, R. (1987) The geopolitics of geopolitical space: towards a critical social theory of international politics, *Alternatives*, **11**, 403–34.

Balibar, X. X. (1991) Es gibt keinen staat in Europa: racism and politics in Europe today, *New Left Review*, **186**, 5–19.

Benton, S. (1993) Founding fathers and earth mothers: women's place at the 'birth' of nations, paper for conference on Gender, Sexuality and Identity: Commonalities and Differences, London.

Charnay, J. P. (1992) *Stratégie générative: de l'anthropologie à la géopolitique*, Paris, PUF.

Connell, R. W. (1990) The state, gender and sexual politics: theory and appraisal, *Theory and Society*, **19**(5), 507–44.

Cooper, D. (1993) An engaged state: sexuality, governance and the potential for change, *Journal of Law and Society*, **20**(3), 257–75.

Corbridge, S. and Agnew, J. (1991) The US trade and budget deficits in global perspective: an essay in geopolitical economy, *Environment and Planning D: Society and Space*, **9**, 71–90.

Dahlerup, D. (1994) Learning to live with the state – state, market, and civil society:

women's need for state intervention in East and West, *Women's Studies International Forum*, **15**, 117–28.

Dalby, S. (1990a) *Creating the Second Cold War*, London, Pinter.

Dalby, S. (1990b) American security discourse: the persistence of geopolitics, *Political Geography Quarterly*, **9**, 171–88.

Dalby, S. (1991) Critical geopolitics: discourse, difference and dissent, *Environment and Planning D*, **9**, 261–83.

Dalby, S. (1994) Gender and critical geopolitics: reading security discourse in the new world disorder, *Environment and Planning D: Society and Space*, **12**(5), 594–612.

Dodds, K. (1994a) Geopolitics and foreign policy: recent developments in Anglo-American political geography and international relations, *Progress in Human Geography*, **18**(2), 186–208.

Dodds, K. (1994b) Geo-politics in the Foreign Office: British representations of Argentina 1945–1960, *Transactions of the Institute of British Geographers*, **19**, 273–90.

Dodds, K. and Sidaway, J. (1994) Locating critical geopolitics, *Environment and Planning D; Society and Space*, **12**(5), 515–24.

Domosh, M. (1991) Towards a feminist historiography of geography, *Transactions of the Institute of British Geographers*, **16**(1), 95–104.

Driver, F. (1991) Political geography and state formation: disputed territory, *Progress in Human Geography*, **15**, 268–80.

Driver, F. (1992) Geography's empire: histories of geographical knowledge, *Environment and Planning D: Society and Space*, **10**, 23–40.

Einhorn, B. (1993) *Cinderella Goes to Market*, London, Verso.

Enloe, C. (1989) *Bananas, Beaches and Bases: Making Sense of International Politics*, Pandora, London.

Enloe, C. (1993) *The Morning After: Sexual Politics at the End of the Cold War*, Berkeley, University of California Press.

Foucault, M. (1980) Questions on geography, in C. Gordon (ed.), *Power/Knowledge: Selected Interviews and Other Writings 1972–1977*, Brighton, Harvester Press, pp. 63–77.

Foucault, M. (1984) *The Foucault Reader*, edited by P. Rabinow, London, Penguin.

Franzway, S., Court, D. and Connell, R. (1989) *Staking a Claim: Feminism, Bureaucracy and the State*, Oxford, Polity.

Funk, N. and Mueller, M. (eds) (1993) *Gender Politics and Post-Communism*, London, Routledge.

Girot, P. and Kofman, E. (1986) *International Geopolitical Analysis: A Selection from Hérodote*, Beckenham, Croom Helm.

Godlewska, A. and Smith, N. (eds) (1994) *Geography and Empire*, Oxford, Basil Blackwell.

Grant, R. and Newland, K. (eds) (1991) *Gender and International Relations*, Milton Keynes, Open University Press.

Hepple, L. (1986) The revival of political geography, *Political Geography Quarterly*, **5**, 521–36.

Jackson, P. (1987) Social geography: politics and place, *Progress in Human Geography*, **12**, 286–92.

Jessop, B. (1990) *State Theory. Putting Capitalist States in Their Place*, Oxford, Polity.

Johnston, R. (1993) The rise and decline of the corporate welfare state: a comparative analysis in global context, in P. Taylor (ed.), *Political Geography of the Twentieth Century: A Global Analysis*, London, Belhaven.

Kearns, G. (1993) Prologue: fin de siècle geopolitics: Mackinder, Hobson and theories of global closure, in P. Taylor (ed.), *Political Geography of the Twentieth Century: A Global Analysis*, London, Belhaven.

Kofman, E. (1993) Vers une théorization féministe de l'état: complexité, contradictions, confusions, in A. Gautier and J. Heinen (eds), *Le Sexe des politiques sociales*, Paris, Côté Femmes.

Kofman, E. (1994) Unfinished agendas: acting upon minority voices of the past decade, *Geoforum*, **26**, 429–43.

Kofman, E. (1996) 'Female birds' of passage a decade later: the politics of international migration in Europe, paper presented at International Studies Association conference, San Diego.

Kofman, E. and Peake, L. (1990) Into the 1990s: a gendered agenda for political geography, *Political Geography Quarterly*, **9**, 313–36.

Kofman, E. and Sales, R. (1992) Towards Fortress Europe? *Women's Studies International Forum*, **15**(1), 129–40.

Kofman, E. and Sales, R. (1996) The geography of gender and welfare in Europe, in M. García Ramón and J. Monk (eds), *South and North: Women's Work and Daily Lives in the European Community*, London, Routledge.

Lacoste, Y. (1976) *La Géographie, ça sert d'abord à faire la guerre*, Paris, Maspero.

Lacoste, Y. (ed.) (1986) *Géopolitiques des régions françaises*, 3 vols, Paris, Fayard.

Lacoste, Y. (1993) *Dictionnaire de géopolitique*, Paris, Flammarion.

Lewis, J. (ed.) (1993) *Women, Work, Family and Social Policy in Europe*, Aldershot, Edward Elgar.

Livingstone, D. (1993) *The Geographical Tradition: Episodes in the History of a Contested Enterprise*, Oxford, Basil Blackwell.

MacKinnon, C. (1989) *Towards a Feminist Theory of the State*, Cambridge, MA, Harvard University Press.

Marchand, M. (1994) Gender and new regionalism in Latin America: inclusion/exclusion, *Third World Quarterly*, **15**(1), 63–76.

Mies, M. (1986) *Patriarchy and Accumulation on a World Scale*, London, Zed Books.

Momsen, J. and Kinnaird, V. (eds) (1993) *Different Places, Different Voices. Gender and Development in Africa, Asia and Latin America*, London, Routledge.

Moreau Defargues, P. (1994) *Introduction à la géopolitique*, Paris, Seuil.

Morokvasic, M. (1984) Birds of passage are also women, *International Migration Review*, **39**, 69–84.

Nijman, J. (1993) *The Geopolitics of Power and Conflict: Superpowers and the International System 1945–92*, London, Belhaven.

O'Tuathail, G. (1993) Pearl Harbor without bombs: a critical geopolitics of the US–Japan 'FSX' debate, *Environment and Planning A*, **24**, 975–94.

O'Tuathail, G. (1994a) (Dis)placing geopolitics: writing on the maps of global politics, *Environment and Planning D: Society and Space*, **12**(5), 525–46.

O'Tuathail, G. (1994b) Problematizing geopolitics: survey, statesmanship and strategy, *Trans. IBG*, **19**, 259–72.

O'Tuathail, G. (1994c) The critical reading/writing of geopolitics: re-reading/writing

Wittfogel, Bowman and Lacoste, *Progress in Human Geography*, **18**(3), 313–32.

O' Tuathail, G. and Agnew, J. (1992) Geopolitics and discourse: practical geopolitical reasoning in American foreign policy, *Political Geography*, **11**(2), 190–204.

Pain, R. (1991) Space, sexual violence and social control, *Progress in Human Geography*, **15**(4), 415–31.

Parker, G. (1985) *Western Geopolitical Thought in the Twentieth Century*, Beckenham, Croom Helm.

Peterson, V. S. (1992) *Gendered States: Feminist (Re)visions of International Relations*, Boulder, CO, Lynne Rienner.

Peterson, V. S. and Runyan, A. (1993) *Global Gender Issues*, Boulder, CO, Westview Press.

Pettman, J. (1993) Gendering international relations, *Australian Journal of International Affairs*, **47**(1), 47–62.

Popke, E. J. (1994) Recasting geopolitics: the discursive scripting of the International Monetary Fund, *Political Geography*, **13**(3), 255–69.

Radcliffe, S. and Westwood, S. (eds) (1993) *Viva: Women and Popular Protest in Latin America*, London, Routledge.

Raffestin, C., Lopreno, D. and Pasteur, Y. (1994) *Géopolitique et histoire*, Lausanne, Éditions Payot.

Reynolds, D. (1992) Political geography: thinking globally and locally, *Progress in Human Geography*, **16**(3), 393–405.

Reynolds, D. (1993) Political geography: closer encounters with the state, contemporary political economy and social theory, *Progress in Human Geography*, **17**(3), 389–403.

Sharp, J. (1993) Publishing American identity; popular geopolitics, myth and *The Reader's Digest*, *Political Geography*, **12**(6), 491–504.

Sidaway, J. (1994) Geopolitics, geography and terrorism in the Middle East, *Environment and Planning D: Society and Space*, **12**, 357–72.

Slater, D. (1992) On the borders of social theory: learning from other regions, *Environment and Planning D: Society and Space*, **10**(2), 309–29.

Slater, D. (1993) The geopolitical imagination and the enframing of development theory, *Transactions of the IBG*, **18**(4), 419–37.

Slater, D. (1994) Exploring other zones of the postmodern: problems of ethnocentrism and difference across the North–South divide, in A. Rattansi and S. Westwood (eds), *Racism, Modernity and Identity*, Cambridge, Polity.

Smith, N. (1984) Political geographers of the past: Isaiah Bowman: political geography and geopolitics, *Political Geography Quarterly*, **3**, 69–76.

Smith, S. (1989) Society, space and citizenship: a human geography for the 'new times'? *Transactions of the Institute of British Geographers*, **14**, 144–56.

Starr, H. (1992) Joining political and geographical perspectives: geopolitics and international relations, in M. Ward (ed.), *The New Geopolitics*, Philadelphia, Gordon and Breach.

Staeheli, L. (1994) Empowering political struggle: spaces and scales of resistance, *Political Geography*, **13**, 387–92.

Sylvester, C. (1993) Feminists write international relations, *Alternatives*, **18**(1), 1–3.

Sylvester, C. (1994) *Feminist Theory and International Relations in a Postmodern Era*, Cambridge, Cambridge University Press.

Taylor, P. (1989) *Political Geography*, 2nd edn, Harlow, Longman.

Taylor, P. (1990) *Britain and the Cold War: 1945 as Geopolitical Transition*, London, Pinter.

Taylor, P. (ed.) (1993a) *Political Geography of the Twentieth Century: A Global Analysis*, London, Pinter.

Taylor, P. (1993b) *Political Geography*, 3rd edn, Harlow, Longman.

Taylor, P. (1994) The state as container: territoriality in the modern world-system, *Progress in Human Geography*, **18**(2), 151–62.

Tickner, A. (1992) *Gender in International Relations: Feminist Perspectives on Achieving Global Security*, New York, Columbia University Press.

Valentine, G. (1992) Images of danger: women's sources of information about the spatial distribution of male violence, *Arca*, **24**(1), 22–9.

Walker, R. B. J. (1993) *Inside/Outside: International Relations as Political Theory*, Cambridge, Cambridge University Press.

Wallerstein, I. (1991) *Geopolitics and Geoculture*, Cambridge, Cambridge University Press.

Wallerstein, I. (1992) Universalism, racism, sexism: ideological tensions of capitalism, in E. Balibar and I. Wallerstein (eds), *Ambiguous Identities: Race, Nation, Class*, London, Verso.

Ward, M. (1992) *The New Geopolitics*, Philadelphia, Gordon Breach.

Watson, S. (ed.) (1990) *Playing the State*, London, Verso.

West European Politics (1994), special issue, **17**(4).

16

Gender Inequalities and Feminist Politics in a Global Perspective

JILL KRAUSE

Introduction

Global economic restructuring, the complex international division of labour and the many dimensions of economic interdependence are integral parts of the phenomenon of 'globalization'. However, the ongoing process of inter-connectedness characteristic of globalization extends beyond the economic sphere. The terms of political debate and action are being transformed as globalization gives rise to a 'new agenda' of issues in international politics. The growing recognition of the relationship between debt, development and environmental degradation, for example, is encouraging, if not the growth of a 'global consciousness', at least an awareness that our lives are in some senses increasingly influenced by activities and events happening well away from the social context in which we carry out our day-to-day activities (Giddens, 1991). At the same time, transnational and supranational institu-tions are playing a role in influencing events both between and within states and in shaping social and political identities. This essay explores global-ization from the perspective of gender. It traces out the global dimensions of gender inequality and the ways in which globalization is changing the terms of feminist politics. First, the essay explores gender issues in a global context and asks what globalization looks like when viewed through the 'lens' of gender (Peterson and Runyan, 1993). It suggests ways in which global-ization transforms social orders and creates the conditions for transnational feminist alliances, and it assesses the degree to which feminists are now playing a role in shaping debates and preparing to be players in international forums.

The second section concerns gender, inequality and feminism in the context of 'critical' approaches to the study of international relations which are attempting to transcend the territorial and conceptual boundaries of state-centric analysis. The processes of globalization are changing our understanding of the world. Recent challenges to 'orthodox' international relations theory have highlighted problems of reductionism in state-centric analysis as economic and social relations become increasingly globalized. Critical approaches also raise questions about the degree to which attempts to theorize global processes are driven by political concerns. Scholars of international relations influenced by feminist thought, critical theory, post-structuralism and postmodernism have insisted that the production of knowledge is itself a historical process which is conditioned by the socio-political, economic and cultural context in which it is constructed. Feminist interventions in international relations are not only seeking to make gender visible, but are also attempting to develop ways of giving a voice to those displaced or marginalized by the impact and operation of global economic processes.

Starting from the position that attempts to understand globalization are inevitably driven by normative concerns, international relations scholars with feminist sympathies might ask what globalization looks like when viewed through the 'lens' of gender. They might be concerned to draw out the global dimensions of gender inequalities. They might ask how global processes change gender relations, or they might be curious about the role played by ideas on gender in producing and reproducing power relations and ask how these relations are structured and transformed. In so far as global-ization transforms social orders and encourages the growth of many and varied new social movements, they might also ask how far globalization has created the conditions for transnational feminist alliances

Gender inequalities in a global perspective

In the 1980s, feminist scholarship in international relations, international political economy and the related field of development studies demonstrated the importance of understanding the gender-specific impact of development policies and of examining the impact on gender relations of the activities of international organizations and multinational corporations.[1] What is the position in the 1990s? Is the 'New World Order', as some commentators claim, characterized by 'gender apartheid'?[2] While there are differences between women across the world, there are also many commonalities and while the pattern of gender inequality varies between regions, it is never-theless a global phenomenon. In general terms, there remains a real dichot-omy between economic and technological changes and social progress. Even in areas of the world where economic growth has been rapid, economic progress has not been matched by social progress in general terms and by improvements in the relative position of women in particular. As the least unionized and poorest-paid of all workers, women are particularly vulner-able to the market policies which have characterized global economic restructuring in the 1990s. Where women are encouraged to take up roles in the paid sector – and women now make up some 41 per cent of paid workers in developed countries and 34 per cent worldwide – it is still the case that on average they earn 30 to 40 per cent less than men for comparable work.[3] Women in general still work longer hours and make up a disproportionate number of those working in the informal sector, though much of this work is unrecorded and thus invisible. Women are concentrated in low-paid jobs. In the developing world, women are still heavily concentrated in export production zones or subsistence agriculture. Women's attempts to translate paid employment into financial independence are often thwarted by lack of access to capital, inadequate education and training and by an unequal burden of family responsibilities. The degree to which women are denied access to land has also been highlighted as a significant barrier to women's full participation in economic reconstruction in some areas.[4]

In many areas of the world the particular problems of debt and structural adjustment for women are still most striking. The burden of debt and of economic policies, which are themselves largely conditioned by international processes, contribute to further gender division within countries in the Caribbean and Latin America (Hooper, 1994a). The impact of a high rate of migration adds to the problem of gender inequalities. In the Caribbean, many of the problems associated with structural adjustment are still felt. In the Asia-Pacific region sustainable development and the negative impact of structural adjustment and migration are also key gender issues. Migration and the drain on resources is also closely associated with increases in child prostitution, tourist prostitution and sex tourism (Thahn Dam, 1983). In the Philippines the need for action on the trafficking of women has been widely recognized, but at the same time the adverse impact of structural adjustment and debt servicing on women has been viewed as central to the problem (Hooper, 1994b). The degree to which women are disproportionately affected by economic restructuring is by no means confined to the 'developing' world or newly industrialized countries. In Central and Eastern Europe and the former Soviet Union there is evidence that women in particular are losing their jobs as the region 'adjusts' to the rigours of the global market-place and are also taking up the burden of care which results from cuts in the social sectors.[5]

The feminization of the global workforce that has accompanied global restructuring, the gender specific impact of structural adjustment and the feminization of poverty are just a few of many global gender issues. The so-called 'new agenda' of the 1990s much discussed by élites in the international community and reflected in debates within international relations has included much discussion of environmental degradation and issues of sustainable development. Sustainable development cannot be achieved unless measures are taken to slow down the growth of the world's population, but the underlying issues that need to be addressed are poverty and inequality. Gender inequalities are central to the debate about sustainable development and poverty alleviation. It has been estimated that the world's population will increase by 93 million by the end of the decade, putting enormous pressure on the environment (UNICEF, 1994). However, some 300 million women worldwide still have no access to effective family planning in a world where an estimated one-fifth of all pregnancies are unwanted. In the global recession of the 1980s, thirty-seven of the world's poorest countries saw their health budgets cut. Cuts in health care also have gender-specific effects. Even in the USA, more women than men die because of a lack of adequate health care (*Feminist Review*, 1991). In many parts of the developing world, girls are still likely to get less food and less health care than boys. The chances of being born and surviving beyond birth in parts of the world are also gender-specific. It has been estimated that 100 million Asian women are missing, a statistic attributed to widespread female infanticide and the abortion of female foetuses (Batou, 1991).

Feminism in global perspective

Feminists have increasingly recognized the need to look at issues of low pay and poverty and the gender-specific impact of economic restructuring in a global context. Furthermore, the fact that issues of population growth, sustainable development, environmental degradation and reproductive rights are now being recognized as crucial gender issues and finding their way on to the agenda of international politics is in no small part due to the efforts of feminists lobbies, both in the form of direct pressure group activity by feminist organizations and through the women's sections of non-governmental organizations. Feminist lobbies have stressed the urgency of overcoming poverty and addressing the needs of rural women, female-headed households and women who work in the so-called informal sector. They have also promoted the key concerns of the impact of global structural adjustment. Engagement with the global economy has made reform of GATT a feminist issue; so, too, with privatization. Feminist scholars have shown that gender relations of inequality and women's double burden are not only important to individual women, but to whole communities worldwide (Seager and Olson, 1986). Women around the world have called for alternative development models which emphasize sustainable, equitable and humane development. They have also argued that women should be given sufficient food, access to water, science and technology. The importance of women's unwaged work to development has also been stressed. Redefining work in the global economy effectively means recognizing both waged and unwaged work as essential to the social and economic well-being of countries. This is very much a feminist issue since the narrow definition of work is in large part responsible for the invisibility of the real contribution that women make to the global economy.

Women are also engaging in debates and international forums. The United Nations accepts that it has responsibilities in promoting women's education and reproductive health care, in improving their economic position and in fully integrating women into development programmes. Furthermore, in recent years the UN has opened up the question of the degree to which cultural patterns discriminate against women. It has thus attempted to balance respect for cultural diversity with the promotion of women's human rights. In the past twenty years the UN has played a role in challenging traditional cultural beliefs, often reinforced in law, which have assigned women to lower social status (Ashworth, 1993).

The issue of violence against women has now found its way on to the global agenda and is challenging established views about what is recognized as a 'human right' or a 'human rights violation'. Women's indirect relationship to the state and their lack of direct political representation means that their interests are neither adequately addressed in theory, practice, nor through monitoring (Ashworth, 1993: 6). Women's relationship to the state is frequently mediated by husbands, fathers and brothers who at same time acquire authority over women either via the state or traditional political communities. While gender relations often appear to be locked in the private realm:

> they are frequently upheld by the modern state through taxation, social security, immigration and nationality laws all of which retain elements of the husband master legacy and where identity and rights are based on property ownership – a traditional source of European law exported through colonialism – the ramifications for women have been enormous. (Ashworth, 1993: 15)

Nevertheless, this is another area where the UN has made inroads in the area of gender politics in recent years. The move to recognize and eliminate violence against women, and to recognize women's rights as human rights, necessarily challenges the sanctity of the patriarchal family structure and the role of men in mediating relations between women and the state. The Declaration on the Elimination of Violence Against Women thus marks a landmark in acknowledging gender-based violence in both public and private spheres as a violation of human rights.

In 1985, at the Nairobi conference that drew to a close the UN 'Decade for Women', a document entitled 'The Nairobi Forward-looking Strategies for the Advancement of Women to the Year 2000' was produced (UN, 1985).

The aims of the strategy were to promote women's interests in health, employment, family life, politics and human rights. The Nairobi FLSAW pressed for the inclusion of unpaid work in national accounts and in social and economic indicators. It also pressed for the allocation of social and economic benefits to take into account this broader definition of work. Since 1985, there have been regular meetings to review progress and decide on strategies for the social and economic advancement of women in the future.

A number of regional sessions were held in preparation for the Fourth UN Conference for Women held in Beijing in September 1995. The aims of these sessions were to review the Nairobi strategy, decide upon regional priority issues and put forward proposals for action for the future. While women met in a number of regional forums to discuss the major concerns for women in those particular regions, the stress was on the need to view the problems of women in a local, national, regional and global context. Clearly, broad disparities between North and South, rural and urban, and rich and poor continue to be of great significance in understanding the nature of global feminism. It is evident that gender inequalities have to be seen in the broader context of class and discrimination on the basis of race – faced by women and men. Furthermore, the degree to which class, race or ethnicity are significant divisions is also recognized both within and across state boundaries. European women have acknowledged that their concern with gender inequalities has to be seen in the context of broad inequalities not only between states and regions, but between women of colour and of different social groups (Hooper, 1994c). European women have argued that unsustainable growth in the European Union region jeopardizes women's lives both in that region and worldwide as the gap between rich and poor grows (Harper, 1994c: 20). The marginalization of women in the former Soviet Union and Eastern Europe is now a major concern for European feminists, but it has been recognized that this needs to be understood in terms of the impact of globalization. Women in Europe have, therefore, joined women in Latin America and in the Asia-Pacific region in rejecting dominant economic paradigms and arguing that the deep contradictions in economic policies of restructuring and globalization are resulting in economic and social policies which are detrimental to the rights of women (Hooper, 1994c: 21). Thus issues of women's rights and sustainable development cannot be seriously addressed unless consumption and production patterns in Europe change.

Significantly women's organizations in Europe have also cited the problems of racism in Europe, noting that women of colour in the region are particularly affected by global restructuring processes and make a particular contribution to unwaged and low-waged work. Thus from a European perspective, thinking about gender in a global perspective entails recognition of the additional problems of racism faced by women both in Europe and the rest of the world.

Thinking about gender in a global context

Theories that have arisen in response to globalization recognize that global processes shape and transform economic activity and that a number of 'actors', both governmental and non-governmental, act as agents of economic, social and political change (Tooze and Murphy, 1991). Since change can no longer be viewed as an entirely 'internal affair', it is necessary to explore its global dimension while recognizing the specificity of some areas (Scholte, 1993). Critical approaches to international relations and international political economy have attacked the dominance of realism within the discipline on the grounds that it serves to legitimize and perpetuate unequal social, economic and power relations. They have stressed the need to develop a counter-hegemonic set of concepts and concerns to deal with the problems of economic and social inequalities. However, the gender dimension of inequality and forms of resistance which arise in response to the experience of gender inequality have been largely neglected (Whitworth, 1993).

There still exists a widespread 'common-sense' assumption that gender discrimination and inequality can only be properly understood in the context of particular cultural practices. Feminists are, therefore, often accused of interfering with culture. The common-sense view that gender relations are essentially either a 'private' or cultural matter is frequently echoed in non-feminist approaches to international relations, where it is assumed that not only can relations between states be understood without reference to gender, but also that gender relations are essentially 'private'. Of course, when the 'international' is viewed through the prism of inter-state relations the degree to which social relations of all kinds are becoming globalized is rendered invisible. Such an accusation also ignores both the ways in which gendered processes have shaped international relations historically and the degree of power involved in constructing and maintaining such relations. Historically, development policies have been built upon neo-colonialist assumptions about the status of women as dependants and men as 'breadwinners', assumptions that have often served to deprive women of traditional rights (Ashworth and May, 1990). Today, Western ideologies, values, technologies and commercialism all interfere with indigenous culture and beliefs. Powerful gendered images are decimated by telecommunications and the global media, while the intrusion of education systems brings alternative value systems, and the introduction of fertility control techniques also poses

fundamental challenges to indigenous cultural values and traditional practices (Ashworth and May, 1990: 6).

It is also often suggested that feminism is a Western ideology which is
'alien' and of no relevance to women in the non-Western world. However,
this is very much an over-simplification. Feminism is no more 'foreign' than
socialism, or indeed nationalism. The rise and growth of feminist movements
has been shown to be related to the rise of nationalist movements in the
Third World and with resistance to imperialism (Jayawardena, 1986).
Feminist movements have emerged in the context of revolutionary changes
which challenged both imperialism and traditional forms of authority. There
is a wealth of woman-centred scholarship that shows that women frequently
support nationalist causes because they hope that in so doing they will
significantly advance the position of women (Ridd and Callaway, 1987).
There remain broad divisions between women in the North and South,
between rural women and urban women, and between women of different
social classes and races. However, global processes can and do create the
conditions for transnational political alliances which in turn affect both
social and economic change. The growth of global capitalism transforms
social orders and gives rise to many and varied new social movements.
Globalization has similarly changed the terms of feminist politics. The
feminization of poverty, the concentration of women in export production
zones, and the use of ideas about gender to legitimize low wages, for example,
have all profoundly affected women and encouraged the growth of groups
which, while sometimes reluctant to adopt the label 'feminist', nevertheless
organize around gender interests. Feminists have also campaigned against
the damaging effects on women and children of transnational activities.

However, while feminists have insisted that gender inequality can no
longer be seen purely in the context of the particularism of local customs or
cultural practices, it is clear that local and specific conditions, social and
cultural factors and the political and legal practices in particular states are
important. Indeed:

> one fundamental challenge for global feminism is that the conception, ob-
> jectives and strategy of feminism in different nations and regions have become
> intertwined with very different economic, socio-cultural and political condi-
> tions (Tohidi, 1994: 111)

That there are many 'feminisms' is perhaps indicative of the degree to which
gender inequality has been intertwined historically with other forms of
inequality. In the context of the global, 'difference' in this sense is magnified
with other major divisions such as class, race or ethnicity cutting across
gender historically. If, therefore, international relations scholars are to
develop ways of understanding gender in global perspective, it is necessary to

develop approaches which recognize the importance of specificity and difference and also the degree to which global processes transform gender relations and create the conditions for feminist alliances.

Gender, identity and difference

The desire to encourage a greater degree of theoretical self-reflexivity[6] in international relations theory has also opened up debates about the degree to which attempts to understand the nature and impact of globalization are inevitably partial. They are partial in the sense that, in the process of constructing a model of the 'global' and identifying the actors and processes which will serve as the subject of study, much will be ignored, marginalized or rendered invisible. Attempts to theorize globalization are also partial in the sense that they reflect particular standpoints or perspectives. The processes of 'inclusion and 'exclusion' inherent in all attempts to understand global processes are inevitable given the difficulties inherent in the task. However, when presented as impartial, value-free and objective, the political nature of knowledge claims is obscured. International relations scholars who adopt what might broadly be described as critical approaches have argued that the subjectivity of the social science should be recognized and historical modes of analysis and explanation encouraged in the discipline.

Feminist interventions in international relations are taking place in the context of a further debate which can in some senses be seen as a response to the need for feminist theory to think beyond the state and nation and grapple with the problem of the global, although increasingly it is recognized that questions of difference are as relevant to the divisions which exist inside state boundaries as 'outside'. Feminists who view the world from a non-Western perspective have recognized the urgent political need to form strategic alliances across class, race and national boundaries, but have also insisted that gender relations are embedded in wider power relations. Feminists operate in the context of wide-ranging inequalities and, therefore, Western feminism must be aware of its own political effects (Mohanty, 1988).

Western feminists have played a larger role in shaping debates within lobbies and within the UN because they have had privileged access to positions of influence. Furthermore, gender-sensitive development policies have been criticized in the past on the grounds that they promote gender interests as articulated by Western women. That feminism is sometimes conflated with imperialism and represented as the ideology of white, middle-class Western women is perhaps in part a consequence of the context in which feminist lobbying has taken place. In recent years, Western feminists have become aware of the need to be sensitive to the context in which the gender interests are promoted. However, it is both disempowering and inaccurate to suggest that women from outside the Western World have played no role in shaping debates.

What is particularly problematic in terms of challenges to Western dominance in this context, however, is the degree to which the analytical principles of Western feminist discourse may in themselves limit the possibilities of coalitions amongst white Western feminists, working-class women and women of colour. Mohanty has argued that while

> feminist discourse may serve as an ideological, mode of intervention into hegemonic discourse and political praxis which counters and resists the totalising imperatives of age old legitimate and scientific bodies of knowledge, there is no universal patriarchal framework which feminist scholarship attempts to counter. (Mohanty, 1988: 62)

Similarly, it cannot be simply assumed that women are constituted as a group before they enter into social relations (p. 68). The 'problem' is not the status of feminism as such but rather the dangers inherent in universalizing the conditions of oppression and of speaking for others. Recent debates in feminist theory have been largely concerned with rethinking approaches to both theory and practice which are historical and which can also allow the articulation of difference while retaining a feminist politics. Much contemporary feminist theory is concerned with thinking through the implications of difference and problematizing the role of the theorist in interpreting and representing the experiences of other women. In order to theorize the global dimensions of gender inequality and feminist politics it is necessary, therefore, to develop a specifically feminist approach that recognizes the links between knowledge, power and interests and which can establish that women's lives and experiences constitute knowledge of the world and that the process of theorizing should begin from women's own experiences, while simultaneously resisting the claim that there is a homogeneous 'women's experience' which can serve as the grounds for knowledge claims. The project entails the need to develop a concept of the subject that does not slide into essentialism, but which never loses sight of the political imperatives of feminism (Alcoff, 1988).

Feminist voices in global 'conversations'

While some feminist writers have warned against the dangerous assumption that women are a strategic group by virtue of their womanhood or their 'dependency', what all feminists share is a conviction that women can become a strategic group when they enter into a common struggle against class, race and gender hierarchies. In this sense the feminist project involves an ongoing struggle to transform oppressive relations of many kinds and in all their complex and diverse manifestations. Feminists are attempting to develop ways of understanding gender identity and power in ways which relate gender to categories of class, race, culture and ethnicity and which recognize that the problems of identity are in some ways better approached historically, but which retain a feminist politics. This involves an ongoing 'conversation' between feminists who consciously reject theoretical projects which offer universal, essentialist or reductionist explanations of multi-faceted and complex social relations, but who are nevertheless committed to finding ways forward to advance the social, economic and political position of women throughout the world. It is based upon a recognition of the many forms of inequality and of the need to build upon the many sites of feminist struggle. This is neither a rejection of theory in favour of pragmatism, nor is it a rejection of the 'emancipatory project' inherent in feminism. However, it does mean that the goals and objectives of feminism cannot be determined on the basis of a priori assumptions or articulated in abstract terms. It entails a genuine willingness to enter into an open dialogue, while addressing the very real inequalities which prevent the experiences of some women from being heard. The challenges which globalization poses for feminist theory are only part of the much larger challenge facing international relations in a postpositive era. However, it is without doubt that feminist scholarship makes a valuable contribution to this project by enriching our understanding of the connections between gender and inequalities of power and the dynamic of social change in a global context.

Notes

1. There is a huge literature in both the areas of women/gender and the global economy, and gender and development. A useful starting-point for examining the gender-specific impact of global restructuring might be Vickers (1988) or Elson (1990). For a more general discussion of the gender-specific impact of global restructuring in the 1980s, see Krause (1995).
2. The Executive Director of UNICEF, James P. Grant, has commented that 'the apartheid of gender is the cruellest and the most pervasive discrimination of all, yet it has not yet generated a sustained condemnation on a global scale', United Nations Department of Public Information DPI/1284-92972, November 1992-6M.
3. See *The Women's World 1970–1990; Trends and Statistics*, New York, United Nations, 1991.
4. See *Focus on Women*, United Nations Department of Public Information 1567, New York, September 1994.
5. Ibid.
6. Part of the critique of the 'orthodoxy' in international relations has centred upon the *positivist* assumptions of mainstream theories and research methods. That is, the assumption that it is possible to explain social phenomena without reference to the meanings which people ascribe to social situations, and that the theorist –

the subject of knowledge – essentially stands apart from the object of study. Critical theories (and I include here most feminist scholarship in International Relations) explicitly recognize the ideological nature of knowledge claims and recognize the intimate connection between theory and practice. The process of theorizing involves reflecting upon the social, historical and political context in which the activity takes place.

References

Alcoff, L. (1988) Cultural feminism and poststructuralism; the identity crisis in feminist theory, *Signs*, **13**(3).

Ashworth, G. (1993) *Changing the Discourse: A Guide to Women and Human Rights*, London, Change Publications.

Ashworth, G. and May, N. (1990) *Of Conjuring and Caring*, London, Change Publications.

Batou, J. (1991) One hundred million women are missing, *International Viewpoint*, 206.

Beneria, L. (1992) Accounting for women's work; the progress of two decades, *World Development*, **20**(11), 1547–60.

Feminist Review (1991) Women in Eastern Europe, **39**, special edition.

Giddens, A. (1991) *The Consequences of Modernity*, Cambridge, Polity Press.

Elson, D. (1990) *Male Bias in the Development Process*, Manchester, Manchester University Press.

Hooper, E. (1994a) (DAC/WID Expert Group Co-ordinator for the 1995 Fourth UN Conference on Women) *Report on the UN ECLAC Regional Preparatory Meeting for the Fourth World Conference on Women*, Mar del Plata, Argentina, 25–29 September.

Hooper, E. (1994b) (DAC/WID Expert Group Co-ordinator for the 1995 Fourth UN Conference on Women) *Report on the UN ECCAP Regional Preparatory Meeting for the Fourth World Conference on Women*, Jakarta, 7–11 June.

Hooper, E. (1994c) (DAC/WID Expert Group Co-ordinator for the 1995 Fourth UN Conference on Women) *Report on the UN ECECE Regional Preparatory Meeting for the Fourth World Conference for Women*, Geneva.

Jayawardena, K. (1986) *Feminism and Nationalism in the Third World*, London, Zed Books.

Krause, J. (1995) The international dimensions of gender inequality and feminist politics: a 'new direction' for international political economy? in J. Macmillan and A. Linklater (eds), *Boundaries in Question; New Directions in International Relations*, London, Pinter.

Mohagadom, V. M. (1994) *Women and National Identity*, London, Zed Books.

Mohanty, C. (1988) Under western eyes; feminist scholarship and colonial discourse, *Feminist Review*, **30**, 61–88.

Momsen, J. (1991) *Women and Development in the Third World*, London, Routledge.

Peterson, V. S. and Runyan, A. (1993) *Global Gender Issues*, Boulder, CO, Westview Press.

Ridd, R. and Callaway, H. (1987) *Caught up in Conflict*, New York, New York University Press.

Scholte, J. A. (1993) *International Relations and Social Change*, Buckingham, Open University Press.

Seager, J. and Olson, A. (1986) *Women in the World: An International Atlas*, New York, Simon and Schuster.

Thahn Dam, T. (1983) The dynamics of sex tourism; the case of South East Asia, *Development and Change*, **14**, 533–53.

Tohidi, N. (1994) Modernization, Islamization and women in Iran, in V. M. Mohagadam (ed.), *Women and National Identity*, London, Zed Books.

Tooze, R. and Murphy, C. (1991) *The New International Political Economy*, Boulder, CO, Lynne Rienner Publications.

Vickers, J. (1988) *Women and the World Economic Crisis*, London, Zed Books.

Whitworth, S. (1993) Theory as exclusion; gender and international political economy, in R. Stubbs and G. Underhill (eds), *Political Economy and the Changing Global Order*, Basingstoke, Macmillan.

UN (1985) *The Nairobi Forward-looking Strategies for the Advancement of Women*: as adopted by the World Conference to review and appraise the achievements of the UN Decade for Women: equality, development and peace, Nairobi, Kenya, 15–26 July 1985, United Nations Department of Public Information, DPI/926–41761, September 1993.

UNICEF (1994) *The State of the World's Children, 1994*, Oxford, Oxford University Press.

17

The Places of Women in Trading Places: Gendered Global/Regional Regimes and Inter-nationalized Feminist Resistance[1]

ANNE SISSON RUNYAN

The gendered nature of globalization, or global economic, political, and social restructuring to facilitate the movement of transnational capital and corporations, is revealed in the following telling characterization of the process by David Mulford, who served as US Under-Secretary of the Treasury during the Bush administration: 'The countries that do not make themselves attractive will not get investors' attention . . . This is like a girl trying to get a boyfriend. She has to go out, have her hair done up, wear make up' (quoted in Cavanagh, 1992: 4). This (hetero)sexual invitation to 'foreign penetration' not only belies the 'date rape' that subsequently occurs with the transfer of 'power and resources from the natural world to human domination, from communities to elites, and from local societies to national and transnational power centers' (Brecher, Childs and Cutler, 1993: xi); it also obscures the realities of women's lives in the context of globalization and the actual resistance of women to these 'advances'.

Interestingly, however, this gendered and sexualized metaphor does signal a fundamental shift in power relations associated with global restructuring. By portraying the state as a feminized spinster/siren and the market as a masculinized roving bachelor on the make, the metaphor speaks to a change from mercantilist global economic relations, presided over most significantly by the hegemonic US state in the post-World War II period, to a transnational corporation and finance-dominated global economy that began to form at least since the 1970s with the breakdown of Bretton Woods and that is not beholden to any state. It also speaks to the mobility of capital vs. the fixedness of the state as a territorial unit, further indicating erosions in state sovereignty to control or even regulate global capital. Finally, it presages the increasing mobility of female labour – 'girls' must 'go out' (typically to urban areas or export-processing zones) and pretty themselves up or rather make themselves highly available and exploitable in order for their states to catch a 'real man'. Alternatively, if the states in which they reside are unable to attract foreign investor 'boyfriends', 'girls' must 'go out' of their states to catch a wage. Of course, this puerile dating is not designed for reproduction – that is, the enhancement of human and planetary life – but rather for a kind of 'love 'em and leave 'em' production that enriches only a few at the expense of far too many and too much.

Gendered global regimes

The transition this apparently 'innocent' dating metaphor captures by the moves of simultaneously gendering (thus naturalizing and domesticating) and sexualizing (thus titillating and romanticizing) continues to unfold with highly problematic consequences for women, particularly within other subordinated groups. The shift from US-dominated mercantilism to a TNC-dominated global political economy was accompanied by a shift from a Fordist to what has been called a 'bloody Taylorist' (Nanda, 1994) form of production in the 1980s. As we know, when TNCs moved assembly-line production from North to South to escape tariffs and worker health and safety and environmental protection laws, women became the preferred labour force in light assembly plants in export-processing zones (EPZs or 'maquiladoras' as they are called in Mexico and the Caribbean), constituting anywhere from 70 to 90 per cent of such workers. What we also know about global factories is that regardless of the state (particularly in the geographic South) which hosts them or the industry (garments, electronics, data processing, etc.) or the national or cultural backgrounds of the management and workers, these 'two-dollars-a-day' women workers (Enloe, 1992), who typically lack the protection of unions and state regulation that is present in the Fordist model, are treated in the same ways.

Local and transnational employers share a patriarchal ideology that sees women (and particularly young and poor ones) as compliant, dextrous and easily exploited labourers working for pin money (despite repeated strikes by women workers too often put down by male bosses, police and even male workers and relatives). As a result, there is much similarity in the wages and working and living conditions of women global factory workers across the geographic South, ranging from the 'two-dollars-a-day' or less standard (which does not constitute a living wage anywhere) to pervasive sexual harassment (the 'lay down or be laid off' policy), unsafe work and work stations (characterized by eyesight-damaging close work, unventilated sweatshops, and repeated toxic chemical exposure), and impoverished and degraded 'home' environments (most vividly illustrated by urban and EPZ shanty towns next to open sewers filled with industrial and residential waste) (Peterson and Runyan, 1993: 101, 109). These scenes, of course, are reminiscent of the 'bloody Taylorism' that marked the rise of the Industrial Revolution in England, complete with unprotected female and child labour as well as appalling working and living conditions that are not conducive to reproducing the working class but do enable the owners of production to extract a great deal of wealth from the process.

This picture, however, is already changing, but not for the better. As Saskia Sassen has found, there have been shifting patterns in foreign direct investment (FDI) and manufacturing throughout the 1980s. Unlike the post-World War II mercantilist world economy, when FDI was concentrated in raw material extractive industries in the geographic South, FDI is now most concentrated in the geographic North, with the USA, the UK, Japan, France and Germany receiving the lion's share (57 per cent) of FDI (Sassen, 1993: 62). At the same time, the share of FDI going to the geographic South has fallen from 25 per cent in the early 1980s to 19 per cent in the late 1980s, with Latin America losing the most (from 49 per cent to 38 per cent of its share) and Southeast Asia gaining a larger share of the smaller piece of the FDI pie going to the South (from 37 per cent to 48 per cent) (Sassen, ibid). Thus, Southeast Asia has become the preferred site for global manufacturing, necessitating, however, a shift to more automated production which can meet the demands for more 'customized' products and 'just-in-time' delivery systems, particularly to the US market. Meera Nanda characterizes this as a shift from 'manufacturing' to 'systemfacturing', in which computers and robotics are used to replace unskilled factory labour, and she has observed that this has had the effect of supplanting female global factory workers with technically skilled male workers (Nanda, 1994; see also Joekes and Weston, 1994: 65). Marianne Marchand has also recently argued that large-scale restructuring of maquiladoras in Mexico is also in the offing to accommodate greater automation (Marchand, 1994: 66–7). Indeed, Sydney Weintraub and Georges Fauriol report that already in Mexico 'transportation and electronic equipment now outstrip clothing production. The labor force of "maquiladoras" used to be upwards of 90 percent women; the male-female ratio is now almost identical' (Weintraub and Fauriol, 1994: 84).

Even as global manufacturing is becoming automated and less dependent on shop-floor female labour, manufacturing itself is becoming devalued. According to Sassen, the debt crisis in the early 1980s – 'actually a crisis for the major transnational banks in the U.S.' (Sassen, 1993: 64) – fuelled the deregulation of international finance:

> Deregulation made finance so profitable that it took investment away from manufacturing. Finance allows superprofits by maximizing the circulation of money (e.g., securitization, multiple transactions over a short period of time, selling debts, etc.) in a way that manufacturing does not. One can bundle a large number of mortgages and sell the bundle many times, even though the number of houses involved stays the same. This option is basically not available in manufacturing, in which a product is made and sold; once it enters

the realm of circulation it enters other sectors of the economy, and it is to these that the profits from subsequent sales accrue. (p. 65)

Sassen goes on to point out that the superprofits connected with international finance 'strengthen the idea that manufacturing needs to be "more" profitable, which in turn can justify the lowering of wages and the extraction of give-backs from workers' (ibid.). This, of course, is what has been happening to factory workers in the geographic North, who either lost jobs as factories went South in search of cheaper labour in the early 1980s or have lost ground throughout the 1980s and into the 1990s as a result of union-busting and forced concessions in the name of global competitiveness. As V. Spike Peterson and I (1993) have pointed out, this process has not only affected the usually portrayed out-of-work male factory worker who has lost his Fordist protections and privileges as the family wage-earner. It has also cost the jobs of a large number of female workers (over 35 per cent of workers who lost jobs in the USA because of plant closings between 1979 and 1983 were women), who face even deeper impoverishment if they are among those who head the growing numbers of single-parent households (Peterson and Runyan, 1993: 101).

One option for more skilled, laid-off women factory workers in the North is the burgeoning service industry in post-industrial urban economies, including clerical services in the international finance industry. As Sassen (1991) has pointed out, 'among the fastest growing jobs' in New York, London and Tokyo, where manufacturing has steadily eroded to be replaced by finance and service industries,

> are professional and clerical occupations, the former paying some of the highest salaries and the latter paying increasingly lower salaries. Furthermore, where the evidence is available, clerical jobs in the new service industries tend to have lower salaries than do clerical jobs in manufacturing and transportation, while the reverse is the case with professional jobs. (p. 244)

However, these professionals whom we most associate with the fast-paced, glamorized world of global finance – cosmopolitan male experts – constitute only about 15 per cent of the workers in global finance industries (Sassen, 1994). They depend heavily on the mostly female labour of clerical workers and other support personnel who make up about 50 per cent of the workers in this industry (Sassen, 1994). Unfortunately, as Sassen also points out, the 'non-professional workforce in finance and in services generally is in a far more subordinate position than the workforce in major mechanized factories, where the shop-floor is a terrain for contestation and workers' struggles' (Sassen, 1993: 65). Moreover, those female workers still engaged in manufacturing are less and less on the shop-floor and more and more relegated to benefit-less, home-based piecework, particularly in garment industries in urban centres, which is increasingly dictated by local subcontractors to TNCs, who can be more ruthless than TNCs themselves. These facts are hidden from view by the proponents of 'cosmocorp' who eulogize over the freedom and upward mobility being created in post-industrial, post-Fordist economies centred in global cities.

What is also obscured by the hegemonic images and practices of global finance is that it is, in fact, highly regionalized across states and within them. As the FDI figures discussed earlier show (see also Henwood, 1993), and as Henk Overbeek has recently argued, 'the globalization process takes place *through* regionalization: most activities by transnational corporations (TNCs) are concentrated more and more in the three core regions of the world: North America (NAFTA), Western Europe (European Single Market), and East Asia' (Overbeek, 1994: 6). At the same time, large parts of the geographic South are being cut off from foreign investment and TNC activity, creating, in effect, a triage process (Overbeek, 1994: 6–7). This is, in part,

> due to the new technological revolution, in which the cycle of capital accumulation depends less and less on intensive use of natural resources, labour, or even productive capital, and more on an accumulation of technology based on the intensive use of knowledge. The intensive concentration and centralization of technological knowledge is more intense and monopolistic than other forms of capital, and only increases the gap between North and South. (Gorostiaga, 1993: 69)

Moreover, large parts of the geographic North are becoming peripheralized economically as the growth of global cities, dominated by international finance industries and 'global' interests, fails to translate into, as it becomes increasingly disconnected from, national economic growth (Sassen, 1991: 13). Thus, welfare states of the North are becoming emptied out in the face of the declines in revenue, infrastructure, export-producing manufacturing and working-class and even middle-class wages, as well as increasing trade deficits brought about by the new orientation to global finance and services circulating within and for the consumption of firms, not people (Sassen, 1991: 10). Indeed, Ricardo Pertella, the European Union's director of science and technology, has predicted:

> 'In just a few decades, nation-states such as the United States, Japan, Germany, Italy, and France will no longer be so relevant. Instead, rich regions built around cities such as Osaka, San Francisco and the four motors of Europe [Stuttgart, Milan, Barcelona, and Lyon] will acquire effective power, because they can work in tandem with the transnational companies who control capital.' (quoted in Drozdiak, 1994: 4)

The only role left for nation-states, in Pertella's view, would be 'multinational security alliances while real government is carried out by ... "the international metropolitans" that would "bring government closer to the people" ' (Drozdiak, 1994: 4).

It is hard to see, however, how these new 'city-states' can be democratic when they are, in fact, controlled by transnational capital. Indeed, David Becker and Richard Sklar (1987) have pointed out how suspect this vision is in their analysis of what they call 'postimperialism' in which 'transnational class formation' is facilitating a political *rapprochement* between and among élites in the North and South in the context of a world capitalist system.

> postimperialism is a theory of international oligarchy. Should the nation-state be increasingly or decisively marginalized as an economic institution by 'Cosmocorp', and should the nationalistic vendettas with which we are all too familiar be overcome, it is not certain that the result would be Utopia foreseen by the ideologists of corporate capitalism. A world dominated by an international bourgeois oligarchy offers little that would appeal to progressives. Its institutions of political power and accountablity might be even more remote from those affected by them than in the case today. What is more, the dominant oligarchy may resort to openly coercive forms of social control if it has to face a sullen or hostile proletariat without the legitimation afforded by nationalism. (p. 14)

Thus, it would seem that even as states are emptied of their welfare capacities, they would continue to be equipped with warfare capacities, not to engage in inter-state conflict, but rather to control labour more effectively to meet the needs of global capital and its agents, transnational corporations.

Gendered regional regimes

States, of course, are still active agents in facilitating global restructuring even as it marginalizes some of their traditional powers and prerogatives. The creation of regional trading blocs or regional integration projects such as the various formations that culminated in the European Union (EU) and the North American Free Trade Agreement (NAFTA) in the past few years has been both a facilitator of, and a (largely rearguard) reaction to, global capital. The construction of the EU has a much longer history than that of NAFTA, as well as a rather different context; however, both are fundamentally economic agreements spurred by concerns about remaining or becoming economically competitive largely to deal with burgeoning national debts. As Overbeek has observed, this competition is twofold. At one level, it is a competition among TNCs sited in Europe, North America and the Pacific Rim (the latter has not as yet been formally articulated as a trading bloc), and at another level it is a competition between states primarily in the North 'to attract transnational capital, preferably in the high value added sectors, in order to provide jobs, income, and security for the population' (Overbeek, 1994: 6). As many critics of the EU and NAFTA have noted, however, few good jobs and high incomes and little security for most people have arisen from these regional integration projects, even though they are successful in attracting transnational capital, primarily because that capital is less and less oriented to the kind of production that can facilitate reproduction.

Feminist critics of the EU and NAFTA have been tallying a number of deficiencies in these agreements for women, particularly those in other subordinated groups, including the poor and working class, communities of colour, and migrant and immigrant populations. In the case of the EU, the deficits feminists in Europe have been cataloguing include a significant transfer of power away from national legislative bodies and the European Parliament to the European Commission and Council of Ministers just as women were gaining increasing access to state legislatures; the construction of women only as workers or production units, which has resulted in relatively strong directives on women's equal treatment in the workplace, but very weak or non-harmonized directives (if any) on violence against women in the home, on the streets, and in the workplace; the promotion of pornography and prostitution as particularly lucrative European industries; the tacit approval of 'abortion tourism' by, for example, allowing Ireland to join the EU without liberalizing its abortion law; the non-harmonization of laws with respect to lesbian and gay rights which restricts the mobility of lesbians and gays within the Union who may be protected in some of their home countries, but not in others; and the treatment of women as a homogeneous category which entitles them to certain protections against sex discrimination in the workplace, but denies women of colour, immigrant women, and lesbians additional harmonized protection against discrimination based on race, national origin, or sexual orientation (Women, the European State and Community Conference Proceedings, 1994).[2]

In short, the so-called Social Charter of the EU, codified in 1989 (but opted out of by the UK), has not gone much beyond the social policy intents of the 1957 Rome Treaty which were to lower the 'risk that governments with inferior standards would not only exploit workers but could also derive cost advantages by spending less on employee welfare' and to avoid 'social dumping' that 'would encourage multinational firms to concentrate their investment in parts of the EC where "social costs" were lower' (Moxon-Browne, 1993: 156). In effect, the primary concern remains that people need to become as undifferentiated and mobile as capital, goods and services to correct distortions in the 'free' market.

However, in order to produce integration and homogenization within, it is necessary to control forces of 'difference'. This lies behind the construction of what has been called 'Fortress Europe'. With the solidification of the EU has come increasing restrictions on immigrants and asylum seekers, reducing their entry and access to citizenship and welfare, as well as a rise in overt racism and racist violence (Kofman and Sales, 1992). Immigrant and migrant women are particularly vulnerable in this context as they often enter the EU as dependants of their husbands, having to remain in this status for years, even with an abusive husband, or risk deportation and/or poverty as social welfare is restricted to citizens (Sales, 1994).

At the same time, however, that movements of many women are restricted into and within the EU, thousands of women are being trafficked into the EU to support the burgeoning prostitution industry. Pauline Bart recently reported that sex trafficking in Europe has increased by 30 per cent since 1984 – coinciding with the increasing deregulation of the industry and the opening of borders within the EU as well as a decline in some European men's sex tourism outside Europe as a result of feminist protest at home and abroad (Bart, 1994). According to Bart, 60 per cent of the 20,000 prostitutes in The Netherlands are from the geographic South now, and 100,000 women from the South have been trafficked into Europe in the last decade. Eastern European women are only the latest wave of trafficked women in Europe, joining East Asian women brought in in the 1970s, Latin American and Caribbean women in the 1980s, and North African women in the 1990s (Bart, 1994). Thus, the free movement of women into and within the EU is heavily restricted, while the forced movement of women is highly facilitated.

In the case of NAFTA, which does not involve even the pretence of a 'social charter', the deleterious effects on women in North America that feminist scholars and activists have been documenting include: a 'maquildorization' of not only the Mexican, but also the Canadian and US economies, driving wages and worker protections downward; a huge net loss in manufacturing jobs, particularly in Canada and the USA, which not only affects women (largely of colour) on the shop-floor, but also large numbers of manufacturing clerical workers; the consignment of immigrant women from Mexico and other locations in the South to urban sweatshops in the North; further declines in family farming and income therefrom, forcing rural women throughout North America to engage in the 'triple day' of harder farmwork, additional waged work, and reproductive work in the home; the intensification of the 'casualization' and 'flexibilization' particularly of women's labour, which consigns women in increasing numbers to part-time and home-based production with low wages and virtually no protections; an increase in the toxicity of workplaces, residential areas, and foodstuffs; a decline in social welfare spending and services, forcing women to fill the gaps in care that the state is abandoning; a growing assault on legislative gains for women, such as pay equity and affirmative action, which, like environmental protection

laws, may be construed as non-tariff barriers resulting in 'unfair' trade
practices; and the unaccountablity of supranational free trade regime élites
to women as state-bound citizens (see, for example, Joekes and Weston,
1994; Duggan and Dashner, 1994; Gabriel and MacDonald, 1994; Alternative Women in Development, 1993; Woman to Woman, 1993; McGinn
and Moody, 1993; Liebowitz, 1993; Ranney and Cecil, 1993; Seguino,
1993; Zabin, 1992; Sparr, 1991; Cohen, 1987). All of these trends are
associated with the larger process of globalization and structural adjustment
for which NAFTA serves as a conveyor belt. Thus much of the resistance
work by women to these processes is focused on the long-term struggle
against these global dynamics, even though particular struggles have gone
on in the context of speaking out against NAFTA and dealing with its
consequences at local levels.

Inter-nationalized feminist resistance

Women's resistance to NAFTA and the more global processes it represents is
beginning to take many forms, ranging from agitating for greater and more
transnational union representation in terms of factory and home-based work
(most notably through the International Ladies Garment Workers Union);
placing global restructuring on the agenda of national women organizations
(primarily in Canada through the National Action Committee on the Status
of Women); cross-border organizing among women workers on the borders
of the USA and Mexico (such as Mujer Obrera in El Paso and Fuerza Unida in
San Antonia), as well as among women workers in similar industries (such
as the Rural Coalition in Washington, DC) and women activists in all three
countries (such as Mujer á Mujer/Woman to Woman in Mexico City,
Toronto, and San Antonio, Alt-WID in Washington, DC, and Labour Notes
in Detroit, all of which sponsor cross-border organizing schools for workers
and activists); and as members of various local, national, and international
coalitions of labour, farmer, church, environmental, development, public
policy, and indigenous people's organizations that have mounted anti-
NAFTA and anti-World Bank, IMF and GATT (now the World Trade
Organization) campaigns.[3]

The cross-border organizing by women going on around NAFTA and
global restructuring may be developing new models 'in the face of proliferating, multiple centers and peripheries' that may be creating 'new analyses of
how gender works in the dynamic of globalization and the countermeasures
of new nationalisms, and ethnic and racial fundamentalism' which 'map
[what Inderpal Grewal and Caran Kaplan call] these scattered hegemonies
and link diverse local practices to formulate a transnational set of solidarities'
(Grewal and Kaplan, 1994: 19). This process is differentiated from 'the old

sisterhood model of missionary work, of intervention and salvation' that 'is clearly tied to older models of center-periphery relations' (ibid.: 19). Facilitating this process is not only the forces of 'integration' which exert downward pressures in similar ways in diverse localities, but also the creation of 'multiply "placed"' and 'multiply "linked"' subjectivities (Grewal, 1994: 235) through the 'forced march' of women's labour into EPZs and urban areas within and increasingly across borders to meet the needs of transnational capital for cheap, casualized labour in both the so-called 'periphery' and 'core'.

Those women who are increasingly on the move are from the geographic South travelling primarily to urban centres, border cities, and Silicon Valley-type areas in the geographic North (specifically, the USA, Canada and Western Europe) to fill low-wage jobs proliferating in these places (ranging from service work as domestics, prostitutes, and restaurant or retail employees in the formal and informal sectors to assembly-line, sweatshop, farmwork, and domestic employment). These legal and illegal immigrant/migrant women, who have often been construed by states in the North as threats – threats to citizens' (men's) jobs, threats to white supremacy (by having 'too many' children of colour), and so on – also pose a challenge to feminist activism in the North. As Rosi Braidotti (1992) has asked with respect to notions of 'European feminism' within the new EU:

> Are women sufficiently present as citizens in our respective countries to start thinking seriously in an international perspective? How aware are European feminists of the realities of migrations in their own countries? Is it not the case that feminists share with the dominant culture a basic resistance to the simple idea that internationalization begins at home? (p. 9).

Indeed, 'cross-border' organizing under conditions of globalization and regionalization needs to take on multiple and more complex meanings. Given that national identities are largely constructions of states, transnational identities are being interpreted by TNCs and states as their political agents, and gender identities are typically the products of these and other 'scattered hegemonies' that lay claim to what is supposed to constitute *the* culture, *the* religion, *the* polity, *the* economy at a given time and place as well as *the* woman or women who will fit into and serve these frameworks, it is vital for women/feminists to 'enact new forms of locating themselves within societies' that 'are both oppositional and nonessentialist, and confront and fracture the self-other opposition in the name of inclusions, multiple identities, and diasporic subject positions' (Grewal, 1994: 234). The mobility of women created by the 'forced marches' instituted by globalization and regionalization – in effect, the trade in women in 'trading places' – is far from liberating. However, the 'mobile subjectivities' (Ferguson, 1993) of women that are being placed in sharp relief and (re)constructed by these same forces, as they reposition women in contradictory ways (for example, dividing individual women's identities by offering worker protections on the basis of sex, but not race or sexual orientation, or by forcing a woman not only out of her 'home', but also out of her country to service debt or finance), are opening up spaces for women to 'trade places' in ways that can build increasingly what I call 'inter-nationalized'[4] solidarities within and across states. As Inderpal Grewal (1994) puts it:

> There can be syncretic, 'immigrant,' cross-cultural, and plural subjectivities, which can enable a politics through positions that are coalitions, intransigent, in process, and contradictory. Such identities are enabling because they provide a mobility in solidarity that leads to a transnational participation in understanding and opposing multiple and global oppressions operating upon them; that is, these subject positions enable oppositions in multiple locations. Multiple locations also enable valuable interventions precisely because the agendas of one group are brought along to interrogate and empower those of another group (Grewal, 1994: 234).

Gatherings like the first Mujer á Mujer's Global Strategies School, which was a Tri-National Conference of Women on Free Trade and Economic Integration that took place in Valle de Bravo, Mexico in February 1992, are able to connect the similarities among 'Reagonomics', 'Salinismo' and the 'Mulroney Plan', but also discuss the differences in the playing out of these architectures in different national contexts in order to arrive at demands that do not undercut women in different locations. For example, during that conference there was much debate on what would constitute 'upward harmonization' as concerns were raised about the problematics of demanding a harmonization of salaries in the context of still very different economies. More contextual approaches suggested included upwardly adjusting salaries 'based on the cost of a basic food basket in each country' as well as ensuring that each country's basic services were not further eroded (Mujer á Mujer, 1992: 22). There was also recognition that organizing within and outside unions are both viable strategies, depending upon the occupational and community context as well as the union involved. Moreover, there was sensitivity about seemingly progressive demands that are actually quite divisive. As one US participant argued,

> 'The problem I see with training as a demand is the underlying belief that it alone will guarantee jobs stay in the country. This undercuts our claim that we don't want to compete with each other. We're basically saying: The problem is us, and if only we can get the right skills, we can save our jobs, our communities, our lives.' (Quoted in Mujer á Mujer, 1992: 21).

On the other hand, one Mexican participant noted that ' "One demand we can make is that the permissible levels for workplace toxics be standardised.

Our bodies are the same (so) it doesn't make sense that the permissible levels in Mexico be so high"' (quoted in Mujer á Mujer, 1992: 23).

These contextualized understandings and strategies arising from the development of a more 'heterogeneous consciousness' (Grewal, 1994: 251) produced by forming 'inter-nationalized' solidarities that build upon women's varying and multiple class, race, national, sexual, age, occupational, community, and gender locations are suggestive of how to construct alternatives to non-existent, insufficient, or exclusionary 'universalist' social charters to mitigate the effects of and reorient regional and global 'integration'. However, the channels for instituting such charters remain highly problematic in the cases of the gendered regimes of both 'North America' and 'Europe'. States, supra-states, city-states that are beholden to TNCs are marching to a different drummer and much faster than are social movements that are trying to intervene to stop the 'forced march' of women as a subordinated group and as part of other subordinated groups. In addition, social movements themselves are also complicit in the process to the degree that they are dependent on state or regional funds to lobby those very entities (as in the case of, for example, the European Women's Lobby), construct exclusive (that is, racist and sexist) or jingoistically competitive organizations (as is the case with too many labour unions and often environmental groups), and/or engage in short-term, single-issue politics with no larger analyses and critiques of the global social, political, and economic forces (modernity and post-modernity, postindustrialism and de-development, capitalism(s), patriarchies, racisms, fundamentalisms, etc.) that give rise to specific policies in specific places (as can too often be the case with such 'liberal' women's organizations as the US National Organization for Women). Relatedly, there is also the danger that social movements can, along with transnational capital, privilege the global at the expense of the local where 'place-bound activities' occur (Sassen, 1993: 65) and where women become visible in households, communities, and work-sites. Internationalized feminist consciousness and practices that are developing in response to globalization and regionalization and which 'disrupt the home/ abroad and the margin/center constructs for more complex positionings' (Grewal, 1994: 234) hold possibilities for less complicit social movement development as well as more contextualized and connected organizing. As a form of multiply located, yet interconnected politics, such consciousness and practices can also yield greater awareness of rapidly shifting patterns in the gendered nature of places and spaces and movements between and through them that require swift reorganization of gender identities and relations, thereby providing continuous remappings of new deployments of power as they unfold.

Notes

1. Research and travel support for the preparation of the paper on which this chapter is based came from New York State/United University Professionals Professional Development and Quality of Work Life Committee, the Research and Creative Endeavors Program of SUNY Potsdam, and the American Political Science Association.
2. Papers arising out of the 'Women, the European State and Community' conference at Kalamazoo College in May 1994 have just been published. See R. A. Elman (1996), *Sexual Politics and the European Union*, Providence, RI, Berghahn Books.
3. These examples come from the files of Karen Kuhn of Development Gap in Washington, DC, which she graciously shared with me.
4. I hyphenate 'inter-nationalized' to stress the politics of difference upon which 'cross-border' feminist alliances necessarily rest. That is, such alliances cannot be based on a homogenized notion of 'woman', but rather must draw their strength from the 'inter-play' of women's multiple identities, experiences, and locations which can reveal multiple yet differing patterns of domination. Moreover, such alliances can only be built 'between', at the interstices of, homogenized national identities that tend to evacuate gender politics.

References

Alternative Women-in-Development Working Group (1993) Breaking boundaries: women, free trade and economic integration, occasional paper, Washington, DC, Alt-WID.

Bart, P. (1994) Introductory remarks for panel on 'Sexual exploitation, violence and death', *Women, the European State, and Community Conference*, Kalamazoo College, Kalamazoo, MI, 13–14 May.

Becker, D. G. and Sklar, R. L. (1987) Why postimperialism? in D. G. Becker, J. Frieden, P. Sayre Schatz and R. L. Sklar (eds), *Postimperialism: International Capitalism and Development in the Late Twentieth Century*, Boulder, CO, Westview Press, pp. 1–18.

Braidotti, R. (1992) The exile, the nomad, and the migrant: reflections on international feminism, *Women's Studies International Forum*, **15**, 7–10.

Brecher, J., Childs, J. B. and Cutler J. (1993) Introduction, in J. Brecher, J. B. Childs and J. Cutler (eds), *Global Visions: Beyond the New World Order*, Boston, South End Press, pp. ix–xxvi.

Cavanagh, J. (1992) Foreword: free trade as opportunity, in J. Cavanagh, J. Gersham, K. Becker and G. Helmke (eds), *Trading Freedom: How Free Trade Affects Our Lives, Work, and Environment*, San Francisco, Institute for Food and Development Policy, pp. 1–11.

Cohen, M. G. (1987) *Free Trade and the Future of Women's Work*, Toronto, Garamond Press and the Canadian Centre for Policy Alternatives.

Drozdiak, W. (1994) Four 'city-states' drive Europe's economy, *Watertown Daily Times*, 16 June, p. 4.

Duggan, P. and Dashner, H. (1994) Introduction: women and economic integration, in P. Duggan and H. Dashner (eds), *Women's Lives in the New Global Economy*,

Notebook for Study and Research No. 22, Amsterdam, International Institute for Research and Education, pp. 7–10.

Enloe, C. (1992) Silicon tricks and the two-dollar woman. *New Internationalist*, issue 227 (January), 12–14.

Ferguson, K. E. (1993) *The Man Question: Visions of Subjectivity in Feminist Theory*, Berkeley, University of California Press.

Gabriel, C. and MacDonald, L. (1994) Women organizing around NAFTA: prospects for a feminist internationality, paper presented at the Annual Meeting of the International Studies Association, Washington, DC, 28 March–1 April.

Gorostiaga, X. (1993) Latin America in the new world order, in J. Brecher, J. B. Childs and J. Cutler (eds), *Global Visions: Beyond the New World Order*, Boston, South End Press, pp. 67–86.

Grewal, I. (1994) Autobiographic subjects and diasporic locations: 'meatless days' and 'borderlands', in I. Grewal and C. Kaplan (eds), *Scattered Hegemonics: Postmodernity and Transnational Feminist Practices*, Minneapolis, University of Minnesota Press, pp. 231–51.

Grewal, I. and Kaplan, C. (1994) Introduction: transnational feminist practices and questions of postmodernity, in I. Grewal and C. Kaplan (eds), *Scattered Hegemonies: Postmodernity and Transnational Feminist Practices*, Minneapolis, University of Minnesota Press.

Henwood, D. (1993) Impeccable logic: trade, development and free markets in the Clinton era, *NACLA Report on the Americas*, **26**, 23–8.

Joekes, S. and Weston, A. (1994) *Women and the New Free Trade Agenda*, New York, UNIFEM.

Kofman, E. and Sales, R. (1992) Towards Fortress Europe? *Women's Studies International Forum*, **15**(1), 29–39.

Liebowitz, D. (1993) Some are winners, but women will lose: the impact of NAFTA on women, paper presented at the Annual Meeting of the International Studies Association – Northeast, Newark, NJ, 11–13 November.

McGinn, M. and Moody, K. (1993) Labor goes global, *The Progressive*, March, 24–7.

Marchand, M. H. (1994) Gender and new regionalism in Latin America: inclusion/exclusion, *Third World Quarterly*, **15**, 61–74.

Moxon-Browne, E. (1993) Social Europe, in J. Lodge (ed.), *The European Community and the Challenge of the Future*, New York, St Martin's Press, pp. 152–62.

Mujer á Mujer (1992) First Tri-National Conference of Women Workers on Economic Integration and Free Trade, *Correspondencia*, **13**.

Nanda, M. (1994) New technologies, new challenges: reimagining the geography of production, presentation for panel on 'Rethinking Global History' for Women in the Global Economy: Making Connections Conference, SUNY Albany, Albany, NY, 22–24 April.

Overbeek, H. (1994) Global restructuring and the emerging regional migration regime in Europe, paper presented at the Annual Meeting of the International Studies Association, Washington, DC, 28 March–1 April.

Peterson, V. S. and Runyan, A. S. (1993) *Global Gender Issues*, Boulder, CO, Westview Press.

Ranney, D. C. and Cecil, W. C. (1993) Transnational investment and job loss in Chicago: impacts on women, African-Americans and Latinos, report prepared for the Center for Urban Economic Development, University of Illinois at Chicago, January.

Sales, R. (1994) Race, gender and European integration, paper presented at the Annual Meeting of the International Studies Association, Washington, DC, 28 March–1 April.

Sassen, S. (1991) *The Global City: New York, London, Tokyo*, Princeton, Princeton University Press.

Sassen, S. (1993) Economic globalization: a new geography, composition, and institutional framework, in J. Brecher, J. B. Childs and J. Cutler (eds), *Global Visions: Beyond the New World Order*, Boston, South End, pp. 61–6.

Sassen, S. (1994) Women in the world economy, 1945 to present, presentation for panel on 'Rethinking Global History' for the Women in the World Economy: Making Connections Conference, SUNY Albany, Albany, NY, 22–24 April.

Seguino, S. (1993) Private profits, social costs: NAFTA, women and the global economy, paper presented at the Annual Union Women's Conference, University of Southern Maine, Lewiston, ME, 1 May.

Sparr, P. (1991) U.S.: why is free trade a women's issue?, *Equal Means*, **1**, 25–6.

Weintraub, S. and Fauriol, G. A. (1994) Migration and economic integration, in K. A. Hamilton (ed.), *Migration and the New Europe*, Washington, DC, Center for Strategic and International Studies, pp. 72–95.

Woman to Woman, Global Strategies (Toronto) (1993) Changing economies: free trade and the global agenda – bringing women into the picture, occasional paper, Toronto, Woman to Woman.

Women, the European State and Community Conference (1994) Proceedings, Kalamazoo College, Kalamazoo, MI, 13–14 May.

Zabin, C. (1992) Binational labor markets and segmentation by gender: agriculture and the North American Free Trade Agreement, paper presented at the Annual Women's Policy Research Conference, Tulane University, New Orleans, LA.

18

Selling NAFTA: Gendered Metaphors and Silenced Gender Implications[1]

MARIANNE H. MARCHAND

Introduction

After approval by the legislatures of Canada, Mexico and the United States, the North American Free Trade Agreement (NAFTA) went into effect on 1 January 1994. As a consequence, NAFTA and the debates surrounding it are no longer front-page news. However, debates about NAFTA have not died: with the recent financial crisis in Mexico we have entered the third phase.[2] And, as was the case with the previous ones, NAFTA's gendered implications are receiving very little attention. Indeed, during the 'second' debate few groups raised objections to NAFTA on feminist grounds.[3] Although there have been exceptions, the question arises why so few feminist groups, such as the US-based National Organization for Women, were actively involved in the NAFTA debates. And, secondly, why were there so few attempts to organize feminist activists at the national or tri-national levels?

One explanation might be that feminists in all three countries were convinced that NAFTA would not differentially affect men and women. This seems a very unlikely explanation for two reasons. First, there was feminist opposition to NAFTA, although not as widespread as we might have hoped. Also, previous feminist research has revealed that global processes of (neo-liberal) political and economic restructuring tend to have a disproportion-ately negative impact on women, as is the case with structural adjustment programmes implemented in the South (cf. Benería and Feldman, 1992). If we accept these reasons, the question as to why so few feminist groups have been actively involved in the NAFTA debates becomes even more puzzling. In this chapter, therefore, I want to explore whether a partial answer to this puzzle might be found in the way NAFTA debates have been framed.

This line of enquiry implies that 'NAFTA', as a set of discursive practices, is a contested area of global restructuring which produces gendered as well as racialized categories of meaning and knowing. In other words, the NAFTA debates reflect attempts to reconstruct, transform and produce (categories of) new meanings about global political, economic and social relations. More specifically, the construction of 'NAFTA' involves drawing boundaries and carving out an economic space to which the socio-political is subordinated; in addition, 'NAFTA' is about gendered and racialized processes of inclusion and exclusion (see also Marchand, 1994).

The construction of NAFTA and in particular the framing of the NAFTA debates have important implications for oppositional strategizing. Using the insights from Carol Cohn's analysis of the language among US defence intellectuals (1989), I will explore whether the discursive framing of NAFTA has primarily served to obscure, silence and marginalize its gendered implications, thus making it more problematic to challenge NAFTA in a gendered voice.

The chapter is divided into three sections. In the first section I will give a brief overview of the debates surrounding NAFTA. The second section will focus more specifically on the possible ways in which gender implications have been silenced, particularly through the language of econometrics. Finally, I will discuss whether using particular metaphors has structured the NAFTA debates in ways which make it difficult to participate on/in 'gendered terms'.

Framing NAFTA

Robert Pastor has argued that the US Congress provided the 'principal forum for addressing NAFTA', because 'the debate in PRI-dominated Mexico and Parliamentary Canada was a foregone conclusion' (1993: 10). Although Pastor might have been too optimistic, particularly with respect to Canada, citizens of all three countries did indeed participate in the NAFTA debates on the Hill. However, this situation placed the NAFTA debates under certain structural limitations. Most importantly, 'inside the beltway' mechanisms were set in motion to ensure that Mexican and Canadian participants (and some of the issues they raised) were largely marginalized. For instance, they received less media coverage than their US counterparts. Moreover, because of this setting it was virtually impossible to raise Canadian or Mexican nationalist or protectionist concerns. In other words, the NAFTA debates have been very US-centred in nature.

When we look at the debates that took place in Washington we see that, thus far, there have been two subsequent waves of NAFTA debates.[4] The first debate centred around procedural issues. The question at hand was whether or not the US Congress should decide on the ratification of a NAFTA deal according to fast-track rules, i.e. to have to vote on the entire agreement without being able to exercise the power of amendment. After heavy lobbying by advocates and opponents, Congress decided in favour of the fast-track authority. Obviously, this decision was more than a procedural matter.

In this first round substantive issues were already brought into the debate by both sides. Moreover, the decision in favour of the fast-track rules influenced and circumscribed future strategies of the participants.

In the second round of debates it is possible to distinguish at least four different positions. Outspoken critics, such as Jeff Faux and David Barkin, opposed any free trade agreement (FTA) among the three states within the near future. Their argument is that the social, economic and political disparities among the three would only be exacerbated by an FTA. Barkin, for instance, argues against the further integration of Mexico into the world economy. Instead he favours a food self-sufficiency strategy for that country:

> The argument stems from the recognition that present development policies will be unable to incorporate the rural population into the productive fold. Rather than toss them off as flotsam, rejecting their humanity and destroying them as the residue of industrial progress, I suggest that they can survive, maybe even flourish, in a world organized by themselves in symbiosis with modernity. At best, existing policies condemn these sizable groups to marginality; at worst, to misery and extinction. Small farmers as a group are too important an actor in Mexico's history for politicians to simply write them off without considering their reactions and exploring alternatives. (1991: 36–37)

Writing in 1991, David Barkin might not have expected his predictions to come true so soon! The Zapatista Liberation Army (EZLN) started its offensive in Chiapas on New Year's eve of 1993, the day before NAFTA went into effect.

Faux takes a more US-oriented view and fears significant job losses, especially in older industries, among low-skilled workers in the United States. Among others, Ross Perot picked up this theme of job losses during his presidential campaign. He argued that the wage differentials between US and Mexican workers would create 'a giant sucking sound in the south'. However, unlike Faux and Barkin's objections, Perot's critique of NAFTA displays nationalist/populist overtones. He wants to preserve and protect 'American values' and the 'American way of life'; clearly, a free trade agreement based on (what Perot considered) 'unfair trading practices' would stand in the way of Perot's ideals.

Moderate opponents do not reject an FTA outright. However, they object to a so-called limited FTA. In the words of William Cunningham, legislative representative of the AFL-CIO, such a limited FTA 'would change the continental economy in ways that would provide great advantages to capital investors at the expense of working women and men throughout North America' (prepared statement, US Congress, 1991, 183). Rather than a limited FTA, moderate opponents are pleading for a regional development strategy (see Quintanilla's prepared statement, US Congress, 1991) which recognizes the increasing integration of the three economies. In their view this integration should be the foundation for 'authentic cooperation to solve mutual problems' among the three states; and, therefore, the negotiations for an extended FTA should include: 'human rights, debt, labor, environment, trade and investment, binding enforcement mechanisms and ways for citizens and residents of each country to oversee the enforcement of the final agreement' (Blake, prepared statement, US Congress, 1991: 158–9).

The supporters of NAFTA can also be divided up into moderates and more outspoken advocates. One of the main differences between these two groups is that the moderates tend to emphasize that NAFTA will result in a 'win–win' situation, thus subscribing to a liberal economic perspective. Those who most strongly favour NAFTA, however, are very candid about the reasons why: they think that in NAFTA's zero-sum game the United States will emerge as the winner. According to them a production-sharing strategy will mostly benefit US companies and thus the United States as a whole. This zero-sum reasoning is also extended beyond the borders of a North American market. The increased competitiveness of US companies, resulting from the production sharing strategy within NAFTA, makes it possible to create a 'North America, Inc.'. This newly created 'Fortress America', in turn, will have the upper hand in dealings with the other members of the Triad, Japan and Europe. R. K. Morris, the director of international trade for the National Association of Manufacturers, clearly postulates this position during the Congressional hearings on the fast-track authority (14 May 1991). In his prepared statement before Congress he initially argues that 'Canadian firms, like American firms and Mexican firms, stand to benefit significantly from the proposed North American Free Trade Agreement' (prepared statement, US Congress, 1991: 172). A little further he recognizes, however, that not all firms will benefit equally: 'the evidence suggests, and NAM's members firmly believe, that on balance American manufacturers will be winners' (ibid.: 174). To make sure that the 'evidence' will not turn out to be faulty in retrospect, Morris urges US negotiators to get a 'clear sense of US economic goals' because 'NAM would oppose any agreement with Mexico that did not clearly advance the economic interests of American manufacturers' (ibid.: 175–6). One of these goals is that 'the benefits of the agreement accrue primarily to the North American participants' (ibid.: 178). Morris's ambiguity about who are to be considered 'North American participants' is clearly manifested in his suggestion to use as the litmus test for NAFTA 'the rule of thumb that if the agreement doesn't work for the American automobile companies, it is probably not a good agreement' (ibid.: 179).

During the debates various issues were raised, ranging from economic to social and political. Interestingly, the advocates of NAFTA primarily emphasized the economic side of NAFTA (cf. Baer, 1991; Morris/US Congress, 1991; Weintraub, 1992a,b). Robert Pastor's (1990, 1992) political arguments, that NAFTA would force Mexico's political regime to become more democratic, were among the few exceptions. Opponents, in contrast, tended to raise the social (and political) implications of NAFTA (Barkin, 1991; Cunningham and Quintanilla/US Congress, 1991). Often these socio-political issues were raised in connection with economic objections, while a few opponents limited themselves to the economic side of the debates (Faux and Rothstein, 1991; Ros, 1992).[5]

In the end NAFTA's proponents carried the day with their arguments about its economic benefits. The economics were so dominant that the opposition had to couch its counterarguments in economic terms as well (Marchand, 1994). In the remainder of the chapter I will explore whether this framing has contributed to the silencing of gender and race implications and made it more difficult to raise gender issues. Two 'framing' practices will be discussed. One is the actual exclusion or silencing of gender issues. This could be done, for instance, by conducting the debates at a certain (aggregate) level of analysis. The second practice concerns the use of gendered metaphors which might inhibit the raising of gender issues.

Silenced gender implications

Within the field of international relations feminist analyses have revealed that the silencing of gender implications occurs in various ways (Enloe, 1990; Peterson, 1992). Most often this silencing is done through the concepts that are used for analysis, through the questions that are asked (and not asked), and through the level of analysis, particularly when the inquiry is situated at the state level. In a previous article I argue that

> The masculinist writing of integration allows, then, for the silencing, exclusion and objectifying of women and feminist values. The integration story being told is one that prioritises economic rationality, involves dichotomised hierarchies, and equates integration with concentration *cum* homogenization. (Marchand, 1994: 73)

The question at hand is whether, besides, NAFTA is constitutive of and constituted by new categories of meaning about global political, economic and social relations.

In her *Manifesto for Cyborgs* Donna Haraway views the 'rearrangements in world-wide social relations' as part of the new, science-and-technology-driven networks which she calls 'informatics of domination' (1990: 203). Communications sciences and modern biology provide key constitutive elements of Haraway's 'informatics of domination':

> Communications technologies and biotechnologies are the crucial tools re-
> crafting our bodies. These tools embody and enforce new social relations for
> women worldwide. Technologies and scientific discourses can be partially
> understood as formalizations, that is, as frozen moments, of the fluid social
> interactions constituting them, but they should also be viewed as instruments
> for enforcing meaning. ... Furthermore, communications sciences and mod-
> ern biologies are constructed by common move – the translation of the world
> into a problem of coding, a search for a common language in which all
> resistance to instrumental control disappears and all heterogeneity can be
> submitted to disassembly, reassembly, investment, and exchange. (Haraway,
> 1990: 205–6)

The extent to which the framing of 'NAFTA' (debates) involves similar moves
of coding and the elaboration of (new) control mechanisms will be explored
below.

A. *Economics is often considered superior to the other social sciences.* The
privileged position held by economics among the social sciences is largely
due to the virtually unopposed application of research methods that are
borrowed from the natural sciences. Its attempt to mirror the natural
sciences is, among other things, reflected in the strong distinction between
object/subject and fact/value and its unfettered belief in rational *homo
economicus.* Among other things, this emphasis has aided (neoclassical)
economics to become the most 'masculine' of the social sciences.[6] Its privileged status is also reflected in society at large, where economic arguments
tend to carry more weight than social and political arguments. In order to be
taken seriously (or to be listened to) it is imperative to raise social or political
issues within the context or framework laid out by the economic debates.
This is exactly what has occurred in the case of NAFTA.

However, feminist scholars have demonstrated that neoclassical economics' claim to 'objectivity' is gendered and racialized in taking (caucasian)
rational economic man as the norm for all economic activity (Bakker, 1994;
Feiner and Roberts, 1990; Kuiper and Oomes, 1994; van Staveren, 1994).
These critiques notwithstanding, the continued dominance of neoclassical
economics ensures that any departure from these norms is still problematic.
For instance, gender and race issues are still largely being excluded or
marginalized in neoclassical theorizing. Neoclassical economists perceive
these issues as departing from assumed standards of rationality and objectivity, and consequently view them as 'social issues' and thus of 'secondary
importance' or external to the economic model under discussion (van
Staveren, 1994). In addition, it is interesting to note that, within the
community of neoclassical economists, the person who raises possible
gender implications of economic policies is often labelled a 'sociologist' or
'soft social scientist'. In other words, the messenger (of feminist concerns) is

being feminized and, as a result, taken less seriously in the (masculine) economists' world of 'Realpolitik'.

B. *NAFTA's economic issues were debated on the basis of (inconclusive) econometric models.* One of the most fascinating aspects of NAFTA is that it has stimulated a growth industry of quantitative or econometric modelling trying to predict its likely impact (Hinojosa-Ojeda and Robinson, 1992: 78).[7] This encoding of the economy into econometric models parallels the move that Haraway (1990: 206) describes:

> In communications sciences the translation of the world into a problem in coding can be illustrated by looking at cybernetic (feedback controlled) systems theories applied to . . . data-base construction and maintenance. In each case, solution to the key questions rests on a theory of language and control; the key operation is determining the rates, directions, and probabilities of flow of a quantity called information. The world is subdivided by boundaries differentially permeable to information. Information is just that kind of quantifiable element (unit, basis of unity) which allows universal translation and so unhindered instrumental power (called effective communication).

Raúl Hinojosa-Ojeda and Sherman Robinson (1992) distinguish three categories of econometric models used to analyse the effects of NAFTA: partial equilibriuim models based on regression analysis, single-country computable general equilibrium (CGE) models and multiple-country CGE models. In their view the partial equilibrium models tend to be less theoretically informed than the CGE-models, which are based on neoclassical trade theory. Despite the differences among the various models in terms of focus, predicted outcome(s), etc., it has been generally acknowledged that the results of these econometric studies have been either incomplete or inconclusive (Faux and Spriggs, 1991; Weintraub, 1992a; van Dijck, 1994).

Another problem with these studies is that they rely on abstract models, which are quite frequently based on erroneous assumptions, like the assumption of full employment. They also prevent the raising of certain issues because of their level of abstraction. This is often recognized by the authors or sympathetic discussants (Crandall, 1992; Weintraub, 1992a). As Conroy and Glasmeier point out, it is difficult to raise distributive issues on the basis of these abstract models:

> formal international trade theory offers little insight into the theoretical distribution of either benefits or costs to different social groups, different regions, or, in many cases, different industries from the freeing of trade. (1992/93: 2)

However, despite the inconclusiveness and incompleteness of these econometric studies, much of the NAFTA debates have been conducted on the basis of their findings. The justification for this is offered by Sidney Wein-traub:

> I am much more disposed to put my trust in those studies that seek to quantify outcomes, whatever the shortcomings of the models than in those that make nonquantifiable assertions. ... I am also much more disposed to put my confidence in those who seek to eliminate barriers to international trade than in those who wish to keep or increase barriers, or who propound 'free' trade circumscribed by many restrictions. (1992a: 133)

Weintraub's reaction is so interesting because he voices a strong *emotional* preference for quantification and econometric models. Thereby, he indirectly appeals to econometrics as the most masculine or 'body-building element' of economics:[8] quantification of data is considered superior to 'soft' qualitative analyses, regardless of whether the results are inconclusive or incomplete.

Weintraub's comments convey again (neoclassical) economics' concerns with rationality and objectivity, but they also convey a concern with control and predictability. Parallel to Haraway's suggestion about communications sciences, econometrics serves to translate economic issues and relations into a coding problem. Econometrics has become our lens through which we 'understand' and 'produce' economics as well as economic relations. It has also become a mechanism for structuring or framing our discussions about economic issues such as NAFTA. In other words, econometrics' translation (of the world) controls our ways of knowing economic relations and delineates their future scope.

In sum, econometrics allows for the privileging of certain stories over others. More specifically, its writing of the economy allows for the silencing of gender implications. Econometric models, for instance, tend not to address distributive issues. The only study which actually does this (Conroy and Glasmeier, 1992/93) shows a negative impact for US women working in rural areas and in the apparel and textile industry. In addition, these models are not very well equipped to measure the effects of NAFTA on the countries' informal sector, which provides employment for many women. Most importantly, econometric models prevent assuming a more comprehensive view of NAFTA's implications. Political and social issues or institutions are considered externalities or exogenous variables and are thus not incorporated in the analysis. In other words, econometric modelling and neoclassical economic theorizing reinforce each other's silencing of gender and race issues.

C. NAFTA's economic debates are pitched at 'aggregate' levels of analysis which obscure gender implications. An indirect effect of the use of abstract models is that it defines at what level of abstraction the discussions are being held. In the case of NAFTA, this was done at the level of the state, industry and labour. With these relatively high levels of aggregation gendered or racialized effects tend to 'disappear' because women and minorities are subsumed under other categories. For instance, analyses at the state level attempt to map NAFTA's likely impact on the entire economy (Lustig *et al.*, 1992). No distinctions are being made among various regions or sectors of the population.

Likewise, sectoral studies, focusing on NAFTA's differential impact on certain industries, tend to take neither gender, ethnicity or class into consideration (Weintraub, 1992a). Of all the contributors to *North American Free Trade: Assessing the Impact* by Lustig, Bosworth and Lawrence (1992), Gustavo Vega-Canovas alone mentions the gendered nature of the maquiladora industry. He emphasizes the changing composition of the maquila workforce, of which currently 35 per cent is male as opposed to 20 per cent ten years ago. According to Vega-Canovas this change is due to the arrival of second-wave maquiladora industries which use more complex technology (1992: 203). Although Vega-Canovas assumes that the changing nature of the industry is the reason for the hiring of more male workers, he does not seem to think that this warrants further gender analysis. This seems to be in line with Kathryn Kopinak's observation that, with fewer women working in the maquiladora industry, analyses have become increasingly gender-blind (1995).

Women have also been subsumed under the category of labour. Although in some studies (Hinojosa-Ojeda and Robinson, 1992) a distinction is being made between skilled and unskilled labour, differentiation on the basis of gender and ethnicity or between primary and secondary labour markets has not occurred. This is exactly the type of differentiation necessary to be able to project the possible gendered impact of NAFTA. Without this kind of information, feminists may find themselves in a double bind. On one level, it is obviously difficult to participate fully in the NAFTA debates, which have been so much informed by the findings of econometric models, if the necessary (gendered) information is not being generated. On another level, trying to raise NAFTA's gendered effects might result in not being taken seriously because they are considered social issues and therefore exogenous variables to the econometric models (see also section A).

The above analysis[9] suggests that the writing and the framing of NAFTA, especially through the privileging of (neoclassical) economic arguments and the use of econometric models, is gendered and racialized. This framing of NAFTA involves its translation into a problem of coding, thus not only circumscribing and structuring but also carving up the space within which NAFTA debates could take place. In so doing, feminist concerns about the gendered implications of NAFTA have been effectively obscured, silenced and kept at the margins of the debates. In the next section I will look at whether the use of gendered metaphors has further delineated and coloured this 'masculinist' discussion/debating space.

Gendered metaphors

From the cognitive point of view, metaphors are used in communication to understand problematic situations in terms of situations we understand and are familiar with. Metaphors, new and old, tend to be built out of basic human concepts arising from bodily interaction with the environment: standing upright, being in a containing space, moving from one point to another. (Chilton and Ilyin, 1993: 9)

Metaphors fulfil an important role in political discourse. For instance, problematic concepts, like states, have been translated into more familiar (everyday) experiences. Paul Chilton and Mikhail Ilyin argue that 'container metaphors' have been used to conceptualize states. The advantage is that 'you can utilise special sorts of containers significant to humans at a basic level, the most potent of which are the body, clothing and shelter' (ibid.: 9).

Current rearrangements of the global political economy are simultaneously problematic and novel. Therefore, we see the utilization of various, often competing metaphors to map these changes. However, conceptualizing new developments through the utilization of metaphors is not necessarily politically neutral, ungendered or non-racist. In the choice of our metaphors we tend to emphasize certain elements at the expense of others. According to Chilton and Ilyin,

What is at issue here is the specification of metaphor at a more or less conscious level of strategic discoursal choice. Since political actors compete for discourse initiative, control of a metaphor through interpretation and stipulation is crucial to political behaviour. (ibid.: 12)

In other words, metaphors are not just language games, but can amount to important political control mechanisms and need to be understood as such.

As is the case with metaphors conceptualizing the European Union, NAFTA metaphors tend either to take as a starting-point its internal dynamics or its (future) interactions with the outside world. In so doing, these metaphors emphasize and thus problematize the boundaries between NAFTA's inside and outside. Among the metaphors used to conceptualize NAFTA, three stand out: 1) a 'hub-and-spoke' imagery dealing with NAFTA's internal dynamics; 2) a structural (or architectural) image of NAFTA as an economic edifice; and 3) the conceptualization of NAFTA as a major business corporation.

Unlike EU metaphors, however, metaphors encoding NAFTA's internal dynamics convey little confusion about the nature of its identity. For instance, the 'hub-and-spoke' image does not leave much room for mistaken identity. To those using this metaphor there is no question that the hub represents the USA and that Canada and Mexico are the spokes: a situation 'in which the U.S. would enjoy free trade with its neighbors to the north and south, while they maintained barriers against each other' (Fisher, 1992: 50). Since Canada joined the NAFTA negotiations, the hub-and-spoke metaphor has not been used as often, possibly because it would give ammunition to Canadian opponents of NAFTA. Interestingly, Robert Pastor evoked the hub-and-spoke image again in a recent paper for the Inter-american Development Bank and the Economic Commission for Latin America and the Caribbean (1993). This time, however, the term was used to indicate the possibility of two hubs, Mexico and the United States. In Pastor's view, Mexico's recent trade agreements with its Latin American and Caribbean neighbours raise the question: 'Will Mexico be a hub or a spoke?' (ibid.: 17). Obviously, there are some doubts whether the image of two hubs (an inner and an outer?) and multiple spokes is politically attractive enough to ensure its continued use. That Mexico's potential new role is problematic for NAFTA's assumed identity and internal dynamics is clear from Pastor's observation that 'NAFTA's rules-of-origin were negotiated to prevent Mexico from being any other country's platform, even though the greatest fear was that Japan, not Latin America, would use it for that purpose' (ibid.: 17). However, the recent financial crisis has eroded Mexico's position sufficiently to make the two-hub scenario for now unlikely.

The second imagery conceptualizing NAFTA as an economic edifice is relatively complex in nature and is not used very often. It does reflect, however, Chilton and Ilyin's suggestion (1993) that many metaphors refer to structures or architectures. Pastor most clearly develops NAFTA's architectural design: 'NAFTA will generate needed growth in Mexico, improve the efficiency of North American corporations, and *lay the foundation for a new economic edifice* that will benefit the three countries' (1993: 2; my italics). Interestingly, Pastor's economic edifice for NAFTA is not a closed, fortress-like building, but a rather open and permeable structure. This is also why he prefers the term trading *area* over trading *bloc* (ibid.: 2). Possibly because of the relatively intricate or complex architecture of Pastor's airy economic edifice, the metaphor never really caught on during discussions about NAFTA.

It appears, then, that the metaphor most often used to encode NAFTA is 'North America, Inc.'. As with the metaphor of 'Fortress Europe', the metaphor 'North America, Inc.' captures and describes processes of inclusion and exclusion in which gender, race and ethnicity play an important role (Kofman and Sales, 1990; Marchand, 1994; Sales, 1994). The construction of 'North America, Inc.' involves a process of externalizing, partially based on gender and ethnicity, of those groups and entities that are excluded. Moreover, the metaphor 'North America, Inc.' simultaneously captures NAFTA's internal dynamics, or inside, and its external relations, or outside. It is, therefore, not surprising that it has become the dominant metaphor used by NAFTA's advocates and opponents alike.

One of the interesting aspects of 'North America, Inc.' is that it conceptualizes NAFTA as a company, analogous to and in competition with 'Japan, Inc.'. The terms to describe NAFTA/North America, Inc. are consequently also borrowed from the business world. In his statement before the Budget Committee of the House of Representatives, Congressman Jim Kolbe summarizes NAFTA as follows:

> Looking at the bigger picture, the United States, Canada, and Mexico form a strategic alliance which will ultimately create an economic union stretching from the Yukon to the Yucatan. The net result would be the creation of an integrated North American economy with a combined population of 362 million people, a combined GNP of $6 trillion, and total combined trade flows of $235 billion. 'North America, Inc.' would become the single most powerful economic region in the world. (US Congress, 1991: 141)

A similar and even clearer conflation of state/society and business interests is voiced by R. K. Morris, the director of international trade for the National Association of Manufacturers:

> As I have said, to one degree or another, the economies of all three countries depend upon the same firms for their economic well being. Most of those firms are engaged in intensive, unremitting, global competition. It is in the interest of all three societies that they be as efficient as possible. The principal arguments for negotiating a North American free-trade agreement are that it could enhance competitiveness and increase economic activity in all three countries. (US Congress, 1991: 172)

Opponents of NAFTA also recognized its corporate nature. William Cunningham of the AFL-CIO argues that 'an FTA between the U.S. and Mexico would change the continental economy in ways that would provide great advantages to capital investors at the expense of working women and men throughout North America' (US Congress, 1991: 183). In his view 'North America, Inc.' would clearly not benefit society's interests, but would facilitate companies to (continue to) pursue strategies of production sharing, flexibilization of labour, etc.

The creation of 'North America, Inc.' as a metaphor for NAFTA could not have occurred without the simultaneous creation of an opponent or 'other', often from a different cultural and ethnic background. It is not surprising that in this process of 'othering' corporate language and images are prominent as well. In discussions on NAFTA Japanese and South Korean companies are singled out as the most threatening competitors, especially in the automotive and electronics industry. In the (masculinist) world of business competition and corporate envy it is, therefore, imperative to bolster (North) American companies and to prevent Japanese and South Korean companies from penetrating the region. In other words, defining the 'other' lays the groundwork for setting in motion certain mechanisms of exclusion. The main mechanism for excluding 'Japan, Inc.' is the rules of origin provision. As Morris sees it

> The agreement should provide mechanisms for ensuring that the benefits of the agreement accrue primarily to the North American participants. We expect the negotiators to spend a lot of time on the rules of origin to be applied in an agreement with Mexico. We cannot afford to offer uncompensated free trade to manufacturers anywhere in the world simply because they set up assembly operations in Mexico. (US Congress, 1991: 178)

On the other hand, the exclusion of foreign companies is not static. House representative Jim Kolbe from Arizona acknowledges that foreign companies can become included in 'North America, Inc.' as long as they abide by the rules (of origin). In his view, this would ultimately benefit the North American economy (US Congress, 1991).

As Robert Pastor has argued in various articles, NAFTA is about more than trade or investment (1990, 1992). Likewise, 'North America, Inc.' is about more than the exclusion of foreign companies. It also involves processes of exclusion that are informed by gender and ethnicity (Marchand, 1994). M. Delal Baer (1991) is among the most sanguine about these aspects of 'North America, Inc.'. In discussing pre-NAFTA bilateral relations between the US and Mexico, she evokes a powerful image in Mexican (political) culture:

> Mexico's traditional political culture viewed U.S. proximity as a curse not an opportunity. Bilateral cooperation was limited or conducted under a cloak of secrecy; Mexican leaders did not wish to be accused of consorting with the enemy. In pursuing a free-trade agreement, however, Mexico has focused on common interests and the opportunities of the U.S. market. It is laying the ghost of Malinche to rest (p. 138).

The image of Malinche, the indigenous Mexican woman who had been given to conquistador Hernan Cortés in concubinage by her own leaders, is often used in Mexico to portray an act of betrayal. One could argue that, for Baer, Mexico had to shed its feminized and indigenous image in order to join 'North America, Inc.' which stands for white, male (Anglo-Saxon) values. This interpretation is supported by Baer's comment that 'NAFTA signifies that Mexico has become a North American country, ready to share Western entrepreneurial values and participate in Western capital markets' (ibid.: 147). Robert Pastor concurs (1993: 14), emphasizing the adoption of Western values by Latin Americans:

> Old stereotypes are being replaced. A new image of modern, democratic technocrats is taking hold. Free, contested elections have been held in every country in South America, Central America, and all but Cuba in the Caribbean ... But democracy is wider, if not deeper, than ever before, and the new democracies are groping on the frontier of an old order of sovereign states to devise collective mechanisms to defend each other from authoritarian reversals.

However, Pastor's new region is characterized by a highly rational, technocratic, businesslike and homogeneous environment allowing little room for difference (Marchand, 1994).

In sum, the metaphor of 'North American, Inc.' used to capture NAFTA informs various processes of inclusion and exclusion. The 'othering' that takes place is couched in corporate language and creates a (discursive) space that is primarily white, Anglo-Saxon and masculine in outlook. Questions of gender and ethnicity are therefore difficult to raise within this context, especially when one is pressured to utilize the economistic language of corporate (North) America.

Conclusion

Processes of inclusion and exclusion on the basis of gender, race and ethnicity are not new. Feminists have faced similar constraints in the past. Under those constraints they have not hesitated to raise the gender implications of certain economic policies. However, it should be noted that these silencing mechanisms continue to be very strong. Often one finds oneself in a double bind where raising gender issues in the dominant economistic language is virtually impossible and raising these issues in a different gendered language often falls on deaf ears (Cohn, 1989). Moreover, the debates surrounding NAFTA were not always very transparent, i.e various interests might not have been obvious from the beginning. This is in part due to the use of abstract econometric models and their incomplete and inconclusive results.

There are certain lessons for feminist oppositional strategies that can be drawn from this account. The first one is that language, whether appearing as (neoclassical) economic theorizing, under the disguise of econometric models, or in the form of metaphors, can become a control mechanism by which gendered and racialized implications can be obscured or silenced. Therefore, the naming, categorizing, mapping and coding of political and economic processes are important sites for feminist oppositional strategies.

Second, in targeting the political uses and manipulations of metaphors feminists should develop a basic understanding about the various possibilities for developing (discursive) counter-strategies. Chilton and Ilyin make some useful suggestions in this respect. They argue that a speaker has several options in dealing with metaphors, ranging from 1) outright rejection and replacement by a different metaphor, 2) re-specifying the theme (or target) domain, cognitive script or frame, to 3) retaining the script or frame of the metaphor, but altering its entailment or target (Chilton and Ilyin, 1993: 13). In other words, it is important to develop discursive counter-strategies that highlight the contradictions as well as the gendered and racialized nature of dominant metaphors and that may provide openings towards new understandings of political and economic processes.

Notes

1 Earlier versions of this chapter were presented at the international conference, Global Politics: Setting Agendas for the Year 2000, held at the Nottingham Trent University, Nottingham, UK, 25–27 July 1994 and at the annual meeting of the International Studies Association, Washington, DC, 28 March – 1 April 1994.
2 I am referring to the various waves of debates within the United States: the first wave was focused on the issue of fast-track negotiations and the second wave consisted of the debates during the actual negotiating phase of NAFTA.
3 Exceptions to this lack of opposition have been: 1) the Canadian National Action Committee on the Status of Women, which has co-ordinated its opposition to the bilateral Free Trade Agreement between Canada and the United States as well as NAFTA with other anti-free trade groups in Canada; 2) various grassroots organizations on the Mexican–US border, including the Coalition for Justice in the Maquiladoras and the Border Committee of Women Workers (supported by the American Friends Services Committee), which have focused their attention on the maquiladora industry; and 3) the tri-national women's group Mujer a Mujer. For more information on these organizational efforts, see Christina Gabriel and Laura Macdonald (1994) as well as Matthew Sparke (1994).
4 I am using the debates in the United States as a benchmark because it is the most dominant actor of the three participants in the NAFTA negotiations. With the Mexican financial crisis of December 1994/January 1995, the onset of the third wave of NAFTA debates has become visible.
5 See also my article (1994) on the prevalence of 'economism' in discussions about NAFTA and integration theory.
6 It is beyond the scope of this chapter to explore in detail why economics occupies this dominant position. However, economics' continuing emphasis on rationality and objectivity is a clear expression of (modernist) Enlightenment thinking, which has only recently come under attack by postmodernists. However, it is still predominant in the natural sciences (which is the model (neoclassical) economics tries to emulate).
7 For an overview, see Faux and Spriggs, 1991; Lustig, Bosworth and Lawrence, 1992; Ros, 1992; Weintraub, 1992b; Conroy and Glasmeier, 1992/93.

8 I am grateful to Marc Williams who suggested this term to me at the Nottingham Trent University Conference.

9 One aspect which I have not discussed, but which needs mentioning, is that econometric modelling is a highly specialized trade with its own language: few people are conversant in it (and needless to say disproportionately few women and minorities). This raises some important issues about the power relations between the initiated and non-initiated, about the alienation and exclusion of the 'illiterate' and about the democratic nature of the NAFTA decision-making process if only a few were able to participate.

References

Baer, M. D. (1991) North American free trade, *Foreign Affairs*, **70**(4), 132–49.

Bakker, I. (1994) Introduction: engendering macro-economic policy reform in the era of global restructuring and adjustment, in I. Bakker (ed.), *The Strategic Silence*, London and Ottawa, Zed Books and the North–South Institute, pp. 1–30.

Barkin, D. (1991) About face, *NACLA Report on the Americas*, **24**(6) (May), 30–7.

Benería, L. and Feldman, S. (eds) (1992) *Unequal Burden: Economic Crises, Persistent Poverty, and Women's Work*, Boulder, CO, Westview Press.

Chilton, P. and Ilyin, M. (1993) Metaphor in political discourse: the case of the Common European House, *Discourse and Society*, **4**(1), 7 and 32.

Cohn, C. (1989) Sex and death in the rational world of defense intellectuals, in D. E. H. Russell (ed.), *Exposing Nuclear Phallacies*, New York, Pergamon Press, pp. 127–59.

Conroy, M. E. and Glasmeier, A. K. (1992/93) Unprecedented disparities, unparalleled adjustment needs: winners and losers on the NAFTA fast track, *Journal of Interamerican Studies and World Affairs*, **34**(4), 1–37.

Crandall, R. W. (1992) Comment, in N. Lustig, B. Bosworth and Z. Lawrence (eds), *North American Free Trade: Assessing the Impact*, Washington, DC, The Brookings Institution, pp. 133–5.

Dijck, P. van (1994) NAFTA and the North American agreement on labor cooperation, paper presented at the Seminar on Trade, Aid and Social Clauses, Free University of Amsterdam, Amsterdam, 19–20 May.

Enloe, C. (1990) *Bananas, Beaches and Bases: Making Feminist Sense of International Politics*, Berkeley, CA, University of California Press.

Faux, J. and Rothstein, R. (1991) 'Fast Track, Fast Shuffle: the Economic Consequences of the Administration's Proposed Trade Agreement with Mexico', Briefing Paper. Washington, DC, Economic Policy Institute.

Faux, J. and Spriggs, W. (1991) 'US Jobs and the Mexico Trade Proposal', Briefing Paper, Washington, DC, Economic Policy Institute.

Feiner, S. F. and Roberts, B. (1990) Hidden by the invisible hand: neoclassical economic theory and the textbook treatment of race and gender, *Gender and Society*, **4**(2), 159–81.

Fisher, R. C. (1992) NAFTA: a U.S. perspective, *SAIS Review*, **12**(1), 43–55.

Gabriel, C. and Macdonald, L. (1994) NAFTA, women and organising in Canada and Mexico: forging a feminist internationality, *Millennium*, **23**(3), 535–62.

Haraway, D. (1990) A manifesto for cyborgs: science, technology, and socialist feminism in the 1980s, in L. J. Nicholson (ed.), *Feminism/Postmodernism*, New York, Routledge, pp. 190–233.

Hinojosa-Ojeda, R. and Robinson, S. (1992) Labor issues in a North American Free Trade Area, in N. Lustig, B. P. Bosworth and Z. Lawrence (eds), *North American Free Trade: Assessing the Impact*, Washington, DC, The Brookings Institution, pp. 69–98.

Kofman, E. and Sales, R. (1992) Towards Fortress Europe? *Women's Studies International Forum*, **15**(1), 29–39.

Kopinak, K. (1995) The continuing importance of gender as a vehicle for the subordination of women maquiladora workers in Mexico, *Latin American Perspectives*, **22**(1), 30–48.

Kuiper, E. and Oomes, N. (1994) Femina academia absens: de onzichtbaarheid van Vrouwen in de economische wetenschap, in H. Maassen van den Brink and K. Tijdens (eds), *Emancipatie en Economie: Is Nederland Inmiddels een Land Waar Vrouwen Willen Wonen?* (Liber Amoricum M. Bruyn-Hundt), Amsterdam, Universiteit van Amsterdam, Leerstoel Vergelijkende Bevolkings-en Emancipatie-economie, pp. 157–70.

Lustig, N., Bosworth, B. P. and Lawrence, R. Z. (eds) (1992) *North American Free Trade: Assessing the Impact*, Washington, DC, The Brookings Institution.

Marchand, M. H. (1994) Gender and new regionalism in Latin America: inclusion/exclusion, *Third World Quarterly*, **15**(1), 63–76.

Mies, M. (1986) *Patriarchy and Accumulation on a World Scale: Women in the International Division of Labor*, London, Zed Books.

Pastor, R. A. (1990) Post-revolutionary Mexico: the Salinas opening, *Journal of Interamerican Studies and World Affairs*, **32**(3), 1–22.

Pastor, R. A. (1992) NAFTA as the center of an integration process: the nontrade issues, in N. Lustig, B. P. Bosworth and Z. Lawrence (eds), *North American Free Trade: Assessing the Impact*, Washington, DC, The Brookings Institution, pp. 176–99.

Pastor, R. A. (1993) The North American Free Trade Agreement: hemispheric and geopolitical implications, *IDB-ECLAC Working Papers on Trade in the Western Hemisphere*.

Peterson, V. S. (1992) Introduction, in V. S. Peterson. (ed.), *Gendered States: Feminist (Re)Visions of International Relations Theory*, Boulder, CO, Lynne Rienner, pp. 1–30.

Ros, J. (1992) Free trade area or common capital market? Notes on Mexico–US economic integration and current NAFTA negotiations, *Journal of Interamerican Studies and World Affairs*, **34**(2), 53–91.

Sales, R. (1994) Race, gender and European integration, paper presented at the annual meeting of the International Studies Association, Washington, DC, 28 March–1 April.

Sparke, M. (1994) Negotiating national action: feminist critique and compromise on multiple Canadian publics, paper presented as part of the Place, Space, and Gender series at the University of Syracuse, Syracuse, NY, 18 February.

Staveren, I. van (1994) Neoclassical economics as a barrier for gender equality in a human centered world economy, introductory paper for the Expert Meeting 'On the Penny' at the Conference The Future: Women and International Cooperation of the Vrouwenberaad Ontwikkelingssamenwerking, Amsterdam, 27 May, pp. 1–30.

US Congress, House Committee on the Budget (1991) *Economic Impact of the Mexico Free Trade Agreement, Hearings before the Taskforce on Economic Policy, Projections and Revenues of the Committee on the Budget*, 6-1, 102nd Cong., 1st session, 14 May.

Vega-Canovas, G. (1992) Comment, in N. Lustig, B. P. Bosworth and Z. Lawrence (eds), *North American Free Trade: Assessing the Impact*, Washington, DC, The Brookings Institution, pp. 199–204.

Weintraub, S. (1992a) Modeling the industrial effects of NAFTA', in N. Lustig, B. P. Bosworth and Z. Lawrence (eds), *North American Free Trade: Assessing the Impact*, Washington, DC, The Brookings Institution, pp. 109–33.

Weintraub, S. (1992b) US–Mexico free trade: implications for the United States, *Journal of Interamerican Studies and World Affairs*, **34**(2), 29–52.

Part 4

Other Domains of the Global: Issues of Inequality

———

19

Other Contexts of the Global: A Critical Geopolitics of North–South Relations

DAVID SLATER

> The globalizing process ... is located within a much longer history; we suffer increasingly from a process of historical amnesia in which we think that just because we are thinking about an idea it has only just started.
>
> (Hall, 1991: 20)

> It obviously still strikes us as a paradox to consider an idea of 'knowledge' that is not in the end of occidental origin.
>
> (Chambers, 1994: 22)

Introduction

According to a certain reading of the contemporary scene we are experiencing an eclipse in universalist thinking: Lingis (1994: 10), for example, comments that the metanarratives of emancipation and the universal system are being forgotten – 'only a few cranky groups of the right are trying to make us remember the Enlightenment and Hegel'. In a more sophisticated theoretical mode, Laclau (1994: 1), in an introduction to the issues of political identity, argues that in our post-Cold War world we are seeing a 'proliferation of particularistic political identities, none of which tries to ground its legitimacy and its action in a mission predetermined by universal history', and 'any kind of universal grounding is contemplated with deep suspicion'. The proliferation of explosive particularisms, the dissolution of erstwhile master narratives of social change, the plurality of positionalities, the decentring of the social subject, the end of unitary conceptions of emancipation and the emergence of new archipelagos of resistance all tend to give body to the sense of rupture and unstable, precarious reconstruction. In times of shattered foundations and ever extending fragmentation, one sign, one meaning of the post-modern, particularly to be located in the work of Baudrillard, is captured in an indifference to the political future. In other instances of Western writing one finds examples of a pervasive cynicism of reason and dystopian visions that express a sense of political paralysis.[1]

In times of difference, plurality and fragmentation there is a strong tendency to assume that one important trend can be taken as constitutive of the whole. But our times are also marked by the presence of a neoliberal regime of truth that is driven by a clearly defined universalist ambition. Although produced and practised inside societies of the North, the major deployment and impact of neoliberal discourse has been in the South. Seen from one society of the periphery, the Argentinean philosopher Reigadas (1988) argues that in the 1980s Latin America was impacted by two waves of Western truth; first by a neoliberal doctrine that purported to offer the sole prescription for development and progress – the only possible horizon – and, secondly, by a postmodernism that destabilized the ground for any alternative horizon, whilst celebrating an ever-proliferating pluralism. Although Reigadas, unlike other Latin American writers, opts for a uniformly negative view of postmodernism, failing to acknowledge its potentially enabling and liberating aspect,[2] it can well be argued that, as Soper (1991: 99–101) has suggested, a postmodern perspective that evades any critical consideration of the prevailing modes of neoliberal thought can be interpreted as complicit with the established order.

The absence of any critical acknowledgement of the continuing power of neoliberal ideas is not only a characteristic of much post-modern and post-structuralist writing; similarly, in the continually expanding literature on globalization or what Robertson (1992) refers to as the 'global condition', one encounters a rather remarkable silence or, as I shall argue, a series of silences. Overall, I want to make the following argument.

In challenging certain influential and well-diffused Western visions of the global, I shall suggest that these 'global perspectives' tend to conceal a limiting, enclosed and particularly centred position that is characterized by a crucial historical and geopolitical amnesia. This forgetting is conducive to the preservation and continued development of a distorted 'world view', since it allows for the historical erasure of imperial politics, and additionally represses the record of contemporary forms of Western power over the non-West, forms which have led some authors to refer to a 'new imperialism' (Bienefeld, 1994; Füredi, 1994). The omissions or silences that can be found within much of the Western-based literature on globalization and global politics can be examined in terms of three interrelated absences: a) the failure to connect contemporary issues of power and politics in a global context to the history of the geographical relations between West and non-West or North and South; b) the lack of any serious treatment of neoliberal discourses of development as they are deployed in peripheral societies, as one powerful modality of a will to global order; and c) the non-inclusion of any serious treatment of the newer forms of Western intervention in Third World societies, including those under a United Nations aegis. By examining these frequently forgotten themes, we can create a new basis for extending the scope of global political analysis, whilst at the same time broadening our understanding of the inequalities and conflicts that characterize the contemporary global scene.

Global imaginations: Whose globe? Whose imagination?

According to Bauman (1993: 226), the time-space invented by modern memory is linear and vertical rather than horizontal and cyclical; in this time-space, 'before' means 'lower' and 'inferior' and also 'outdated'. Bauman goes on to note that in the process whereby time-space emerges as the battleground between the (superior) future and the (inferior) past, there is a 'carefully concealed variable' called power. Here in this area, 'superiority is tested and proved in victory; inferiority in defeat … the story of progress is told by the victors' (ibid.). Interestingly, and perhaps symptomatically in Bauman's narrative, the questions of power and of victory and defeat in the prosecution of progress are not linked to colonialism nor to the key geopolitical penetrations carried by imperial missions. Remembering the connectivity in Foucault between the 'power to' and the 'power over', we can emphasize the point that the 'power over' has been assertively expressed in the history of progress and modernity through Western incursions and ruptures of non-Western societies. The geopolitical power over other societies, legitimated and codified under the signs of manifest destiny and civilizing missions, has been a rather salient feature of earlier Western projects of constructing new world orders. These projects or domains of truth, as they emanated from Europe or the United States, attempted to impose their hegemony by defining normality with reference to a particular vision of their own cultures, whilst designating that which was different as other than truth and in need of tutelage.[3]

At the beginning of the present century, for example, President T. Roosevelt, when referring to the 'weak and chaotic people south of us', proclaimed that it was 'our duty, when it becomes absolutely inevitable, to police these countries in the interest of order and civilisation' (quoted in Niess, 1990: 76).[4] The emergence in the nineteenth century of the phenomenon of what I might call a sense of geopolitical predestination, the belief in the necessity of an imperial mission to civilize the other and to convert other societies into inferior versions of the same exemplified a lack of respect for difference, and, above all the autonomy of difference, that marched through into the next century. Honig (1993: 193) writes that 'the other awakens differences and resistances within us, inviting us to experience as contingencies the identities and proclivities that constitute us so deeply that we often experience them as natural'. But in the making of empire, the drive is to convert the other into a copy of the colonizer, to reinforce the identities and proclivities that constitute us as definitively natural and universal. For Campbell (1992), writing on security and US foreign policy, the moral space of inside/outside is both made possible by and helps constitute a moral space of superior/ inferior. Hobbes, for instance, not only delineated a domain of the rational, ordered polity from the dangerous, anarchic world in which it was situated, he also 'enumerated the character of each realm by arguing that the former was the residence of the good, sane, sober, modest and civilised people, while the latter was populated by evil, mad, drunk, arrogant and savage characters' (Campbell, 1992: 85). For Campbell the ordering of a moral space by an inside/outside logic provides a basis for understanding the imperative of security and the power mechanisms deployed to contain and neutralize imagined threats to the preservation of order. Equally, however, the concern with security ought not to distract our attention away from the underlying desire to civilize and possess the other culture and society.[5] Threats to a sense of mission fuel a neurotic concern for security, but initially it is the construction of a civilizing project that moulds the subsequent concern with security. And the civilization of the other necessitates expansion – in fact, in the words of Hannah Arendt (1975: 125), expansion 'as a permanent and supreme aim of politics is the central political idea of imperialism'. But rather than link this idea of expansion to an economic logic, or as Arendt did, to the realm of business speculation, it can be alternatively argued that the underlying Western will to expand was rooted in the desire to colonize, civilize and possess the non-Western society; to convert what was different and enframed as inferior and backward into a subordinated same. In this context, I would argue that imperialism and the geopolitical penetration of other societies were constituted through the development of an invasive discourse of Western liberalism, sometimes captured in the phrase 'the project of Western modernity'. Crucial to this project, as I shall argue below, was and remains the effects of a binary logic of superior/inferior, civilized/barbaric, father/child, peoples with history and those without, modern and traditional. But surely in global times, in our era of time-space compression, these binary divisions have been eclipsed?

McGrew (1992a: 23) provides a succinct definition of globalization which he sees as having two distinct dimensions: scope (stretching) and intensity (or deepening). It is a process which refers to the 'multiplicity of linkages and interconnections between the states and societies which make up the modern world system', being in essence a phenomenon by which events, decisions and activities in one part of the world can significantly impact on individuals and communities in quite distant parts of the globe. In one sense, it implies a grouping of processes whereby politics and social activities are 'becoming stretched across the globe'; and, in another sense, it captures an 'intensification in the levels of interaction, interconnectedness or interdependence between states and societies which make up the world community' (ibid.). Thus, global processes are seen as expressing a double movement of 'stretching' and 'deepening'. The intellectual fascination with globalization and its effects was partly stimulated by a concern to understand the variety of socio-economic changes affecting the West. The global economic recession of the early 1980s, the deeply rooted fears of nuclear war and the growing concern with environmental degradation on a world scale all tended to accentuate an awareness of an emerging global condition. Furthermore, an expanded consciousness of global connectivity was reinforced by the electronic media, which were capable of bringing to an audience's immediate attention events in distant locations, hence generating a sense of global belonging and imagination. The global condition poses at the same moment the questions of the national and the local, as well as more recently the regional.

In the contemporary world, social relations and interaction are not dependent upon simultaneous actual 'presence' within a specific location, since the structures and organizations of modern societies, facilitated by instantaneous communication, stimulate intense relations between 'absent' others. In this way, globalization can be interpreted as articulating this imbrication of 'presence' and 'absence' through its systematic interlocking of the 'local' and 'global' (Giddens, 1990).[6] For Harvey (1989) today's 'global village' results from a historical process penetrated by discrete phases or bursts of intense time-space compression. These phases are seen as rooted in the periodic crises and restructuring of capitalism which involve an acceleration of economic and social processes. One of the consequences of this speeding up of socio-economic change is an intensification of time-space compression, and the concomitant acceleration in the pace of globalization, which Harvey sees as being most pronounced in the spheres of manufacturing production and finance (Harvey, 1989: 61). It is here, too, that we have a number of key implications for the nation-state and the preservation of sovereignty. Held (1991: 222), for example, in considering democracy in the context of globalization underlines the ways in which the nation-state is being pressurized from above and below. Pressures of economic, political, legal and military interconnectedness are changing the nature of the sovereign state from above, whilst the manner in which 'local and regional nationalisms' are eroding the nation-state from below reflects a growing destabilization of previously constituted national sovereignties, especially those established in peripheral societies. The disruption and erosion of sovereignties is a theme that reminds us of that other hidden dimension of many Western discussions of the global: the relative lack of interest in the construction and deployment of a neoliberal discourse of development. But, in addition, it is important to note that much contemporary 'global talk' ignores the connections with earlier phases of the occidental will and capacity to intervene and destabilize other governments and subvert other sovereignties. Either in the form of overt acts of military intervention on a worldwide basis, or as more covert, invisible acts of continuing penetration and subversion,[7] the West and especially the United States developed a powerful series of institutional and logistical mechanisms in order to be able to influence events and confront its enemies in a turbulent Third World (Kolko, 1988).

Tracing the connections between today's global condition and past phases of the West's outward expansion and evolving geopolitical power on a world stage can help us better to understand the specificities of the current era, including the identification of discontinuities juxtaposed to continuities. Stuart Hall (1991: 28) points to one facet of the continuity when he writes that 'global mass culture' has, in spite of a variety of different characteristics, two features in common: i) it remains centred in the West and always speaks English, although English as an international language, as Anglo-Japanese, Anglo-French or Anglo-German, as an almost hybrid English, and ii) its peculiar form of homogenization which does not work for completeness but rather recognizes and absorbs differences within a larger overriding framework of what is essentially an American conception of the world. Hall gives the relationship between the United States and Latin America as an example of the argument; here forms which are different, which have their own specificity, can also be 'repenetrated, absorbed, reshaped, negotiated, without destroying what is specific and particular to them' (ibid.: 29) – one element of a 'global postmodern' which is trying to live with, and at the same moment overcome, sublate, grasp, assimilate difference.

Hall's underscoring of the centrality of the West and of the presence of an Anglo-American project of homogenizing difference through processes of penetration, absorption and assimilation is not only relevant to a treatment of global mass culture; it also goes to the heart of that other hidden dimension of much First World-based analysis of globalization – the impact of neoliberal doctrine on a whole range of peripheral societies. If we take as a point of reference certain key texts on globalization (Featherstone, 1990; Giddens, 1990; Harvey, 1989; Held, 1991; McGrew, 1992b; Robertson, 1992) it becomes readily apparent that the issue of neoliberal thought and its deployment in the South is not considered as a significant part of global analysis. McGrew (1992b: 92) does draw our attention to the ways in which 'global and regional institutions, such as the IMF and the EC, may directly challenge the sovereignty and authority of member states when they impose decisions and policies upon them', but this flows out of a general consideration of the weakening of the state in advanced industrial countries, and little is mentioned by way of North–South relations. Robertson (1992: 27) does indicate contra Giddens that the present concern with globalization cannot be comprehensively considered simply as an outcome of the Western 'project' of modernity. For Robertson there has been a heightening of civilization, societal, ethnic, regional and individual self-consciousness that makes globalization and Westernization a problematic duo. However, as a whole, these authors show little interest in the possible significance of either the global effects of the neoliberal discourse of development or North–South relations in general.[8] Similarly, the emergence of reinvigorated forms of intervention and penetration in societies of the periphery tend to remain outside the analytical orbit of most of the Western proponents of the globalist turn in social science enquiry.

Neoliberalism, as it informs the enframing of orthodox development theory, is characterized by the combined significance attached to private property, market relations and possessive individualism. Initially, it was most keenly felt in peripheral societies through the implementation of 'structural adjustment' programmes with their well-known ensemble of devaluation, increased producer prices and reduced wage bills, wage freezes, decline in real wages and salaries, elimination of subsidies and privatization. In the 1980s, the strategic concepts were to cut, to differentiate, to dismiss and to discipline (Slater, 1993). More recently, the terrain for intervention has been considerably extended so that by the early 1990s the subject of participating development and good governance came to occupy much greater importance in the official agenda of development. In relation to the 'developing world' the OECD (1992) Report argued that what was required was a general framework for establishing key characteristics of good governance (see Mohan, this volume) within which support for the strengthening of judiciary systems, election monitoring, administrative decentralization and ethnic relations, and protection of minorities, conflict resolution and demobilization are all key features. Fundamental to this approach is the priority given to building institutional and economic capacities in the developing countries; in the Report, 'the key to *mastering development* and other global challenges' lies precisely in this task of construction (OECD, 1992: 7) emphasis added). Moreover, the Report subsequently notes that policy-makers in the West are finding that solutions to the domestic problems they face are increasingly associated with the economic and institutional functioning of other societies; in the words of the Report, 'this creates new scope for mutual understanding and synergy among policy-makers in donor governments as they tackle development as part of *achieving a global agenda,* (ibid.: 49, emphasis added).

'Mastering development' as part of a 'global agenda' is one of the most emblematic of phrases to be found in texts of the World Bank, OECD, IMF and other official donor agencies and international organizations. No longer is the discussion restricted to the soundness of economic policy and the need to roll back the state: today's official discourse encapsulates a role for civil society, for good governance, Western-style democracy, decentralization and 'effective participation'. In an African context, Barya (1993) critically discusses the emergence of a political conditionality to aid, and in a broader collection of essays edited by Sørenson (1993) the varied elements of this new more overt form of conditionality are usefully dissected. My purpose here is to signal the contours of a significant absence in the Western contextualization of the global condition. Just as the earlier significance of modernization theory and its partial linkage to the Cold War is ignored in the theorizations of global power, so, too, do we tend to find that neoliberal doctrine as a will to geopolitical power over the societies of the South is hidden in the interstices of the global agenda, as written in the West.

Whilst the modernization theory of the late 1950s and 1960s emphasized the relevance of a strong state in peripheral societies, not only for internal security but also as a basis for national economic development, the neoliberalism of today seeks to roll back all key influences connected with the peripheral state. The relation between the public and private sectors has been very much shifted in the direction of a centring on the private. For example, in the World Bank's (1994) Report on infrastructure for development, concepts of business, competition and integration into the world market continue to be given the determining weight. Although it is recognized that there is a trend in many countries 'toward democratization, pluralism and decentralization' (World Bank, 1994: 35), when it comes to economic strategy, there is an implacable adherence to a uniformly conventional perspective rooted in neoliberal doctrine.

The strategy of 'structural adjustment', which has been in place for well over a decade, has been accompanied by a massive redistribution of financial resources from the South to the North. The structural resubordination of the South to the North has been accompanied by the dismantling of the economic role of the state in countries with leaders as diverse as Carlos Menem in Argentina, Michael Manley in Jamaica, Hosni Mubarak in Egypt, Jerry Rawlings in Ghana and Carlos Salinas de Gortari in Mexico. From Argentina to Ghana state participation in the economy has been drastically curtailed, protectionist barriers against Northern imports have been predominantly eliminated, restrictions on foreign investment have been lifted, and through export-first policies the internal economies of Third World countries have been more tightly integrated into the capitalist world market.

Neoliberal doctrine has been assigned a universalist relevance that starkly contrasts with other approaches. For example, when discussing the possibility of the so-called 20–20 plan presented at the United Nations summit on poverty, held in Copenhagen in early 1995, the London *The Economist* argues that countries differ, that each has its own development problems. The 20–20 plan calls for the rich countries to spend at least 20 per cent of their aid budgets, and developing countries 20 per cent of their public spending, on basic social development. There is, then, a certain normative, potentially universalist implication from the proposal, and it is exactly against such an implication that it is contended that 'it would have been absurd economics – to say nothing of an infringement of sovereignty – to impose the same spending rule on all' (*The Economist*, 18 March 1995: 19). And yet structural adjustment policies have been welcomed by the protagonists of economic orthodoxy precisely because they include the imposition of rules and regulations for as many peripheral economies as possible. Within this orthodoxy, no argument has been advanced which suggests that the overall development of structural adjustment policies may constitute an 'infringement of sovereignty'. But World Bank and IMF tutelage and monitoring of the economic health of Third World countries can certainly be represented as a form of infringement of sovereignty, since they undermine and displace the independent capacity and economic capability of legally constituted state entities.

Although the above comments focus on economic strategy and refer to neoliberalism in the context of structural adjustment policies, it is important to remember, as I suggested earlier on, that the enunciated doctrine of key international organizations such as the World Bank, the IMF, OECD, USAID, cannot only be seen as reflections of the economic. Latouche (1993), for example, reminds us of the continuing relevance of seeing the economic as part of the cultural. He argues against the idea that economy and culture conform to two antagonistic logics, one linked to egoism and individual interest, the other expressing the quest for identity grounded in experience of a collective life and solidarity. He suggests that first of all this dualistic perspective does not take into consideration the phenomenon of ethnocide, and secondly it treats the economic as weightless compared to the social. For Latouche, the economic is a historical and cultural invention, which in the West has been allocated an unprecedented pre-eminence. In this sense, the economic is nothing other than one dimension of Western culture. Moreover, in the West the economic is tending to become the substitute for culture, by absorbing all expressions of culture into itself (e.g. management of capital, cost-effectiveness, trade-offs, choices of lifestyle, etc.). The domain of 'calculating rationality' increasingly colonizes the spheres of art, feeling and beliefs.

These comments reinforce my argument that a crucial part of the globalization process is constituted by a continuance of the North's will to gain geopolitical power over the South, and neoliberalism is a key reflection of this will. Neoliberal development doctrine, remembering Latouche's (1993: 160) phrase that 'development ... is still the *Westernization of the World*', is reflective of 'globalization from above'. In any critical reappraisal of the global condition we cannot afford to evade analysis of this aspect of globalization since it affects, on a continuing everyday basis, the lives of the majority of the globe's citizens.

Finally it is necessary to indicate the interlocking of neoliberalism with the development, post-1989, of a new geopolitical conjuncture within which notions of global order and global governance are being superimposed on to a world in increasing turmoil. Simultaneously, but within the realm of critical social science, older notions of 'dependency' and 'imperialism' are being resuscitated, albeit with a qualifying prefix of the 'new'.[9]

For Bienefeld (1994), the 'new world order' has brought in a new age of visible imperialism since it is based on a hegomonic power that has a much greater capacity and willingness to subvert the national sovereignty of other societies, particularly non-Western societies, for reasons of its own geopolitical strategy. The limits that were previously imposed by the existence of a rival world power have been dissolved. At the same time, ethical constraints emanating from the demands and opposition of well-informed and morally vigilant electorates have tended to be eroded, as apathy, confusion, cynicism and socio-economic insecurity have become more marked inside the societies of the North. When Panama was invaded in 1989, or when the USA carried out massive air strikes against Baghdad in 1992, designating extensive civilian casualties as 'unavoidable collateral damage', it was quite evident that despite contrasting contexts of intervention hegemonic power was free to use force in its self-defined interest, and against the sovereignty of other nation-states. Of course, it is one practice to enforce rules and another to fix the chaos that might ensue. The analysis of a 'new imperialism' is taken much further by Füredi (1994) who strongly argues the case that instead of merely discrediting Third World societies there is now a new attempt positively to celebrate the record of the West – to create the ground for a 'moral rehabilitation of imperialism'. Füredi situates this return of imperial desire to three varied but mutually reinforcing causes: a) the failure of Third World nationalism or so-called 'Third Worldism'; b) the emergence of a much more conservative intellectual climate; and c) the end of the Cold War and the collapse of the Second World which has effectively removed one of the major restraints on Western intervention in Third World societies. Recovering some interesting lines of thought from Hobson's study of imperialism, Füredi rightly emphasizes the importance of a sense of moral superiority which endows the West with the presumed ability to provide a solution to the problems of other societies. Older notions of 'manifest destiny' and 'imperial mission' can be quite easily blended into a new will to have global power. However, in the post-Cold War era, with a redevelopment of the United Nations, Western intervention is projected in a multilateral or international form. UN resolutions are routinely deployed to legitimize military intervention, so that UN troops in Somalia or Cambodia are described as 'peace-keeping' forces involved in 'humanitarian' tasks. Substantial military operations can be depicted as acts of disinterested generosity by reluctant Western actors.

New forms of intervention are also legitimized in the context of a variety of Third World threats or sources of global insecurity; the threat of nuclear proliferation, environmental pollution, the dangers of the drug trade; the spread of AIDS, the rise of Islamic fundamentalism, the growth of terrorism and the perils of over-population and migration, especially in the direction of the West. As Füredi shows, these themes are fertile ground for a series of Western-created moral panics in which it becomes vital to protect Western culture from destabilization and disruption from outside. Expressed in more measured terms, Paul Kennedy stresses the decline of the population of the West in relation to other societies and suggests that this development has raised the question of whether 'Western values' – a liberal social culture, human rights, religious tolerance, democracy, market forces – 'will maintain their prevailing position in a world overwhelmingly peopled by societies which did not experience the national scientific and liberal assumptions of the Enlightenment' (quoted in Füredi, 1994: 117).

In an atmosphere marked by notions of the 'clash of civilizations' and perceived threats to Western culture from the emergence of a much more unpredictable and turbulent non-Western world, new forms of imperialist thought do not reflect the confidence and secure sense of power and vitality once found in the Victorian era. There is a new sense of insecurity, pessimism and uncertainty which emanates from a combined perception of the social maladies affecting the societies of the West together with a realization that the world outside, culturally and politically, is becoming increasingly heterogenous, polyvocal, turbulent and chaotic.[10] Paradoxically, this anxious perception of flux and danger co-exists with the undiminished power of the neoliberal doctrine of development and modernization. Whilst, in a certain sphere, Füredi might be right to point to the insecurities that give Western attitudes towards Third World societies an 'irrational and unpredictable character' (Füredi, 1994: 119), at the same time, the Western discourse of neoliberalism displays a continuing confidence and stability, if not dogmatic certitude that contrasts quite markedly with the underlying current of angst depicted by Füredi. This contrast, I would argue, has much to do with the varied provenances and institutional contexts of cultural challenge on the one hand and development doctrine on the other. Briefly, there are three dimensions that can be identified.

First, as Hills (1994), for example, has recently shown, within the poorer nation-states of the world, the hegemony of the IMF and the World Bank, and the privatization and liberalization which they legitimize incorporate political mechanisms for representing the interests of the industrialized West and their transnational corporations. Moreoever, US structural dominance over communications goes together with the fact that in the communication sector the world is being shaped in the US market image. Hills concludes by stating that the concept of 'dependency', in the sense that the autonomy of the individual poorer states is minimal and that their internal domestic arrangements are increasingly shaped by the international economy, is more relevant today than ever.

Second, in the post-1989 period, with the collapse of the Second World, the corresponding opening-up of space to the remaining world power, and the severe weakening of the economic and political autonomy of the peripheral societies of the South, there has been a recrudescence of imperial sentiment and a general mood of Western supremacy. This has been particularly marked in the military arena,[11] but also in business circles there have been clear signs of a return to an earlier validation of an imperial politics.

Third, in an uneasy juxtaposition with expressions of Western superiority, the current era is also marked by a sense of Western unease. New questions of political identity and difference haunt the traditional landscapes of Western privilege, and the clash over the canon in the literary domain, as well as more broadly the multi-cultural thematic, point to a climate of contestation and change.[12] All three dimensions and their interwoven nature could be analysed far more in this context. My objective has been simply to signal their relative exclusion from many studies of globalization, and to suggest that the lack of concern for these sorts of issues inevitably limits the effectiveness of analysis, and also the potential for a genuine extension of global understanding.

Conclusions

Falk (1993), in his examination of global citizenship, makes the useful distinction between 'globalization from above' and 'globalization from below'. He defines the former in terms of the collaboration between leading states and the main agents of capitalism; it is the New World Order reflected in either the geopolitical project of the US government or as a technological and marketing project of large-scale capital. The second type of globalization is characterized as both a reaction to these developments as well as a response to different influences which emanate from the concerns of grass- . roots movements and new visions of the human community. For Falk, this type of globalization from below inclines towards a 'one-world community premised on a politics of aspiration and desire', and 'rests upon the strengthening over time of the institutional forms and activities associated with global civil society' (Falk, 1993: 39).

This latter type of globalization closely relates to the question of social movements and the constitution of citizenship. If alternate visions of the global are to gather weight, the connections of solidarity between social movements in different countries need to be given greater priority. Struggles around issues, for example, the environment, human rights, decentralized forms of government, gender politics and indigenous communities, express an increasingly common agenda and in the South these sorts of struggles, often ignored by Western social scientists (Slater, 1994), provide an emerging basis for new and alternative visions of justice and ethics in a global context. Hence, whilst I have highlighted only three kinds of absence in the Western discussions of the global, I would like to conclude by suggesting that in the discussion of alternative visions of the global and challenges to Western notions of 'new world orders' it is important to avoid the assumption that it is only in the North that more questioning alternatives to the global condition will emerge. Again, it is in the context of North–South relations that we can find other starting-points that originate in the South and help refocus our attention on the need to challenge the established geopolitical imaginations of the dominant powers in today's world (Shiva, 1993). Listening critically to other voices can hopefully be broadened to move beyond a still predominant tendency to situate analysis of the global within an implicitly occidental frame.

For a more detailed version of this paper, see 'Challenging Western visions of the global', *European Journal of Development Research*, December 1995.

Notes

1. One recent example can be found in the work of Hans Magnus Enzensberger – see his short piece entitled 'No More Heroes' in *The Guardian Weekend*, 9 July 1994. For a detailed treatment of 'cynical reason', see Sloterdijk (1988).
2. For an eloquent presentation of such a position, see Bauman's (1993) text on postmodern ethics. For a discussion of the varied strands of the Latin American debates on modernity and postmodernity, see Slater (1994).
3. The Cuban writer Mosquera (1993: 531) remarks that 'Eurocentrism is the only ethnocentrism that has been universalized by the domination, on a global scale, of a metaculture whose power is secured by the traumatic transformation of the globe through economic, social and political processes centred in one corner of it'. We might add here that 'Euro-North Americanism', a rather clumsy, albeit more valid term for the twentieth century, can be interpreted similarly; at the same time, however, it does pose the need to examine the specification of

American Empire and the nature of US manifest destiny – see the excellent collection of essays in Kaplan and Pearse (1993).

4. Such an imperative of mission and destiny had deep historical roots; Thomas Jefferson, for example, averred towards the end of the eighteenth century that 'our confederation must be viewed as a nest, from which all America, north and south, is to be populated' (Niess, 1990: 2).

5. The drive to annex and to possess was neatly expressed by Cecil Rhodes in the phrases 'expansion is everything . . . I would annex the planets if I could' (quoted in Arendt, 1975: 124).

6. Hall (1991: 27) makes a similar point, commenting that one of the things which happens when the nation-state weakens is that the response goes in two simultaneous directions; it goes above the nation state and it goes below it . . . it goes global and local in the same moment . . . Global and local are the two faces of the same movement'.

7. One reminder of this reality is to be found in one of Arendt's (1975: xx) footnotes where she refers to a quotation from a former head of the CIA, Allen Dulles, who wrote that the Agency had to model itself upon the Soviet State Security Service which was an 'instrument for subversion, manipulation and violence, for secret intervention in the affairs of other countries'. More recent information and analysis of these sorts of operations can be found in Chomsky's prolific work (for instance, Chomsky, 1992).

8. In one instance, it is suggested that American and Western hegemony in the world system declined at the end of the 1960s (Friedman, 1990: 323); whether we are to assume that this decline has remained in force is not clear. In the same reader the contributions of Wallerstein and Worsley do place the issue of the Third World on to the agenda, but very much in the context of the world-systems model.

9. Although, in this case, I take my example from the social and political science literature, it needs to be pointed out that in general the terms 'imperialism', 'imperial politics' or 'the imperial encounter' are used far more frequently in literary theory, especially within the post-colonial genre than in the development studies or social science literatures where such terms have tended to fall into disuse. In critical development theory it was the Marxist perspective that gave meaning and theoretical substance to imperialism and the critique of capitalism, but in the post-Cold War era, with 'market triumphalism' and the waning of the Marxist tradition, these older critical concepts seem stranded on an analytical terrain that appears quite outmoded. Conversely, critical literary theory does not seem to be weighed down by such a conceptual history, and has breathed new life into the questioning of empire and imperialist power. Said's (1993) most recent work on this subject is a classic example.

10. And of course *within* societies of the North, especially the United States, realizations of the growing ethnic diversity of social life, the debates on multiculturalism and the decline as a percentage of the population of the Anglo-American category have also contributed to a sense of 'cultural erosion' within the dominant white Anglo-American grouping. However, feelings of being undermined have also ignited more militant expressions of cultural 'purity' and

fundamentalist passion. Recently, for instance, some Florida schools have introduced a new curriculum which teaches that Americans are 'unquestionably superior' to any other nation now, or at any time in history. Introduced by Christian fundamentalists as a backlash against a multicultural approach to education, it emphasizes America as 'the best of the best' (reported in *The Guardian*, 16 May 1994: 10).

11. One Pentagon draft position paper defines the main military objectives of the United States in the post-Cold War period as 'preventing the emergence of rival powers' (Bienefeld, 1994: 44). In order to accomplish such a goal a continuous process of surveillance, monitoring and control would be required. No matter how extensive and intensive such a military and intelligence gaze might become, the potential threat is always present and there will always be, in this context, a perpetual need for the power to discipline, intervene and prevent.

12. A sense of anger, doubt and perplexity can be found reflected in the wide range of sources, both popular and scientific. In one special number of *Time*, the lead article is entitled 'Whose America? – multicultural education calls the nation's shared sense of history into question', and 'American kids are getting a new – and divisive – view of Thomas Jefferson, Thanksgiving and the Fourth of July' (*Time*, **138**(1), 8 July 1991). The hostile academic responses to Said's (1993) text on *Culture and Imperialism* reflect a similar mood of angry defence of the traditional canon.

References

Arendt, H. (1975) *The Origins of Totalitarianism*, San Diego, A Harvest/HBJ Book.

Barya, J.-J. B. (1993) The new political conditionalities of aid: an independent view of Africa, *IDS Bulletin*, **24**(1), 16–23.

Bauman, Z. (1993) *Postmodern Ethics*, Oxford, Blackwell.

Bienefeld, M. (1994) The new world order: echoes of a new imperialism, *Third World Quarterly*, **15**(1), 31–48.

Campbell, D. (1992) *Writing Security: United States Foreign Policy and the Politics of Identity*, University of Minnesota Press, Minneapolis.

Chambers, I. (1994) *Migrancy, Culture, Identity*, London, Routledge.

Chomsky, N. (1992) *Deterring Democracy*, New York, Hill and Wang.

Falk, R. (1993) The making of global citizenship, in J. Brecher *et al.* (eds), *Global Visions: Beyond the New World Order*, Montreal, Black Rose Books, pp. 39–50.

Featherstone, M. (ed.) (1990) *Global Culture: Nationalism, Globalization and Modernity*, London, Sage.

Friedman, J. (1990) Being in the world: globalization and localization, in M. Featherstone (ed.), pp. 311–28.

Füredi, F. (1994) *The New Ideology of Imperialism*, London, Pluto.

Giddens, A. (1990) *The Consequences of Modernity*, Cambridge, Polity.

Hall, S. (1991) The local and the global: globalization and ethnicity, in A. D. King (ed.), *Culture, Globalization and the World-System*, London, Macmillan, pp. 19–39.

Harvey, D. (1989) *The Condition of Postmodernity*, Oxford, Blackwell.

Held, D. (1991) Democracy, the nation state and the global system, in D. Held, *Political Theory Today*, Cambridge, Polity, pp. 197–235.

Hills, J. (1994) Dependency theory and its relevance today: international institutions in telecommunications and structural power, *Review of International Studies*, **20**, 169–86.

Hitchcock, P. (1993/94) The othering of cultural studies, *Third Text*, **25**, 11–20.

Honig, B. (1993) *Political Theory and the Displacement of Politics*, Ithaca, NY, Cornell University Press.

Kaplan, A. and Pearse, D. E. (eds) (1993) *Cultures of United States Imperialism*, Durham, NC, Duke University Press.

Kolko, G. (1988) *Confronting the Third World: United States Foreign Policy 1945–1980*, New York, Pantheon Books.

Laclau, E. (1994) Introduction, in E. Laclau, *The Making of Political Identities*, London, Verso, pp. 1–8.

Latouche, S. (1993) *In the Wake of the Affluent Society: An Exploration of Post-Development*, London, Zed Books.

Lingis, A. (1994) Some questions about Lyotard's postmodern legitimation narrative, *Philosophy and Social Criticism*, **20**(1/2), 1–12.

McGrew, A. (1992a) Conceptualizing global politics, in A. McGrew, A. Lewis *et al.* (eds), *Global Politics*, Cambridge, Polity, pp. 1–28.

McGrew, A. (1992b) A global society? in S. Hall, D. Held and T. McGrew (eds), *Modernity and Its Futures*, Cambridge, Polity/Open University, pp. 61–116.

Nandy, A. (1992) *Traditions, Tyranny and Utopias: Essays in the Politics of Awareness*, Delhi, Oxford University Press.

Niess, F. (1990) *A Hemisphere to Itself – A History of US–Latin American Relations*, London, Zed Books.

OECD (1992) *Development Cooperation: 1992 Report*, Paris.

Reigadas, M. (1988) Neomodernidad y posmodernidad: preguntado desde América Latina, in Mari (ed.), *¿Posmodernidad?*, Buenos Aires, Editorial Biblos, pp. 113–45.

Robertson, R. (1992) *Globalization: Social Theory and Global Culture*, London, Sage.

Said, E. (1993) *Culture and Imperialism*, London, Chatto and Windus.

Shiva, V. (1993) The greening of the global reach, in J. Brecher *et al.* (eds), *Global Visions*, pp. 53–60.

Slater, D. (1993) The political meanings of development: in search of new horizons, in F. Schuurman (ed.), *Beyond the Impasse: New Directions in Development Theory*, London, Zed Books, pp. 93–112.

Slater, D. (1994) Power and social movements in the other Occident: Latin America in an international perspective, *Latin American Perspectives*, **21**(2), 11–37.

Sloterdijk, P. (1988) *Critique of Cynical Reasoning*, London, Verso.

Soper, K. (1991) Postmodernism and its discontents, *Feminist Review*, **39**, 97–108.

Sørenson, G. (ed.) (1993) *Political Conditionality*, London, Frank Cass.

Wallerstein, I. (1990) Culture as the ideological battleground of the modern world system, in M. Featherstone (ed.), *Global Culture: Nationalism, Globalization and Modernity*, London, Sage, pp. 31–55.

World Bank (1994) *World Development Report 1994*, Oxford, Oxford University Press.

Worseley, P. (1991) Models of the modern world-system, in M. Featherstone (ed.), *Global Culture: Nationalism, Globalization and Modernity*, London, Sage, pp. 83–95.

20

Globalization and Governance: The Paradoxes of Adjustment in Sub-Saharan Africa

GILES MOHAN

Introduction: the theoretical and political marginalization of sub-Saharan Africa

Recently geographers have realized that many of the assumptions which underpin their subject are universalizing (Blaut, 1993). Despite this, the incorporation of perspectives from the 'non-West' into mainstream geographical theory from the 'West' has still not occurred to any great extent (Slater, 1992 and this volume). This is even worse in the case of sub-Saharan Africa (SSA). This chapter addresses this bias by analysing SSA's development predicaments and is guided by themes in the globalization literature. As such the chapter seeks to create a dialogue between hitherto disparate fields of study and addresses two key questions. First, what can the globalization literature offer for an analysis of Africa's marginalization? This is addressed in the next two sections. The second question is what can Africa's development dilemmas offer for an analysis of globalization? This is addressed in the penultimate and final sections.

Globalization and governance: learning from the West

Does the recent literature on globalization and governance offer a useful model for an analysis of SSA's multiple crises? If we accept Jessop's general assertion regarding the state, that there has been a 'complex triple displacement of powers upward, downward, and to some extent, outward' (Jessop, 1993: 10) then we need a 'redefinition of the study of politics . . . [and] . . . the concept of power, too, has to be radically enlarged' (Strange, 1995: 169–70). What might this reconfigured study of power and politics look like? Four key themes emerge.

The first refers to the move away from formulations which normalize the state as the definitive political unit (Ashley, 1987; Held, 1990; Peck and Tickell, 1994). As Strange (1995: 173) asserts, we must 'move the field away from too exclusively state-centred a focus'. Jessop (1993: 9) adds that

These reflections suggest that state actions should not be attributed to the state as an originating subject but should be understood as the emergent, unintended and complex resultant of what rival 'states within the state' have done and are doing on a complex strategic terrain.

Clearly any major socio-economic development such as economic liberalization or democratization cannot be seen as simply an 'internal' or an 'external' decision.

This first theme begs the question, if the state is decreasingly an originator of political actions, where does power lie and who sets political agendas? One response, and the second theme, lies in the realm of the international political economy and studies of imperialism (Murphy and Tooze, 1991; Stubbs and Underhill, 1994; Booth and Smith, 1995). For the analysis of Africa it is necessary to focus upon the trends towards the globalization of finance capital, the 'Triadization' of regional politics and trade, and the increasingly political role of the formerly 'economic' Bretton Woods institutions. Peck and Tickell (1994) describe political regulation in this emerging world (dis)order as a twofold division between local *responsibility without power* and the supra-national exercise of *power without responsibility* (see also Leyshon, 1992). The Bretton Woods institutions are increasingly playing the latter role in the former socialist and developing worlds (Toye, 1993; Strange, 1994; Bird, 1995).

The third theme overlies the previous two and relates to the relationship between power and knowledge and the diffusion of neoliberal discourses. This builds upon the previous theme regarding neoliberalism as a (the only?) development path (Slater, this volume). One of the useful outcomes of debates around postmodernism is an awareness of the way in which discourses normalize power relations. In geography this has spawned an area known as critical geopolitics (Dalby, 1991; O'Tuathail and Agnew, 1992; Mohan, 1994) which 'does not take existing ... power relations for granted, but problematizes their important quality of being unremarkable' (O'Tuathail, 1987: 197). In this way deconstruction of dominant discourses can be part of an attack on the hegemony of neoliberalism by exploding the myths about the inevitability of marketization (Bienefeld, 1994; Little, 1995).

The fourth theme builds from the first in locating a 'new' realm of politics, but it is different from the second theme in that it focuses upon *the local*. The local has, in some ways, come to replace class as the definitive social category with its ability to capture a multitude of non-exclusive social relations. The most recent set of lender reforms centre on an ill-defined notion of 'governance' involving institutional strengthening and 'civil society' which encompasses local participation and decentralization. The issue is usually couched in terms of liberal democracy and follows from a fairly rigid reading of Fukuyama's dubious 'end of history' thesis (Fukuyama, 1989). However, these prescriptions are readily transparent. As Lynda Chalker exclaims, 'Above all, government must provide stable, predictable conditions in which to do business' (1993: 24) – what the World Bank refers euphemistically to as the 'enabling environment' (World Bank, 1992). The most recent discovery by World Bank pundits is 'civil society' which is seen as a necessary counter-balance to the 'autonomous' state. As Harbeson (1993: 1) of USAID notes 'Promoting civil society is a key ingredient of donor-supported democratization initiatives in many, if not most, African countries'.

Neoliberalism and adjustment in Africa: exploring the paradoxes

It remains to be seen whether these themes are useful in analysing development in the region. I have chosen to structure this section around two interrelated tensions. The first relates to the role of the state while the second revolves around civil society and democracy. The post-independence crisis in SSA needs to be seen as the result of a complex and contextual interlocking of factors. The dynamics of post-colonial politics can be characterized as *statist nationalism* rather than *nation-statism* (Chachage, 1994: Wamba-dia-Wamba, 1994). What emerged was a weak state-based development model where 'politics is the state and the state is politics' (Wamba-dia-Wamba, 1994: 250). However, in attempting to achieve hegemony 'it was necessary to strengthen the state power and make it monolithic on the one hand, and weaken the civil society in terms of its organizational capacities on the other' (Chachage, 1994: 55). In the process of this strategy, forces within civil society were being shaped in opposition to the state and cannot simply be seen as 'disengaging' from politics. The net result was political and economic crises which for many SSA countries reached a trough in the late 1970s.

Against this demise we have seen the changing role of the Bretton Woods institutions and the rise of neoliberalism in Fordist Atlantic countries. The SAPs of the 1980s saw the IBRD and IMF working more closely than at any other time in the past thirty-five years, so much so that they became known in SSA as 'the Terrible Twins'. The neoliberal model is based on an outward-looking economic strategy where non-tradables are moved into the tradable sector (Balassa, 1981; Mamdani, 1994). In pursuit of this logic the average SAP is centred on a Holy Trinity of demand-management conditions: devaluation, credit squeezes towards the public sector and trade liberalization (Logan and Mengisteab, 1993; Olukoshi and Nwokwe, 1994). Alongside this demand-management strategy is an attack on the state and the valorization of the market (World Bank, 1991; Bienefeld, 1994; Watts, 1994). Privatization of inefficient and nepotistic nationalized industries is seen as one way of sanctioning corruption and reducing the state's financial obligations. Other supposedly 'institutional' reforms centre on the deregulation of state services which usually involves the introduction of user charges.

Table 20.1 gives an overview of the extent of SAPs in SSA. It shows that thirty-eight out of forty-three countries, or 88 per cent, have entered an agreement with the IMF. Of the twenty-nine countries for which a classification of strong or weak reform effort is available, twenty-one (or 72 per cent) are strong reformers. Given this pervasive influence on development in SSA, it is all the more surprising that its effects have not been noted to any great extent in the globalization literature.

The rest of this chapter explores primarily the political aspects of adjustment at a variety of levels. However, I have stressed the point that any separation between 'politics' and 'economics' is an artificial one. Before moving on it needs stating, perhaps above all else, that the record of economic gains from SAPs has been neutral to negative. As Bienefeld (1994: 35) notes, 'Few of the specific policy instruments that make up the neoliberal policy package enjoy strong or persuasive empirical support, while that of the package as a whole is all but non-existent.' Watts (1994: 374–5) adds that 'the record of IMF-IBRD reform has been a failure ... Overall, however, the economic outcomes have been stunningly unimpressive.' In the absence of convincing data, the IMF and World Bank tend to rely on a theoretical faith in the market or parade the one or two 'success stories', namely Ghana and The Gambia (Leechor, 1994). The following section examines two key paradoxes.

Paradox I - Deregulation, reregulation and the state

In the standard neoliberal package it is the state rather than the market that is seen to need 'rethinking' (Slater, 1993; World Bank, 1991). The sixth World Development Report made explicit the links between market reforms and administration whereby 'achieving improvements in economic performance requires both policy reforms and strengthened institutions for management' (World Bank, 1983: 39). Whether to use public or private instruments should, according to the report, have nothing to do with political ideology but simply efficiency, since 'competitive markets permit the necessary flexibility and responsiveness and, because they decentralize the task of handling information, also economize on scarce administrative resources' (ibid.: 53). In this light decentralization 'should be seen as part of a broader market-surrogate strategy' (ibid.: 123).

Table 20.1 The record of structural adjustment in Africa

Nation	IMF agreement (Y/N)[1]	Strong (S) or weak (W) reform effort[2]	Contested elections in last 5 years (Y/N)[3]	Election likely soon (Y/N)
Angola	N	-	N	Y
Benin	Y	W	Y	N
Botswana	N	-	Y	N
Burkina Faso	Y	W	N	N
Burundi	Y	S	N	N
Cameroon	Y	-	N	Y
Cape Verde	N	-	Y	N
Central African Republic	Y	S	N	N
Chad	Y	-	N	N
Congo	Y	S	N	Y
Côte d'Ivoire	Y	S	Y	N
Djibouti	N	-	N	N
Equatorial Guinea	Y	W	N	N
Ethiopia	Y	W	N	N
Gabon	Y	-	Y	N
Gambia	Y	S	N	Y
Ghana	Y	S	N	Y
Guinea	Y	S	N	Y
Guinea-Bissau	Y	S	N	N
Kenya	Y	S	N	Y
Lesotho	Y	-	N	N
Liberia	Y	W	N	N
Madagascar	Y	S	N	Y
Malawi	Y	S	N	N
Mali	Y	S	N	Y
Mauritania	Y	S	Y	N
Mauritius	Y	S	N	N
Mozambique	Y	-	N	N
Niger	Y	S	N	Y
Nigeria	Y	S	N	Y
Rwanda	Y	-	N	N
São Tomé & Príncipe	Y	-	Y	N
Senegal	Y	S	Y	N
Seychelles	N	-	N	N
Sierra Leone	Y	W	N	Y
Somalia	Y	S	N	N
Swaziland	Y	-	N	N
Tanzania	Y	S	N	N
Togo	Y	S	Y	N
Uganda	Y	-	N	N
Zaire	Y	S	N	N
Zambia	Y	W	Y	N
Zimbabwe	Y	W	N	N

[1] Riddell (1992)
[2] Logan and Mengisteab (1993)
[3] *The Economist* (1992)

Sovereignty, socialism and development trajectories

Taking it to its extreme, national state–society interaction and central–local relations become meaningless where policy is externally driven and rigidly circumscribed (Slater, 1989). This process has serious implications for ideological struggles since acceptance of the neoliberal package is predicated upon an erasure of competing political visions. As Frederick Chiluba, the Zambian trade union leader, asked rhetorically, 'Where on earth has the IMF financed socialism?' (cited in Callaghy, 1990: 297). Similarly, Mosley *et al.* (1991: 287) note that 'where there is articulate opposition to policy reform, as there usually is, that opposition must be overcome somehow if implementation is to take place'. In Ghana, for example, the PNDC embarked upon a 'radical populist' path following the *coup* in 1981 (Kraus, 1987). However, by 1983 they had all but accepted a standard SAP, and Bing (1984: 102) noted that 'The task of securing financing for the participatory approach might well have been more difficult than the technical approach'. These comments suggest that IMF conditionality is not consequent upon the loan but in fact precedes it. They also refute Fukuyama's triumphalism since 'socialism' had not been proved untenable but incompatible with the implementation of market liberalism.

Austerity and delegitimation

The second major problem emerges in the contradiction between austerity and legitimacy. Demand-management policies tend to hurt the urban formal sector harder than the export-producing rural sector as it reverses urban–rural terms of trade. They also hurt vociferous professional groups who work through state or parastatal organizations such as doctors, lawyers, university lecturers and students. In reducing state expenditure the level of investment drops which can increase absolute and relative scarcity and further undermines policy intervention (Parfitt and Riley, 1989).

The result is often social protest against the government so that the IMF's illegitimacy is transferred to a lower political level and effectively insulates it from the contradictions it has unleashed. Hence, there is a blurring of national and international boundaries between the initiators and implementors of austerity packages. The most notable example of protest came in Zambia in 1986. Following an adjustment programme in 1985, maize prices increased and subsidies were partially removed. Subsidies were retained on lower-grade maize but the details were unclear so millers were reluctant to mill the lower-grade maize, resulting in severe shortages in the Copperbelt. The riots which followed saw fifteen people die and protest spread to the capital Lusaka where Kaunda reversed the subsidy decision and promptly nationalized the large flour mills (Callaghy, 1990).

I discuss the issue of democratization in more detail in the following section. However, it needs to be said at this juncture that democratization efforts often come at a time when anti-adjustment feeling is at its height and the government is trying to cling on to power. Hence, the pressures of electoral success add to an already heavy political burden which exacerbates the types of conflicts already outlined. For example, Ivory Coast President Houphouet Boigny clamped down so heavily on opposition parties that a situation arose of 'multi-partyism without opposition' (Aribisala, 1994: 140).

State capacity, technocracy and 'official discourse'

These questions around sovereignty, austerity and legitimacy open up a further set of questions around the policy process. The most important of these are how is consensus achieved for neoliberal policies? through which organizations are policies negotiated and implemented? and does the state have the institutional capacity to implement complex policies?

First, we need to focus on the power–knowledge nexus as it relates to the policy process. In a variety of ways research agendas have been used to legitimate political intervention. Hoogvelt *et al.*'s (1992) analysis of World Bank empiricism and Samoff's (1992) account of the 'intellectual–financial complex' both examine the way in which seemingly objective studies promote the neoliberal cause. With regard to decentralization and development administration there has been a growth in public choice approaches and the emergence of the 'New Development Administration' school (Werlin, 1992) which stresses deregulation, privatization, minimal government, popular participation and incrementalism. Mohan's (1994) study shows the ways that the market and liberal democracy are normalized as the pillars upon which growth are to be achieved.

Secondly, we need to analyse the ways in which state officials formulate and implement adjustment-related policies. In SSA there has been a problem of institutional capacity in terms of implementing development initiatives (Hyden, 1983; Rothchild and Foley, 1983; Conyers and Hills, 1984). These tendencies were clear under the statist nationalism where the state assumed the burden for development planning and implementation. Under neoliberalism this has taken a different direction. The crudest version of neoliberalism sees the market replacing the state as the primary redistributive mechanism. However, Bienefeld (1994: 32) notes that marketization 'requires extensive intervention in the affairs of previously sovereign states' and this process is being waged within the state apparatus. Hutchful's analysis of

Ghana is useful in this respect. He writes that 'What has emerged in Accra is a *parallel government* controlled if not created by the lender agencies' (1989: 12; my emphasis). This small, technocratic clique are generally placed in the finance ministries and 'formulate' policy in collaboration with Bank and Fund officials either resident in the country or who visit on missions. Loxley (1992) even cites a case where the World Bank drafted a response to one of its own directives.

Evidence from other countries supports this notion of a parallel government which contradicts the calls for accountability and democracy in the liberalization process. In Tanzania the World Bank-sponsored Tanzania Advisory Group (TAG) consisted of only three people (van der Geest and Kottering, 1994). In the Ivory Coast, Aribisala (1994: 135) noted 'the growing regional trend of African heads of government being former IMF or World Bank officials', while 400 staff months of foreign consultancy were used to prepare the privatization plan. This amounts to a situation very similar to the colonial period where a scaled-down form of 'indirect rule' is being used to bolster an imperialist project.

The corollary of this increased centralization and non-accountability is the problem of implementation. The neoliberal agenda is, by its very nature, highly centralized because it seeks to free markets which are viewed as ubiquitous and spaceless, unlike state apparatuses which are place-bound and spatially uneven. In this way deregulation of markets entails the reregulation of political space. The logic of using central ministries for implementation is justified on the grounds that subnational levels of the state are too weak to implement policies. There is no doubt that institutional weaknesses have exacerbated the effects of adjustment policies which represents another paradox of the technocratic model. The state institutions through which de- and reregulation are taking place are also part of the political apparatus which will lose power to markets and therefore fight to protect their position. Some institutional 'weaknesses' are therefore more like filibusterism whereas others are genuine weaknesses because of poorly trained staff, sketchy data and inadequate technological infrastructure. For example, in 1984 in Niger responsibility for the privatization programme was placed in two ministries leading to 'unhealthy and unnecessary rivalry between the State, Board of Directors and the Director-Generals of the companies' (Akinterinwa, 1994: 159). We have already seen the confusion that arose in Zambia over maize subsidies which was the result of 'extreme administrative weaknesses of the Zambian state' (Callaghy, 1990: 296).

Paradox II - Democracy, participation and civil society

As Cox (1994: 50) noted, 'The issues of globalization have an important implication for the meaning of democracy'. I have already looked at the linkages between sovereignty and legitimacy. This section builds upon this by looking at the relationships between conditionality and good governance. The political analysis of the IFIs is, as Riley (1992) notes, based upon two flaws. First, the political difficulties of Africa are viewed simplistically in terms of state versus society. Second, democracy is conceived of in very limited terms, largely as an electoral process. This section unpicks a number of the main contradictions.

Austerity, informalization and new political spaces

We have already seen that austerity has produced violent protest, especially in urban areas. However, there are other important political responses to neoliberalism which go beyond simple 'survival strategies'. These centre on the growth of the 'informal' sector, ethno-regionalism and a related issue of guerrilla violence.

An important conceptual issue here relates to the formal–informal dichotomy. In the same way that the statist school posits a divide between state and society there are implicit assumptions about the mutual exclusivity of formal and informal sectors. Such a division is important where liberalization programmes aim to move commodities from the informal/non-tradable sector into the formal/tradable sector. Such divisions are overly simplistic. As Chachage (1993: 88–9) notes,

> groups involved in the 'second economy' do not occupy separate market and production systems; rather they are part and parcel of an entire system of production, exchange and distribution around which particular forms of social and political relations are embedded.

Hence, developments in the 'adjusted' formal sector cannot be separated from changes in the 'informal' sector because the two are intertwined in complex ways.

Evidence suggests that austerity measures such as wage freezes and redundancy force many people to seek alternative incomes through the informal sector. The result is that the informal sector has grown under SAPs. In Sierra Leone, Zack-Williams (1990) analyses the *dregg* economy where women especially secure incomes through informal activities. In Niger, Akinterinwa (1994: 149) notes 'the increasing informalization' of the economy. The same is true of the Ivory Coast (Aribisala, 1994) and Tanzania (Chachage, 1993). The conclusion is that 'adjustment has generally strengthened existing accumulation forms rather than supported the development of new, more dynamic ones' (Chachage, 1993: 90).

Alongside these enhanced economic relations, political spaces have emerged based on ethno-regionalism in the uncertain context of Cold-War demilitarization. For example, in Liberia, Somalia, South Africa, Rwanda and among the Ogoni of the Niger Delta, we have seen the emergence of politics based around some form of ethnic identity. This has been further complicated by the availability of cheap weapons following the collapse of the US and Soviet military–industrial complexes. One of the peace 'dividends' has been an escalation of armed movements in SSA. These guerrilla groups are an increasing feature of the adjustment era as the post-colonial state comes under further attack from disenfranchized and impoverished social groups (Shaw and Inegbedion, 1994). The media portray this as tribalism and blame the hot-headedness of 'tribal' leaders. However, reality is more complex. For example, up until 1991 Somalia was regarded as one of the few successful democracies in SSA (Clapham, 1993). The breakdown of order was seen in terms of 'clanism' with warlords battling it out. However, Samatar (1993: 35) shows that 'The colonial and post-colonial systems subverted the Heer-based social and moral order' yet 'invented' clanism in order to mobilize the nation.

Civil society and neoimperialism

From the statist perspective civil society is seen to be the counter-balance to the repressive, overbearing state (Bratton, 1989). Liberal theory sees civic politics as the seed-bed and training ground for a dormant political culture. This is at a time when development theorists outside the IFIs are suggesting that New Social Movements (NSMs) are the best way to achieve a politics of development and a politics for development (Escobar, 1992; Schuurman, 1993). Does this polycentrism hold out any real prospects for SSA? Clapham (1993: 435) is cautiously optimistic where civil society 'could be used to underpin an effective democratic order'. As we have seen, the IFIs attack the state in pursuit of unleashing markets and 'civil society', but these prescriptions are based around an assumption that state and civil society at present hardly interact.

Beckman's (1993) analysis of the process is instructive in drawing out the ways in which neoliberals are using seemingly radical concepts to promote their cause and picks up on themes throughout this chapter. Firstly, he argues that the state is analysed as redundant and useless developmentally. Hence, there is an immediate move to delegitimize the state. Beckman goes on to argue that the state represents the only viable focus of resistance to world market subordination so that efforts to promote civil society over the state are yet another means of facilitating the deepening of capitalist relations. He says that 'The "liberation of civil society" plays a vital role in the struggle to legitimate the shift in the balance of forces, both internally and globally, and to delegitimize resistance and contending options' (1993: 22). In this light the emphasis on civil society is part of the broader neoliberal project.

We saw above that the IFIs' vision of the state includes a measure of decentralization and participation in the building-up of civil society. This section examines briefly the issue of local government, service provision and welfare. According to a World Bank-sponsored conference, the role of local government is to 'provide cost-effective municipal services through public, private or informal sectors ... [and likewise to] ... find ways to incorporate, where appropriate, the initiatives of the private sector, the informal sector and NGOs' (1990: 3). These initiatives centre on the introduction of user charges and involve little real understanding or dialogue with the users (Wunsch, 1991). Political issues arising out of the ensuing social hardship are not considered since it is the unquestioned application of market mechanisms which is important. In this sense strengthening of local government and increasing fiscal accountability are used as a means of deflecting attention from the fact that these debilitating policy measures were devised and implemented centrally and undemocratically (Slater, 1989).

Conclusion: learning from Africa

In the decidedly one-sided flow of ideas from the West regarding globalization we must ask ourselves what can a study of Africa tell us about these processes? Conversely, any solution to SSA's development paradoxes will not be easy given the complexity of the 'post-Westphalian' order.

The emphasis on local politics within civil society appears promising. However, as this chapter has shown, the state should not be regarded as independent of this process. As Beckman states (1993: 21–9) 'the state plays a central role in the construction of civil society ... and ... Both state and civil society are formed in the process of contestation', the corollary being that any attempt to use the state effectively will not be premised on donor-funded support of civil society which aims magically to develop it as an 'autonomous' sphere. Such prescriptions are naïve. The liberals believe that the linking of society to state will be achieved through periodic and transparent elections. However, we have seen that *the local* can be manipulated, insulated and bypassed in a neoliberal agenda which stresses ubiquitous markets over place-bound state apparatuses.

Wamba-dia-Wamba (1994: 258) suggests that an 'emancipatory politics will be a politics without parties but through political organizations'. The key becomes alliance-building between local organizations at a multiplicity of local political sites – factories, villages, etc. This politics will also be built upon the everyday experiences and consciousness of Africans themselves so that hegemonic thought and politics is more effectively 'de-colonised' (Chachage, 1994). However, this does not rule out the need for a state since the state sets the rules in which this popular democracy can function. In the longer term, alliances may form which can lead to 'a reconstitution of state–civil society relations, and not one but many, depending on concrete experiences and openings' (Beckman, 1993: 31).

For the IFIs the main problem lies in eroding the sovereignty of state through conditionalities and rolling back its boundaries, yet still requiring its technocratic and repressive elements. This suggests a tension in the global-ization literature over the displacement of the state's power. While power has been moved 'upwards' the state remains a vital link in the system and therefore will not wither away. This realization is central to the notion of deregulation and reregulation. It also points to the fact that power is not 'contained' in nationally sealed political containers but does indeed flow through increasingly 'plastic' boundaries. On the other hand, for SSA countries the problem is in entering the world economy on their own terms which is largely, but by no means exclusively, a state-level project. As Bienefeld (1994) notes, there are critical areas where the state can usefully guide integration into the world economy. These include promotion of new industry, welfare expenditure, and support for agriculture. The overall conclusion is that the state does indeed have a role for all vested interests – the IFIs, the states themselves and local actors.

References

Akinterinwa, B. (1994) The experience of Niger: adjusting what structure? in A. Olukoshi, A. Olaniyan and P. Gibbon (eds), *Structural Adjustment in West Africa*, Lagos, Pumark.

Aribisala, F. (1994) The political economy of structural adjustment in Côte d'Ivoire, in A. Olukoshi *et al.* (eds), *Structural Adjustment in West Africa*, Lagos, Pumark.

Ashley, R. (1987) The geopolitics of geopolitical space: towards a critical social theory of international politics, *Alternatives*, **12**, 403–34.

Balassa, B. (1981) *Structural Adjustment Policies in Developing Economies*, Washington, DC, World Bank.

Beckman, B. (1993) The liberation of civil society: neo-liberal ideology and political theory, *Review of African Political Economy*, **58**, 20–33.

Bienefeld, M. (1994) The New World Order: echoes of a new imperialism, *Third World Quarterly*, **15**(1), 31–48.

Bing, A. (1984) Popular participation versus people's power: notes on politics and power struggles in Ghana, *Review of African Political Economy*, **31**, 91–104.

Bird, G. (1995) *IMF Lending to Developing Countries: Issues and Evidence*, London, Routledge.

Blaut, J. (1993) *The Colonizer's Model of the World: Geographical Diffusionism and Eurocentric History*, New York, Guildford Press.

Booth, K. and Smith, S. (eds) (1995) *International Relations Theory Today*, Cambridge, Polity Press.

Bratton, M. (1989) Beyond the state: civil society and associational life in Africa, *World Politics*, **41**(3), 407–30.

Callaghy, T. (1990) Lost between state and market: the politics of economic adjustment in Ghana, Zambia and Nigeria, in J. Nelson (ed.), *Economic Crisis and Policy Choice: The Politics of Adjustment in the Third World*, Princeton, NJ, Princeton University Press.

Chachage, C. (1993) New forms of accumulation in Tanzania: the case of gold mining, in C. Chachage, M. Ericsson and P. Gibbon (eds), *Mining and Structural Adjustment: Studies of Zimbabwe and Tanzania*, Uppsala, Nordiska Afrikainstitutet.

Chachage, C. (1994) Discourse on development among African philosophers, in U. Himmelstrand, U. K. Kinyanjui and E. Mburugu (eds), *African Perspectives on Development: Controversies, Dilemmas and Openings*, London, James Currey.

Chalker, L. (1993) The proper role of government, in D. Rimmer (ed.), *Action in Africa: The Experience of People Actively Involved in Government, Business and Aid*, London, James Currey.

Clapham, C. (1993) Democratization in Africa: obstacles and prospects, *Third World Quarterly*, **14**(3), 423–38.

Conyers, D. and Hills, P. (1984) *An Introduction to Development Planning in the Third World*, Chichester, John Wiley.

Cox, R. (1994) Global restructuring: making sense of the changing international political economy, in R. Stubbs and G. Underhill (eds), *Political Economy and the Changing Global Order*, Basingstoke, Macmillan.

Dalby, S. (1991) Critical geopolitics: discourse, difference, and dissent, *Environment and Planning D: Society and Space*, **9**, 261–83.

The Economist (1992), 2 February.

Escobar, A. (1992) Imagining a post-development era? Critical thought, development and social movements, *Social Text*, **31/32**, 20–56.

Forrest, J. (1988) The quest for state 'hardness' in Africa, *Comparative Politics*, **20**(4), 423–42.

Fukuyama, F. (1989) The end of history? *The National Interest*, **18**, 21–8.

Harbeson, J. (1993) Civil society and democratization in Africa, *African Voices*, **2**(3), 1–3.

Held, D. (1990) The decline of the nation state, in S. Hall and M. Jacques (eds), *New Times: The Changing Face of Politics in the 1990s*, London, Lawrence and Wishart.

Hoogvelt, A., Phillips, D. and Taylor, P. (1992) The World Bank and Africa: a case of mistaken identity, *Review of African Political Economy*, **54**, 92–7.

Hutchful, E. (1989) From 'revolution' to monetarism: the economics and politics of the Structural Adjustment Programme in Ghana, in B. Campbell and J. Loxley (eds), *Structural Adjustment in Africa*, New York, St Martin's Press.

Hyden, G. (1983) _No Shortcuts to Progress: African Development Management in Perspective_, London, Heinemann.

Jessop, B. (1993) Towards a Schumpeterian workfare state? Preliminary remarks on post-Fordist political economy, _Studies in Political Economy_, **40**, 7–39.

Kraus, J. (1987) Ghana's shift from radical populism, _Current History_, **86**, 205–28.

Leechor, C. (1994) Ghana: frontrunner in adjustment, in I. Husain and R. Faruqee (eds), _Adjustment in Africa: Lessons from Country Case Studies_, Washington, DC, World Bank.

Leyshon, A. (1992) The transformation of regulatory order: regulating the global economy and environment, _Geoforum_, **23**(3), 249–67.

Little, R. (1995) International relations and the triumph of capitalism, in K. Booth and S. Smith (eds), _International Relations Theory Today_, Cambridge, Polity Press.

Logan, I. and Mengisteab, K. (1993) IMF–World Bank adjustment and structural transformation in sub-Saharan Africa, _Economic Geography_, **69**(1), 1–24.

Loxley, J. (1992) _Ghana: The Long Road to Recovery (1983–1990)_ Ottawa, The North–South Institute.

Mamdani, M. (1994) A critical analysis of the IMF programme in Uganda, in U. Himmelstrand, K. Kinyanjui and E. Mburugu (eds), _African Perspectives on Development: Controversies, Dilemmas and Openings_, London, James Currey.

Meillassoux, C. (1970) A class analysis of the bureaucratic process in Mali, _Journal of Development Studies_, **6**(2), 97–110.

Mohan, G. (1994) Manufacturing consensus: (geo)political knowledge and policy-based lending, _Review of African Political Economy_, **62**, 525–38.

Mosley, P., Harrigan, J. and Toye, J. (1991) _Aid and Power: The World Bank and Policy-based Lending_, London, Routledge.

Murphy, C. and Tooze, R. (eds) (1991) _The New International Political Economy_, Boulder, CO, Lynne Rienner.

Olukoshi, A. and Nwoke, C. (1994) The theoretical and conceptual underpinnings of structural adjustment programmes, in A. Olukoshi, A. Olaniyan and P. Gibbon (eds), _Structural Adjustment in West Africa_, Lagos, Pumark.

O'Tuathail, G. (1987) Beyond empiricist political geography: a comment on van der Wusten and O'Loughlin, _Professional Geographer_, **39**(2), 196–7.

O'Tuathail, G. and Agnew, J. (1992) Geopolitics and discourse: practical geopolitical reasoning in American foreign policy, _Political Geography_, **11**(2), 190–204.

Parfitt, T. and Riley, S. (1989) _The African Debt Crisis_, London, Routledge.

Peck, J. and Tickell, A. (1994) Jungle law breaks out: neoliberalism and global-local disorder, _Area_, **26**(4), 317–26.

Riddell, B. (1992) Things fall apart again: structural adjustment programmes in sub-Saharan Africa, _Journal of Modern African Studies_, **30**(1), 53–68.

Riley, S. (1992) Political adjustment? Democratic politics and political choice in Africa, paper presented at Liverpool University, February.

Rothchild, D. (1993) Rawlings and the engineering of legitimacy in Ghana, paper presented to the conference on elections in Ghana, University of London, August.

Rothchild, D. and Foley, M. (1983) The implications of scarcity for governance in Africa, _International Political Science Review_, **4**(3), 311–26.

Samatar, A. (1993) Structural adjustment as development strategy? Bananas, boom, and poverty in Somalia, *Economic Geography*, **69**(1), 25–41.

Samoff, J. (1992) The intellectual-financial complex of foreign aid, *Review of African Political Economy*, **53**, 60–75.

Schuurman, F. (1993) Modernity, post-modernity and the new social movements, in F. Schuurman (ed), *Beyond the Impasse: New Directions in Development Theory*, London, Zed Press.

Shaw, T. and Inegbedion, E. (1994) The marginalization of Africa in the New World (Dis)order, in R. Stubbs and G. Underhill (eds), *Political Economy and the Changing Global Order*, Basingstoke, Macmillan.

Slater, D. (1989) Territorial power and the peripheral state: the issue of decentralization, *Development and Change*, **20**, 501–31.

Slater, D. (1992) On the borders of social theory: learning from other regions, *Environment and Planning D: Society and Space*, **10**, 307–27.

Slater, D. (1993) The political meanings of development: in search of new horizons, in F. Schuurman (ed.), *Beyond the Impasse: New Directions in Development Theory*, London, Zed Press.

Strange, S. (1994) From Bretton Woods to the casino economy, in S. Corbridge, R. Martin and N. Thrift (eds), *Money, Power and Space*, Oxford, Basil Blackwell.

Strange, S. (1995) Political economy and international relations, in K. Booth and S. Smith (eds), *International Relations Theory Today*, Cambridge, Polity Press.

Stubbs, R. and Underhill, G. (eds) (1994) *Political Economy and the Changing Global Order*, Macmillan, Basingstoke.

Toye, J. (1993) *Dilemmas of Development*, Oxford, Basil Blackwell.

van der Geest, W. and Kottering, A. (1994) Structural adjustment in Tanzania: objectives and achievements, in W. van der Geest (ed.), *Negotiating Structural Adjustment in Africa*, London, James Currey.

Wamba-dia-Wamba, E. (1994) Africa in search of a new mode of politics, in U. Himmelstrand, K. Kinyanjui and E. Mburugu (eds), *African Perspectives on Development: Controversies, Dilemmas and Openings*, London, James Currey.

Watts, M. (1994) Development II: the privatization of everything? *Progress in Human Geography*, **18**(3), 371–84.

Werlin, H. (1992) Linking decentralization and centralization: a critique of the new development administration, *Public Administration and Development*, **12**, 223–35.

World Bank (1983) *World Development Report*, Washington, DC, World Bank.

World Bank (1990) *Strengthening Local Government in Sub-Saharan Africa*, Washington, DC, World Bank.

World Bank (1991) *World Development Report*, Washington, DC, World Bank.

World Bank (1992) *Strategy for African Mining*, Washington, DC, World Bank.

Wunsch, J. (1991) Institutional analysis and decentralization: developing an analytical framework for effective Third World administrative reform, *Public Administration and Development*, **11**, 431–51.

Zack-Williams, A. (1990) Sierra Leone: crisis and despair, *Review of African Political Economy*, **49**.

ωspects for Sustainable Development: Experiences of Small Island Developing States

ROY SMITH

Introduction

Sustainable development has become a key term in international relations at the levels of both theory and practice. In theoretical terms there remains considerable debate surrounding the definitions of 'sustainability' and 'development'. In practice there are clear implications for failing to implement policies which allow for the long-term viability of resources. The processes of globalization and the increasing influence of the world's major economic and political institutions relate closely to the pursuit of sustainable development policies. In particular these factors can be seen as highly significant in relation to the policy option choices available to the less powerful states in the contemporary international political system.

This chapter will consider two related themes. First, it will briefly review the intergovernmental process of promoting economic growth whilst attempting to minimize environmental degradation. Second, this process will be set within the context of the particular experiences of several small island states. Many of the states referred to exhibit diverse characteristics. They have widely varying natural resource bases, population levels, technological capabilities and social, economic and political structures. However, it will be argued that they share a basic common denominator. That is the necessity to evolve development policies that do not sacrifice environmental integrity in favour of short-term economic goals.

As with the terms 'sustainable' and 'development' there are disagreements over what criteria should be used to determine various standards of living. Value judgements come into play. Cultural differences will also influence these assessments. In particular there are widely differing views on what value to put on various aspects of the environment. For example, how should the protection of particular endangered species and their habitats be related to the impact that such protective measures have on human activities?[1] These are questions that are implicitly recognized in the majority of states' policies towards environmental protection. It was with these issues in mind that the whole United Nations Conference on Environment and Development (UNCED) process was founded. The UN Conference on the Human Environment, held in Stockholm in 1972, was notable for the emphasis that developing countries put on their relative poverty as the root cause of environmental degradation (McCormick, 1989).

The legacy of both the Stockholm and Rio (1992) Conferences has been that governments continue to emphasize the economic growth interpretation of what development entails. The World Bank continues to use economic growth rates as the base indicator for how successful development policies are (World Bank, 1991). In terms of promoting sustainability the initiative remains largely in the hands of individual governments. The United Nations Commission on Sustainable Development (CSD) has responsibility for monitoring the extent to which the directing document of the Rio Conference, Agenda 21, is being implemented (Roberts and Kingsbury, 1993). The first test of governments' post-Rio commitment to the promotion of sustainable development came at the United Nations Global Conference on Sustainable Development in Small Island Developing States (UNGCSDSIDS) held in Barbados, 25 April–6 May 1994. The outcome of this conference will be looked at in more depth shortly. However, it should be noted that the Barbados Conference provided an excellent opportunity to assess both the difficulties of achieving sustainability and the international commitment of the more developed states to promote this goal.

The concept of sustainable development

Before looking more closely at UNGCSDSIDS it is worthwhile paying some attention to how sustainable development is variously understood. Several disciplines have contributed towards providing overviews of how humans have viewed their natural environment, both in terms of a relationship and as an integrated whole (Torrance, 1993). One of the key interpretations goes beyond recognizing the integrated relationship between humans and their natural environment. There is a questioning of the extent to which the present population has duties and responsibilities towards future generations (Baier, 1980). This is an essential attribute of policies of sustainable development. It acknowledges the level of environmental degradation promoted by the majority of development policies that prioritize economic growth. Moreover, it features the significant factor of adopting a longer-term view of the impact of development policies. There is also an awareness shown that the rate of environmental decay is an important element that should be included in any cost/benefit analysis of development policies.

The post-Stockholm Conference period of the early 1970s did see some significant developments with the setting up of the UN Environmental

Programme (UNEP), the call for a New International Economic Order (NIEO) and the signing of three major international treaties on the protection of Wetlands, World Cultural and Natural Heritage and the prohibition of trade in Endangered Species (Smith, 1993). These are events that cannot be discounted within the debate on global governance. Despite these moves, however, the overwhelming trend throughout the 1970s and 1980s was one of increasingly rapid environmental degradation (UNEP, 1994). Furthermore, the continuing dominance was of economic models highlighting economic growth. Even where there was an awareness of the environmental damage being caused in many developing and industrialized states the priority remained economic growth over environmental protection.

The Stockholm Conference explicitly raised the question of linking poverty with environmental degradation, particularly within the context of developing states. However, it was not until 1983 and the establishment of the World Commission on Environment and Development that the UN created a body specifically to deal with the implications of recognizing the relationship between these two areas. The report of this Commission, commonly known as the Brundtland Report, was published in 1987. Although development within this UNCED framework continued to be viewed in terms of economic growth, there was a far greater awareness of the significance of protecting the natural environment in order to achieve continuing prosperity, both for current and future generations. Popular expectations of greater governmental concern and action for tackling environmental issues rose with the announcement of an 'Earth Summit' to be held in Rio in 1992.

Foremost among the political outcomes from the Rio Conference were the signing of the Framework Conventions on Climate Change and on Biological Diversity; the production of Agenda 21 with its programme of action; the creation of the Global Environment Facility (GEF) to fund a wide variety of projects and the institutional support of the Commission on Sustainable Development (CSD) to oversee the GEF and promote the aims outlined in Agenda 21. The CSD has particular significance as an ongoing body charged with maintaining the momentum of the UNCED process (Jordan, 1994). There was also an explicit acknowledgement that the role of non-governmental organizations should be seen as an integral part of the promotion of sustainable development (Makhurane, 1993).

The non-governmental Global Forum, which ran parallel with the Earth Summit, proposed more radical solutions than had emerged from the government delegations. With far less need to adopt pragmatic positions to satisfy competing domestic interest groups the NGOs were able to call for zero-growth rates and even capital investment into environmental reclamation and protection projects. The failure of the majority of these projects to receive governmental backing partially accounts for the disillusion with the

UNCED process felt by some of the NGO membership. Despite this disillusionment in some quarters the UNCED process has continued with sustainable development maintaining a key role as a central and guiding concept.

The CSD, via the GEF, has become the prime conduit for channelling funding from the main industrialized donor states to sustainable development projects, predominantly in the South. At an institutional level the fact that the GEF is based at, and partly administered by, the World Bank raises some questions about the extent to which these projects differ from those previously funded by the World Bank. There have been increasingly vocal calls for a major overhaul of the main international financial institutions (Swift, 1994). Yet, despite NGO reservations about the institutional culture within which the GEF operates, the Pilot Phase of GEF-funded projects appears to reflect a genuine attempt to promote relatively small-scale operations that enhance both local and global criteria for sustainable development (Global Environmental Facility, 1994).

On a global scale the GEF operations will have minimal impact. They are mainly based around the protection of wildlife habitat preserves and fostering practices such as sustainable forestry. Whilst these are positive developments they are not sufficient in themselves to counter ongoing trends in environmental decay. Far more is needed in terms of technology transfers, the alleviation of developing states debt burdens and the rationalization of energy usage and patterns of consumption. Broadly this refers to a radical rethinking of North–South relations and an acceptance of the global environmental consequences of both industrialized and developing states continuing with policies that consistently give short-term economic considerations priority over the sustainability of their natural resources.

With these issues in mind attention will now be turned to the first major international conference on sustainable development in the post-Rio era. UNGCSDSIDS was significant partly as a benchmark for the level of momentum maintained for environmental issues on the international political agenda. Moreover, the unusual circumstances of various small island states lend themselves particularly well to assessing the extent to which sustainable development policies are both feasible and likely. Despite the great variety exhibited by the many Small Island Developing States (SIDS) attending the Barbados Conference, numerous similarities were also to be found.

Being a small island state

Whilst acknowledging the broad disparity between several SIDS, the convening of UNGCSDSIDS illustrates the recognition that many of these states face particular problems in achieving sustainable development. Issues such as limited resource bases, remoteness from markets, proneness to natural disasters, poor infrastructure and the lack of capital investment resources and appropriate labour skills have been cited as major drawbacks in promoting development. In 1985 the Commonwealth Consultative Group published a report highlighting how these factors disadvantaged SIDS in many aspects of international relations. In an attempt to offset these problems there have emerged regional organizations in both the Caribbean and the Pacific regions. The Caribbean Community (CARICOM) was established in 1973 and remains the predominant co-ordinating body for its members (Griffith, 1993). A similar role has been played by the South Pacific Forum (SPF) since its inception in 1971 (New Zealand Ministry of External Affairs and Trade, 1992).

Both of these regional organizations have been active in the UNCED process. In particular the South Pacific Forum oversees the Pacific Islands Development Programme (PIDP) and the South Pacific Regional Environment Programme (SPREP). These programmes have both addressed the issue of sustainable development in the Pacific Islands. In addition to full SPF members these programmes also include French overseas territories (French Polynesia, New Caledonia) and territories in Free Association with the United States (Federated States of Micronesia, Marshall Islands). This element draws in the metropolitan powers, thus enabling easier access to funding and the major international institutions. Of course, it can also be argued that it allows the major powers to promote their own interests from within an essentially regional organization. This may be so but, on balance, the benefits of this additional financial and technical support currently outweigh the potential costs.

The relationships between many SIDS and the major powers have a significant bearing on both the UNCED process in general and UNGCSDSIDS in particular. Many of these states are former colonies. Some continue to be so. Others remain caught in a dependency relationship with their former colonial rulers. In the case of the French overseas territories, despite more recent attempts to improve France's image in the Pacific region, it is clear that major policy decisions emanate from Paris. Attempts at self-determination in these territories have been strongly resisted by the French (Robie, 1989). A relatively large measure of internal self-government exists in the former UN Trust Territories of the Pacific Islands. However, these territories, now in Free Association with the USA, remain restricted in their independence by the dependency relationship that evolved during more than forty years of Trusteeship (Smith, 1994).

The reason for raising the question of autonomy from the major powers is to draw attention to the relatively weak bargaining position the majority of SIDS operate from. This is a natural result of their weakness in the areas cited above. In an effort to overcome this disadvantaged position the principle of strength through unity was extended beyond CARICOM and the SPF and led to the formation of the Alliance of Small Island States (see the Appendix for a list of AOSIS member states). This body had first been formulated to present joint position papers at the Earth Summit. In particular, the issues of global warming and sea-level rise were highlighted as being of extreme concern to low-lying island states, such as the Maldives and the Marshall Islands. Further to this point there was an awareness that the solutions to these problems lay outside of the jurisdiction of SIDS. If the scientific data were to be accepted the root cause of these problems was to be found in the energy consumption patterns of the most developed states. Under these circumstances there was a need to lobby the richest and most powerful states in the world.

One of the difficulties for AOSIS is presenting a united position drawn from such a diverse membership. Whilst not suggesting that there is a conspiracy by the major powers to undermine the AOSIS' position it remains the case that it would be relatively easy to seduce individual members by way of financial or other incentives. In particular, the states with the weakest economies are further weakened in terms of finding it harder to resist both positive incentives and negative pressures from stronger states. An example of the types of compromises SIDS may consider was the focus of some of the more heated debate at UNGCSDSIDS. The Marshall Islands government is currently reviewing a plan to use one of its atolls as a dumping site for nuclear waste (North, 1994). The Marshalls' President Kabau outlined the logic in capitalizing on the only productive use that could be made of atolls already contaminated by the US nuclear test programme. Despite this argument many of the other island states retain an avowed anti-nuclear stance and viewed such a plan as a serious compromise of this position.

At the same time as UNGCSDSIDS was taking place the International Whaling Commission was holding a meeting in Mexico. It was reported that, in an attempt to win votes on the resumption of commercial whaling, the Japanese government was offering substantial aid packages to several Caribbean states (Whale and Dolphin Conservation Society, 1994). Again this is illustrative of the enormous number of issues and pressures that complicate international relations. Greenpeace and several other environmental groups were on the verge of calling for a consumer and tourist boycott of the targeted states if they accepted the aid packages. Although this position was eventually modified, it brings attention to the complex nature of lobbying and governmental policy options. While many SIDS governments may have the awareness and political will to resist major power intervention, or to adopt sustainable development policies, these in themselves will not guarantee that such policies will enter into force. The immediacy of chronic indebtedness or the need to offset the costs of hurricane damage or similar natural disaster can have the effect of moving longer-term environmental concerns further down SIDS political agendas. The following section will consider what factors must be in place before sustainability can be achieved.

Criteria for sustainable development

Theoretically sustainability can be achieved without prior knowledge of the various ecological processes that maintain the global biosphere. However, with human activity increasingly disrupting ecosystems there is a pressing need to understand how various policies may be detrimental to the environment. This point is all the more serious in SIDS where ecosystems tend to be more fragile and less resilient to disruption. Also the relatively limited land areas mean that there are greater limitations on approaches such as shifting cultivation or allowing land to lie fallow until it recovers. A high reliance on subsistence agriculture, and marine resources, will also reflect a greater need to avoid the disruption of food supplies. Although there is a move away from reliance on domestically produced food supplies in SIDS they still partially contribute to many households. Moreover, there are arguments for regenerating the domestic cultivation of crops such as taro to counter a diminishing awareness of the significance of protecting the natural environment (Women Working for a Nuclear-Free and Independent Pacific, 1987).

As mentioned in the previous section, many SIDS are severely restricted in the policy options available to them. For example, the need to improve balance-of-payment deficits may require developing sectors with relatively quick returns such as cash-crop agriculture or tourism. The overall impact of the majority of these types of projects is that they adversely affect subsistence agriculture and pollute the environment. The UN's Food and Agriculture Organization (FAO) prepared a report for UNGCSDSIDS which details the environmental pressures associated with these two sectors in the Caribbean region (FAO, 1994). Although both could become sustainable the current pattern shows that major improvements would be needed in both sectors. This would only be possible with a large outlay of capital investment to reorganize these sectors. It is possible to point to individual projects such as eco-tourism ventures that have sustainability built into them from their conception. However, such schemes are currently a small minority within most island economies.

The above point illustrates a fundamental requirement for attaining sustainability in SIDS. That is that it should be an available and realistic policy option. Obviously a necessary requirement for sustainability is the physical resource base to maintain in the first place. However, almost as important is the ability to exercise political control over how this environment is affected. In the case of greenhouse gas emissions and their alleged linkage to sea-level rise the SIDS have virtually no control beyond participating in international negotiations. However, even within their own jurisdiction SIDS governments are limited in their levels of technology, expertise and available capital. Assuming that all of the above criteria can be met, island governments will still be faced with political decisions to give priority to particular projects.

Jonathan Lindsay has pointed out that there is a necessary trade-off between promoting both economic growth and environmental protection (Lindsay, 1993). The World Bank describes the apparent conflict between development and the environment as a 'false dichotomy' (World Bank, 1992). These two elements, the Bank argues, should be seen as the two sides of one coin. They complement each other rather than compete. Ideally this should be true and there is no denying the basic logic of the Bank's argument. However, as Lindsay points out, developing states are not starting with a 'clean slate'. They must deal with the situation in which they find themselves. Very often this is with economies still closely tied to their experience of colonialism, an already degraded environment, confusion regarding preferable policy options and restrictions in terms of what options are available.

The criteria for sustainable development policies in SIDS can thus be summarized as follows:

1. Knowledge of the processes that lead to environmental decay;
2. The means to influence these processes (technology, expertise and funding);
3. The political will to make the compromises and trade-offs that will have an economic cost as well as an environmental benefit.

In view of the above criteria the final section will assess the extent to which current trends suggest that SIDS can expect to achieve sustainable development.

Prospects for SIDS

The very fact that UNGCSDSIDS took place at all demonstrates that SIDS have legitimacy as a distinct body of states with particular needs and a pro-active political agenda. With regard to the first criterion listed above the amount of technical knowledge available was staggering. Each governmental delegation submitted a report that included Environmental Impact Assessments for various planned and ongoing projects. Agencies such as UNEP and UNDP supplied vast amounts of information, not only on SIDS but also on the global trends that were cited as having implications for developments in the islands (UNDP, 1994). As with the Global Forum at the Rio Conference there was a parallel NGO gathering at Barbados. This was called the Global Village and it also provided large amounts of technical data on environmental trends. A further exhibition, 'SusTech 94', was held by international businesses promoting goods designed to save energy and enhance environmental conservation.

A striking feature of the various forums discussing sustainability was the high percentage of natural scientists compared to social scientists. Understandably there were many marine biologists and associated scientists. They undoubtedly played a vital role supplying survey data and discussing integrated coastal management plans. Yet such plans are of limited value when there is little likelihood that they will be implemented. A recurring theme in workshop discussions within the Global Village was that the key concepts of environmental decay were well understood, the technology was available to offset this decay and yet a major obstacle remained with the failure to motivate political decision-makers to alter their policies. This gave rise to some frustration amongst NGO delegates who felt the government representatives, particularly from the more developed states, were not taking sufficient steps to bring about sustainability.

As within all disciplines there remain ongoing debates between environmental scientists regarding the causes, rates and solutions for environmental damage. However, UNGCSDSIDS reflected a broad consensus in most areas on the urgent need to respond to current patterns of decay in SIDS. Where this consensus breaks down is when the debate moves into the political sphere and governments are required to undertake wholesale reviews of their economic policies and commit significant funding towards environmental protection projects. At this level resistance from government is more appropriately analysed from a social science perspective. The logic of promoting sustainability is undeniable from an apolitical scientific standpoint. Problems arise when political choices have to be made by decision-makers operating with 'non-scientific' rationality.

In an assessment of development policies in Fiji John Overton has referred to the significance of cultural factors in determining both the policies and their likely outcome (Overton, 1993). The racial demography of Fiji is a significant social/cultural factor. However, Overton's conclusions would be equally applicable to many other SIDS. He argues that the reform of élite-dominated structures and institutions will not come about from within. Vested interests of élite groups are unlikely to be altered even where the longer-term consequences of maintaining the *status quo* would be ecological collapse. The reasoning behind this élite view is that up until the point of complete collapse they will be able to maintain a relatively privileged position. If this analysis also holds for élite groups in other SIDS and in the industrialized states the prospects for significant reforms relevant to sustainability are bleak. The first criterion referred to, that of adequate knowledge, is largely met, or could be with relatively straightforward education programmes. The issue of political will to alter policies divides into two distinct, but related, areas. First, there are aspects of SIDS policies that fall within their own jurisdiction and influence. Again this is an area where political decision-making and prioritizing is all-important. There will be variety on a case-by-case basis as to how individual administrations incorporate sustainability into their policies. However, there is at least the opportunity for SIDS governments to recognize how sustainability could be incorporated into their development programmes. Their ability to act on this recognition largely depends on a secondary factor. That is their position in relation to the major powers who exert a disproportionate influence on SIDS in this area. As mentioned previously, a fundamental aspect of SIDS being able to achieve sustainability revolves around the basic structure of their economies and the extent to which they feel they can *afford* to protect their environment. Obviously there is a strong argument for saying no government can afford not to protect its environment. However, the political reality for many of these governments is that hard currency has a greater appeal, in the short term, than a protected environment.

The eventual outcome of the Rio Conference, at least in financial terms, was that there would be some additional funding made available for environmental protection but that this should be distributed through existing channels. To all intents and purposes this meant further funding would replenish the GEF. The key phrase in the Barbados Declaration was that there should be 'adequate, predictable new and additional financial resources in accordance with chapter 33 of Agenda 21' (United Nations, 1994). No precise figures were given in terms of how much additional funding would be available. There was also a recommendation that SIDS should be given a higher priority in the allocation of GEF funding. Some SIDS have already been the location for the first round of GEF projects. The second phase of funding, GEF II, has yet to be implemented. The World Bank is currently defining policy guidance, strategies, programme priorities and eligibility criteria. Under restructuring the new GEF Council, which will decide future policies, has representation from both the Caribbean and Micronesia. However, these states have only been allocated one and a half seats out of thirty-two.[2] This is not insignificant but it is clear that the more developed states will retain control of the distribution of funding.

In addition to the direct allocation of funding a significant factor in the vulnerability of SIDS involves broader developments in the international economic system. The conclusion of the Uruguay Round of the GATT negotiations and the development of a World Trade Organization have potentially serious implications for SIDS. There are concerns that some SIDS may be net losers in the emerging economic order. GATT Director-General, Peter Sutherland, has attempted to ease these worries (Sutherland, 1994). However, it remains to be seen if the greater liberalization of trade will actively benefit SIDS. A further concern is the impact of the renegotiations of the Lomé Convention. These talks are ongoing but the EU Council has agreed a negotiating mandate which some commentators have described as a 'take it or leave it' position (Horner, 1994).

Under Lomé the African, Caribbean and Pacific (ACP) states are at a relative disadvantage to the EU. Similarly within the GATT framework the majority of SIDS do not possess great negotiating strengths. Under these circumstances SIDS rely heavily on positive actions from the more developed states. Reviewing UNGCSDSIDS it is possible to point to some positive trends with further support demonstrated for GEF-funded projects. However, these are of little significance compared to the demands called for in the NGO Action Plan formulated during sessions at the Global Village and presented to the governmental delegates at the official Conference. This document draws attention to gross disparities of wealth between countries of the North and South, the disadvantaged position of many indigenous peoples, the impact of military spending on development and a broad range of injustices under the general heading of 'neocolonialism'. The language used in this document tends towards the emotive and some of the demands, for example the return of Diego Garcia to Mauritius, are extremely unlikely to be met. However, in looking at the agenda set by the NGO representatives it becomes clear how limited the official Action Plan actually is.

Conclusion

Overall the UNGCSDSIDS was of greatest value in terms of reinforcing co-operation between AOSIS members. It also allowed SIDS governments access to state of the art scientific data on environmental degradation and informa-tion on the technology available to counter this degradation. The down side of this is that without assistance from donor states this knowledge and technology is unlikely to be put into operation.

The UNCED process continues with the CSD and the GEF playing pivotal roles. However, given the enormity of the task of achieving sustainability on a global scale the advances made in the last two years have fallen far short of what is required. If UNGCSDSIDS is to be taken as the first test of the major states' commitment to promoting sustainable development policies, the prognosis for life on earth is not good. One of the advantages of assessing sustainability within the context of SIDS is that they provide relatively closed systems for analysis. Theoretically if sustainability can be achieved anywhere it should be on a small island state where the processes affecting ecosystems are more clearly seen. Their relatively small scale also lends itself to enhanced study of these processes. Similarly, relatively smaller adjustments to economic patterns need to be made than would be necessary in larger states and those more integrated into the international economic system. The ongoing GEF-funded projects may provide useful information on what policies to adopt to promote sustainable development. However, there are strong indications that the current commitment to these projects by the donor states represents 'too little, too late'.

The criteria identified for achieving sustainability in SIDS can be equally applied at the global level. The knowledge regarding global environmental decay is open to some dispute, but only in the details rather than the general trend. The expertise and technology exist to remedy the vast majority of this decay. Again the key variable is the political will to act on the previous two factors. UNGCSDSIDS can be seen as a microcosm of the issues that need to be addressed on a global scale. The Earth Summit was the first step in meeting this challenge. Yet, if the attempt to start by way of the SIDS is any indication, the second step has been somewhat faltering. It is, perhaps, too early to be completely dismissive of the major powers' true commitment to a significant alteration of their economic policies and attitudes towards environmental protection. However, by the time a conclusive analysis can be put forward it may already be too late for environmental recovery to be achieved.

The processes of globalization are ongoing. The major political and economic international institutions continue to dominate the setting of global agendas. The above analysis has highlighted the degree to which small island states are at the forefront of the debate surrounding the need to adopt sustainable development policies. It has also demonstrated that, to a great extent, these states are limited in their policy options and constrained by a range of external factors. Globalization and non-sustainable development practices impinge directly on the small island states. However, this is disproportionate to the ability of these states to exert significant influence within key areas of political decision-making.

Notes

1. The conflict between environmentalists and the logging industry in the United States' Northwest with regard to the protection of the Spotted Owl illustrates this point. Similar conflicts abound in areas surrounding, and within, nominally protected wildlife reserves in Africa, Asia and Latin America.
2. Personal correspondence with M. Ramos, Biodiversity Officer of the GEF, World Bank.

References

Baier, A. (1980) The rights of past and future persons, in E. Partridge (ed.), *Responsibilities to Future Generations*, Buffalo, NY, Prometheus.

Brundtland, H. (1987) *Our Common Future*, Oxford, Oxford University Press for the World Commission on Environment and Development.

Commonwealth Consultative Group (1985) *Vulnerability: Small States in the Global Society*, London, Commonwealth Secretariat.

Danielsson, B. and Danielsson M.-T. (1986) *Poisoned Reign: French Nuclear Colonialism in the Pacific*, Melbourne, Penguin.

Declaration of Barbados (1994) UN Doc. A/Conf. 167/L.4/Rev.1, 5 May.

FAO (1994) *Agriculture, Tourism and Sustainable Development in Small Island States in the Caribbean*, Santiago, Chile, Regional Office for Latin America and the Caribbean.

Global Environmental Facility (1994), *Quarterly Operational Report*, May, Washington, DC, GEF.

Griffith, I. L. (1993) *The Quest for Security in the Caribbean*, London, Sharpe.

Horner, S. (1994) Spotlight on Lomé IV mid-term review, *Courier*, 144, March/April.

Jordan, A. (1994) The international organizational machinery for sustainable development: Rio and the road beyond, *Environmentalist*, **14**(1).

Lindsay, J. M. (1993) Overlaps and tradeoffs: coordinating policies for sustainable development in Asia and the Pacific, *Journal of Developing Areas*, October.

McCormick, J. (1989) *The Global Environmental Movement*, London, Belhaven.

Makhurane, L. (1993) The role of non-governmental organizations in sustainable development, *Development*.

New Zealand Ministry of External Relations and Trade (1992) *The South Pacific Forum: Regional Cooperation at Work*, Information Bulletin No. 41, Wellington, New Zealand, Public Affairs Division.

NGO Plan of Action Committee (1994) *NGO Plan of Action*, UNGCSDSIDS, Barbados.

North, D. (1994) Cashing in on nuclear waste, *Pacific Islands Monthly*, **64**(6).

Overton, J. (1993) Fiji: options for sustainable development, *Scottish Geographical Magazine*, **109**(3).

Roberts, A. and Kingsbury, B. (eds) (1993) *United Nations, Divided World: The UN's Role in International Relations*, Oxford, Clarendon.

Robie, D. (1989) *Blood on Their Banner: Nationalistic Struggles in the South Pacific*, London, Zed.

Simmons, I. G. (1993) *Interpreting Nature: Cultural Constructions of the Environment*, London, Routledge.

Smith, R. (1993) *International Treaties, Conventions and Agreements Relevant to Biodiversity Conservation*, University of Bradford, Development and Project Planning Centre.

Smith, R. (1994) Aspects of security in Micronesia, in P. Sutton and A. Payne (eds), *Size and Survival: The Politics of Security in the Caribbean and the Pacific*, London, Frank Cass.

Streeton, P. (1993) Institutions for sustainable development, *Interdisciplinary Science Reviews*, **18**(4).

Sutherland, P. (1994) In the Uruguay Round everybody is a winner, *Courier*, **144**, March/April.

Swift, R. (1994) Squeezing the south: World Bank, IMF, GATT . . . 50 years is enough, *New Internationalist*, **257**.

Thakur, R. (1991) *South Pacific: Problems, Issues and Prospects*, London, Macmillan.

Torrance, J. (ed.) (1993) *The Concept of Nature*, Oxford, Clarendon.

UNDP (1994) *Sustainable Development in Small Island Countries*, New York, UNDP.

UNEP (1994) *Environmental Data Report, 1993–94*, Oxford, Blackwell.

Whale and Dolphin Conservation Society (WDCS) (1994) The IWC: killing time? *WDCS Campaign Newsletter*, July.

Women Working for a Nuclear Free and Independent Pacific (WWNFIP) (1987) *Pacific Women Speak*, Oxford, Greenline.

World Bank Country Study (1991) *Pacific Island Economies: Toward Higher Growth in the 1990s*, Washington, DC.

World Bank (1992) *World Development Report 1992: Development and the Environment*, New York, Oxford University Press.

Appendix

The Alliance of Small Island States

1.	American Samoa	23.	Mauritius
2.	Antigua and Barbuda	24.	Micronesia
3.	Aruba	25.	Nauru
4.	Bahamas	26.	Netherland Antilles
5.	Bahrain	27.	Niue
6.	Barbados	28.	Palau
7.	Cape Verde	29.	Papua New Guinea
8.	Comoros	30.	Samoa
9.	Cook Islands	31.	São Tomé & Príncipe
10.	Cuba	32.	Seychelles
11.	Cyprus	33.	Singapore
12.	Dominica	34.	Solomon Islands
13.	Dominican Republic	35.	St Kitts and Nevis
14.	Fiji	36.	St Lucia
15.	Guam	37.	St Vincent
16.	Grenada	38.	Tokelau
17.	Haiti	39.	Tonga
18.	Jamaica	40.	Trinidad and Tobago
19.	Kiribati	41.	Tuvalu
20.	Maldives	42.	US Virgin Islands
21.	Malta	43.	Vanuatu
22.	Marshall Islands		

22

Globalization, Culture and Land: The Case of the Caribbean[1]

TRACEY SKELTON

Introduction

What happens to local cultures in the face of globalization? Can they resist global processes? How does a 'local' which is part of the Third World react to a 'global' process stimulated within the First World? This chapter considers such questions through analysis of the Caribbean, issues of land and how these combine with culture. I suggest ways of reading some contemporary conceptual work on the local and the global and the complex ways in which these interrelate. In considering the Caribbean I provide examples which are non-Western and which are genuine, lived examples. The chapter is part of an attempt to answer often neglected questions about what globalization means in real life for people who are pushed to the margins in global systems of change.

To answer my questions I combine conceptual ideas relating to globalization, global/local and culture from sociology, with matters of concern within cultural studies and cultural geography, with political and ethical debates within development studies and Caribbean studies. This chapter therefore uses established concepts around the subject of globalization and interrogates them through the consideration of land, cultures of land and people's relationships with, and sentiments about, land. It illustrates the inequalities which are either created or exacerbated by global processes which clash with local perceptions and cultures.

Definitions

'Culture' is a subject of considerable debate and multitudinal definitions, indeed, in order to resist élitist definitions of culture one has to admit that there can be no absolute way of defining the term. Here I identify key concepts as a grounding of the term for the specific purpose of this chapter. Culture is not fixed and static but rather dynamic and changes according to time and space. It is socially constructed and so an individual's experience and creation of culture is determined by many social factors such as gender, 'race', class, sexuality and so forth. Culture is also contingent upon history and the contemporary social, economic and political factors (Clarke *et al.*, 1976; Hall, 1980; Williams, 1958). As a social and cultural geographer I also acknowledge the importance of place and spatiality in both the construction of culture and the ways in which space is constructed by culture (Jackson, 1989). When I talk of the culture of land within the Caribbean this implies a dynamism around relationships with the meaning and value of land, but also a connection with the land which is constructed through a particular history of slavery and the plantation economy and culture. Understandings of the contemporary relations around land have to be understood at several levels which acknowledge both the history and the 'here and now'. While there are central elements of Caribbean relations with land which link back to history, there is also a changing quality of contemporary relationships. However, in the face of external change, traditional cultural relationships to land may re-emerge as a form of resistance against, and retreat from, the global and a move towards the local.

Discussion of 'land' in the context of the Caribbean revolves around not only questions of ownership but also around everyday use, of common memory connected with land which may be a common memory within the family, within a village or a larger community. 'Land' is also linked to identity through history and experience. The vast majority of the peoples of the Caribbean have an ancestral memory of the role of land because they were brought to the islands either as slaves from Africa or as indentured labour from India,[2] specifically to labour on the plantations for commodity production. For the freed slaves the ownership of a piece of land was a symbol of their new identity; for indentured Indian labour the promise of a land plot once the indenture period was over was what drew poor rural, landless labourers into such a contract (Beckles and Shepherd, 1993; Besson and Momsen, 1987; Thomas, 1988).

The Caribbean is a region in which land, land ownership and labour were inextricably linked, initially, in a wide-scale regional system of exploitation. It was a system which linked the Caribbean into a wider global relationship of the Atlantic Triangle – Africa, the Caribbean and Europe. Land in the Caribbean is therefore saturated with memories of exploitation at the same time as being a symbol for the meaning of freedom. Such contradictory relationships have a resonance with contemporary Caribbean cultures of land and are part of the reason why global processes, specifically those of global capital, which threaten to commoditize, privatize and compartmentalize the land, face such opposition. It is why the supposed rationalities of economics within the global system face the presumed irrationalities of cultural interpretations of the meaning and value of land which cannot be fully understood without an awareness of Caribbean history and contemporary life.

Theoretical approaches

The call to include 'culture' in academic discourse on globalization, global political economy and development is gaining strength. It has been a plea within selected writing on development practice and critique for some time. Verhelst (1987), a senior project officer with the Belgian Development Agency, criticizes development practices and talks of culture as the forgotten dimension. He argues that 'the indigenous cultures of the peoples of the Third World have been largely neglected. There is an urgent need to pay much greater attention to these than we have in the past.' (Verhelst, 1987: 22). Interestingly he stresses that the attack on Third World cultural identities has been twofold, and that capitalism is not all to blame, but that left-wing and NGO approaches have often neglected the cultural and spiritual heritage of the people they work with (ibid.: 20).

Roland Robertson (1992) provides an example of academic discourse demanding that culture be written into analyses of globalization and world politics:

> I believe that it is directly necessary to adopt a cultural focus to what is often called world politics ... We have come increasingly to recognise that while economic matters are of tremendous importance in relations between societies and in various forms of transnational relations these matters are ... subject to cultural contingencies and cultural coding. (p. 4)

It was from this academic context that I went on to read a quote from a World Bank economist for Jamaica which triggered me to ask questions about cultural attitudes towards land, the complexities of development and how this could relate to the Caribbean:

> Look at an island, say, like Montserrat, or the others. If their governments could be persuaded to sell land for retirement homes for wealthy Americans the place could be another Monte Carlo! The ones who stay would have higher incomes. But they don't want to do it. They regard the land as some sort of birthright. (Quoted by McAfee, 1991: 10)

This approach to Caribbean land by those from the West, in particular the USA, was echoed by George Shultz, US Secretary of State in the Reagan administration. Soon after the US invasion of Grenada in October 1983, he visited the island and was taken to the capital St George. One of his first remarks upon seeing the town with its backdrop of green mountains and the calm harbour was, 'It's a lovely piece of real estate' (McAfee, 1991: 97). Both quotations raise serious questions and issues.

Why would Caribbean people want to sell their land for the retirement homes of people from the States and Canada? Why would Montserrat want to be another Monte Carlo? Why is the assumption that the Caribbean is 'For Sale' so prevalent in development and economic thinking of the North?

What the above quotes demonstrate in simplistic terms are highly complex cultural differences in the attitudes towards, and relationships with, the land between those of the North and those of the South. I also include here the indigenous peoples of countries of the North such as Native Americans, Canadian Indians and Inuit peoples, Australian Aborigines and Maoris of New Zealand. Other dimensions of the complexities occur when there are distinctive attitudes towards land according to class, gender, 'race' and ethnicity, which may play a part within both the North and the South. Here I want to establish debate around the cultural meanings of land for the people of the Caribbean and why such cultural interpretations have to be considered within development and globalization discourse. What concerns me is how to integrate the experience of Caribbean peoples and their land within academic debate on the global. If the Caribbean experience is to be taken seriously, and to have any extrapolative meaning for development discourse, then it has to be theoretically linked with social theory which debates aspects of globalization. Reading writers on the global such as Mike Featherstone (1990, 1993), Anthony King (1990) and Stuart Hall (1991) enabled me to conceptualize ways in which processes in the Caribbean could be theorized within globalization discourse.

Global and local cultures

Here I interrogate some of the key points found in selected writing on the global and the local and examine some of the concepts within the context of the Caribbean in general, and Montserrat in particular. One of the difficulties I have with much of the writing on globalization, global theory and discourses of global change is that many of the everyday examples used as illustration are drawn from Western experience – hence my focus on the Caribbean.

Featherstone argues that one consequence of globalization is not just the production of homogeneity but also familiarization with greater diversity, the knowledge that there is an extensive range of cultures (1993: 169). However, major players in the global economy, the International Monetary Fund (IMF) and the World Bank, do not seem to have shared in an understanding of such diversity. They seem either determined not to, or unable to, fathom the complexities of cultural relations between Caribbean peoples and the land. This is perhaps because both institutions are locked into the West's conceptualization of itself as 'the guardian of universal values on behalf of a world formed in its own self image' (Featherstone, 1993: 172). As products of Western cultural hegemony, as well as economic predominance, the two institutions are determined that Caribbean governments, and Caribbean people if considered at all, should perceive land in the same way they do. The land is there to be sold, the land is 'a lovely piece of real estate'. Land is to be seen in monetary terms, with investment in mind, to be possessed and owned, compartmentalized into lots and sold off piecemeal. An example of this cultural clash is given below.

In Grenada the US Agency for International Development (USAID) had a central principle of 'privatization'. Kathy McAfee (1991) researched what happened in the name of 'development' after the US invasion of Grenada. USAID was determined to return the land to private ownership but what they had failed to understand was that the land had been government-owned even before the New Jewel revolution of March 1979. Their anti-revolutionary zeal blinded them to recognizing that the basis of Grenada's economy is its 8000 independent, mostly small-scale farmers. By the end of their effective involvement in Grenada in 1988 USAID had spent US$1.7 million but left more rural workers without jobs, more small-scale farmers with no future prospects for development and improvement of their land, and farmers who used to be part of the Farms Corporation uncertain of whether they would get the right to buy their land, or whether they would in fact lose it altogether. USAID failed to understand both the political and social cultures related to land and farming in Grenada and left the situation in a worse position than before it became involved.

Returning to Featherstone (1993), he presents a definition of local culture which would certainly describe many small islands of the Caribbean region. Local culture, he suggests, is

> a culture of a relatively small bounded space in which individuals who live
> there engage in daily face-to-face relationships ... the emphasis is upon the
> taken-for-granted, habitual and repetitive nature of the everyday culture ...
> the common stock of knowledge ... has persisted over time and may incorpo-
> rate rituals, symbols and ceremonies that link people to a place and a common
> sense of the past. (p. 176)

For many Montserratians rituals and ceremonies are linked with the land and the villages connected to a particular area. For example, St Patrick's Day is celebrated to remind the islanders of their link with Eire (Irish Catholics expelled from Virginia were the first European settlers of Montserrat). At the same time it serves as a memorial to the first slave uprising on the island, which took place on St Patrick's Day in the late eighteenth century. Such a dual significance demonstrates the complexities of cultural histories and the way they are mapped out in space. The space of St Patrick's has different historical meanings – the name of the space acknowledges the colonial settlers, and the actual day of St Patrick reminds the present-day islanders of their colonial past and their slave past. Layers of historical and cultural meaning are sedimented down upon the land. The day is also an opportunity for the southern part of the island, the parish of St Patrick's, to host people from all over the island. People of the parish prepare food for sale from their own provision grounds – all kinds of vegetables, cassava bread traditionally baked in stone ovens, goat water (stew), and juices made from tree and fruit production of the area. The cultural connection of the place, the land and people's relationship with that land are very clear.

When we consider the encounter between globalization forces and local culture we find that localities are integrated

> into more impersonal structures in which the dictates of market or administrative rationalities maintained by national élites or transcultural professionals and experts have the capacity to override local decision-making processes and decide the fate of the locality. (Featherstone, 1993: 177)

In Montserrat there has been a process of selling land to those from the USA and Canada for retirement or second home building for the past three decades. This process has caused contradictions in understandings about, and perceptions of, the land – specifically access to and ownership of the land. In Montserrat land that was not built upon and not used for any agricultural production was perceived as common land and was used as grazing land by individual Montserratians who had a few cattle and goats. When the government and the Montserrat Company (which dates back to the times of slavery and full colonial domination of the island) began to sell lots to rich business people in the USA and Canada the local culture of Montserratian villagers had their fates decided by Montserratian élites and professional real estate developers. Montserratians lost access to land they had always had since the decline of the estates. For them land was about freedom and a link with an ancestral past, a collective memory of the misery and inhumanity of slavery and the subsequent wage–labour exploitation. Where there were unfenced lots, Montserratians continued to graze their animals, and the expatriates who now lived in the houses they had built complained. Animals would often break their tethers and choose to go into gardens where the well-watered lawns provided better grass than the bush areas. Legislation was passed which allowed for the impounding of animals found on sold lots, fines had to be paid, often necessitating the sale of other animals. With fewer and fewer places to tether their animals individuals had to sell off their stock and so lost an important traditional source of livelihood.

Hence the global processes of 'Land for sale' (as long as you are buying in US dollars it appears) had a dramatic knock-on effect upon the local lifestyles, the local economy and cultural attitudes of access to land. Montserratians could not afford to buy the land, nor was it offered to them, and they did not reap the benefits of its sale. External capital organized alongside a sympathetic government to purchase land and re-sell it as real estate.

In his essay on global and local issues Stuart Hall (1990) talks of the return to the local as a response to globalization. He suggests that it is something people do when faced with a particular form of modernity; he argues that people 'opt out'. Featherstone reiterates this argument (although interestingly does not refer to Hall) when he talks of a 'deglobalizing reaction to global compression and the intensity of global flows' (Featherstone, 1993: 177). Hall stresses that it is at the 'retreated to' local place that there are struggles for cultural representation. It is respect for local roots which is drawn in and used against the anonymous impersonal forces of globalization. The neighbourhood, the community is what people know, understand and can talk about. Stuart Corbridge (1993) talks of the Third World experiencing 'a fractured modernity in Western terms' (p. 200) – the modernization of the economy is incomplete, political systems are usually linked to private gain and yet the penetration of Western ideas and modes of thought is much more complete. A response to this 'fractured modernity' and such insecurity may be the retreat to historical meaning, a retreat to something which modernity has yet to taint and destroy.

I argue that a 'retreat to the local', a 'deglobalizing reaction', a response to 'fractured modernity' for many who live in the Caribbean involves a cultural relationship with the land. With the history of slavery the 'possession' of land – which may take a variety of forms, not necessarily always formally recorded – is an important part of Caribbean identity. As slaves Caribbean people were property, allowed to own nothing. Upon emancipation they formed their own communities on marginal lands. Still indentured to work on the plantations they began their own provision agriculture close to their homes and separate from the white-owned plantations. Indian indentured labour also followed a similar pattern of village development and the lure of a piece of land for their own use was important in fulfilling the indentured contract. Thus began a long-standing tradition of 'ground cultivation' for self-sufficiency. Market trade in the form of higglering and huckstering began linking the 'new' Caribbean peoples with each other from the level of the free village, the local town, throughout the island, and between the islands. Hence in the Caribbean the culture of land is not one based solely on economics but rather one connected with history, ancestry, independence and freedom. The land has a spiritual meaning as well as being of practical importance. Many of the women I interviewed were indeed retreating to the local, finding security in the face of 'fractured modernity' through their ownership of and access to their families' land (Skelton, 1989).[3]

Almost all the women had what they called 'mountain ground'. For most this land was not where they now lived or worked but located in their home villages. This was especially true of professional women in banking, insurance and the civil service. They were women who had physically, educationally and behaviourally moved away from their rural homes into the urban and suburban areas and into employment contexts which integrated them into the global economy and gave them experience of globalization. Although many of them did not own the land, their mothers or grandmothers did, so that there was a sense of it being 'family land'. These are women who have aspirations about their careers and their futures and yet they retain firm links with their roots and their personal and family history – they retain such a link through their continued attachment to the land. Such an attachment is at once physical, spiritual and emotional. A few women talked of going to their land to relax their mind, remind themselves about where they came from, to get away from the stresses of their work, their lives in the urban areas. Many of the professional women had a comprehensive understanding of real estate opportunities for the sale of land, but there was no question that this 'family land' would ever be sold.

The importance of land to Caribbean identity can be acute at times of natural disaster, usually a hurricane. In Montserrat the role of land in the constructions of identity, culture and sense of place manifested itself in the aftermath of Hurricane Hugo which completely devastated the island on 17 September 1989. Many people lost everything they possessed. When they were interviewed for television reports, wrote letters of their experience to me or told their individual stories when I returned to the island ten months after Hugo, they talked of their personal losses but a great part of their discourse included grief for the land itself. The post-Hugo experience was an extremely unsettling and disturbing time. Not only did the islanders have to begin the lengthy task of rebuilding but they also had to cope with an inundation of foreign aid workers, advisers, experts almost all from the USA, Canada and the UK. Other Caribbean islands helped with work-parties who worked alongside Montserratians to rebuild. In the face of such an influx of personnel, ideas, practices and decisions Montserratians had little to retreat to that was Montserratian. The only common experience that they had was the hurricane itself and that stimulated a cultural production not experienced on the island before. Collections of poems, stories and recollections have been published with participation from all over the island. The local culture was threatened and altered, either temporarily or permanently, through an integration with wider global cultures, but new forms of cultural expression about the land also appeared.

A future agenda?

What should a future agenda concerning land and culture in the Caribbean address? Just as there are critiques of the way development practice in the region has been carried out so far, especially in respect of agriculture and land use, so, too, are there alternatives offered which allow for the indigenous development of the region which maintains the cultural integrity of the people. However, in the face of the process of globalization the implementation of local strategies for change are going to be extremely difficult.

The Caribbean currently faces spiralling national debts of more than US$21 billion, owed predominantly to the World Bank, the IMF, USAID and the Interamerican Bank. Faced with programmes of structural adjustment policies, the rural poor in the region become increasingly dependent upon their small plots of land to provide basic food sources for themselves. At the same time the land is under increasing pressure. External 'development' advice concerned with agriculture is to move towards or continue with export crops. More and more land is brought under cultivation in order to maintain the income earned from a single crop – for example, bananas in Dominica (McAfee, 1991). Land is also under pressure to be sold to external buyers. A more recent threat to Caribbean land comes from transnational companies offering large sums of money to governments in severe external debt for the right to use land for the dumping of toxic waste from the North. Montserratians heard in 1994 that their government was in negotiations with one such company. The outcry and resistance that have developed across the island have been unanimously against the proposal (*New Internationalist*, July 1994). Such global processes will throw Caribbean islanders into constant conflict with the North and globalization processes and such is their position within the global political economy that it will become increasingly difficult to resist.

A future agenda has to include an integrated understanding of the cultures of land in the Caribbean, a recognition of the social, historical, spiritual, cultural and emotional importance of land and a consideration of the patterns of gender relations associated with the land. Discourse of development for the region has to take account of Caribbean cultures in their broadest sense and give space for indigenous strategies for self-reliance and empowerment.

Notes

1. Two versions of this chapter have been given as papers, one at the Caribbean Studies Association conference, Grenada in 1992 and the second at the Global Politics: Agendas for the Year 2000 conference held in July 1994 at Nottingham Trent University. I am most grateful to the Department of International Studies at

Nottingham Trent which provided funding to attend both these conferences.
2. When this chapter talks of the Caribbean it does so from the perspective of the Anglophone Caribbean, although the experience of slavery from the West Coast of Africa is a common one throughout the Dutch, French and Spanish Caribbean. The system of indentured labour from India is a feature of the Anglo-Caribbean and particularly affected the countries of Trinidad and Tobago and Guyana.
3. I am not suggesting that such cultures of land are exclusive to the Caribbean; many similar meanings and attachments to the land may exist in a whole range of societies and cultures, in both the North and the South. However, the historical and cultural complexity of such relations with the land is unique to the Caribbean.

References

Appadurai, A. (1990) Disjuncture and difference in the global cultural economy, in M. Featherstone (ed.), *Global Culture: Nationalism, Globalization and Modernity*, London, Sage, pp. 295–310.

Beckles, H. and Shepherd, V. (eds) (1993) *Caribbean Freedom*, London, James Currey.

Besson, J. and Momsen, J. (eds) (1987) *Land and Development in the Caribbean*, Basingstoke, Macmillan.

Bird, J., Curtis, B., Putnam, T., Robertson, G. and Tickner L. (eds) (1993) *Mapping the Futures: Local Cultures, Global Change*, London, Routledge.

Clarke, J., Hall, S., Jefferson, T. and Roberts, B. (1976) Subcultures, cultures and class: a theoretical overview, in S. Hall and J. Henderson (eds), *Resistance Through Rituals*, London, Hutchinson/Centre for Contemporary Cultural Studies, pp. 9–74.

Corbridge, S. (1993) Colonialism, post-colonialism and the political geography of the Third World, in P. J. Taylor (ed.), *Political Geography of the Twentieth Century*, London, Belhaven Press, pp. 171–205.

Featherstone, M. (ed.) (1990) *Global Culture: Nationalism, Globalization and Modernity*, London, Sage.

Featherstone, M. (1993) Global and local cultures, in J. Bird *et al.* (ed.), *Mapping the Futures: Local Cultures, Global Change*, London, Routledge, pp. 169–87.

Hannerz, U. (1990) Cosmopolitans and locals in world culture, in M. Featherstone (ed.), *Global Culture: Nationalism, Globalization and Modernity*, London, Sage, pp. 237–51.

Hall, S. (1980) Cultural studies and the Centre: some problematics and problems, in S. Hall, D. Hobson and A. Lowe (eds), *Culture, Media, Language*, London, Hutchinson/Centre for Contemporary Cultural Studies, pp. 15–47.

Hall, S. (1990) The local and the global: globalization of ethnicity, in A. King (ed.), *Culture, Globalization and the World-system*, London, Macmillan, pp. 19–39.

Jackson, P. (1989) *Maps of Meaning*, London, Routledge.

King, A. (ed.) (1990) *Culture, Globalization and the World-system*, London, Macmillan.

McAfee, K. (1991) *Storm Signals: Structural Adjustment and Development Alternatives in the Caribbean*, London, Zed.

New Internationalist Magazine (1984) July, p. 16.

Robertson, R. (1992) *Globalization: Social Theory and Global Culture*, London, Sage.

Skelton, T. (1989) *Women, Men and Power: Gender Relations in Montserrat*, unpublished Ph.D. thesis, University of Newcastle upon Tyne.

Thomas, C. (1988) *The Poor and the Powerless*, London, LAB.

Verhelst, T. (1987) *No Life Without Roots: Culture and Development*, London, Zed.

Williams, R. (1958) *Culture and Society, 1780–1950*, London, Chatto and Windus.

Index